TEACHING FOR BLACK LIVES

EDITORS

DYAN WATSON

JESSE HAGOPIAN

WAYNE AU

PRODUCTION EDITOR

ARI BLOOMEKATZ

A RETHINKING SCHOOLS PUBLICATION

Teaching for Black Lives
Edited by Dyan Watson, Jesse Hagopian, and Wayne Au

A Rethinking Schools Publication

Rethinking Schools, Ltd., is a nonprofit publisher and advocacy organization dedicated to sustaining and strengthening public education through social justice teaching and education activism. Our magazine, books, and other resources promote equity and racial justice in the classroom.

To request additional copies of this book or a catalog of other publications, or to subscribe to *Rethinking Schools* magazine, contact:
Rethinking Schools
6737 W. Washington St.
Suite 3249
Milwaukee, WI 53214
800-669-4192
rethinkingschools.org

Follow @RethinkSchools
teachingforblacklives.org

© 2018 Rethinking Schools, Ltd.
First edition
Third printing

Cover and Book Design: Nancy Zucker
Cover Illustration: Ekua Holmes
Production: Ari Bloomekatz
Proofreading: Lawrence Sanfilippo
Indexing: Carol Roberts

All rights reserved. Except as permitted below, no part of this book may be reproduced in any form or by any means, including electronic, without the express prior written permission of the publisher, except for brief quotation in an acknowledged review. Individuals may photocopy excerpts from this book for use in educational settings (physical settings only; internet use is not permitted), as long as such material is furnished free to students or workshop participants. For sale of any portion of this book as part of course packets, contact the Copyright Clearance Center for permissions and appropriate fees. If you have any questions, contact Rethinking Schools at the address above.

ISBN: 978-0-942961-04-1

Teaching for Black Lives
Library of Congress Control Number: 2018936887

DEDICATION

This book is dedicated to Black families, and to educators everywhere
who are working to make Black lives matter in our schools.

ACKNOWLEDGEMENTS

We are grateful to the many people who helped make this work come to fruition. Thank
you to all of the chapter authors and artists for your contributions to this book, including the cover artist, Ekua Holmes. This book is stronger because of you. Thank you to
our Rethinking Schools family: Bill Bigelow, Linda Christensen, Grace Cornell Gon-
zales, Stan Karp, David Levine, Deborah Menkart, Larry Miller, Marcelia Nicholson,
Gina Palazzari, Bob Peterson, Adam Sanchez, Lindsay Stevens, Michael Trokan, Ursula
Wolfe-Rocca, and Moé Yonamine. We also thank Ben Secord for his support, as well as
Lawrence Sanfilippo, Elizabeth Barbian, Emily C. Bell, Samantha Fine, Turquoise L.
Parker, Isaac Brosilow, and Paige Foreman for their help with proofreading and other
work needed to complete this book. To our individual family members, Mira and Mako;
Caleb and Nehemiah; Sarah, Miles, and Satchel; David, Laurie, Josh, and Rachel: We
love you and are grateful for your love and support. In addition, we acknowledge the
loved ones who gave us their opinions in the editorial process or provided other support
so that we could be free to work. We absolutely could not do this without you.

Teaching for Black Lives was made possible, in part, by substantial donations from
Michael Bennett and Ben Haggerty (aka Macklemore), as well as donations from Mia
Henry, David Bloome, University Prep, Parker Felton-Koestler and family, the Badass
Teachers Association, and more than 230 other donors. Although we cannot list all 230
names, we know that every dollar given was a sacrifice and we appreciate your trust. Thank
you for believing in this project.

Finally, we are honored by, and indebted to, Ari Bloomekatz and Nancy Zucker,
without whose tireless work this book would not have happened.

Contents

SECTION 2
ENSLAVEMENT, CIVIL RIGHTS, AND BLACK LIBERATION

SECTION 3
GENTRIFICATION, DISPLACEMENT, AND ANTI-BLACKNESS

SECTION 4
DISCIPLINE, THE SCHOOLS-TO-PRISON PIPELINE, AND MASS INCARCERATION

SECTION 5
TEACHING BLACKNESS, LOVING BLACKNESS, AND EXPLORING IDENTITY

For handouts, lesson plans, and other teaching resources for the articles in this book, go to teachingforblacklives.org

THE ARTISTS OF TEACHING FOR BLACK LIVES

Khalid Albaih: 331, 335
Hanna Barczyk: 231, 235, 321
Howard Barry: 32, 42–43
Micah Bazant: 327
Keith Henry Brown: 114–115, 349
Kesha Bruce: 361, 363
Sharon Chang: 22–31
Molly Crabapple: 286
Damon Davis: 16
Emory Douglas: 143
Michael Duffy: 199

Bob Fitch: 147
Maya Freelon: 310
Matt Herron: 123
Ekua Holmes: Cover
Chris Kindred: 173, 245
Rafael López: 341
Danny Lyon: 129
Ricardo Levins Morales: 59
Hanna Neuschwander: 357
Richie Pope: 150, 299
Erin Robinson: 307

Erik Ruin: 273
Boris Séméniako: 71, 221, 223
Simone Shin: 278
Brian Stauffer: 89, 215
Katherine Streeter: 137
Seth Tobocman: 265
Adolfo Valle: 187
Olivia Wise: 257
Shannon Wright: 183

Introduction

Black students' minds and bodies are under attack.

Fifteen-year-old Black student Coby Burren was in geography class at Pearland High School near Houston in the fall of 2015. As he read the assigned page of his textbook, he noticed something that deeply disturbed him: A map of the United States with a caption that said the Atlantic slave trade brought "millions of workers from Africa to the southern United States to work on agricultural plantations." Coby took a picture of his textbook and texted it to his mother, adding, "We was real hard workers wasn't we," along with a sarcastic emoji. It was bad enough that the McGraw-Hill textbook erased the enslavement of African people by simply calling them "workers," implying they were paid. But they also placed the portion on the enslavement of Africans in the section of the book titled "Patterns of Immigration" — as if Africans came to the United States looking for a better life.

In the winter of 2017, a mother in Connecticut wrote about how she was troubled by a worksheet on slavery that her daughter had completed for school. The question asked, "How were the slaves treated in Connecticut?" Her daughter had initially written, "The slaves were treated badly and cruelly," but crossed that out and replaced it with the answer that was written in the textbook, which stated slaves were "often cared for and [the slave owners] protected them like members of the family."

From the North to the South, corporate curriculum lies to our students, conceals pain and injustice, masks racism, and demeans our Black students. But it's not only the curriculum that is traumatizing students.

In October of 2015, a Black girl in South Carolina was ripped out of her desk and thrown across the room by a police officer in the school for allegedly refusing to put away her cell phone. The video captured by a classmate of the incident went viral. The officer who brutalized the girl was not charged with a crime and instead both the girl videotaping and the girl thrown across the room were arrested and charged with "disturbing schools." In May of 2017, surveillance video revealed a police officer at Woodland Hills High School in Churchill, Pennsylvania, choked and body-slammed a Black boy in the office.

Recent data reveals that school security officers outnumber counselors in three out of five — and four out of the top 10 — of the biggest school districts in the country, including New York City, Chicago, Miami-Dade County, and Houston.

These examples reveal some of the policies that result in pushing kids out of school, making it difficult to graduate, then difficult to get a job, and finally more likely that they will end up in jail. This school-to-prison pipeline begins with a curriculum that conceals the struggles and contributions of Black people and other people of color. It is a curriculum that fails to respect young Black people as intellectuals, and ignores their cultures, communities, and concerns. In the majority of textbooks, African Americans' struggles and contributions are minimized, portrayed as blatant stereotypes, or confined to a few roles that are acceptable to mainstream white society. This absence (or destructive presence) begins in preschool and continues throughout a Black student's schooling.

Even when teachers include African American history, they often fail to consider the methods used to teach about Black lives to Black and non-Black children. Command and control lecture and rote memorization are not effective means of teaching for Black lives. Indeed, teaching for Black lives means just the opposite: engaging students in critical self-reflection, grounding our curriculum and teaching in their lives and communities, and orienting them toward community activism and social transformation.

Teaching for Black lives means that we can't relegate Black history to certain historical time periods or events and we must include Black lives in all aspects of curriculum, including science, math, literature, and the arts. Teaching for Black lives also means considering the loneliness of learning about one's history when you might be one of a few students in class (or few teachers in a school) that this history represents.

When Black history and Black contributions are denied in the curriculum and by those who teach it, Black people are themselves denied. Consequently, students who become disinterested in a course or vocal about its shortcomings and historical erasure are often labeled defiant and pushed out of the classroom. These students may then get swept up by police officers stationed in school and be hit with criminal charges for behavior that was once handled by school administration. If the offending student is sent to administration, they are often required to implement zero-tolerance discipline policies prescribed by the school district that mandate suspension or expulsion for various infractions. When a decision to suspend a student is left up to an administrator's discretion, Black students are far more likely to be punished than their white peers. When students miss school, they fall behind in their classes and are more likely not to pass. The pipeline continues with the lack of tutoring programs, counseling services, college access programs, after-school programs, healthcare, proper nutrition, and other support services that would assist students who are falling behind. And if a student makes it through that gauntlet of perils, high-stakes end-of-course exams are waiting to deter them from graduating.

The school-to-prison pipeline is a major contributor to the overall epidemic of police violence and mass incarceration that functions as one of sharpest edges of structural racism in the United States.

The Rise of the #BlackLivesMatter Movement

A new rebellion against structural racism is under way in the form of the Black Lives Matter movement, galvanized by extrajudicial executions of Black people by the police and racist vigilantes. The murder of Trayvon Martin in 2012 and the ensuing national protests that followed showed the potential for a mass social movement — and the hashtag #BlackLivesMatter was launched by three Black women, Patrisse Khan-Cullors, Alicia Garza, and Opal Tometi. Their demand that all Black lives have value was simple, yet visionary — especially in its call to highlight the most marginalized Black lives, including LGBTQ folks, women, and Black immigrant lives.

In August of 2014, Michael Brown was killed in the streets of Ferguson, Missouri, his body left there for hours as a reminder to the Black residents in the neighborhood that their lives are meaningless to the American Empire. But this time the potential for a national uprising was actualized as thousands of mostly Black residents of Ferguson took to the streets and inspired rallies across the country and around the world. Only weeks after the non-indictment decision of Michael Brown's killer, Darren Wilson, a New York grand jury failed to indict the officer who strangled Eric Garner to death on camera, and the movement went into high gear. Student walkouts, mass marches, and urban rebellions swept the country as people's anger boiled over at the racist criminal (in)justice system.

In 2015, the African American Policy Forum coined the hashtag #SayHerName in an effort to raise awareness about state violence against women — including Black queer women and Black transgender women — and the campaign took off in the aftermath of the death of Sandra Bland, who died in jail while in police custody after being detained by an officer for a traffic stop.

Despite the ongoing protests, police killings of Black people have continued unabated, including the widely known cases of Freddie Gray, Philando Castile, Alton Sterling, and Charleena Lyles, a pregnant mother who was killed in front of three of her four children. In addition to these adults, police have also killed many Black children in the past few years, including 7-year-old Aiyana Stanley-Jones, 12-year-old Tamir Rice, 17-year-old Laquan McDonald, 15-year-old Jordan Edwards, 13-year-old Tyre King, and 15-year-old Darius Smith.

The continuing police murders of Black people, and the refusal of the court system to punish police for these crimes, has continued to fuel an explosion of protests — from the streets to the schools. Protest even erupted on NFL fields in 2016 when then-San Francisco 49ers quarterback Colin Kaepernick sat and then took a knee during the national anthem in protest of police brutality. Following Kaepernick's lead, student athletes from middle school through college took a knee against racism.

In Seattle, on Oct. 19, 2016, the movement for Black lives burst into the struggle for equitable education when some 3,000 educators came to school wearing shirts that said "Black Lives Matter, We Stand Together," with many of them teaching lessons about the long history of the struggle against racism. This movement spread across the country with educators in Philadelphia and Rochester, New York, holding similar actions. Then, during the first school week of February 2018, educators from around the country organized the first national "Black Lives Matter at School" week of action. Educators taught lessons throughout the week that corresponded to the 13 principles of the Black Lives Matter Global Network organization and raised several demands:

1. End Zero-Tolerance Discipline, Implement Restorative Justice.
2. Hire More Black Teachers.
3. Black History/Ethnic Studies Mandated K–12.
4. Fund Counselors Not Cops (this demand was added later).

Teaching for Black Lives is a direct response to the movement for Black lives. We recognize that anti-Black racism constructs Black people, and Blackness generally, as not counting as human life. The chapters here in *Teaching for Black Lives* push back directly against this construction by not only providing educators with critical perspectives on the role of schools in perpetuating anti-Blackness, but also by offering educators concrete examples of what it looks like to humanize Black people in curriculum, teaching, and policy. Throughout the book, we demonstrate how teachers can connect the curriculum to young people's lives and root their concerns and daily experiences in what is taught and how classrooms are set up. We also highlight the hope and beauty of student activism and collective action.

The first section of *Teaching for Black Lives*, "Making Black Lives Matter in Our Schools," frames how police violence and the movement for Black lives can explicitly be brought to schools and classrooms by educators through organizing mass action and through curriculum. The pairing of these is purposeful: Not only is it critical that we teach about the systemic violence against Black people and the travesty of Black deaths, it is also important for students and teachers to understand their roles in organizing in support of Black life and Black communities, and against anti-Black racism.

In Section 2, "Enslavement, Civil Rights, and Black Liberation," *Teaching for Black Lives* takes a historical turn. Here the chapters focus on how Black history is taught in the classroom. We recognize, for instance, that the enslavement of Africans and their descendants, the Civil War, and the Civil Rights Movement are all regularly taught in schools, but, as we alluded to at the beginning of this introduction, we also know that these subjects are too often taught in ways that further dehumanize Black people and perpetuate anti-Black racism. Thus the chapters we include in this section reframe the teaching of these histories in ways that challenge white supremacy and reject many of the popular, yet racist, myths that all too often paint Black people as non-actors in their own liberation. To that end, through textbook critique, role plays, and other classroom-based activities, several chapters in this section focus on how racism and white supremacy have operated historically, and highlight how Black people have organized in the interest of their own freedom.

However, we know that anti-Blackness isn't just historical: It is spatial too. Through gentrification and the violence of displacement, anti-Blackness terraforms Black communities into white ones, and working-class communities into spaces for wealthy elites. Anti-Black racism also starves Black communities of resources, either turning them into neoliberal marketplaces for profit — as in New Orleans post-Hurricane Katrina, or simply allowing them to remain toxic for Black residents. *Teaching for Black Lives* takes this up in Section 3, "Gentrification, Displacement, and Anti-Blackness." In particular, the chapters in this section highlight how these issues can and should be taught through a critical lens of racial and economic justice.

Displacement is not just a socioeconomic process. It is real and concrete because it happens to Black bodies. Specifically, this happens in part through our schools' roles in the mass incarceration of Black people. In Section 4, "Discipline, the Schools-to-Prison Pipeline, and Mass Incarceration," the authors explore the ways that school discipline policy and practice contribute directly to the disproportionate punishment and incarceration of Black students. This section examines what it means to teach students whose family members are incarcerated, as well as how to teach about the system of mass incarceration impacting Black communities. Section 4 concludes with chapters that highlight the ways that schools can challenge mass incarceration, including some possibilities for restorative and transformative justice.

Finally, Section 5, "Teaching Blackness, Loving Blackness, and Exploring Identity," recognizes that *Teaching for Black Lives* encompasses more than just teaching critique and social action. It is also about teaching Black identity and the beauty of Blackness both as self-care for Black students and as a way to directly confront anti-Blackness. Here, we pivot toward looking at ways we can and should affirm Black identity in our classrooms and with our children, as we explore the varied and complex relationships between teaching, learning, and being Black. This includes respecting and affirming the language that bathes our existence, and explores the intersectionality with other identities. Here the authors celebrate Blackness and all of its hues while explicating the tensions between being seen and unseen all at once.

We do not expect *Teaching for Black Lives* to end police violence against Black communities, stop anti-Black racism in schools, or end the school-to-prison pipeline. We do, however, see this collection as playing an important role in highlighting the ways educators can and should make their classrooms and schools sites of resistance to white supremacy and anti-Blackness, as well as sites for knowing the hope and beauty in Blackness. The ferocity of racism in the United States against Black minds and Black bodies demands that teachers fight back. We must organize against anti-Blackness amongst our colleagues and in our communities; we must march against police brutality in the streets; and we must teach for Black lives in our classrooms. We call on others to join us in this fight. ■

A Note on Language in *Teaching for Black Lives*

Following the practice of *Rethinking Schools*, the editors of *Teaching for Black Lives* have capitalized the "B" in Black in order to respect and honor the "fight for the right to a proper name" as Lori L. Tharps called it in her *New York Times* op-ed, "The Case for Black with a Capital B." As such, we will also continue the practice to acknowledge people's rights to be legitimated through proper names and have largely left it to individual authors to delineate how they will name themselves. Thus, the reader will see Latinx as well as Latina/o, and Black interchanged with African American, along with more conventional naming practices. We also want to note that student names throughout *Teaching for Black Lives* have been changed except in circumstances where we have received permission to include them or they were quoted in the media.

For more information about *Teaching for Black Lives*, including teaching materials and resources that accompany many of the articles in this book, visit teachingforblacklives.org.

1

MAKING BLACK LIVES MATTER IN OUR SCHOOLS

DAMON DAVIS

Black Students' Lives Matter
Building the school-to-justice pipeline

By the editors of *Rethinking Schools*

We're at a tipping point. The killings of Trayvon Martin, Jordan Davis, Michael Brown, Tamir Rice, Renisha McBride — and far too many other African Americans — have put to rest the myth of a "post-racial" America. In death, these Black youth — shot down with impunity because of the color of their skin — have provided a tragically thorough education about police terror and institutional racism, and ignited the Black Lives Matter movement.

The hashtag #BlackLivesMatter was originally created by Black women activists Alicia Garza, Patrisse Khan-Cullors, and Opal Tometi as a call to action after George Zimmerman was acquitted of the murder of Trayvon Martin in July 2013. Their battle cry went viral and then turned into a national uprising when Darren Wilson, a police officer in Ferguson, Missouri, killed Michael Brown, an unarmed Black teenager. The movement exploded when NYPD officer Daniel Pantaleo was not indicted for choking to death Eric Garner.

As the Black Lives Matter movement has grown, Black students have played a pivotal role. For example, at Seattle's Garfield High School, some 1,000 students, led by the Black Student Union (BSU), walked out the day after the non-indictment of Wilson was announced. As 17-year-old Issa George, vice president of the Garfield BSU, told the *Seattle Times*: "This is our time, as youth, to speak. . . . The waking up that America has done in the past couple of months — something that us as youth get to witness and get to be a part of — has been extremely powerful."

College, high school, and even middle school students have staged protests and school walkouts in cities around the country. According to reporting by the *Nation's* George Joseph and others, student activists of the Baltimore Algebra Project held a die-in when their local school board voted to shut down the first of five schools. The board fled, and the students took over their chairs to lead a community forum on the closures.

Black students take these risks because they know their lives and futures are at stake — from police violence on the street; from the dismantling of their communities through foreclosures, gentrification, and unemployment; and from the destruction of their schools through corporate reform.

The School-to-Grave Pipeline

For the past decade, social justice educators have decried the school-to-prison pipeline: a series of interlocking policies — whitewashed, often scripted curriculum that neglects the contributions and struggles of people of color; zero-tolerance and racist suspension and expulsion policies; and high-stakes tests — that funnel kids from the classroom to the cellblock. But, with the recent high-profile deaths of young African Americans, a "school-to-grave pipeline" is coming into focus. Michael Brown had just graduated from high school and was preparing to go to college when police killed him. According to a 2012 investigation by the Malcolm X Grassroots Movement, a Black person is killed by law enforcement, security guards, or vigilantes every 28 hours. A recent ProPublica report found that "Blacks, age 15 to 19, were killed at a rate of 31.17 per million, while just 1.47 per million white males in that age range died at the hands of police."

In death, these Black youth — shot down with impunity because of the color of their skin — have provided a tragically thorough education about police terror and institutional racism, and ignited the Black Lives Matter movement.

The Black Lives Matter movement inspires us to fight the school-to-grave pipeline as an example of structural racism, after decades in which anti-racism has been defined in excessively personal terms through anti-bias or diversity training. Anti-bias work focuses primarily, and often exclusively, on internal and interpersonal racism. In other words, if you strive to not be racist in your personal relationships, that's good enough.

There is definitely a place for personal reflection and discussion of racist attitudes and beliefs. And there is no doubt that many individual police officers need anti-bias training and to be held responsible for their actions. But that's not enough, as the statistics on police violence, incarceration, school suspension and dropout rates, inequitable school financing, and school closures make clear. These are all sharp indicators of structural racism. When Michelle Alexander says mass incarceration is "the new Jim Crow," she insists that the racist structures that have existed since slavery have mutated and changed, but they have not been eradicated. We can't understand, teach about, or change what's happening in this country if we don't face this fact. And our students know that. Being an effective teacher in today's society means taking the Black Lives Matter movement seriously.

For all the "students first" rhetoric of the corporate education reformers — who claim their policies are directed at closing the "achievement gap" — they are conspicuously absent from the Black Lives Matter movement. In fact, the corporate reform agenda is in direct conflict with the goals of the movement. In city after city, Black students are those most affected by the decimation of neighborhood schools, the "no excuses" discipline and rote teaching of charters like KIPP, the substitution of endless test prep for meaningful curriculum, and the imposition of two-years-and-I'm-gone Teach for America corps members on our highest needs students.

Black Lives Matter doesn't just mean Black people don't want to be shot down in the streets by unaccountable police. As anti-racist teachers and students, we need to expand the slogan to include:

- Stop closing schools in Black neighborhoods.
- Fund schools equitably.
- Support African American studies programs and substantive multicultural curriculum.

After activists staged a Black Lives Matter die-in in Michigan in December 2014, Will Daniels, from United Students Against Sweatshops, told the *Nation*: "As a Black student, my rationale for doing the die-in was that structural racism causes not only police brutality, but also the starving of majority Black schools. This is a subtler form of violence."

Let Black Children Be Children

The murder of Tamir Rice exposes a connection between individual racism and structural racism with important implications for teachers. Tamir was only 12 years old when police showed up at the Cleveland park where he was playing with a toy gun and shot him down within two seconds of their arrival. When his 14-year-old sister ran over, she was tackled to the ground and handcuffed. The officer who called in the shooting described Tamir to the dispatcher as a "Black male, maybe 20."

Overestimating the age, size, and culpability of Black children is a widespread phenomenon, according to *The Essence of Innocence: Consequences of Dehumanizing Black Children*, based on research led by UCLA's Phillip Atiba Goff and Matthew Christian Jackson. One of their studies involved 264 mostly white female undergraduates who were asked to assess the age and innocence of white, Black, and Latino boys. The students saw the Black boys as more culpable and overestimated their age by 4.5 years. "Perceptions of the essential nature of children can be affected by race and, for Black children, this can mean they lose the protection afforded by assumed childhood innocence well before they become adults," said Jackson. "Black children may be viewed as adults when they're just 13 years old."

> "This is our time, as youth, to speak. . . . The waking up that America has done in the past couple of months — something that us as youth get to witness and get to be a part of — has been extremely powerful."

It's not much of a stretch to see how this affects Black children in schools where the majority of their teachers are not African American. Any time teachers or administrators see Black children as older than they are, "just being teenagers" (or pre-teens, or little kids) becomes something threatening that has to be controlled or disciplined. How can children grow and learn if the adults around them see them as older and "guiltier" than they are? What will it take for school communities to eradicate this deeply embedded prejudice?

Why Not "All Lives Matter?"

As the Black Lives Matter movement has grown, some participants have questioned whether "All Lives Matter" is a more inclusive slogan. Although we recognize the serious impact of racism and other forms of oppression on many groups of people in the United States, we think it's important to understand and talk with others about the historical and current realities behind this specific demand. As Alicia Garza, one of the movement's originators, explains:

> When we say Black Lives Matter, we are talking about the ways in which Black people are deprived of our basic human rights and dignity. . . . It is an acknowledgment that 1 million Black people are locked in cages in this country. . . . It is an acknowledgment that Black women continue to bear the burden of a relentless assault on our children and our families. . . . #BlackLivesMatter doesn't mean your life isn't important — it means that Black lives, which are seen as without value within white supremacy, are important to your liberation. Given the disproportionate impact state violence has on Black lives, we understand that when Black people in this country get free, the benefits will be wide-reaching and transformative for society as a whole.

> "When we say Black Lives Matter, we are talking about the ways in which Black people are deprived of our basic human rights and dignity. . . . Given the disproportionate impact state violence has on Black lives, we understand that when Black people in this country get free, the benefits will be wide-reaching and transformative for society as a whole."
> — Alicia Garza, co-founder #BlackLivesMatter

A civil disobedience demonstration that closed down the federal building in Oakland, California, during Martin Luther King Jr. weekend in 2015 highlighted the connections. Behind a banner reading "Third World for Black Power," protesters identified themselves as Arabs, Filipinas/os, Latinas/os, Koreans, Chinese, Palestinians, and South Asians "for Black resistance." As Filipina activist Rhonda Ramiro said: "The wealth accumulated through the enslavement of Black people in the United States enabled the United States to go around the world and colonize countries like the Philippines. We see our struggle for independence as linked 100 percent."

Within that framework, how teachers apply this understanding will obviously vary from classroom to classroom, depending on how old the children are, their experience and knowledge about the issues involved, and the level of community that has been built in the classroom.

How to Make Black Lives Matter in Our Schools

So what does all this mean in individual classrooms and schools? Here are a few ideas for bringing Black Lives Matter into our teaching:

1. Provide a social justice, anti-racist curriculum that gives students the historical grounding, literacy skills, and space to explore the emotional intensity of feelings around the murder of Black youth by police. At the same time, deep discussion of these heavy issues needs to build on strong classroom community. Students can't launch into discussions of racism without a basis of trust and sharing among students and between students and teacher. That is the slow, steady work of meaningful classroom conversation, purposeful group work, reading and writing about critical social and personal issues, shared writing, and more. Teachers need to nurture communities of mutual respect and empathy.

2. Support students who want to have conversations about the Black Lives Matter movement outside the classroom, in school forums or school clubs. Educators supporting the work of BSUs in schools across the country have helped transform the school climate. Black students' sense of pride and self-worth have helped ignite this new civil rights movement.

3. Raise the Black Lives Matter movement with other teachers at our schools and in our unions. It's not enough to provide students with historical lessons. History is being made today by teachers planning Black Student Lives Matter forums and die-ins, advocating for hiring more Black teachers, and participating in many other actions around the country.

> This is the moment social justice educators have been waiting for. . . . The topic of police violence against Black people and systemic racism is on the table in a way it hasn't been for a generation. It's time to put aside the test prep and build a school-to-justice pipeline.

This is the moment social justice educators have been waiting for. When pro football players ran onto the field with their hands up in a demonstration of solidarity with the "Hands Up, Don't Shoot" protests that followed Michael Brown's murder, some people in the audience supported them; others were opposed. But everyone knew what they meant. This is a sea change. The topic of police violence against Black people and systemic racism is on the table in a way it hasn't been for a generation. It's time to put aside the test prep and build a school-to-justice pipeline. ■

How One Elementary School Sparked a Citywide Movement to Make Black Students' Lives Matter

By Wayne Au and Jesse Hagopian

SHARON CHANG

t was the morning of Sept. 16, 2016, and a conscious party of resistance, courage, and community uplift was happening on the sidewalk in front of John Muir Elementary in Seattle. Dozens of Black men were lined up from the street to the school doorway, giving high-fives and praise to all the students who entered as part of a locally organized event called "Black Men Uniting to Change the Narrative." African American drummers pounded defiant rhythms. Students smiled and laughed as they made their way to the entrance. And teachers and parents milled about in #BlackLivesMatter T-shirts, developed and worn in solidarity with the movement to make Black lives matter at John Muir Elementary.

You never would have known that, just hours before, the school was closed and emptied as bomb-sniffing dogs scoured the building looking for explosives.

That September morning was the culmination of a combination of purposeful conversations among John Muir administration and staff, activism, and media attention. John Muir Elementary sits in Seattle's Rainier Valley, and its student population reflects the community: 68 percent of Muir's roughly 400 students qualify for free or reduced lunch, 33 percent are officially designated transition bilingual, 10 percent are Hispanic, 11 percent are Asian American, 11 percent identify as multiracial, and almost 50 percent are African American — mostly a mix of East African immigrants and families from this historically Black neighborhood.

By that autumn, John Muir Elementary had been actively working on issues of race equity, with special attention to Black students, for months. The previous year, Muir's staff began a deliberate process of examining privilege and the politics of race. With the support of both the school and the PTA, Ruby Bridges — who as a child famously desegregated the all-white William Frantz Elementary School in New Orleans in 1960 — had also visited Muir as part of a longer discussion of racism in education among staff and students. During end-of-the-summer professional development, with the support of administration and in the aftermath of the police killings of Alton Sterling and Philando Castile, school staff read and discussed an article on #BlackLivesMatter and renewed their commitment to working for racial justice at Muir.

As part of these efforts, DeShawn Jackson, an African American male student support worker, organized the "Black Men Uniting to Change the Narrative" event for that September morning, and in solidarity, school staff decided to wear T-shirts that read "Black Lives Matter/We Stand Together/John Muir Elementary," designed by the school's art teacher.

A local TV station reported on the teachers wearing #BlackLivesMatter T-shirts, and as the story went public, political tensions exploded. Soon the white supremacist, hate group-fueled news source *Breitbart* picked up the story, and the right-wing police support group Blue Lives Matter publicly denounced the effort. Hateful emails and phone calls began to flood the John Muir administration and the Seattle School Board, and then the horrifying happened: Someone made a bomb threat against the school. Even though the threat was deemed not very credible by authorities, Seattle Public Schools officially canceled the "Black Men Uniting to Change the Narrative" event at Muir out of extreme caution.

All of this is what made that September morning all the more powerful. The bomb-sniffing dogs found nothing and school was kept open that day. The drummers drummed and the crowd cheered every child coming through the doors of John Muir Elementary. Everyone was there in celebration, loudly proclaiming that, yes, despite the racist and right-wing attacks, despite the official cancellation, and despite the bomb threat, the community of John Muir Elementary would not be cowed by hate and fear. Black men showed up to change the narrative around education and race. School staff wore their #BlackLivesMatter T-shirts and devoted the day's teaching to issues of racial justice, all bravely and proudly celebrating their power. In the process, this single South Seattle elementary galvanized a growing citywide movement to make Black lives matter in Seattle schools.

Organizing Across the District

Inspired by that bold action, members of the Social Equity Educators (SEE), a rank-and-file organization of union educators, invited a few John Muir staff to a meeting to offer support and learn more about their efforts. The Muir educators' story explaining how and why they organized for Black lives moved everyone in attendance, and the SEE members began discussing taking the action citywide.

Everyone was there in celebration, loudly proclaiming that, yes, despite the racist and right-wing attacks, despite the official cancellation, and despite the bomb threat, the community of John Muir Elementary would not be cowed by hate and fear.

Everyone agreed that there were potential pitfalls of doing a citywide Black students' lives matter event. The John Muir teachers had a race and equity team and dedicated professional development time the previous year to discuss institutional racism, and they had collectively come to the decision as an entire school to support the action and wear the shirts. What would it mean at a different school if some teachers wore the shirts and taught anti-racist lessons, and others didn't? What if only a few dozen teachers across Seattle wore the shirts — would that send the wrong message? What if other schools received threats? What if those threats materialized?

These and other considerations fueled an important discussion and debate among SEE members, and highlighted the need to educate our communities about why this action was urgently needed. However, with the videos of police killing Philando Castile and Alton Sterling fresh in the minds of SEE members, the group decided that to not publicly declare that Black lives matter would be a message in and of itself.

And it wasn't just about the police murder of Black people that motivated SEE to organize an action across the school system. It was also because of the institutional racism infecting Seattle's public schools. Seattle has an alarming pattern of segregation both between and within schools, with intensely tracked advanced classes overwhelmingly populated with white students. Moreover, the Department of Education's 2013 investigation found that Seattle Public Schools suspended Black students at about four times the rate of white students for the same infractions.

SEE members decided that on Oct. 19, 2016, they would all wear Black Lives Matter shirts to school and voted to create a second T-shirt design that included "#SayHerName." The African American Policy Forum created this hashtag in the wake of Sandra Bland's death while in the custody of Waller County (Texas) police, to raise awareness about police violence against women, to raise awareness about police violence against Black women, and to raise awareness about police violence particularly against Black queer women and Black transgender women.

As part of this action, SEE also developed a three-point policy proposal that would serve as an ongoing campaign to support Black Lives Matter in schools and aid in the struggle against institutional racism:

1. Support ethnic studies in all schools.
2. Replace zero-tolerance discipline with restorative justice practices.
3. De-track classes within the schools to undo the racial segregation that is reinforced by tracking.

In addition, SEE voted to bring a resolution to the Seattle Education Association (SEA), the union representing Seattle's educators, to publicly declare support for the action of the John Muir teachers and community, and to call on all teachers across the district to actively support the Oct. 19 action.

At the September SEA Representative Assembly, SEE member Sarah Arvey, a white special education teacher, brought forward the following resolution:

> Whereas the SEA promotes equity and supports anti-racist work in our schools; and,
>
> Whereas we want to act in solidarity with our members and the community at John Muir who received threats based on their decision to wear Black Lives Matter T-shirts as part of an event with "Black Men United to Change the Narrative"; and,
>
> Whereas the SEA and SPS promote Race and Equity teams to address institutionalized racism in our schools and offer a space for dialogue among school staff; and,
>
> Therefore be it resolved that the SEA Representative Assembly endorse and participate in an action wearing Black Lives Matter T-shirts on Wednesday, October 19, 2016, with the intent of showing solidarity, promoting anti-racist practices in our schools, and creating dialogue in our schools and communities.

SEE members expected a difficult debate at the SEA Representative Assembly, and many didn't think the resolution would pass. But they underestimated the impact of the ongoing protests against police brutality and racism that were sweeping school campuses. Inspired by San Francisco 49ers quarterback Colin Kaepernick, the Garfield High School football team captured headlines around the city and nation when every single player and coach took a knee during the national anthem — and maintained that action for the entire season. The protest spread to the girls' volleyball team, the marching band, the cheerleaders, and many other high school sports teams across Seattle. When it came time for the SEA vote, the resolution to support Black Lives Matter at School day passed unanimously.

As word got out about the SEA Representative Assembly vote, and in reaction to the threats against John Muir Elementary earlier in the month, allies also began to step forward in support of making Black Students' Lives Matter. The Seattle NAACP quickly endorsed the event and lent its support. Soup for Teachers, a local parent organizing group formed to support the 2015 SEA strike, as well as the executive board of the Seattle Council Parent Teacher Student Association, also endorsed the action and joined in solidarity.

SEE helped gather representatives from these organizations for an Oct. 12 press conference to explain why parents, educators, and racial justice advocates united to declare Black lives matter at school. Predictably, news outlets repeatedly asked teachers if they thought they were politicizing the classroom by wearing BLM shirts to school. Seattle NAACP education chair Rita Green responded directly: "We're here to support families. We're here to support students. When Black lives matter, all lives matter."

Arvey told reporters, "It's important for us to know the history of racial justice and racial injustice in our country and in our world . . . in order for us to address it. When we're silent, we close off dialogue and we close the opportunity to learn and grow from each other." Other teachers pointed out that students were having discussions all the time in the halls, during sports practice, and outside of school about racism, police violence, and the Black Lives Matter movement. A better question to ask, teachers asserted, would be "Is school going to be relevant to the issues that our students are discussing every day?"

In an effort to build greater solidarity for Seattle educators taking part in the Black Lives Matter at School day, one of us — Wayne — organized a national letter for professors to sign in an effort to build support for the action. After only a few days, close to 250 professors, many of them well-recognized scholars in educational research locally and nationally, had signed on. Another letter of support was signed by luminaries such as dissident scholar Noam Chomsky, former MSNBC anchor Melissa Harris-Perry, 1968 bronze medalist and activist John Carlos, Black Lives Matter co-founder Opal Tometi, noted education author Jonathan Kozol, and Pulitzer Prize-winning journalist Jose Antonio Vargas.

As support for Seattle's Black Lives Matter at School action swelled, in a move that surprised many, the Seattle Public Schools' administration, with no formal provocation from activists or the school board, officially endorsed the event. An Oct. 8 memo read:

During our #CloseTheGaps kickoff week, Seattle Education Association is promoting October 19 as a day of solidarity to bring focus to racial equity and affirming the lives of our students — specifically our students of color.

In support of this focus, members are choosing to wear Black Lives Matter T-shirts, stickers, or other symbols of their commitment to students in a coordinated effort. SEA is leading this effort and working to promote transformational conversations with staff, families, and students on this issue.

We invite you to join us in our commitment to eliminate opportunity gaps and accelerate learning for each and every student.

At that point, we in Seattle felt that we had accomplished something historic, because for perhaps the first time in Seattle's history, the teachers and the teacher union, the parents and the PTSA, students and the Seattle Public Schools administration had all reached a consensus support for a very politicized action for racial justice in education.

As the Oct. 19 Black Lives Matter at School day approached, orders for the various Black Lives Matter T-shirts soared. John Muir set up a site where T-shirt purchases would directly benefit the school's racial justice work. SEE's online T-shirt site received some 2,000 orders for the BLM shirts, with proceeds going to support racial justice campaigns and a portion going to John Muir. Other schools created their own T-shirt designs specific to their schools. Seattle's schools were now poised for unprecedented mass action for racial justice.

Black Lives Matter at School Day

As Oct. 19 arrived, Garfield High School senior Bailey Adams was in disbelief. She told Seattle's KING 5 News, "There was a moment of like, is this really going to happen? Are teachers actually going to wear these shirts? All of my years I've been in school, this has never been talked about. Teachers have never said anything where they're going to back their students of color."

But sure enough, every school across the city had educators come to school wearing the shirts. Hundreds of teachers took advantage of the day to teach lessons and lead discussions about institutional racism. SEE and Soup for Teachers partnered to make a handout called "Teaching and Mentoring for Racial Justice" that suggested BLM resources for both teachers and parents. The SEA also emailed suggested resources to teachers.

Some schools changed their reader boards to declare "Black Lives Matter." Parents at some elementary schools set up tables by the front entrance with books and resources to help other parents talk to their kids about

And it wasn't just about the police murder of Black people that motivated SEE to organize an action across the school system. It was also because of the institutional racism infecting Seattle's public schools.

racism. Many schools coordinated plans for teaching about Black lives, including lessons about movements for racial justice and lessons about the way racism impacts the school system today. Several teachers across the district showed the film *Stay Woke* about the origins of the Black Lives Matter movement, and held class discussions afterward. Some educators used the opportunity to discuss intersectional identities and highlighted how Black and queer women had first launched the #BlackLivesMatter hashtag.

Schools such as Chief Sealth International High School and Garfield High School put up Black Lives Matter posters/graffiti walls, which quickly filled up with anti-racist commentary from students and educators. A teacher at Dearborn Park International Elementary built a lesson plan from a photo of Colin Kaepernick kneeling. To capture the power of the day, educators from most of the schools around the district took group photos wearing the BLM shirts and sent them to the union for publication.

While the educators who launched this movement were quite aware that the institutions of racism remained intact, they also knew those same institutions had been shaken.

During lunchtime, the Garfield faculty, staff, and students rallied on the front steps of the school. In one of the most moving and powerful moments of the day, Black special education teacher Janet Du Bois decided she finally had to tell everyone a secret she had been quietly suffering with. In front of all the assembled school community and media she revealed that the police had murdered her son several years ago — and this had happened after he had been failed by the education system and pushed out of school. Fighting through tears, Du Bois said, "When our kids are failed, they have to go to alternative places and end up with their lives hanging in the balance because someone does not care."

To cap off the extraordinary and powerful day, SEE organized a community celebration, forum, and talent showcase that evening that drew hundreds of people. The event was emceed by educator, organizer, poet, attorney, and soon-to-be Seattle mayoral candidate Nikkita Oliver. Spoken word poets, musicians, and the Northwest Tap Connection (made up of predominantly Black youth performers) delighted and inspired the audience. Black youth activists from middle schools and high schools engaged in an onstage discussion about their experience of racism in school and what changes they wanted to see to make the education system truly value their lives. Seahawks Pro Bowl defensive end Michael Bennett came to the event and pledged his support of the movement, saying, "Some people believe the change has to come from the government, but I believe it has to be organic and come from the bottom."

By the end of the day, thousands of educators had reached tens of thousands of Seattle students and parents with a message of support for Black students and opposition to anti-Black racism — with local and national media projecting the message much farther. While the educators who launched this movement were quite aware that the institutions of racism remained intact, they also knew those same institutions had been shaken.

Lessons Learned

In many ways we had a successful campaign around making Black lives matter in Seattle schools, and, from an organizing perspective, we learned several important lessons. To begin, we learned that one school can make a big difference: A single elementary school bravely took a stand that provided a spark for an already simmering citywide movement, and influenced national discussions as educators in Philadelphia, Rochester (New York), and elsewhere followed suit with similar educationally based #BlackLivesMatter actions.

We also learned that acting in the context of a broader social movement was critical. The police killings of Philando Castile and Alton Sterling in the summer of 2016, as part of the long-standing pattern of Black death at the hands of police, ensured that there were ongoing protests and conversations associated with #BlackLivesMatter. This broader movement created the political space and helped garner support for the actions of both John Muir Elementary specifically, and Seattle Public Schools more generally.

In addition, we learned that sometimes when the white supremacists, "alt-right," and right-wing conservatives attack, it can make our organizing stronger and more powerful. In the case of Seattle, it was the avalanche of hateful emails and calls, the right-wing media stories, and the bomb threat against John Muir Elementary that ultimately galvanized teachers and parents across the city.

We also learned that developing a broad base of support was essential to the success of the campaign to make Black student lives matter in Seattle schools. Garnering the official support of the teacher union, the executive board of the Seattle Council PTSA, and even Seattle Public Schools, as well as gathering acts of solidarity from scholars and others nationally, helped build a protective web of political support to shield Seattle educators as they moved forward with their action.

In the end, we also learned that, with more time and resources, we could have done better organizing. For instance, we had to grapple with the fact that when the John Muir Elementary staff made the decision to wear their #BlackLivesMatter T-shirts, it was after being a part of sustained discussion and professional development that took place over multiple years. Ideally, all schools should have had the opportunity to have similar discussions as part of their typical professional development so that, when a moment like this happens, all school staff have stronger basic understandings of racial justice to guide their decision-making.

Another improvement would have been to be able to offer a clearer vision of curriculum across the district for the Black Lives Matter at School day. Despite the strength of the "Teaching and Mentoring for Racial Justice" resource handout developed by SEE and Soup for Teachers, the quality and depth of what children at different schools learned on the day of the districtwide event varied wildly from school to school. With just a little more time and resources, we could have provided teachers with a cluster of grade-level appropriate teaching activities that they could have used on that day if they wanted. In particular, this is something that might have helped teachers around the district who wanted to support the action but struggled with ways to explicitly make Black lives matter in their own classroom curriculum.

It wasn't until the end of the school year that we learned two more lessons. The first was that, despite widespread community support for the Black Lives Matter at School day, the passive-aggressive racism of some of Seattle's notoriously liberal, white parents had been lurking all along. In a June 2017 story, local news radio station KUOW reported on a series of emails from white parents who live in the more affluent north end of Seattle. According to the story, white parents complained not just about the perceived militancy and politics of the Black Lives Matter in School day in Seattle, but that children couldn't handle talking about racism, and that we should be colorblind because "all lives matter." Importantly, many of these parents openly questioned the existence of racial inequality in Seattle's schools.

The second lesson we learned well after the Black Lives Matter in School day was that our action helped strengthen the political groundwork for a continued focus on racial justice in Seattle Public Schools. On July 5, 2017, the Seattle School Board unanimously passed a resolution in support of ethnic studies in Seattle Public Schools in response to a yearlong campaign from the NAACP, SEE, and other social justice groups, including formal endorsement from the Seattle Education Association. While this policy shift happened on the strength of the community organizing for ethnic studies specifically, Seattle's movement to make Black Lives Matter in School demonstrated to the district that there was significant public support for racial justice initiatives in Seattle schools, effectively increasing the official space for other initiatives like ethnic studies to take hold.

Putting the Shirts Back On

The school year ended with a horrific reminder of why we must continue to declare the value of Black lives when on Sunday, June 18, 2017, Seattle police shot and killed Charleena Lyles, a pregnant mother of four, in her own apartment after she called them in fear her home was being burglarized. She was shot down in a hail of bullets in front of three of her kids, two of whom attended public elementary schools in Seattle. The immediate media narrative of her death dehumanized her by focusing on the fact that the police alleged Charleena was wielding a kitchen knife, that she had a history of mental illness, and a criminal background. This was the usual strategy of killing the person and then assassinating their character in an attempt to turn public opinion in support of the police.

But in Seattle, there were the countervailing forces of Charleena's organized family, community activists, and Seattle educators who forced a different public discussion about the value of Black lives and the callous disregard of them by unaccountable police. SEE and the SEA immediately put out a call for teachers to put their Black Lives Matter shirts back on — many of which also featured #SayHerName

— for a districtwide action in solidarity with Charleena and her family on June 20. Within three days of Charleena's death, hundreds of teachers came to school wearing heartbreak, rage, and solidarity in the form of their Black Lives Matter T-shirts — with shirt sales this time going to Charleena's family.

A couple hundred educators swelled the ranks of the after-school rally that day with Charleena's family and hundreds of other supporters at the apartment complex where she had been killed. With educators from her son's schools and all across the district rallying to Charleena's side, the press was compelled to run stories talking about her as a woman, as a parent of Seattle schoolchildren, and as a person with talents and struggles like everyone else.

Seattle's Black Lives Matter at School day is only a beginning. Having nearly 3,000 teachers wear T-shirts to school one day doesn't magically end anti-Black racism or white supremacy. If that were the case, then perhaps Charleena Lyles would still be alive today to drop her kids off at school, chat with other parents on the playground, and watch the children play.

But something powerful and important did happen in Seattle. At John Muir Elementary, the school staff and community stood strong against white supremacist hate, and across Seattle schools,

We learned that sometimes when the white supremacists, "alt-right," and right-wing conservatives attack, it can make our organizing stronger and more powerful.

teachers and parents found a way to stand in solidarity with Black students and their families. In the process, the public dialogue about institutionalized racism in Seattle schools was pushed forward in concrete ways. And while we have so much more work to do, in the end, what happened in Seattle showed that educators have an important role to play in the movement for Black lives. When they rise up across the country to join this movement — both inside the school and outside on the streets — institutions of racism can be challenged in the search for solidarity, healing, and justice. ∎

Wayne Au and Jesse Hagopian are editors of Rethinking Schools. *Au, a former public high school teacher, is a professor in the School of Educational Studies at the University of Washington Bothell. Hagopian teaches ethnic studies at Seattle's Garfield High School and is a member of Social Equity Educators (SEE). You can follow him @ JessedHagopian.*

ST. LOUIS AMERICAN • SEPT. 28 – OCT. 4, 2017

SPORTS EYE

With Alvin A. Reid

Black players brought the N America to its knees during anthe

HOWARD BARRY

Student Athletes Kneel to Level the Playing Field

By Jesse Hagopian

'rotests

Paying the Bills - Former Buffalo Bills quarterback and Hall of Famer **Jim Kelly** was critical of the national anthem protests in Buffalo – and brought religion into the equation in a social media post with a photo of him standing with his hand over his heart. "The only time I will ever take a knee is to pray and to thank the Good Lord for what he's given me. We all have our issues. ... But I do know that we need to UNITE not SEPARATE. I hope next week we can STAND, LOCK ARMS and become ONE FAMILY."

Bills defensive end **Jerry Hughes**, who is black, countered saying "I was very disappointed in him. I was very disappointed in how he approached the whole situa-

...y was ...the national ...lly set Kelly

Sean McCoy, ...rong, but I total ...isagree with ...Kelly, who ...side- ...stood for the ...nt to kneel?

It started one Friday night in September 2016 with the jocks, the coaches, the marching band, and the cheerleaders. It was just two weeks after San Francisco 49ers quarterback Colin Kaepernick took a knee during the national anthem before a game against San Diego, and the Black Student Union, the teachers, and the administration soon joined in too.

These disparate high school groups don't often come together in common cause, but they did at Garfield High School where I teach in Seattle. And in times of great peril and great hope, barriers that may have once seemed concrete can collapse under a mighty solidarity.

The crisis of police terror in Black communities across the country is just such a peril, and the resistance to that terror, symbolized by athletes protesting, is just such a hope.

The power of athletes collectively joining the movement for Black lives first found expression on July 9, 2016, when the members of the WNBA's Minnesota Lynx showed up at a game in warm-up shirts printed with the phrases "Black Lives Matter," "Change Starts with Us," and "Justice and Accountability," along with the names of Alton Sterling and Philando Castile, who had recently been killed by police. The movement spread quickly across the WNBA, with the New York Liberty, Indiana Fever, and Washington Mystics all refusing to answer reporters' postgame questions unless they related to the Black Lives Matter movement or other social issues.

Then, in the initial weeks of the 2016 football season, as Kaepernick's fledgling protest began to also take shape, critics bombarded him with insults and it was unclear what the response around the country would be.

And that's when Garfield, and high schools and students around the nation, stepped up to the challenge.

On Sept. 16, the entire Garfield football team, including the coaches, joined in the protest that Kaepernick set in motion by taking a knee during the national anthem. As Garfield football player Jelani Howard said, "It really affected people and showed that kids can actually make a difference in the world." Head football coach Joey Thomas said of the action, "One thing we pride ourselves on is we have open and honest conversations about what is going on in this society. It led kids to talk about the social injustice they experience."

The team's bold action for justice made headlines. Their photo appeared in the October 2016 issue of *Time* magazine that featured Kaepernick on the cover, and CBS News came to Garfield to do a special on the protest.

And the Garfield Bulldogs weren't alone. A dozen high school football players in Sacramento also took a knee that same day. About 24 hours later the cheerleading squad at Howard University refused to stand, and a couple days after that several members of the Oakland Unified School District Honor Band kneeled with their clarinets, trombones, tubas, and behind their cellos while playing the national anthem before an Oakland A's game.

In times of great peril and great hope, barriers that may have once seemed concrete can collapse under a mighty solidarity.

Kaepernick knew how important these youth protests were.

"We have a younger generation that sees these issues and want to be able to correct them," Kaepernick told the *Seattle Times* about the Garfield Bulldogs taking a knee. "I think that's amazing. I think it shows the strength, the character, and the courage of our youth. Ultimately, they're going to be needed to help make this change."

For the Garfield students, the protest was not only a move in solidarity with Kaepernick and against the ongoing crisis of state violence against Black people, it also served as a rejection of the rarely recited third verse of the "Star Spangled Banner," which celebrates the killing of Black people. As the Garfield football team said in a joint statement:

> We are asking for the community and our leaders to step forward to meet with us and engage in honest dialogue. It is our hope that out of these potentially uncomfortable conversations positive, impactful change will be created.

The conversation in the locker room led the team to analyze the ways racism is connected to other forms of oppression and the ways those forms of oppression disfigure many aspects of their lives, including the media and the school system. Yes, football players publicly challenging homophobia may be rare, but the Bulldog scholar-athletes wanted it known that it was time to upend all forms of oppression. Here was the team's six-point program to confront injustice:

1. Equality for all regardless of race, gender, class, social standing, and/or sexual orientation — both in and out of the classroom as well as the community.

2. Increase of unity within the community. Changing the way the media portrays crime. White people are typically given justification while other minorities are seen as thugs.

3. Academic equality for students. Certain schools offer programs/tracks that are not available at all schools or to all students within that school. Better opportunities for students who don't have parental or financial support are needed. For example, not everyone can afford Advanced Placement (AP) testing fees and those who are unable to pay those fees are often not encouraged to enroll in those programs. In addition, the academic investment doesn't always stay within the community.

4. [Opposition to] Lack of adequate training for teachers to interact effectively with all students. Example, "Why is my passion mistaken for aggression?" "Why when I get an A on a test does the teacher tell me, 'Wow, I didn't know you could pull that off'?"

5. [Opposition to] Segregation through classism.

6. Getting others to see that institutional racism does exist in our community, city, state.

And the rebellion at Garfield didn't stop with the Bulldogs' football team.

The Garfield High School girls' volleyball team all took a knee before a game that same week. At the following football game, the marching band and the cheerleaders joined the players on bended knee for justice. At the homecoming game — a space that is more associated with mascots and rivalry than with protest and solidarity — Black Student Union members lifted a sign during the national anthem proclaiming:

When we kneel you riot, but when we're shot you're quiet.

The sign referenced death threats directed at Kaepernick as well as cowardly wishes of harm made against the Garfield football team for their actions. One Black Student Union officer told me:

The anthem doesn't represent what is currently happening in the U.S. and what has happened in the past — from slavery to police brutality and mass incarceration. Don't be mad at us for protesting against these issues, be mad at the people who caused them.

Garfield's protest was indicative of campuses around the country in the weeks after Kaepernick began his protest, and the movement burst onto the field of play nationwide. As *Time* magazine wrote:

Athletes across the country have taken a knee, locked arms, or raised a fist during the anthem. The movement has spread from NFL Sundays to college football Saturdays to the Friday night lights of high school games and even trickled down into the peewee ranks, where a youth team in Texas decided they, too, needed to take a stand by kneeling.

By the third week of the NFL season, the protests had been echoed everywhere from volleyball courts in West Virginia to football fields in Nebraska. Then on Sept. 15, the movement reached the international stage when Megan Rapinoe, an openly gay member of the U.S. women's soccer team, kneeled for the anthem before a match against Thailand. "I thought a lot about it, read a lot about it, and just felt, "How can I not kneel too?" Rapinoe tells *Time*. "I know what it's like to look at the flag and not have all your rights."

There is a deep fear from the sports establishment (which often overlaps with the richest 1 percent of Americans) and from politicians of the potential of this protest. Team owners and school officials worry the protest will disrupt the branding of their sports and cut into the bottom line. The wealthiest 1 percent and the politicians who serve their interests have even deeper fears. The ability to reproduce a vastly unequal society, generation after generation, requires a populace that believes in the infallibility of the nation. These protests expose the great contradiction of a country that professes to be the freest on earth and yet has always brutalized Black people. Institutional racism, from slavery, to segregation, to redlining, to our own era of mass incarceration, has played a seminal role in creating vast amounts of wealth for a mostly white owning class at the top of society. And yet far too often, the beneficiaries of this arrangement have gotten away with public declarations of living in the "world's greatest democracy."

These protests expose the great contradiction of a country that professes to be the freest on earth and yet has always brutalized Black people.

Sports have long played a pivotal role in our nation as promoting blind patriotism and the myth of a meritocratic society. These protests threaten more than just the sensibilities of people who find the silent gestures distasteful. They threaten more than just the profit margins of some of the wealthiest corporations in the country. These protests hold the potential to expose the very deceit upon which oppression and exploitation rest.

So as with any movement to disrupt oppression and demand human rights, the reaction against it by those in power has been forceful and brutal. The U.S. Soccer Federation quickly changed its rules to mandate all players stand for the anthem. Youth across the country have been reprimanded and even kicked off teams for protesting. And Colin Kaepernick has lost his job.

For the 2017 NFL season, Kaepernick has been shut out of the league, with the owners actively refusing to sign him to any team, even as a backup quarterback. Owners may have been hoping that with the example of Kaepernick losing his job over the protest that it would intimidate others from taking up the cause. But despite the attack on Kaepernick, players such as Seattle Seahawk Michael Bennett, San Francisco 49er Eric Reid, and Philadelphia Eagle Malcolm Jenkins continued to protest during the anthem.

Even several white NFL players, such as Chris Long and Justin Britt, took to standing next to these protesting athletes with a hand on their shoulder in solidarity.

Then before week three of the 2017 NFL season, President Donald Trump used a speech in Huntsville, Alabama, to attack players who protest during the national anthem. Trump said, "Wouldn't you love to see one of these NFL owners, when somebody disrespects our flag, to say 'Get that son of a bitch off the field right now, out. He's fired. He's fired!'"

Trump had hoped these words would lead to the disciplining of any player who had the audacity to exercise free speech. But instead, his words were a lit match to the tinderbox of rebellion that swept across the league. Some 200 players protested that week. Almost the entire Oakland Raiders team sat or kneeled for the anthem. The Seattle Seahawks and Tennessee Titans refused to come out of the locker room during the national anthem, with the Seahawks releasing a statement saying:

> As a team, we have decided we will not participate in the national anthem. We will not stand for the injustice that has plagued people of color in this country. Out of love for our country and in honor of the sacrifices made on our behalf, we unite to oppose those that would deny our most basic freedoms. We remain committed in continuing to work towards equality and justice for all.

And in the wake of Trump's comments and the horrible reaction by NFL team owners, student athletes around the country have continued to rise up for Black lives as well.

Members of the Traip Academy girls' soccer team in Kittery, Maine, kneeled in protest during the anthem. So did high school football players on both teams at a game in Evanston, Illinois. And a few hundred students at an Alameda, California, high school took a knee after classes on the Monday following the weekend of NFL controversy, as proposed by the high school's student body president — a move no doubt inspired by the student athletes who protested during the anthem the previous year.

Increasingly, threats are being made — and even carried out — against those who engage in these protests.

On Sept. 28, 2017, Waylon Bates, the principal of the public Parkway High School in Bossier City, Louisiana, said the school "requires student athletes to stand in a respectful manner throughout the national anthem during any sporting event in which their team is participating. . . . Failure to comply will result in loss of playing time and/or

If Colin Kaepernick had been the only one to kneel in protest of police brutality during the anthem, it would have been an important act of moral courage. But when young athletes around the nation found the same bravery, it helped launch a mass movement of athletes at every level of sports in what has become one of the leading edges of the movement for Black lives.

participation as directed by the head coach and principal."

In Cahokia, Illinois, youth football coach Orlando "Doc" Gooden was suspended from coaching after his team of 7- and 8-year-olds took a knee during their Sept. 17, 2017, game in response to the acquittal of St. Louis cop Jason Stockley for the killing of Anthony Lamar Smith.

And in Houston, Cedric Ingram-Lewis and his cousin Larry McCullough were both kicked off their high school football team because of their protest during the anthem at a game on Sept. 29, 2017. "We had to get our message across: End racial injustice and the oppression of Black people," Ingram-Lewis told the *New York Times*.

> **When the story of the Civil Rights Movement is told, too often the many great leaders of the movement obscure the hundreds of middle and high school students who protested and filled the jails in opposition to legal segregation.**

While the threats and intimidation have been real, the protests continue because the oppression that caused the protests hasn't ceased. And while the professional players and student athletes are not on the same field, they are side by side in the struggle.

If Colin Kaepernick had been the only one to kneel in protest of police brutality during the anthem, it would have been an important act of moral courage. But when young athletes around the nation found the same bravery, it helped launch a mass movement of athletes at every level of sports in what has become one of the leading edges of the movement for Black lives. There can be no doubt that this movement is having an impact when you consider an Oct. 2, 2017, *USA Today* poll that found 68 percent of respondents believe Trump's call for NFL owners to fire the players and fans to boycott their games was inappropriate.

When the story of the Civil Rights Movement is told, too often the many great leaders of the movement obscure the hundreds of middle and high school students who protested and filled the jails in opposition to legal segregation. But let us not forget that it was the mass mobilization of youth in cities like Birmingham, Alabama, that played a pivotal role in breaking the back of Jim Crow. And let us not forget to tell the story of our youth today who, at great personal risk, are fighting to level the playing field by taking a knee in the struggle for Black lives. ∎

Jesse Hagopian teaches ethnic studies at Seattle's Garfield High School, is a member of Social Equity Educators (SEE), and is an editor of Rethinking Schools. *You can follow him on Twitter @JessedHagopian. A previous version of this article was published by the* Progressive *in October 2016.*

Happening Yesterday, Happened Tomorrow

Teaching the ongoing murders of Black men

By Renée Watson

Emmett Till.

Medgar Evers.

Henry Dumas.

Fred Hampton.

Mulugeta Seraw.

Amadou Diallo.

Sean Bell.

Oscar Grant.

Trayvon Martin.

Jordan Davis.

Eric Garner.

Michael Brown.

There is a history in our country of white men killing unarmed Black boys and men with little to no consequence. I taught the murders of Sean Bell and Amadou Diallo, using Willie Perdomo's "Forty-One Bullets Off-Broadway" as the model poem, to a class of 7th graders. But then there was Trayvon Martin, then Jordan Davis, then Michael Brown, and the list keeps growing.

After the murder of Trayvon Martin, I taught a version of a lesson I called "From Pain to Poetry" again using Perdomo's "Forty-One Bullets Off-Broadway." I wanted to use Perdomo's poem again — it is a strong example of how writers use facts and their imaginations to tell a story. I wanted to add a research component because my students needed to develop researching and note-taking skills and, just as important, I needed to show students that racial profiling and police brutality are not new.

Aracelis Girmay's poem "Night, for Henry Dumas" is a perfect pairing with "Forty-One Bullets Off-Broadway." We get the intense immersion into one man's story in Perdomo's poem, while Girmay plays with time and place, making us acknowledge that the list of Black men who have been unjustly killed is long and painful and ongoing. I wanted students to see both as approaches in their own work.

One of my objectives was to have students explore ways that poets use their work to respond to injustice. I also wanted them to create a collaborative performance by the end of the unit, so scaffolding in opportunities to work together was something I needed to think about. I decided to ask students to work in small groups for the entire unit and focus on a person who was killed as a result of racial profiling or police brutality.

Over time, I have added the stories of women and girls such as Aiyana Stanley-Jones and Renisha McBride. I talk with my students about the #SayHerName movement and make sure the names of Black women and their stories are not erased.

> **Lakeesha noticed that they were all Black.**
>
> **"And they're all men," Sami added.**
>
> **"And they probably didn't deserve to die," James blurted out.**

"They Were Murdered"

When they came to class on the first day of the unit, there was a plastic bag with jigsaw puzzle pieces in the center of each table. Each group's puzzle, when put together, was a photo of one of five of the slain men: Henry Dumas, Oscar Grant, Amadou Diallo, Sean Bell, or Trayvon Martin. I made the puzzles by printing the photos on cardstock, turning them over to the blank side, drawing jigsaw pieces, and cutting them out. The pieces were big and easy to assemble, about 10–15 pieces for each photo.

The goal was to get the students to collaborate on creating something. "You have five minutes to work as a group to put the puzzle together," I told them as they began to pour the pieces out. I walked around the classroom, checking to make sure everyone in the groups was actively participating.

When each group finished, they received an index card with the name of their person written on it. I called out to the class, "Who has Henry Dumas?" The members of that group raised their hands. I taped his photo on the board and wrote his name underneath so that the whole class could see Dumas. I continued this, making a chart on the board with five columns. The last person we added to the board was Trayvon Martin.

I asked the class: "Do you recognize anyone on the board?"

All of the students knew who Trayvon Martin was.

There were a few students who felt they had seen Oscar Grant before. "There's a movie about him, right?" one student asked. *Fruitvale Station*, a movie that reconstructs the last 24 hours of Grant's life, had been released the same weekend as the Zimmerman verdict. (George Zimmerman, who killed Martin, was found not guilty by a jury in Sanford, Florida.)

I asked someone to give a very brief account of what they knew about Martin.

"He was shot by a neighborhood watch guy," a student answered.

"He was shot because he was wearing a hoodie," another student shouted.

I asked the class to hold off on adding more. "Based on what you know about Trayvon and Oscar, why do you think these other men are on the board?"

"Because they got shot, too?" James suggested.

"Yes. They were all murdered," I told the class. "Looking at these photos, what do you notice? What do they have in common?"

Lakeesha noticed that they were all Black.

"And they're all men," Sami added.

"And they probably didn't deserve to die," James blurted out.

I asked him, "What makes you say that?"

He considered what he knew about Martin and Grant. "They didn't even have weapons on them when they got shot. The others probably didn't, either."

"You all are being great critical thinkers. Let's find out more about these men — what happened to them, how their stories are similar, and where there are differences." I passed out an article to each of the five groups about the person whose photo they had. "Your group should take turns reading the article out loud. Underline important facts that stand out. If there are strong images in the article, underline those too." I ask students to mark up their papers, whether it's an article or a poem. I think it's important for them to engage with their handouts, to write questions in the margins, to highlight phrases that grab them. "When you are finished reading the article, let me know."

Students were eager to learn what happened to the men in the photos. When the groups finished reading, I gave them a handout with three columns — Facts, Emotions, Images — and asked them to write at least four words under each heading. I explained that the images could be from their imaginations. "Even if the article doesn't mention blood-stained cement, that might be something that comes to your mind as you read the article. Think about the pictures your mind sees as you read the article and write them down." For the list of emotions, I told them they could write their own emotion or an emotion that they believe people in the article felt. "So, when I read about Henry Dumas, I felt shocked. I'm going to write 'shock' on my chart. I'm also going to write

Ishmael H. Sistrunk

height, weight, reach, speed, strength and agility. On the streets of Ferguson, the St. Louis Metro Area and all across America, those same attributes can be a death sentence.

When Ferguson police officer Darren Wilson decided to end the life of Michael Brown he did so with an excessive amount of force. No, the full details of what happened that fateful Saturday afternoon have not emerged, thanks to a Grand Jury investigation shrouded in secrecy. The fact

remains, however, that Brown, an unarmed black teenager, was shot at least six times including twice in the head. He didn't have a gun, a knife or any other weapon, but was in the middle of the street, in broad daylight. To some, the 6-foot-4, 292 pound teenager's size and skin color offer enough of an excuse the officer the benefit of the doubt.

The shooting, of course, which has gained global attention, has been the first response

N speak

Teams and players show solidarity and

The shooting death of unarmed teenager Michael Brown on August 9 by police officer Darren Wilson and subsequent civil unrest has put the city of Ferguson in the eye of the national storm.

It seems as if that entire country has been paying attention to the continuous protests that have been happening on West Florissant Ave. since the day Brown was That includes play

National Football League, who preparing for the upcoming regular season, but are fully aware of what's since cent of players are American, ally is centage of American Ferguson night. should not

members Introductions "Don't Shoot" p

HOWARD BARRY

'frustrated' because I think his family might have felt that way."

Students went back to their articles and searched for compelling facts, strong emotions, and vivid images. Shavon was in the group that read about Martin. Under Facts she wrote "acquitted" and "a voice can be heard screaming for help." Fania, who studied Diallo, listed "betrayal" and "resentment" under Emotions. Lakeesha, who focused on Bell, wrote "a wedding dress hanging on a hanger" and "a child standing at a casket" under Images.

After they filled out the charts, I asked for a representative from each group to share what they learned. "Give us at least three important facts," I said. I wrote on the board under the picture of each person. "Make sure you copy this list in your notebook," I told the class. I wanted to keep them engaged, and I also needed them to have this information for the poems they would be writing.

> **Seeing the faces of five Black men who had been murdered side by side, with facts about their lives written under their names, was sobering. Once all groups had shared, we had a class discussion. "What did you learn? What more do you want to know?"**

Seeing the faces of five Black men who had been murdered side by side, with facts about their lives written under their names, was sobering. Once all groups had shared, we had a class discussion. "What did you learn? What more do you want to know?"

Sami wanted to know why this kept happening. Jason wanted to know why, in the cases of Diallo and Bell, there was such excessive force. "I mean, 41 bullets being shot is just not right!"

I asked students to share how they felt. I took the first risk and shared that I felt angry and sometimes hopeless. That I cried when I heard the verdict because I thought about my 17-year-old nephew and how it could have been him walking home with snacks from a corner store but never making it. Maria said she felt sad. Jeremiah shared that it made him afraid sometimes. Fania told the class: "It just makes me angry. It makes me so angry."

Poetry Holds Rage and Questions

It was important to me not to censor students, but to welcome their emotions into the space. Just as I invited their boisterous laughter, their hurt was allowed here too. Even if that meant tears. I believe young people need space to learn and practice positive ways of coping with and processing emotions. Art can provide a structured outlet for them to express how they feel.

I wanted them to know that poetry could hold their rage and their questions. The first poem we read was "Forty-One Bullets Off-Broadway." I played the audio poem and students read along. As I had asked them to mark up their articles, I asked them to do the same on the poem. "I'd like you to think about when Willie is using facts from the article and when he is using his own imagination."

Usually, as a ritual, we give snaps after a poem is shared in class, following the tradition of poetry cafés. But after listening to Perdomo's poem, students clapped.

Before discussing the poem, I asked them to number the stanzas. "I'd like us to talk like poets, OK? So name the stanza you're referring to and, if you notice any literary devices that Willie is using here, we can talk about that too." We noted when he used a fact from the case. "In the second stanza, he mentions the exact number of bullets," Maisha pointed out.

Jeremiah read from stanza four:

> Before you could show your
> I.D. and say, "Officer — "
> Four regulation Glock clips went achoo
> and smoked you into spirit

He recognized that Diallo reaching for his wallet was factual and noted Perdomo's use of personification in making a gun sneeze. He also noticed that Perdomo used his imagination to describe the "bubble gum-stained mosaic" floor where Diallo's body fell.

The next poem we read was Girmay's "Night, for Henry Dumas." Just as we did when discussing "Forty-One Bullets Off-Broadway," we talked about where Girmay used facts, where she used her imagination. Students liked how she referenced Dumas' science fiction writing by saying he did not die by a spaceship. Most of them had underlined the moment of the poet's imagination when she writes that Dumas died "in the subway station singing & thinking of a poem/what he's about to eat."

We talked about the different approaches each poet took. "Willie Perdomo focused on one incident and took us into Amadou Diallo's story," Lakeesha said. "Aracelis Girmay wrote about Henry but also talked about other Black men who have been murdered."

I asked the class: "What do you think the phrase 'happening yesterday, happened tomorrow' means?"

Maisha touched the puzzle at her table, moved the pieces even closer together. "I think she's saying that it happened in 1968 and in 2008 and in 2012 — "

"And it's probably going to keep happening," James blurted out.

> It was important to me not to censor students, but to welcome their emotions into the space. Just as I invited their boisterous laughter, their hurt was allowed here too. Even if that meant tears. I believe young people need space to learn and practice positive ways of coping with and processing emotions. Art can provide a structured outlet for them to express how they feel.

I asked him why he thought that.

"Well, there was Emmett Till," he said. James was in my class last year when we studied Marilyn Nelson's "A Wreath for Emmett Till" and watched excerpts of *Eyes on the Prize*. I was glad to see him making connections to previous lessons. "And in her poem, I think that's what she's saying. It happened way back in the day and it happens now and it will continue to happen everywhere."

"Where do you see that in the poem?" I asked.

"This part," Jason said. He read the lines to the class:

under the ground & above the ground
at Lenox & 125th in Harlem, Tennessee,
Memphis, New York, Watts, Queens.
1157 Wheeler Avenue, San Quentin, above which
sky swings down a giant rope, says
Climb me into heaven, or follow me home

Lakeesha noted Girmay's list of Black martyrs. "There could be so many names added to that list," she said.

"How does this make you feel?" I asked the class.

"It makes me want to be careful."

"It makes me worry about my brother."

"I feel really angry because it isn't fair and it's not a coincidence that this keeps happening."

Then I asked: "Why do you think Aracelis Girmay and Willie Perdomo wrote these poems? Does it change anything? What's the point?"

"It makes people aware of what's going on."

"I think the point is to make people remember. If people don't write their stories they could be forgotten."

"And it honors them."

Writing from Facts, Emotions, and Images

With that, it was time to write. "You can choose to write your poem like Willie did, and focus on one person. Or you can include the stories or names of others, like Aracelis." I told them to be sure to use the brainstorming chart to help them with writing their poem. "Your poem should include at least three facts, three emotions, and three images from your chart." I also gave them options for point of view. "You can write in first, second, or third person. You can write a persona poem in the voice of one of the people involved in the story — for example, you can be Oscar Grant or maybe his daughter. You could even speak from the bullet's perspective or the ground."

I wrote line starters on the board, but most students didn't use them. They had a lot to say and already knew how they wanted to craft their poems. Since that day, I have taught this to racially diverse groups of students, as well as to professionals who work with young people, including teachers, counselors, and administrators at the college level; the words have spilled out of almost everyone.

I was deeply moved by the poetry my students wrote. For example:

NEVER WRITTEN
By A. M.
for Henry Dumas

1968, underground,
day or night,
coming or going,
under the eternal florescent
flicker of subway lights

the clamor of wheels,
crackle of electric current
maybe muffled the shooting
sound that silenced.

One cop's "mistake"
two boys now to forever
wait for their father's face.

A mind full of memory and make believe,
stretched from sacred desert sands
to sci-fi space and mythic lands,
spilled out, running thick
on worn concrete spans

as subway doors open and close
empty cars rattle ahead
blank pages blown behind
nothing but another man's
black body laid down
in haste and waste.

FOR ALL OF THEM
By L. V.

Who scrubs the blood-stained train track, tile, lobby, car, sidewalk?
Who tears down the yellow tape?
Who sends the flowers and cards?
Who sings at the funeral?
Who watches the casket sink into the ground?
Who can get back to their normal life?
Who is holding their breath waiting for the next time?
Who takes a stand?
Who demands justice?
Who knows justice may never come?
Who keeps fighting anyway?
Who fights by protest?
Who fights by teaching?
Who fights by writing a poem?
Who fights by keeping their names alive?

After students revised their poems, I encouraged them to take a small action. "The first brave thing you did was make yourself vulnerable enough to write this poem. Now what are you going to do with it?" I asked. "Remember the reasons you said it was important for poems like these to be written. How can you share your poem to get it out into the world?" We made a quick list that included posting the poem on Facebook, tweeting a line or phrase from the poem, recording the poem and posting the video, reading the poem to a teacher, parent, or friend.

Later in the semester, a few students shared their poems at our open mic, when we invited parents and the community to witness the art their young people had created. Some students shared their poems through social media outlets. I encouraged them to not let this just be an assignment but something they took out of our classroom. I challenged them to pay attention to the news, to continue to use their pens and their voices to respond to what is happening in their world. ∎

"The first brave thing you did was make yourself vulnerable enough to write this poem. Now what are you going to do with it?" I asked.

"Remember the reasons you said it was important for poems like these to be written. How can you share your poem to get it out into the world?"

Renée Watson is an author, educator, and activist. Her young adult novel, Piecing Me Together, *received a Newbery Honor and Coretta Scott King Award. She is the founder of I, Too Arts Collective, a nonprofit housed in the brownstone where Langston Hughes lived and created.*

FORTY-ONE BULLETS OFF-BROADWAY
By Willie Perdomo

It's not like you were looking at a
vase filled with plastic white roses
while pissing in your mother's bathroom
and hoped that today was not the day
you bumped into four cops who
happened to wake up with a bad
case of contagious shooting

From the Bronx to El Barrio
we heard you fall face first into
the lobby of your equal opportunity
forty-one bullets like silver push pins
holding up a connect-the-dots picture of
    Africa
forty-one bullets not giving you enough
    time
to hit the floor with dignity and
justice for all forty-one bullet shells
trickling onto a bubble gum-stained
    mosaic
where your body is mapped out

Before your mother kissed you goodbye
she forgot to tell you that American kids
get massacred in gym class
and shot during Sunday sermon
They are mourned for a whole year while
people like you go away quietly

Before you could show your
I.D. and say, "Officer — "
Four regulation Glock clips went achoo
and smoked you into spirit and by the
time a special street unit decided what
    was
enough another dream submitted an
application for deferral

It was *la vida te da sorpresas/sorpresas
te da la vida/ay dios* and you probably
    thought
I was singing from living *la vida loca*
but be you prince/be you pauper
the skin on your drum makes you
the usual suspect around here
By the time you hit the floor
protest poets came to your rescue
legal eagles got on their cell phones
and booked red eyes to New York
File folders were filled with dream team
pitches for your mother who was on TV
looking suspicious at your defense
knowing that Justice has been known
to keep one eye open for the right price

By the time you hit the floor
the special unit forgot everything they
learned at the academy
The mayor told them to take a few
days off and when they came back he
sent them to go beat up a million young
black men while your blood seeped
    through
the tile in the lobby of your equal
opportunity from the Bronx to El Barrio
there were enough shots to go around

From *Smoking Lovely* by Willie Perdomo. Copyright © 2003. Used by permission of author.

NIGHT, FOR HENRY DUMAS

By Aracelis Girmay

Henry Dumas, 1934–1968,
did not die by a spaceship
or flying saucer or outer space at all
but was shot down, at 33,
by a New York City Transit policeman,
will be shot down, May 23rd,
coming home, in just 6 days,
by a New York City Transit policeman
in the subway station singing & thinking of a poem,
what he's about to eat, will be, was, is right now
shot down,
happening yesterday, happened tomorrow,
will happen now
under the ground & above the ground
at Lenox & 125th in Harlem, Tennessee,
Memphis, New York, Watts, Queens.
1157 Wheeler Avenue, San Quentin, above which
sky swings down a giant rope, says
Climb me into heaven, or follow me home,
& Henry
& Amadou
& Malcolm
& King,
& the night hangs over the men & their faces,
& the night grows thick above the streets,
I swear it is more blue, more black, tonight
with the men going up there.
Bring the children out
to see who their uncles are.

This poem originally appeared in Girmay, Aracelis. 2011. *Kingdom Animalia*. BOA Editions Ltd.

Space for Young Black Women

An interview with Candice Valenzuela

By Jody Sokolower

A few years ago, Candice Valenzuela created and facilitated a group for young Black women at Castlemont High School in Oakland, California. She grounded her work in womanist, Black feminist, and critical pedagogy, as well as her own lived experience as a Black multi-ethnic woman of working-class origins and a history of trauma. Valenzuela currently coaches early career teachers in culturally relevant teaching, critically conscious pedagogy, holistic wellness, and earth-based spiritual healing.

JODY SOKOLOWER: How did you end up running a group for African American girls?

CANDICE VALENZUELA: I was teaching English at Castlemont High School. The school was transitioning to a focus on social justice, equity, and social change, and it was our pilot year. We noticed certain populations were struggling. And the group that stood out most was African American girls — they were the ones most out of class, the ones their teachers found to be the most challenging, and the ones who had the most complaints about school. We decided to form a class to support them specifically. At the time I was in grad school, so it wasn't my first choice to be running such an intense group, but the principal convinced me to take it on.

SOKOLOWER: There is so much focus on the crisis among African American boys. Very few people — and most of those seem to be African American women — are talking about African American girls. It's interesting that at Castlemont, Black girls were identified as the group that was really struggling. Do you think there's a connection between the focus on Black boys and how much crisis these girls were in?

VALENZUELA: I do think it's connected. I want to preface by saying, based on my years of working with students in Oakland, almost all students feel unseen. Period. Across lines of color and gender. Ageism is real, and youth in our society suffer from a lack of voice and a lack of adults seeing them as full human beings with rights and capacities.

And then, too many of our young people experience added layering to that invisibility. With young Black women, it's extreme.

The research does indicate that African American males are being targeted as far as suspension rates, policing in schools, incarceration. There is a historical racialized fear of Black males that plays into those overt and covert strategies to marginalize them.

But there's also a gendered way research happens. At least in Oakland, I don't think that Black girls are doing substantially better than Black boys when it comes to academics. And what happens if you bring truancy into the picture? Are Black girls actively pushed out or are they just not showing up? We're not looking at rates and impact of sexual harassment on academic achievement and social development; we're not looking at rates of sexual trauma. If you look at that stuff, you're going to get a whole other picture. Black girls specifically, and then queer Black youth additionally, are facing marginalization and attack throughout society.

I boil inside because there's such a high need with the girls. It's not to say that Black males don't need to have their own holding space. What I have issue with is when we promote that as the priority above all others, instead of finding ways to serve all young people, even if that means creating targeted campaigns for various subgroups.

SOKOLOWER: What is the impact on Black girls?

VALENZUELA: One student said: "I feel invisible." I can't find a better way to say it. Even when a Black male is harmed, he has a mother, he has sisters, all these women who care for him are harmed when he's harmed. You are putting these girls in between a rock and a hard place. Obviously they love their brothers and their cousins, and they want the best for them. But why is it always at the expense of Black girls?

So that narrative has to be reframed. Yes, you're trying to help a certain population, but the perspective is too narrow-minded and you're again privileging males.

SOKOLOWER: How did you decide who would be in the class?

VALENZUELA: Initially the administrators wanted to choose the girls they saw as having the most issues. I pushed against that. I feel that we benefit the most with diversity, when we can all learn from one another. Young people don't all struggle in the same ways, so we often see the ones who are loud, not in class, and making a big noise. But the children who are yelling still have their voices. There's something inherently healthy about openly resisting a system that's not built for you. Sometimes it's the quiet ones, who might even be making straight A's, who are struggling in different ways or directing their hatred inward. We miss them when we only focus on the loud ones.

So I reached out to teachers and asked them to recommend Black girls who they thought might benefit from community, who might need support to develop as leaders or to come into their voices, those who might be able to help guide others, who might benefit from added support and be open to receiving it. I wanted to create a core group in the midrange of students who might get passed over.

SOKOLOWER: How was the class defined?

VALENZUELA: It was originally listed as an advisory. But that looks like nothing on a high school transcript when students apply to college. We listed it as women's studies so they could get social studies credit.

I took a holistic approach because that's who I am, and I think that's what women need, especially in that age group. It wasn't text-heavy. I wanted to give them exposure to different concepts and theories, but that was a small percentage of what we ended up doing. It was more of a support group. I focused on being present for whatever need was showing up in that moment.

"I'm Not Black"

SOKOLOWER: How did you get started?

VALENZUELA: The young women in the group were under such constant trauma and triggering of past traumas — in school and in the rest of their lives — that creating a safe space to talk and help each other was a huge challenge.

To build community, instead of having rules, we had a code. We called it the Sisters' Code. I created it before school started. If I were to teach this class again, I would have that be one of our first projects — to co-create our code — but I was trying to establish some foundations. We discussed it, memorized it, performed it as a class, and revisited it throughout the year. We had T-shirts made.

The girls' initial reactions were mixed. They felt happy to have that space, but then they often tested and challenged it. We know that happens in the classroom, but this was a little different. I felt there was deep fear or uncertainty about what it meant to have a space that was only young Black women. That wasn't something they had been in, not intentionally so — amongst their friends maybe, but not like this class, which was just for them.

In the beginning, it was hard for them to sit with that and figure out what it meant. It brought up a lot of their internalized self-hatred, their internalized sense of not being worthy. They weren't sure why it mattered for them to develop their own race and gender consciousness.

So some of them would come to my class late, or come in and be silly. There was a lot of passive resistance.

Much of the initial work was helping them uncover for themselves: Why do we need to do this work? Why do I need it? What do I think? I had them talk and talk and talk. I brought in media, readings, and poems — anything I could think of to prompt them to do their own discovery around what it means to be a young Black woman.

SOKOLOWER: And what did they say?

VALENZUELA: In the beginning, a lot of the girls said, "I'm not Black." They didn't like the term. That was hard for me. I had to hold back because I feel very strongly about Black liberation. But they had experienced it as a label of harm. So they'd say, "I'm not Black, I'm Brown."

I asked them: "What are all the negative things that are associated with Blackness?" We did a huge brainstorm that I left on the wall. It was painful, but I wanted them to remember and ask themselves: Is this who we are or is this a misrepresentation that we don't agree with? Externalizing those reflections was helpful because they had internalized it so much.

Now it's true that race has no scientific validity. By the end of the year they understood that it's a social construct, but also that we have a great history of building solidarity around our experience within that construct. What we live and breathe every day as racialized beings is real.

Then, once those initial walls were down, when I would touch something deeper, they often tried to avoid what was painful by making fun of someone else in the class. The infighting and backbiting were fierce. Even on a good day, they would often throw verbal jabs at each other.

I would call their awareness to the way those jabs accumulate over time and tear at our self-esteem. We have to treat each other better than that if we want to be treated better ourselves. We know we're worth it. It took a long time to get to that place. A lot of it was returning over and over and over to the conversation. And then modeling something different for them — being conscious of how I engaged with them and how I talked to them, always coming from a place of love and respect so that they knew that was the standard.

What was most difficult for me were the emotions they brought in — the deep pain or sense of hopelessness, their sense of not being worthy, of not being seen. The need for social-emotional support was so high; even those receiving therapy needed more. That created a whole different challenge for me than being a general ed teacher. I talked to my own therapist about it. She told me that the teacher holds the hope and the therapist holds the hopelessness. Being in a space where people can actually show you their despair is not as rewarding in a day-to-day way. As a teacher, I always engaged in a hopeful way and brought that out in young people, but in this group, I wasn't the one who got to witness most of their transformation.

Their teachers would come to me and say: "What's going on in that class? Are you drugging them? They're doing so much better. They're being so helpful to the other students. They're acting as leaders." Over and over again, I heard rave reviews from their teachers. Although the girls often resisted me and each other during class, they couldn't stop talking about the class to folks outside of it.

But that wasn't what I saw. When we were together, what I often saw was the pain. I had to hold hope for myself because the manifestation of them being able to purge what they were feeling was so powerful when they went out into the community.

Confronting Conflict

SOKOLOWER: Did you have a curriculum for the class?

VALENZUELA: I decided that the most meaningful thing I could give them was a space that was unapologetically different from everything else they were doing — a space that was completely different from school as they knew it.

We had reflective writing and journaling when they came into class. And then an open share; we would gather in a circle and use a talking piece. Sometimes, as long as it was respectful, I would let them keep talking and talking. Then I might guide the conversation with another question to more critically investigate whatever was coming up. And then we'd send the talking piece around again.

Of course, that meant the teacher inside me was often screaming, "But we're not reading anything!" That was my own internalized voice saying that reading and writing are the most important ways of learning. But that's not always true.

The first content area that I pulled out was looking at conflict: How are we dealing with conflict now and does that approach serve us? We spent two solid weeks on it and then kept coming back to it. The reflective writing assignments included: What is conflict? What kinds of conflict have you been in? Describe a conflict that you thought went well. Describe a conflict that you thought ended horribly. What was the impact of each? Who do you tend to get into conflict with the most? Why do you think that is?

They had so much to say, so much to discuss. As they talked, I would listen and write. I have three notebooks full of the girls' words.

When I got home, I'd sit with what had been shared and I'd think. Where do we go from here? What's the need they're expressing? Is there some area where they can be pushed to learn something new or to see themselves in a more holistic and more humanizing way? The girls' words were my text.

> **Whenever I came too close to my teacher role, they said, "No, we don't want you as a teacher, we want you as a mentor, we want you as a counselor, and we want you as a mom."**

The girls were very clear that what they needed and what they wanted was the social-emotional support. Whenever I came too close to my teacher role, they said, "No, we don't want you as a teacher, we want you as a mentor, we want you as a counselor, and we want you as a mom." Since I knew from the beginning that the purpose was to support them, I took their feedback seriously.

SOKOLOWER: What other topics were important to the group?

VALENZUELA: We talked about friends and the way they treated each other. Sometimes their friendships included a lot of talking behind each other's backs, making fun of each other, betraying one another, lying to each other. So I asked them: "What does it mean to be a friend? What does that word mean to you?" We had to keep coming back to that. Some were able to say, "I'm going to try and act a little differently." Others realized that every time they hung out with a particular friend, they got in trouble or there was drama. Often it boiled down to repressed hurt and anger. Each time we came around to the same topics, we peeled back more layers.

Every week we had free art days when the students created collages or paintings about different areas of their lives — family, love, relationships, culture, the media. Two days a week we did movement: African dance, yoga, Tae Bo. I was blessed to have a volunteer, Kihana Ross, who was doing research for her PhD on strategies for African American wellness. She helped me bring in guest speakers and co-led different activities. We both fundraised so the girls could have food every day, so they'd focus and feel cared for.

SOKOLOWER: It sounds like the beginning was difficult. How did you know that the group was starting to have a positive impact?

VALENZUELA: About two months in, the younger students started running to my class. I started getting text messages throughout the day, letting me know what was going on in the community or what they were doing. Then I knew that things had shifted and they had accepted me as being on their side, being in their corner.

One girl often found herself in a lot of conflict. When she reached out to me before going up to someone and challenging them, I knew that was an important shift. She was seeking counsel. And she had opened herself up to growing and changing. It wasn't perfect, but she grew throughout that year in how she addressed conflict. It was incremental.

Other girls in the school started coming up to me and saying, "I want to have a Polynesian girls group," "I want to have a Native American girls group." That's when I knew they were talking about it with their friends and other girls were seeing the need in themselves to speak out and claim a space that was just for them.

One of the young women who had said "I'm not Black, I'm not Black" in the beginning focused her final junior English project on Black women's empowerment. Now here she was saying, "I am proud to be a Black woman. I am proud of who we are."

All of them at the end of the year said unequivocally they were so thankful for the space, and they believed that every Black girl should have that space.

What Does It Take?

SOKOLOWER: This was a great thing you were able to do for these girls. But wasn't it an exceptional situation? You got to say how many kids, you had extra people coming in. There was money for food. What are the implications for teachers at schools that don't have those options?

VALENZUELA: Our situation was in no way ideal. We were in East Oakland, in a school that had just had three principals in three years, in a hostile environment and an extremely traumatized neighborhood, where Black girls were last on the list for services.

I would say the No. 1 thing is to not be afraid to advocate for what you know the students need, and to do so in a way that's creative, collective, and forward-thinking. I wasn't going to the principal and saying, "Give me this, please, please." If you're always putting yourself at the beck and call of those in power, then you're never going to have anything. The resources we had weren't coming from the school, they were things I advocated and fought for, alongside other allies at the school site. The money we raised was through crowdsourcing.

My advice to teachers is to always push back against the isolation. They set us up in these situations where we feel isolated and overwhelmed. I make an effort to know each person at the site and have a personal relationship. It's important to figure out who are your comrades, who are your allies, and who is politically opposed to what you're doing. Then it's the same advice I give to students. You don't have to like everyone, but it's important to ask: "How can we work together? How do we leverage the resources we have amongst ourselves to work toward a common goal, even in the face of differences?

SOKOLOWER: Then the district changed the school's direction again, and you didn't get to do a second year. What was that like?

VALENZUELA: That year was so hard because I started at zero. It was all about building trust and community amongst the girls. In the second year we could have done some of the revolutionary projects that I envisioned. I know I would have seen them step up as leaders and begin to show up more in the community, not just in our circle.

I wish we could've had another year. And I wish that folks could have taken on working with the other groups of girls so we could build solidarity. How can I show up for you and your struggle when I can't even see my own? It would be great to build different groups up strong and then bring them together to dialogue and build a deeper unity across all of the cultures. I would love to see that. That's one of the major problems with how much churn there is in schools these days — we rarely get to build on the foundations we've laid. It's always starting from zero.

This course was a labor of love for me. I often felt personally, emotionally, and physically challenged by the group in ways that were uncomfortable. The group landed in a place that was far from where I ultimately wanted to go in terms of theory and practice, but the end result was a place that reflected both my and the girls' authentic growth and needs. The experience taught me to honor where people are at, starting with myself. ∎

Jody Sokolower is a former managing editor of Rethinking Schools*, editor of* Teaching About the Wars*, and co-editor of* Rethinking Sexism, Gender, and Sexuality. *She is currently a teacher educator and coordinator of the Teach Palestine Project at the Middle East Children's Alliance in Berkeley, California.*

SISTERS' CODE

» We respect, love, and care for each other as sisters would. We keep our conversations confidential and don't spread gossip from this class. We listen to each other when we speak.

» We understand that our struggles are connected, but our people are divided. We do our best to resolve conflict and come together. We stand in solidarity, making connections to sisters of other races and backgrounds.

» We are growing and changing all the time, inside and out. We make the commitment to change for the better. We understand that when we transform, our families and communities transform too.

» We take the time out to focus on the positive and encourage one another through our struggles.

» We don't quietly accept our oppression. We stand up for ourselves and for each other. We challenge ourselves, and those around us, to resist all the things that hold us down.

» We put our education first and do our best. We know that no one can save us but ourselves. We look for jobs, we work hard in school, we prepare for college, and we NEVER GIVE UP on our path to succeeding!

Trayvon Martin and My Students

Writing toward justice

By Linda Christensen

A t a local protest over the killing of Trayvon Martin and the delayed arrest of George Zimmerman, Kelsey Turner, one of my students at Jefferson High School in Portland, Oregon, brought many of us to tears when he said, "I wore a Ninja Turtle hoodie today because I wish I could go back to a day in time when I didn't have to worry about these problems, to a time when I didn't have to worry about me being an almost grown man and people feeling like they have the right to shoot me."

When the jury acquitted Zimmerman of Trayvon Martin's murder in July 2013, I remembered Kelsey's words and felt rage at the judicial system's betrayal, the ongoing betrayal of Black students like Kelsey, who have sat in classrooms over the decades as the deaths of Emmett Till, Medgar Evers, Amadou Diallo, Sean Bell, and Oscar Grant — other Black people killed in racist interactions — run like ticker tape under the screen of school curriculum across the country. When school started in the fall, I knew that students needed to talk about the verdict, to have time to "wail," as academic/activist Cornel West says, to be part of a national debate on racial profiling. And, as always, I wanted to meld this critical discussion with the development of students' essay writing skills.

"Seeing what happened to Trayvon was traumatic," explains Marc Lamont Hill, a professor of education at Columbia University, in an *Essence* magazine interview. He describes the message sent to Black youth: "'You're less valuable and less worthy of protection, love, and investment than other folks.' And when that message is received, it wears on your spirit. It's tough to live in a world where you're seen as less than."

Later in the article, Hill discusses the need to create spaces for young Black men to talk about the impact of being profiled:

> There need to be conversations about what it feels like to be followed in the store, chased out of the mall, or to not be welcomed on the other side of town. Give boys the space to ask questions, vent and cry and be vulnerable in a world that almost demands them to be hard at all times. Because sometimes that very toughness, that hypermasculinity, is the very thing that could get them in trouble.

When any national disaster occurs, students watch their teachers to see our reaction: Is this important? Do you care? I still recall my teachers' responses to the murders

UNTIL THE KILLING OF BLACK MEN, BLACK MOTHER'S SONS, BECOMES AS IMPORTANT TO THE REST OF THE COUNTRY AS THE KILLING OF A WHITE MOTHER'S SON. WE WHO BELIEVE IN FREEDOM CANNOT REST UNTIL THIS HAPPENS.

ELLA BAKER 1964

RICARDO LEVINS MORALES

of Kennedy and King. The hushed, reverential tones in my 7th-grade classroom as my teacher delivered the news of President Kennedy's death, the flag waving at half-mast through the slanted blinds. And the silence during my junior year as not one teacher talked about Martin Luther King Jr.'s assassination.

I watched President Obama's talk about Trayvon Martin after the verdict, after thousands of demonstrators had gathered in cities across the country to remember Trayvon's death and to protest the outcome. I was struck by the difference in tone in this speech — the pace of the speech is slower, almost hesitant, without Obama's more typical oratorical style. He looks down instead of looking into the camera. He speaks of his personal experiences with racism, the experience of African Americans, the history of race in this country:

> There are very few African American men in this country who haven't had the experience of being followed when they were shopping in a department store. That includes me. There are very few African American men who haven't had the experience of walking across the street and hearing the locks click on the doors of cars. That happened to me — at least before I was a senator.

In fact, during the speech Obama explores what Benjamin Todd Jealous, then-president of the NAACP, spoke about when he said, "Our people have been free for 150 years and yet our young men are still treated like criminals. Racism is the original sin of our country." Obama's speech acknowledges "that some of the violence that takes place in poor Black neighborhoods around the country is born out of a very violent past in this country, and that the poverty and dysfunction that we see in those communities can be traced to a very difficult history." Obama's speech moved me. I thought, "Finally, a president is acknowledging the pervasive racism in our country."

But when I heard Cornel West's critique of Obama's speech during an interview with Amy Goodman on *Democracy Now!* a few days after the president's talk, I recognized how much I had missed, how much I wanted Obama's speech to do more than it did. I also realized West's discussion of the speech provided a great example of how to critique — an article, a novel, a speech by the president. Goodman showed West chunks of Obama's speech and asked him to respond in the same way I want students to annotate any kind of text: critically, using evidence from the original text, both acknowledging and questioning the merits of the evidence.

> **When any national disaster occurs, students watch their teachers to see our reaction: Is this important? Do you care?**

The Opening Act: Trayvon's Photo

Because I retired from full-time teaching several years ago, I adopt a class each year, usually at Jefferson High School, where I spent most of my 30-year teaching career. Jefferson is located in a gentrifying African American neighborhood in North Portland. About 60 percent of the school is African American, 20 percent white, and 12 percent Latina/o; 84 percent are on free and reduced lunch. This year, Dan Coffey and Amy Wright, two 11th-grade language arts teachers, invited me to share their classrooms.

When we started this unit on Trayvon, we wondered how much background knowledge students would need. Amy and I created an opening PowerPoint lesson plan that included photos of Trayvon and Zimmerman, as well as a timeline activity in case students needed more information. They didn't.

We projected Trayvon's photo and asked, "Who is this? List everything you know about this person. If you know a lot, write a lot. If you don't know, describe him." Students bent their heads and pens to the task, writing furiously. Almost all the students knew chapter and verse about the events: the profiling, Zimmerman's call to 911, the Arizona Iced Tea and Skittles, Trayvon's phone conversation with his friend, the struggle, the gunshot, the delayed arrest, the trial, the verdict, and even subsequent information about Zimmerman and his wife, and his purchase of a new gun. The two students who did not know about Trayvon's murder and the trial took notes during the discussion.

> At the end of the class, Clayborn remarked, "We should stop thinking about Zimmerman and start thinking about the system that allowed Zimmerman to go free after murdering an unarmed teenager." The class agreed; this remark later became Clayborn's thesis in his essay.

When I asked, "How do you know so much?" Mahogany said she watched the news with her mother and grandmother. Others added similar stories of discussing the case in summer school, with family or friends. When I talked with students one on one during a fire drill, one young woman said, "I searched on the internet for information over the summer. I'm really glad we're discussing this because I've been wanting to talk about it."

Analyzing President Obama's Remarks

Before students watched the video of Obama's speech, I distributed a hard copy of the talk for them to write on. Let me say, I experienced some hesitation in launching a piece that asked students to criticize Obama because, as the first African American president, he represents hope to many of our students. Also, he has been viciously and unfairly attacked from the right. That said, West's critique addresses actions that a string of presidents, including Obama, have committed — from drone attacks to prosecution of whistle-blowers to failure to address "the new Jim Crow" to promoting corporate agendas.

I began by talking about where we were heading with this unit: "We're going to write a critique of this talk. A critique doesn't mean to just shred apart; it also means to be alert to what you like or agree with — and why. For example, you might approve of a solution that the president proposed. As you watch the speech, think about the content of the talk: What do you agree with in this speech? What resonates for you in the talk? What do you find problematic? What is missing?" And, while I was in danger of overloading them, I also added, "Think about the audience of the speech. Who is Obama talking to? How do you know?"

Although the speech is relatively short, only 15 minutes, I chunked out the viewing because I wanted students to pause to write and talk after significant points instead of waiting until the end. Also, because I was teaching this in September, I wanted to model how to take notes and discuss texts. I stopped the video about four minutes in, just after Obama relates his own history with racial profiling. I asked students to write notes about this first section: "What resonates for you in this section? What do agree with? What do you argue with?"

After students wrote, they talked. Obama's personal experiences echoed in their lives. They, too, had experiences being followed or viewed as suspicious. One young man, an African immigrant, mentioned that he lives in an almost all white community and said, "My neighbors' eyes follow me when I walk in the neighborhood." Another young man wrote, "I know how it feels to feel like you are less than someone else. I remember one time I was in the mall with eight of my friends, and the mall security told us we have to separate into groups of three because they thought we were a gang." Kell brought us back to mourning Trayvon: "The president said, 'Trayvon Martin could have been me 35 years ago.' Trayvon can't be nothing now."

> **This unit resonated for students because they care about racism, poverty, and racial profiling. Trayvon was one of their own. Both Obama and West spoke directly to their lives. They understand the shame and anger caused by stop-and-frisk laws, by "looking suspicious" because of their skin and their clothes.**

We continued through the remainder of Obama's comments, stopping several more times to write and talk our way through the speech. Although the speech is short, this activity took most of the 90-minute period.

At the end of the class, Clayborn remarked, "We should stop thinking about Zimmerman and start thinking about the system that allowed Zimmerman to go free after murdering an unarmed teenager." The class agreed; this remark later became Clayborn's thesis in his essay.

When we returned the following class, I distributed a two-column handout. In the left-hand column, I asked students to return to the hard copy of the president's speech, re-read it, and pull out five quotes they wanted to discuss — five key pieces of the talk. I asked them to use the right-hand column to write an analysis of each quote: what it meant, why they chose it, why it was important, why they agreed or disagreed with it, what issues it addressed, what issues it missed. Although this might seem redundant to the previous day's assignment, this close reading of the text is where I had noticed that students in previous years experienced difficulty. Too often they summarized the text and/or related it to their own lives, but they didn't analyze it. I wanted them to practice that skill. Since they had watched the video and read along, they could go deeper in a second reading.

After I noted that most students had one quote but some students were struggling with the analysis, I asked a couple of students to bring their papers to the document camera and to share their quote and analysis. We looked at why their analysis worked and what could be added. For example, Trina wrote about Obama's "it could have been me" quote: "He is showing emotion; Obama tells his experience of being stopped and frisked before he was a senator or president. He's trying to relate to Trayvon and all African Americans that he has been through the same thing."

In this analysis, Trina demonstrates an understanding of why Obama includes this section in his speech and also *who* his speech was aimed at. Could she have said more? Sure. But as we discussed her analysis, the students began to understand how to move beyond summarization and into locating audience, context, and the purpose of the speech.

Maya wrote that, when Obama spoke about demonstrations and vigils and protests, he was trying to calm people down: "If I see any violence, then I will remind folks that that dishonors what happened to Trayvon Martin and his family."

We stopped writing and analyzing 10 minutes before the end of the period. At that time, I asked a few more students to come up to the document camera to share one of their quotes and the related comments. Most students wrote about similar places in Obama's speech: his identification with Trayvon, his remarks about the history of racial disparities, his question about what would happen if Trayvon had been white and Zimmerman Black, his statement that he and Michelle talk frequently about the need to give young Black men "the sense that their country cares about them and values them and is willing to invest in them," and his final note that "each successive generation seems to be making progress in changing attitudes when it comes to race." While the students shared, I encouraged their classmates to talk about what worked in the analyses, and to add quotes or more commentary to their own papers.

Cornel West: A Sharper Perspective

The next day I layered in West's critique of the speech, using the interview with Amy Goodman. This was students' first introduction to Cornel West, a professor who at the time was at the Union Theological Seminary in New York City, and who is also a radio commentator, an activist, an author, and a spoken word artist. They fell in love with him and insisted that we watch the entire interview, not just the clips I had selected. This interview is not easy. West speaks rapidly and makes many historical and contemporary allusions without providing context. For example, he mentions Assata Shakur, Chelsea Manning, Edward Snowden, Ray Kelly, and many other contemporary and historical figures. Amy developed a cheat sheet so that students could have some background about the people West discusses as they followed along with his talk.

Because I wanted students to understand that the format of Goodman's interview parallels the critiques that they would write, we looked at the excerpts from Obama's speech that she selected, then at West's responses to those selections. How did he critique? What did he say about the segments that we had discussed on previous days? We followed the same protocol of stopping after each segment to discuss it.

West stunned students from the first time he opened his mouth and stated, "I think we have to acknowledge that President Obama has very little moral authority at this point, because we know anybody who tries to rationalize the killing of innocent people is a criminal. George Zimmerman is a criminal, but President Obama is a global George Zimmerman because he tries to rationalize the killing of innocent children, 221 so far, in the name of self-defense, so that there are actually parallels here." I had to stop and discuss drone missile attacks; many students were unaware of the U.S. drone strikes in Pakistan and Yemen, and the resulting deaths of innocent people.

> **If we are serious about nurturing students' academic skills, then we need to keep them wrestling with ideas that speak to deep themes in society and in their own lives.**

Students had read an article on stop-and-frisk laws prior to the beginning of the unit to give them background on the racial profiling laws discussed in both men's speeches, but their understanding of the harm of these laws grew when West made connections between the stop-and-frisk laws and the increased incarceration of Black and Brown kids:

> [New York City Police Commissioner Ray Kelly] racially profiled millions of young Black and Brown brothers. The question is: Will [Obama's racial] identification hide and conceal the fact there's a criminal justice system in place that has nearly destroyed two generations of very precious poor Black and Brown brothers? [Obama] hasn't said a mumbling word until now. Five years in office and can't say a word about the new Jim Crow.

The difference between Obama's claim about wanting to end racial profiling and West's statistical citation of the numbers of youth of color who have been incarcerated — and the fact that Obama had not discussed this during his five years in office — became a theme in many student essays. This critique of a point many students initially agreed with in Obama's speech helped them see the difference between an assertion without evidence and the strength of an argument when real evidence enters the conversation.

West also attacked Obama's remarks about his and Michelle's talks about how to make Black males feel more a part of society:

> If you are concerned about Black boys being part of our society . . . I would say we're going to have to talk seriously about massive employment programs; high-quality public education, not the privatizing of education; dealing with gentrification and the land grab that's been taking place; ensuring that young Black boys . . . have access [to] a sense of self-respect and self-determination, not just through education and jobs, but through the unleashing of their imaginations

— more arts programs in the educational system. They've been eliminated, you see. Those are the kind of things hardly ever talked about. But we can only talk about transpartnerships in terms of global training for capital and multinational corporations and big banks. That's been the priority: the Wall Street-friendly and the corporate-friendly policies that I think are deeply upsetting for somebody like myself vis-à-vis the Obama administration.

Dazha's analysis of this section echoed many students' essays:

I agree with West because as much as Obama talked about what African American boys go through, what is he doing for them? Nothing. It's clearly not a priority. It's like Obama says things with little to no action. I was on Obama's side until I heard West's rebuttal. Even as Obama addressed the issue, he spoke as if he didn't belong to the Black American side.

Group Work on Quote Analysis

When I reviewed student essays from last year, I noticed that I had not done a good enough job of teaching evidence paragraphs. It wasn't just that students' "analysis" of the evidence was more often summary than analysis. They also didn't always include the context of a quote or anything about the person who made the quote. So I created an assignment to develop students' awareness and skills about how to write evidence paragraphs in an essay.

After giving the assignment, Dan and I modeled the process of writing an evidence paragraph with the group. The assignment asked students to provide:

1. Context for the quote.
2. Identification of the speaker: Who is it? What is his/her authority on this topic?
3. An introduction to the quote (which might be contained in the previous sections).
4. Analysis of the quote: Do you agree or disagree with the quote? Why? What is missing? What else do readers need to know?

Using Obama's quote about today's youth's changing attitudes based on his observations of his daughters Malia and Sasha, I asked the class how we could write a paragraph that included Obama's quote, West's analysis, and our four required elements. "How would we begin the paragraph? We need to discuss the context of the quote. When and where did he say this? Who said it?"

Mahogany said, "We could start by writing that President Obama gave a talk after the verdict came back." Going back and forth in this way, the class and I constructed a model paragraph:

President Obama finishes his speech following the George Zimmerman verdict by stating, "Things are getting better. Each successive generation seems to be making progress in changing attitudes when it comes to race." I both agree and disagree with this quote by the president. Yes, things are getting better: Jim Crow laws are no longer in place and segregation was abolished. Yet astounding numbers of African Americans are still incarcerated and victim to stop-and-frisk laws and other kinds of racial profiling. These issues will be forced on the next generation. As president, Obama should say less "they are going to" and more "I will" and "we should."

We left this paragraph on the document camera as a template for students to refer back to as they constructed their own paragraphs in small groups.

Then we gave each group a quote from Obama's speech and West's interview. In retrospect, I would let them choose their own. Students had interesting discussions as they wrote their paragraphs. Some argued over the wording that slid them into the quote; others discussed what they wanted to say about the quote. This was a crucial and missing step from my previous work on essay writing, especially when students need to layer evidence from multiple texts. At the end of the period, we shared these collective paragraphs. As testimony to the importance of the process, many students used one of these paragraphs in their final essays.

The Essay

Before they started writing the essays, Dan and I asked students to review their notes. What did they want to say about the speech? Which quotes or ideas were most significant to them? "Remember, your assignment is to critique the president's speech. A critique doesn't just mean to tear apart. It also means what you agree with, what pieces of the speech you support. Perhaps you like a solution President Obama proposes. But critique also means to cast a critical eye. Dr. West brings a wealth of background knowledge to his critique: What's left out or unacknowledged in the president's speech about his policies? Go back through your notes and highlight ideas that link together." Then, as a class, we brainstormed possibilities.

This is why, as teachers and schools, we need to move beyond the simplistic notions of "text complexity" given to us by Common Core, worry less about MLA format, and care more about developing curriculum that builds students' intellectual capacity to engage in national dialogues.

From the beginning, Maya knew she wanted to write about how Obama's speech was meant to pacify: "Obama didn't want the people to rise up and take matters into their own hands; he made his speech to merely cool the fires, not to kindle." We discussed — and wrote on the document camera — which quotes would support her thesis. Kell wanted to discuss the twin issues of stop-and-frisk laws and the mass incarceration of Black youth. Some students picked up on West's critique of Obama's lack of action on issues and wrote about his "timidity." Sydney wrote, "Obama addressed his citizens like a quiet old grandpa, only chiming into the conversation because he could, rather than being raw and passionate. To make change, we cannot *think* we need to do something, we have to do something." Only one student returned to the drones and global issues that West brought up in his critique.

West's repeated lines that Obama claims to care about Black and Brown youth, but his lack of action demonstrates that he's not serious because he hasn't built any programs, reverberated for the majority of our class. For they are students at a high school that has no music program, no drama program, worn-down computer labs, floors with missing tiles, and classrooms with Home Depot shower stall "whiteboards" mounted by teachers. Obama's "hollow" language and West's outrage delivered in almost slam poetry style became a theme of their essays.

Kell's essay demonstrates the passion that fueled much of the writing produced during the unit, but also the sense of anger over Obama's lack of action on issues that affect their lives:

> Considering the fact that African American boys are seen as disposable, President Obama should stop talking so much and start acting on these problems. He should either make a new law or put some type of restrictions on the ones that already exist. As a young, Black male, I don't want anything like this to happen to me. I know I live in another state, but I don't want to end up a victim like Trayvon Martin.

Clearly, this unit resonated for students because they care about racism, poverty, and racial profiling. Trayvon was one of their own. Both Obama and West spoke directly to their lives. They understand the shame and anger caused by stop-and-frisk laws, by "looking suspicious" because of their skin and their clothes. They attend an under-resourced school, they experience the lack of programs for youth in their neighborhoods, and they live with the criminalization of Black and Brown youth, watching classmates disappear into jail cells and hospitals.

If we are serious about nurturing students' academic skills, then we need to keep them wrestling with ideas that speak to deep themes in society and in their own lives. This is why, as teachers and schools, we need to move beyond the simplistic notions of "text complexity" given to us by Common Core, worry less about MLA format, and care more about developing curriculum that builds students' intellectual capacity to engage in national dialogues with the power and poetry of Cornel West. ∎

Linda Christensen (lmc@lclark.edu) is director of the Oregon Writing Project at Lewis & Clark College in Portland, Oregon, and a Rethinking Schools *editor. She is author, most recently, of* Reading, Writing, and Rising Up: Teaching About Social Justice and the Power of the Written Word (*2nd edition*).

Two Sets of Notes

By MK Asante

I find myself feeling
as if I am touching both ground and ceiling,
in schools that do not engage in healing,
they simply open the wounds and entrap me in rooms
where I am consumed by hypocrisy
like, who authored Greek philosophies?

And the statues on campus be watchin me,
Washington, Jefferson, Williams, clockin me.
As if to say "times up"
but I don't run laps on tracks,
I run laps around the scholars of tomorrow
because their new schools of thought
are merely old histories borrowed.

So they label me militant, and Black national radical,
trying to put my learning process on sabbatical.
But I don't apologize,
I spit truth into the whites of eyes infected by white lies.

Then they try to get me to see
Their point of view from a cat that looks like me,
but he don't
walk like me
    talk like me
        or
          act like me,
and he started running
when I asked if he was
Black like me.

Mastering their thoughts
and forgetting our own
and we wonder why we always feel alone,
from the media to academia
hanging us like coats,
that's why in they schools:

I always take two sets of notes.
One set to ace the test
        and
one set I call the Truth,
and when I find historical contradictions
I use the first set as proof,
proof that Black youths
minds are being
polluted,
    convoluted,
            diluted,
not culturally rooted.

In anything
except the Western massacre
that's why in school, we were scared of Africa,
we viewed our mother's land
Through the eyes of racists like Hume and Kant.
But Immanuel Kan't tell me anything about a land he's never seen
a land rich with history
beautiful kings and queens.

They'll have you believe otherwise
the history they taught me was stood atop high rise lies
they never told me the pyramids were completed
before Greece or Rome were conceptualized.
Then they said the Egyptians' race was a mystery
you tell them to read Herodotus Book II of the histories.

Can it be any clearer?
Black children
look in the mirror
you are the reflection of divinity
don't let them fool you with selective memory
walk high,
listen to the elders who spoke
Black students, Brown students, all students,
always take two sets of notes.

MK Asante is a best-selling author, award-winning filmmaker, recording artist, and distinguished professor. His most recent book, Buck: A Memoir, *was on the* Washington Post *Bestseller List in 2014 and 2015, and is being adapted into a major motion picture.*

Taking the Fight Against White Supremacy into Schools

By Adam Sanchez

A s a history teacher, there are times when the past reasserts itself with such force that you have to put aside your plans and address the moment. Charlottesville in 2017 is one of those times. The image of white supremacists openly marching in defense of a Confederate general, viciously beating and murdering those who are protesting their racism — is an image we hoped had died with Jim Crow. That this image is not a relic of the past is a reality that teachers and students must face.

In his defense of the white supremacists marching against the removal of a statue of Robert E. Lee, Donald Trump pointed out that George Washington owned people and asked, "So this week, it is Robert E. Lee. I noticed that Stonewall Jackson is coming down. I wonder, is it George Washington next week? And is it Thomas Jefferson the week after? You know, you really do have to ask yourself, where does it stop?"

Many responded to this question by pointing out that unlike Lee, Washington and Jefferson were not best known for their defense of slavery. But *The Onion* cut to the heart of the President's position with its headline: "Trump Warns Removing Confederate Statues Could Be a Slippery Slope to Eliminating Racism Entirely." And activists have been making it clear that they hope this moment won't end with the removal of Confederate monuments. In the wake of Charlottesville, former *Rethinking Schools* editor and current Philadelphia city councilmember Helen Gym has called for the removal of the statue of former mayor Frank Rizzo, known for terrorizing Black and gay communities. In New York City, protesters have demanded the removal of a Central Park statue of Dr. J. Marion Sims, who experimented on enslaved women in the 19th century.

Weighing in on this debate, historian Eric Foner writes, "Historical monuments are, among other things, an expression of power — an indication of who has the power to choose how history is remembered in public places." In that case, what better way to empower students and teachers in schools across the country than by actively taking part in the debate over whether symbols of white supremacy should be taken down — whether a statue at a nearby park, a classroom poster, a hallway mural, or even a school name. In fact, according to the Southern Poverty Law Center, 109 public schools, a quarter of which have student bodies that are primarily Black, are named after Confederate icons. In addition to efforts aimed at challenging symbols that represent racism, an equally powerful activity could be discussing, and ultimately taking action around, what names, pictures, and monuments would more accurately reflect the values of your school community.

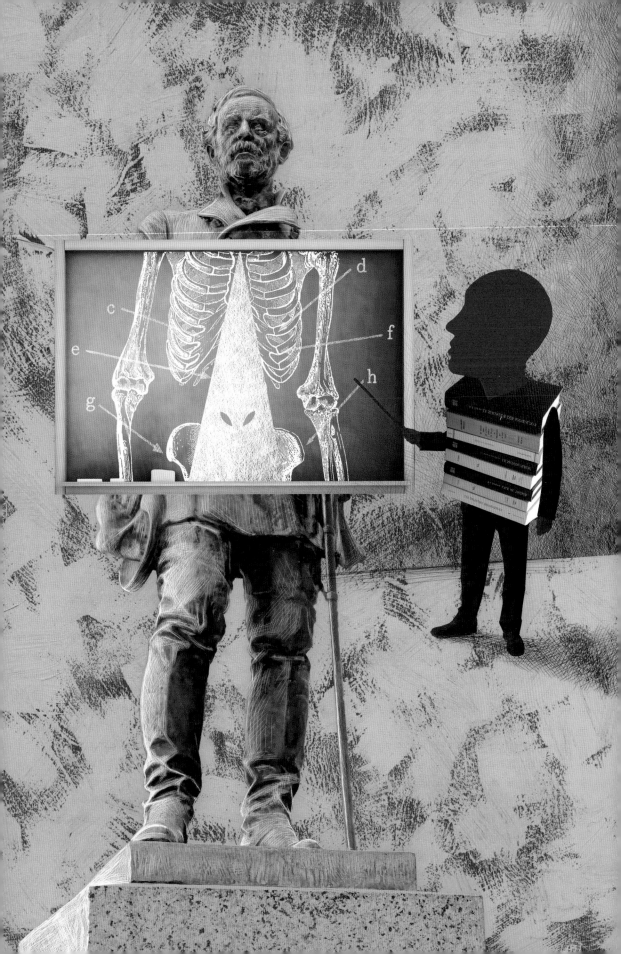

But eventually, we need to move beyond discussions about tearing down symbols of white supremacy, and begin to strategize about how to tear down the systems that still prop it up. In response to Trump's query, educator and activist Brian Jones writes, "Where does it stop? Let's answer him: *It goes all the way to the beginning.* If we're serious about uprooting racism and racist violence, we have to write a new American history for every student in every classroom, for every monument and museum."

If you doubt the need for such a drastic reclaiming of history, you need to look no further than the textbooks adopted by the state of Virginia, where this recent racist violence took place. One of the adopted textbooks, *The American Journey*, has previously been critiqued by James Loewen for inaccurately implying that states' rights, not slavery, was the reason Southern states seceded at the beginning of the Civil War. Another, Pearson's *America: History of Our Nation*, ends its chapter on Reconstruction with a section titled "A Cycle of Poverty" that begins "At emancipation, many freedmen owned little more than the clothes they wore. Poverty forced many African Americans, as well as poor whites, to become sharecroppers."

But neither poverty nor sharecropping was an inevitable outcome of emancipation. In fact, sharecropping was the result of a compromise between emboldened freedmen who refused to work in gangs under white supervision and ex-slaveholders who needed a workforce to till their land. It wasn't until the end of Reconstruction, the same period when all those Confederate monuments were built and Jim Crow laws put in place, that a new landlord-merchant class was able to turn sharecropping into a system that kept many Blacks and poor whites in a permanent state of debt, poverty, and dependence.

> **What better way to empower students and teachers in schools across the country than by actively taking part in the debate over whether symbols of white supremacy should be taken down — whether a statue at a nearby park, a classroom poster, a hallway mural, or even a school name.**

Furthermore, what's suspiciously absent from this passage is the discussion of why people who had labored all their lives for no pay, on whose backs the nation's wealth was built, ended up in poverty — many working for their former "masters" after finally winning freedom from slavery. This textbook — and so many others — offers no suggestion that there were alternatives, like in the Georgia Sea Islands, where 400 freedmen and women divided up land, planted crops, started schools, and created a democratic system with their own constitution, congress, supreme court, and armed militia — that is, until the U.S. Army forced them out and handed their land back to the former slave owners who had abandoned it. Also left out are the millions of Blacks and poor whites who organized together across the South in the Union Leagues through strikes, boycotts, demonstrations, and educational campaigns that fought to make freedom more than simply the freedom to be poor.

In fact, what all the major textbooks have in common — whether adopted in Virginia or New York — is that they give a top-down history of events. This history emphasizes and memorializes presidents, legislators, generals, and the wealthy — the same people who are typically honored with monuments. As Howard Zinn so eloquently wrote:

> The result of having our history dominated by presidents and generals and other "important" people is to create a passive citizenry, not knowing its own powers, always waiting for some savior on high. . . . History, looked at under the surface, in the streets and on the farms, in the GI barracks and trailer camps, in factories and offices, tells a different story. Whenever injustices have been remedied, wars halted, women and Blacks and Native Americans given their due, it has been because "unimportant" people spoke up, organized, protested, and brought democracy alive.

As teachers, we need to dedicate ourselves to teaching Charlottesville along with a more honest, full history of the United States. That story can't be told without centering racism and oppression as crucial to the development of the country, but it also can't be told without acknowledging those who have fought and died fighting racism and oppression. We need a history that honors the Takiyah Thompsons and Heather Heyers, not the Robert E. Lees. But more than that, we need a history that helps us learn how to move beyond tearing down statues and toward tearing down the racist system that those statues represent. ∎

As teachers, we need to dedicate ourselves to teaching Charlottesville along with a more honest, full history of the United States. That story can't be told without centering racism and oppression as crucial to the development of the country, but it also can't be told without acknowledging those who have fought and died fighting racism and oppression.

Adam Sanchez (asanchez@zinnedproject.org) is an editor of Rethinking Schools. *Sanchez teaches at Harvest Collegiate High School in New York City and works as curriculum writer and organizer with the Zinn Education Project.*

A Vision for Black Lives
Policy demands for Black power, freedom, and justice

By the Movement for Black Lives coalition

I n 2016, a coalition of more than 50 organizations released a revolutionary platform as the Movement for Black Lives with more than 30 policy demands. The collective said they hoped the document would be "both an articulation of our collective aspirations as well as a document that provides tangible resources for groups and individuals doing the work. We recognize that some of the demands in this document will not happen today. But we also recognize that they are necessary for our liberation." We urge readers to visit policy.m4bl.org and to read through the entire platform and all of the policy demands, but we also wanted to highlight one section that, among others, focuses on the liberation of Black youth.

AN IMMEDIATE END TO THE CRIMINALIZATION AND DEHUMANIZATION OF BLACK YOUTH ACROSS ALL AREAS OF SOCIETY INCLUDING, BUT NOT LIMITED TO, OUR NATION'S JUSTICE AND EDUCATION SYSTEMS, SOCIAL SERVICE AGENCIES, MEDIA, AND POP CULTURE

What Is the Problem?

- Across the country, Black children attend under-resourced schools where they are often pushed off of an academic track onto a track to prison. Zero-tolerance policies — a combination of exclusionary disciplinary policies and school-based arrests — are often the first stop along the school-to-prison pipeline and play a key role in pushing students out of the school system and funneling them into jails and prisons.
- Each year more than 3 million students are suspended from school — often for vague and subjective infractions such as "willful defiance" and "disrespect" — amounting to countless hours of lost instructional time. As a result, Black students are denied an opportunity to learn and punished for routine child and adolescent behaviors that their white peers are often not disciplined for at all.
- For Black youth, the impact of exclusionary school discipline is far-reaching — disengaging them from academic and developmental opportunities and increasing the likelihood that they will be incarcerated later in life. In addition, current research emphasizes the need to examine the unique ways in which Black girls are impacted by punitive zero-tolerance policies.[1] There are higher disciplinary disparities between Black girls and white girls than disciplinary disparities between Black boys

and white boys; yet, Black girls have historically been overlooked in the national discourse around youth impacted by the school-to-prison pipeline.

- Black youth are also more likely to experience higher rates of corporal punishment. According to the U.S. Department of Education's Office for Civil Rights (OCR), Black students constitute 17.1 percent of the nationwide student population, but 35.6 percent of those paddled. In addition, while girls are paddled less than boys, Black girls are more than twice as likely to be paddled than white girls. In the 13 states that paddle more than 1,000 students per year, Black girls are 2.07 times as likely as white girls to be beaten.[2]

- Outside of schools, young Black people are criminalized in ways that limit their life chances at every point. 2010 data shows that while Black youth comprised 17 percent of all youth, they represented 31 percent of all arrests. These disparities persist even as juvenile "crime" rates have fallen. Among youth arrests, young Black people are more likely to be referred to a juvenile court than their white peers, and are more likely to be processed (and less likely to be diverted). Among those adjudicated delinquent, they are more likely to be sent to solitary confinement. Among those detained, Black youth are more likely to be transferred to adult facilities. The disparities grow at almost every step, stealing the dignity of young Black people and forcing them onto lifelong pathways of criminalization and diminished opportunity.[3]

- For Black girls, the U.S.'s failure to address gender-based violence, which they experience at greater levels than any other group, is paramount to the criminalization they experience. In fact, sexual abuse is one of the primary predictors of girls' entry into the juvenile justice system, with girls often being routed to the system specifically because of their victimization. For instance, girls who are victims of sex trafficking are often arrested on prostitution charges. The punitive nature of this system is ill-equipped to support young girls through the violence and trauma they've experienced, which further subjects them to sexual victimization and a lifelong path of criminalization and abuse.[4]

- There is a critical need for a coordinated strategy in local communities that addresses rampant racial disparities in the application of zero-tolerance policies and criminalization practices that impact Black boys and girls. Fortunately, a powerful grassroots movement, led primarily by youth and parents of color, has taken shape across the country to address these harmful policies — but much more work remains.

- Tens of thousands of youth under the age of 21 are currently incarcerated for offenses ranging from truancy to more serious charges. Every crime bill passed by Congress throughout the 1980s and 1990s included new federal laws against juvenile crimes and increased penalties against children. Similar trends can be seen throughout state legislation. There is mounting research that children under the age of 23 do not have fully developed brains and that the cheapest, most humane, and most cost-effective way to respond to juvenile crime is not incarceration, but programs and investments that strengthen families, increase stability, and provide access to educational and employment opportunities. Prosecuting youth with crimes is not only cruel, but it also permanently disadvantages them with a criminal record — which makes completing their education, getting a job, finding housing, and growing up to be contributing members of society unfairly difficult.

What Does This Solution Do?

• Advances a grassroots organizing strategy at the local and state level that centers the work of ending the criminalization of Black youth through a racial and gender justice framework — led and informed by youth and parents.

• Addresses state-sanctioned violence that stems from over-policed schools and the deprivation of resources to public schools.

• Opens resources for alternative practices like restorative justice as a way to train students, parents, and staff to deal with interpersonal conflict. Restorative justice practices are used as an alternative to zero-tolerance policies by helping to build stronger school communities through: 1) Developing effective leadership; 2) Building trust, interconnection, and deeper relationships amongst students, parents, teachers, and staff; 3) Providing methods to address misbehavior in a way that gets to the root cause of conflicts and holds individuals accountable; 4) Repairing harm in a way that maintains the integrity of the community and doesn't further isolate offenders

• By ending the practice of charging youth with misdemeanors and limiting the ability to charge them with felonies we would save hundreds of millions of dollars annually and provide the opportunity for our children to outlive their mistakes.

Federal Action

• Target(s): U.S. Congress and Federal Agencies (Office for Civil Rights, Department of Education, Department of Justice)

• Process: The potential for policy reforms to zero-tolerance and punitive disciplinary practices at the federal level are somewhat limited. In December 2015, the U.S. Senate approved the most recent iteration of the Elementary and Secondary Education Act, also known as "No Child Left Behind." The new law reduces the role of the federal government in education matters and leaves in place punitive high-stakes testing requirements that have been a force behind removing students from the classroom and closing schools in Black and Brown communities, creating a "test, punish, pushout" effect. However, there are opportunities to demand greater enforcement of civil rights violations, particularly within federal agencies responsible for enforcing claims of racial disparities involving the administration of school discipline.[5] In January 2014, the Department of Education and Department of Justice issued joint guidance outlining school districts' obligations to ensure that school discipline policies are not administered in a manner that fuels racial disparities.[6] There is strong potential for additional guidance documents around these issues that can be used as a lever for local and statewide organizing efforts — although these documents lack the force to truly push real transformation in schools.

• Target: Legislative

• Process: This would require passage of a bill through both houses of Congress and signed by the president. The bill would repeal all federal juvenile crimes and amend the Juvenile Justice and Delinquency Prevention Act. It would also provide incentives to states, including the tying of federal prison and policing grants, to adopt statutes that ban the prosecution of children under the age 23. The bill would also include a mandatory reinvestment strategy where federal and state savings would be captured and reinvested in programs shown to reduce juvenile crime, increase youth educational attainment, and support communities where youth incarceration has been most prevalent.

State Action

- Target: Legislative
- Process: The passage of state law banning exclusionary discipline (suspensions, expulsions, and arrests) for all students pre-K through 12th grade.
- State law banning exclusionary discipline (suspensions, expulsions, arrests) for vague and subjective behaviors including willful defiance, disrespect, insubordination, obnoxious, and disturbing the peace.
- The passage of state law prohibiting the use of corporal punishment in all educational settings.
- State law requiring the use of supportive services for students, including fully funding restorative programs and support for students in crisis in educational settings.
- Improve the child welfare system's identification of victims of abuse, implement a gender-responsive approach to victims of abuse, and use Medicaid funds to improve quality care and trauma-related services for girls in child welfare.
- Target: Legislative
- Process: This would require passage of a bill through the state legislature. The bill would repeal all existing juvenile offenses and would also include a mandatory reinvestment strategy where state savings would be captured and reinvested in programs shown to reduce juvenile crime, increase youth educational attainment, and support communities where juvenile incarceration has been most prevalent.

> **For Black youth, the impact of exclusionary school discipline is far-reaching — disengaging them from academic and developmental opportunities and increasing the likelihood that they will be incarcerated later in life.**

Local Action

- Passage of local school district policy banning exclusionary discipline (suspensions, expulsions, and arrests) for all students pre-K through 12th grade).
- Passage of local school district policy banning exclusionary discipline (suspensions, expulsions, arrests) for vague and subjective behaviors including willful defiance, disrespect, insubordination, obnoxious, and disturbing the peace.
- Passage of local school district policy prohibiting the use of corporal punishment in all educational settings.
- Passage of local school district policy requiring the use of supportive services for students, including fully funding restorative programs and support for students in crisis

in educational settings.

- Invest in creating safe and supportive group homes with specialized services for teenage girls.
- Invest in training for students, parents, teachers, and staff on restorative justice practices as an alternative to zero-tolerance policies.
- Process: At the local level, reducing the prosecution of juvenile misdemeanors can be accomplished in a variety of ways:
  - » Campaigns that target city and county prosecutors and demand that instead of prosecution, youth defendants are diverted to nonpunitive programs.
  - » Campaigns that target police, who often have wide discretion in the arrest of misdemeanors, to publicly de-prioritize the arrest of youth for misdemeanors.

How Does This Solution Address the Specific Needs of Some of the Most Marginalized Black People?

- These solutions address exclusionary and overly punitive school discipline policies in public schools across the nation that deny Black youth an opportunity to learn. These policies have the greatest impact on queer and trans youth, foster care youth, and girls.
- These solutions will propel Black youth toward graduation, and create a school-to-college pipeline.
- Students will not have minor offenses on their academic records.
- Legislation banning the prosecution of youth for all misdemeanors would have the largest impact on people who are made most vulnerable by incarceration, including LGBTQ and undocumented people. It would also reduce the number of incarcerated people significantly. The reinvestment aspect of the legislation would positively impact homeless people by providing increased services.

Model Legislation

- Model school discipline policy
- Trayvon's Law

Resources

- *Black Girls Matter: Pushed Out, Overpoliced, and Underprotected*
- *Pushout: The Criminalization of Black Girls in Schools*
- *The Sexual Abuse to Prison Pipeline: The Girls' Story*
- *Telling It Like It Is! Miami Youth Speak Out on the School-to-Prison Pipeline*
- *Intro to Restorative Practices* (from Power U Center for Social Change)

ORGANIZATIONS CURRENTLY WORKING ON POLICY

NATIONAL

- Advancement Project
- Alliance for Educational Justice
- Dignity in Schools Campaign
- Genders & Sexualities Alliance Network
- NAACP Legal Defense Fund

LOCAL

- Alliance for Quality Education (New York)
- Baltimore Algebra Project (Baltimore)
- Boston Youth Organizing Project (Boston)
- Community Justice Project (Miami)
- Critical Exposure (District of Columbia)
- DeSoto County Parents & Students for Justice (Mississippi)
- Dream Defenders (Florida)
- Desis Rising Up and Moving (New York)
- Families and Friends of Louisiana's Incarcerated Children (New Orleans)
- Girls for Gender Equity (New York)
- Labor Community Strategy Center (Los Angeles)
- Nollie Jenkins Family Center (Mississippi)
- One Voice (Mississippi)
- Padres & Jóvenes Unidos (Denver)
- Philadelphia Student Union (Philly)
- Power U Center for Social Change (Miami)
- Portland Parents Union (Portland)
- Project South (Atlanta)
- Racial Justice Now! (Ohio)
- Rethink (New Orleans)
- SpiritHouse (North Carolina)
- Tenants and Workers United
- Tunica Teens in Action (Mississippi)
- Urban Youth Collaborative (New York)
- Voices of Youth in Chicago Education (Chicago)
- Youth Justice Coalition (Los Angeles)
- Youth United for Change (Philly)
- Local NAACP branches
- And many others!

AUTHORS & CONTRIBUTORS OF THIS POLICY OVERVIEW*

Thena Robinson Mock
Education Law Center

Ruth Jeannoel
Power U Center for Social Change

Rachel Gilmer
Dream Defenders

Chelsea Fuller
Advancement Project

Marbre Stahly-Butts
Center for Popular Democracy

*Affiliations at the time of writing this policy.

ENDNOTES

[1] *Black Girls Matter: Pushed Out, Overpoliced, and Underprotected.* African American Policy Forum and Center for Intersectionality and Social Policy Studies (February 2015). atlanticphilanthropies.org/sites/default/files/uploads/BlackGirlsMatter_Report.pdf

[2] *A Violent Education: Corporal Punishment of Children in U.S. Public Schools.* American Civil Liberties Union and Human Rights Watch (February 2009).

[3] The Sentencing Project. sentencingproject.org/wp-content/uploads/2015/11/Disproportionate-Minority-Contact-in-the-Juvenile-Justice-System.pdf

[4] The Sexual Abuse to Prison Pipeline: The Girls' Story. Human Rights Project for Girls, Georgetown Law Center on Poverty and Inequality, Ms. Foundation for Women. rights4girls.org/wp-content/uploads/r4g/2015/02/2015_COP_sexual-abuse_layout_web-1.pdf

[5] The Office for Civil Rights (OCR) has the mission of ensuring "equal access to education and to promote educational excellence through vigorous enforcement of civil rights in our nation's schools." ed.gov/about/offices/list/ocr/index.htm

[6] U.S. Department of Education/Department of Justice Federal Discipline Guidance (released January 2014). ed.gov/policy/gen/guid/school-discipline/index.html

Permission to publish this portion of the platform was provided by the M4BL coalition.

2

ENSLAVEMENT, CIVIL RIGHTS, AND BLACK LIBERATION

The Color Line

How white elites sought to divide and conquer in the American colonies

By Bill Bigelow

Colonial laws prohibiting Blacks and whites from marrying one another suggest that some Blacks and whites *did* marry. Laws imposing penalties on white indentured servants and Black slaves who ran away together likewise suggest that whites and Blacks *did* run away together. Laws making it a crime for Indians and Blacks to meet together in groups of four or more indicate that, at some point, these gatherings must have occurred. As Benjamin Franklin is said to have remarked during the Constitutional Convention, "One doesn't make laws to prevent the sheep from planning insurrection," because this has never occurred, nor will it occur.

The social elites of early America sought to manufacture racial divisions. Men of property and privilege were in the minority; they needed mechanisms to divide people who, in concert, might threaten the status quo.

The social elites of early America sought to manufacture racial divisions. Men of property and privilege were in the minority; they needed mechanisms to divide people who, in concert, might threaten the status quo. Individuals' different skin colors were not sufficient to keep these people apart if they came to see their interests in common. Which is not to say that racism was merely a ruling class plot, but as Howard Zinn points out in chapters 2 and 3 of *A People's History of the United States*, and as students see in this lesson, some people did indeed set out consciously to promote divisions based on race.

Because today's racial divisions run so deep and can seem so normal, providing students an historical framework can be enlightening. We need to ask, "What are the origins of racial conflict?" and "Who benefits from these deep antagonisms?" A critical perspective on race and racism is as important as anything students will take away from a U.S. history course. This is just one early lesson in our quest to construct that critical perspective.

Suggested Procedure

I'd suggest doing this activity before students read Zinn's chapters 2 or 3. With students, review the reading "Colonial Laws: Divide and Conquer" (see p. 86). How they work with the problems posed in the reading is a matter of preference. Students could come up

"THE BOSTON MASSACRE" | THE NATIONAL ARCHIVES AND RECORDS ADMINISTRATION

with some tentative ideas on their own and then work in pairs or small groups to assemble a more complete list. Or they might work in small groups from the very beginning.

However they approach the "Colonial Laws" problems, ask students to compare their answers with the information contained in chapters 2 and 3. Some actual laws and policies initiated to respond to the problems described in the student reading follow. Where indicated, students can find this information in either chapter 2 or 3 in *A People's History of the United States*. Not all of these are included in chapters 2 and 3. (For valuable insights on the first question, see William Loren Katz, *Black Indians: A Hidden Heritage*, chapter 8: "Their Mixing Is to Be Prevented." This chapter is easily read by most high school students, and is highly recommended.)

1. Predict the measures that were taken to keep Indians and Blacks from uniting, or that may have even made them to feel hostile toward one another.

- As one white Carolinian put it, we need a policy "to make Indians & Negros a checque upon each other lest by their Vastly Superior Numbers we should be crushed by one or the other." Laws were passed to prohibit free Blacks from traveling in Indian country. Treaties with Indian tribes required the return of fugitive slaves (ch. 3).

- A 1683 New York law made it a crime for "Negro or Indian slaves" to meet any-where together in groups of four or more or to be armed "with guns, swords, clubs, staves, or any other kind of weapon." A 1690 Connecticut law forbade Indians and Blacks from walking beyond the town limits without a pass. Connecticut, Rhode Island, and Massachusetts all had a 9 p.m. curfew for Blacks and Indians. A 1773 New York law was passed "to prevent Negro and Indian slaves from ap-pearing in the streets after 8 at night without a lantern with a lighted candle in it."
- Whites often hired local Indians to hunt down escaped African slaves. In 1676, Mary-land offered rewards to Indians for capturing Black slave runaways. In 1740, South Carolina offered Indians £100 for each slave runaway captured alive and £50 for "ev-ery scalp of a grown negro slave." In 1729, South Carolina hired Catawba Indians to recapture or kill enslaved Blacks who had rebelled in Stono, South Carolina (ch. 3).
- In 1725, South Carolina outlawed bringing any Black slaves to the frontier. As a British colonel said, "The slaves . . . talk good English as well as the Cherokee lan-guage and . . . too often tell falsities to the Indians which they are apt to believe."
- A large number of Indians were sold as slaves to the West Indies. In a single year, more than 10,000 Indian slaves were shipped in chains to the West Indies from the port of Charleston, South Carolina.
- The British sent Black troops to fight the Natchez Indians in the Yamasee War of 1715.
- The British encouraged the so-called Five Civilized Tribes — the Cherokee, Creek, Chickasaw, Choctaw, and Seminole — to enslave Africans, as the whites were do-ing. Ultimately, slaves made up between 10 and 20 percent of all five groups but the Seminoles. The Cherokee adopted a "slave code" to prevent Blacks from learning to read and write and provided that if a slave ran off, other tribe members were ob-ligated to catch the runaway. Slavery contributed to inequality within each Indian nation. Only a relatively small elite of 12 percent of the Cherokees owned slaves.

2. Predict laws or policies adopted to discourage white indentured servants and Black slaves from running away together.

- A 1661 Virginia law provided that "in case any English servant shall run away in company of any Negroes" he would have to suffer extra years of servitude to the master of the escaped slave (ch. 2).

3a. Predict how poor whites and white indentured servants were taught to believe that they were superior to and didn't have anything in common with Blacks.

- All whites were encouraged to believe that they were superior to Blacks and laws were passed that underscored their superiority. For example, a 1723 Maryland law pro-vided for cutting off the ears of any Black person who struck a white person (ch. 2).
- A Virginia colonial law sentenced whites to 25 lashes for stealing a pig, but in-creased it to 39 lashes if the person were Black or Indian.
- Poor whites were enlisted to hunt down runaway slaves, and were put on slave patrols (ch. 3).

- A 1705 Virginia law required that when a white servant's period of indenture was over, a master must provide men with 10 bushels of corn, 30 shillings, and a gun; and women with 15 bushels of corn and 40 shillings. The freed servants were also to be given 50 acres of land (ch. 2).
- After Bacon's Rebellion in 1676, amnesty was given to whites but not to Blacks (ch. 3).
- White servants were given numerous advantages not given to Black slaves, including the right to testify against their masters in court if they were not treated properly.

3b. Predict how Blacks and whites were kept separate, so that whites would not even imagine getting together with Blacks.
- A 1691 Virginia law provided that "any white man or woman being free who shall intermarry with a negro, mulatoo, or Indian man or woman bond or free" shall be banished (ch. 2).
- Virginia, Massachusetts, Maryland, Delaware, Pennsylvania, the Carolinas, and Georgia all passed laws prohibiting interracial marriage (ch. 3).
- In Southern colonies, according to historian Joseph P. Cullen, if a white female indentured servant had a child by a Black man she would be punished by public whipping and her period of indenture would be doubled.

4. Predict the measures adopted to ensure that on every plantation there were enough white overseers in relation to Black slaves. How might white owners have found more white indentured servants to help supervise Blacks?
- In 1698, South Carolina passed a "deficiency law" that required every plantation owner to have at least one white servant for every six male adult Black slaves (ch. 3).
- As Howard Zinn points out in chapter 3, servants were acquired from Great Britain, and later from Ireland and Germany, by "lures, promises, . . . lies, by kidnapping." Kidnappers would sell servants to the highest bidder in the American colonies.
- In 1717, the British parliament made transportation to the American colonies a legal punishment for committing certain crimes. Tens of thousands of convicts were sent to Maryland, Virginia, and other colonies (ch. 3). ■

Bill Bigelow is curriculum editor of Rethinking Schools *and co-director of the Zinn Education Project. He co-edited* A People's Curriculum for the Earth: Teaching Climate Change and the Environmental Crisis. *This lesson was first published at the Zinn Education Project.*

RESOURCES

Teaching materials that accompany this article can be found in the following pages or online at teachingforblacklives.org

Katz, William Loren. 1986. *Black Indians: A Hidden Heritage.* Atheneum.

Zinn, Howard. 1980. *A People's History of the United States.* HarperCollins.

Colonial Laws

Divide and Conquer

Christmas Day, 1522: On a sugar plantation owned by Christopher Columbus' son, Diego, enslaved Africans united with enslaved Taíno Indians in the first recorded Black/Indian rebellion in the Americas. They killed their white overseers and ran away. In Great Britain's North American colonies Black and Indian slaves and white indentured servants often ran away together.

Throughout the history of early America, white ruling elites worried about what Blacks and Indians might do if they got together. The people with property were also concerned about uprisings of white indentured servants, poor whites, and enslaved Blacks, as occurred in 17th-century Virginia in Bacon's Rebellion. Conditions were different in different colonies, but everywhere people who had some wealth wanted to make sure that no one took it away from them.

Below are a number of specific problems that colonial legislatures faced. *Try to predict the laws they passed to deal with these problems and protect their privileged position.* Some laws may deal with more than one problem, and some problems required several laws. Sometimes legislatures passed no specific laws, but white leaders promoted general policies. *For each problem, except #4, come up with at least three laws or policies — some require more than others.*

The Problems

1. At times, Indians would attack white settlers on the frontier, kill them, and take their slaves. In parts of North America, enslaved Black people and Indians greatly outnumbered whites. If Blacks and Indians united, they could crush the white rulers. **Predict the measures that were taken to keep Indians and Blacks from uniting, or that may have been used to make Indians and Blacks to feel hostile toward one another.**

2. Some white indentured servants along with enslaved Blacks escaped from their masters. **Predict laws or policies adopted to discourage white indentured servants and enslaved Blacks from running away together.**

3. Black slaves, indentured servants, and even some poor but free whites organized together to threaten rebellion.
   a. **Predict how poor whites and white indentured servants were taught to believe that they were superior to and didn't have anything in common with Blacks.**
   b. **Predict how Blacks and whites were kept separate, so that whites would not even imagine getting together with Blacks.**

4. In some areas, there were not enough whites to supervise enslaved Blacks. This made rebellion more likely. In some colonies, there were not many poor whites or indentured white servants in relation to the number of enslaved Blacks. **Predict the measures adopted to ensure that on every plantation there were enough white overseers in relation to Black slaves. How might white owners have found more white indentured servants to help supervise Blacks?**

Presidents and Slaves

Helping students find the truth

By Bob Peterson

During a lesson about George Washington and the American Revolution, I explained to my 5th graders that Washington owned 317 slaves. One student added that Thomas Jefferson also was a slave owner. And then, in part to be funny and in part expressing anger — over vote fraud involving African Americans in the then-recent 2000 election and the U.S. Supreme Court's subsequent delivery of the presidency to George W. Bush — one of my students shouted, "Bush is a slave owner, too!"

"No, Bush doesn't own slaves," I calmly explained. "Slavery was finally ended in this country in 1865."

Short exchanges such as this often pass quickly and we move onto another topic. But this time one student asked: "Well, which presidents were slave owners?"

She had me stumped. "That's a good question," I said. "I don't know." Thus began a combined social studies, math, and language arts project in which I learned along with my students, and which culminated in a fascinating exchange between my students and the publishers of their U.S. history textbook.

After I admitted that I had no clue exactly which presidents owned slaves, I threw the challenge back to the students: "How can we find out?"

"Look in a history book."

"Check the internet."

I realized that I had entered a "teachable moment" when students show genuine interest in exploring a particular topic. Yet I had few materials about presidents and slaves, and no immediate idea of how to engage 25 students on the subject.

I also recognized that this was a great opportunity to create my own curriculum, which might help students look critically at texts while encouraging their active participation in doing meaningful research. Such an approach stands in sharp contrast to the "memorize the presidents" instruction that I suffered through growing up, and which too many students probably still endure. I seized the opportunity.

First, I had a student write down the question — "Which presidents were slave owners?" — in our class notebook under the heading, "Questions We Have." I then suggested that a few students form an "action research group," which in my classroom means an ad hoc group of interested students researching a topic and then doing something with what they learn. I asked for volunteers willing to work during recess. Several students raised their hands, surprising me because I would have guessed that some of them would have much preferred going outside to staying indoors researching.

Action Research by Students

At recess time, Raul and Edwin were immediately in my face. "When are we going to start the action research on the slave presidents?" they demanded. I told them to look in the back of our school dictionaries for a list of U.S. presidents while I got out some large construction paper. The dictionaries, like our social studies text, had little pictures of each president with some basic information.

"Why don't they just tell whether they have slaves here in this list of presidents?" asked Edwin. "They tell other things about presidents."

"Good question," I said. "Why do you think they don't tell?"

"I don't know, probably because they don't know themselves."

"Maybe so," I responded. "Here's what I'd like you to do. Since slavery was abolished when Lincoln was president, and since he was the 16th president, draw 16 lines equal distance from each other and list all the presidents from Washington to Lincoln, and then a yes-and-no column so we can check off whether they owned slaves."

Filling in those columns turned out to be a challenge.

When my students and I began investigating which presidents owned slaves, our attempts focused on traditional history textbooks and student-friendly websites from the White House and the Smithsonian Institution. These efforts turned up virtually nothing. We then pursued two different sources of information: history books written for adults and more in-depth websites.

I brought in two books that were somewhat helpful: James Loewen's *Lies My Teacher Told Me* (Simon and Schuster, 1995) and Kenneth O'Reilly's *Nixon's Piano: Presidents and Racial Politics from Washington to Clinton* (Free Press, 1995). By using the indexes and reading the text out loud, we uncovered facts about some of the presidents. We also did an internet search using the words "presidents" and "slavery." We soon learned we had to be more specific and include the president's name and "slavery" — for example, "President George Washington" and "slavery." Some results were student-friendly, such as the mention of Washington's slaves (and some of their escapes) at mountvernon.org/slavery. There was also a bill of sale for a slave signed by Dolly Madison, the wife of president James Madison. Many websites had a large amount of text and were beyond the reading level of many of my students. So we searched for the word "slave" to see if there was any specific mention of slave ownership.

In their research, students often asked, "How do we know this is true? Our history books aren't telling the truth. Why should we think this does?" I explained the difference between primary and secondary sources and how a primary source — like a bill of sale or original list of slaves — was pretty solid evidence. To help ensure accuracy, the students decided that if we used secondary sources, we needed to find at least two different citations.

Bits and Pieces of Information

Over the next several days the students, with my help, looked at various sources. We checked our school's children's books about presidents, our social studies textbook, a 1975 World Book Encyclopedia, and a CD-ROM encyclopedia. We found nothing about presidents as slave owners. I had a hunch about which presidents owned slaves, based on what I knew in general about the presidents, but I wanted "proof" before we put a check in the "yes" box. And though my students wanted to add a third column — explaining how many slaves each slave-owning president had — that proved impossible. Even when we did find information about which presidents owned slaves, the numbers changed depending on how many slaves had been bought, sold, born, or died.

> After I admitted that I had no clue exactly which presidents owned slaves, I threw the challenge back to the students.

In our research, most of the information dealt with presidential attitudes and policies toward slavery. It was difficult to find specific information on which presidents owned slaves. To help the investigation, I checked out a few books for them from our local university library.

Overall, our best resource was the internet. The best sites required adult help to find and evaluate, and I became so engrossed in the project that I spent a considerable amount of time at home surfing the web. The "student-friendly" websites with information about presidents — such as the White House's gallery of presidents (whitehouse.gov/1600/presidents) — didn't mention that Washington and Jefferson enslaved African Americans. Other popular sites with the same glaring lack of information are the Smithsonian Institution (smithsonianeducation.org/educators/lesson_plans/idealabs/mr_president.html) and the National Museum of American History (americanhistory.si.edu/presidency).

As we did the research, I regularly asked, "Why do you think this doesn't mention that the president owned slaves?" Students' responses varied, including "They're stupid"; "They don't want us kids to know the truth"; "They think we're too young to know"; and "They don't know themselves." (Given more time, we might have explored this matter further, looking at who produces textbooks and why they might not include information about presidents' attitudes about racism and slavery.)

During our research, my students and I found bits and pieces of information about presidents and slavery. But we never found that one magic resource, be it book or website, that had the information readily available. Ultimately, though, we discovered that two presidents who served after Lincoln — Andrew Johnson and Ulysses S. Grant — had been slave owners. While the students taped an extension on their chart, I explained that I was not totally surprised about Johnson because he had been a Southerner. But

> "How do we know this is true? Our history books aren't telling the truth. Why should we think this does?"

it was a shock that Grant had owned slaves. "He was the commander of the Union Army in the Civil War," I explained. "When I first learned about the Civil War in elementary school, Grant and Lincoln were portrayed as saviors of the Union and freers of slaves."

When I told the entire class how Grant's slave-owning past had surprised me, Tanya, an African American student, raised her hand and said, "That's nothing. Lincoln was a slave owner, too." I asked for her source of information and she said she had heard that Lincoln didn't like Blacks. I thanked her for raising the point, and told the class that while it was commonly accepted by historians that Lincoln was not a slave owner, his attitudes toward Blacks and slavery were a source of much debate. I noted that just because a president didn't own slaves didn't mean that he supported freedom for slaves or equal treatment of people of different races.

I went into a bit of detail on Lincoln, in part to counter the all-too-common simplification that Lincoln unequivocally opposed slavery and supported freedom for Blacks. I explained that although it's commonly believed that Lincoln freed enslaved Americans when he signed the Emancipation Proclamation, the document actually frees slaves only in states and regions under rebellion — it did not free slaves in any of the slaveholding states and regions that remained in the Union. In other words, Lincoln "freed" slaves everywhere he had no authority and withheld freedom everywhere he did. Earlier, in Lincoln's first inaugural address in March of 1861, he promised slaveholders that he would support a constitutional amendment forever protecting slavery in the states where it then existed — if only those states would remain in the Union.

Slave-Owning Presidents

By the time we finished our research, the students had found that 10 of the first 18 presidents were slave owners: George Washington, Thomas Jefferson, James Madison, James

Monroe, Andrew Jackson, John Tyler, James K. Polk, Zachary Taylor, Andrew Johnson, and Ulysses S. Grant. Those who didn't: John Adams, John Quincy Adams, Martin Van Buren, William Henry Harrison, Millard Fillmore, Franklin Pierce, James Buchanan, and, despite Tanya's assertion, Abraham Lincoln. The student researchers were excited to present their findings to their classmates, and decided to do so as part of a math class. I made blank charts for each student in the class, and they filled in information provided by the action research team: the names of presidents, the dates of their years in office, the total number of years in office, and whether they had owned slaves. Our chart started with George Washington, who assumed office in 1789, and ended in 1877 when the last president who had owned slaves, Ulysses S. Grant, left office.

We then used the data to discuss this topic of presidents and slave-owning within the structure of ongoing math topics in my class: "What do the data tell us?" and "How can we construct new knowledge with the data?" Students, for example, added up the total number of years in which the United States had a slave-owning president in office, and compared that total to the number of years in which there were non-slave-owning presidents in office. We figured out that in 69 percent of the years between 1789 and 1877, the United States had a president who had been a slave owner. One student observed that only slave-owning presidents served more than one term. "Why didn't they let presidents who didn't own slaves serve two terms?" another student pondered.

> **By the time we finished our research, the students had found that 10 of the first 18 presidents were slave owners.**

Using the data, the students made bar graphs and circle graphs to display the information. When they wrote reflections on the math lesson, they connected math to content. One student wrote: "I learned to convert fractions to percent so I know that $\frac{10}{18}$ is the same as 55.5 percent. That's how many of the first 18 presidents owned slaves." Another observed, "I learned how to make pie charts and that so many more presidents owned slaves than the presidents who didn't own slaves."

During a subsequent social studies lesson, the three students who had done most of the research explained their frustrations in getting information. "They hardly ever want to mention it [slaves owned by presidents]," explained one student. "We had to search and search."

Specific objectives for this mini-unit, such as reviewing the use of percent, emerged as the lessons themselves unfolded. But its main purpose was to help students to critically examine the actions of early leaders of the United States and to become skeptical of textbooks and government websites as sources that present the entire picture. I figure that if kids start questioning the "official story" early on, they will be more open to alternative viewpoints later. While discovering which presidents were slave owners is not an in-depth analysis, it pokes an important hole in the godlike mystique that surrounds the "Founding Fathers." If students learn how to be critical of the icons of American past, hopefully it will give them permission and tools to be critical of the elites of America today.

Besides uncovering some hard-to-find and uncomfortable historical truths, I also wanted to encourage my students to think about why these facts were so hard to find, and to develop a healthy skepticism of official sources of information. I showed them two quotations about Thomas Jefferson. One was from a 5th-grade history textbook, *United States: Adventures in Time and Place* (Macmillan/McGraw-Hill, 1998), which read: "Jefferson owned several slaves in his lifetime and lived in a slave-owning colony. Yet he often spoke out against slavery. 'Nothing is more certainly written in the book of fate than that these people are to be free'" (p. 314). The other quotation was from James Loewen (*Lies My Teacher Told Me*):

> Textbooks stress that Jefferson was a humane master, privately tormented by slavery and opposed to its expansion, not the type to destroy families by selling slaves. In truth, by 1820 Jefferson had become an ardent advocate of the expansion of slavery to the western territories. And he never let his ambivalence about slavery affect his private life. Jefferson was an average master who had his slaves whipped and sold into the Deep South as examples to induce other slaves to obey. By 1822, Jefferson owned 267 slaves. During his long life, of hundreds of different slaves he owned, he freed only three and five more at his death — all blood relatives of his. (p. 140)

We talked about the different perspective each quote had toward Jefferson and toward what students should learn. I then explained what an omission was, and suggested that we become "textbook detectives" and investigate what our new social studies text *United States* (Harcourt Brace, 2000) said about Jefferson and slavery. I reviewed how to use an index and divided all page references for Jefferson among small groups of students. The groups read the pages, noted any references to Jefferson owning slaves, and then reported back to the class. Not one group found a single reference. Not surprisingly, the students were angry when they realized how the text omitted such important information. "They should tell the truth!" one student fumed.

No Mention of Racism

I wanted students to see that the textbooks' omissions were not an anomaly, but part of a pattern of ignoring racism in America — in the past and in the present. In the next lesson, I started by writing the word "racism" on the board. I asked the kids to look up "racism" in the index of their social studies book. Nothing. "Racial discrimination." Nothing.

"Our school should get a different book," one student suggested. "Good idea," I said, "but it's not so easy." I told my students that I had served on a committee that had looked at the major textbooks published for 5th graders and that none of them had dealt with racism or slavery and presidents.

Students had a variety of responses:

"Let's throw them out."

"Let's use the internet."

"Write a letter to the people who did the books." I focused in on the letter-writing suggestion and reminded them that before we did so, we had to be certain that our criticisms were correct. The students then agreed that in small groups they would use the textbook's index and read what was said about all the first 18 presidents, just as we had done previously with Jefferson. None of the groups found any mention of a president owning a slave.

Letters as Critique and Action

In subsequent days, some students wrote letters to the textbook publisher. Michelle, a white girl, was particularly detailed. She wrote: "I am 11 years old and I like to read and write. When I am reading I notice every little word and in your social studies book I realize that the word "racism" is not in your book. You're acting like it is a bad word for those kids who read it." She went on to criticize the book for not mentioning that any presidents had slaves: "I see that you do not mention that some of the presidents had slaves. But some of them did. Like George Washington had 317 slaves. So did Thomas Jefferson. He had 267 slaves." She continued: "If you want to teach children the truth, then you should write the truth." (Michelle's letter and some of the student-made charts were also printed in our school newspaper.)

> **We do students a disservice when we sanitize history and sweep uncomfortable truths under the rug.**

We mailed off the letters, and moved on to new lessons. Weeks passed with no response and eventually the students stopped asking if the publishers had written back. Then one day a fancy-looking envelope appeared in my mailbox addressed to Michelle Williams. She excitedly opened the letter and read it to the class.

Harcourt School Publishers Vice President Donald Lankiewicz had responded to Michelle at length. He wrote that "while the word 'racism' does not appear, the subject of unfair treatment of people because of their race is addressed on page 467." He also argued: "There are many facts about the presidents that are not included in the text simply because we do not have room for them all."

Michelle wrote back to Lankiewicz, thanking him but expressing disappointment.

"In a history book you shouldn't have to wait until page 467 to learn about unfair treatment," she wrote. As to his claim that there wasn't room for all the facts about the presidents, Michelle responded: "Adding more pages is good for the kids because they should know the right things from the wrong. It is not like you are limited to certain amount of pages. . . . All I ask you is that you write the word 'racism' in the book and add some more pages in the book so you can put most of the truth about the presidents."

Michelle never received a reply.

Improving the Lesson

Michelle and the other students left 5th grade soon after the letter exchange. In the flurry of end-of-year activities, I didn't take as much time to process the project as I might have. Nor did I adequately explore with students the fact that most non-slave-owning presidents exhibited pro-slavery attitudes and promoted pro-slavery policies.

But the larger issue, which critical teachers struggle to address, is why textbook publishers and schools in general do such a poor job of helping students make sense of the difficult issues of race. We do students a disservice when we sanitize history and sweep uncomfortable truths under the rug. We leave them less prepared to deal with the difficult issues they will face in their personal, political, and social lives. Granted, these are extremely complicated issues that don't have a single correct response. But it's important to begin with a respect for the truth and for the capacity of people of all ages to expand their understanding of the past and the present, and to open their hearts and minds to an ever-broadening concept of social justice.

> While discovering which presidents were slave owners is not an in-depth analysis, it pokes an important hole in the godlike mystique that surrounds the "Founding Fathers."

I believe my students learned a lot from their research on presidents and slaves — and clearly know more than most Americans about which of the first 18 presidents owned slaves. I'm also hopeful they learned the importance of looking critically at all sources of information. I know one student, Tanya, did. On the last day of school she came up to me amid the congratulatory goodbyes and said, "I still think Lincoln owned slaves."

"You are a smart girl but you are wrong about that one," I responded. "We'll see," she said. "You didn't know Grant had slaves when the school year started! Why should I always believe what my teacher says?" ∎

Bob Peterson (bob.e.peterson@gmail.com) is an editor of Rethinking Schools *and former president of the Milwaukee Teachers' Education Association. He taught 5th grade in Milwaukee Public Schools for 30 years.*

AUTHOR'S NOTE: *About two years after I completed the research on slave-owning presidents with my students, a wonderful website called UnderstandingPrejudice.org was put up by folks at Wesleyan University. This site includes extensive information on presidents who owned slaves (see understandingprejudice.org/slavery). I learned from this website that three presidents not on my list also owned slaves: Martin Van Buren, William Henry Harrison, and James Buchanan. I am grateful for the additional information on this website, which opens up all sorts of new teaching possibilities.*

RESOURCES

For teaching materials related to this article, including the two letters referenced, go to teachingforblacklives.org

When Black Lives Mattered
Why teach Reconstruction

By Adam Sanchez

Every day seems to bring new horrors, as President Donald Trump's racist rhetoric and policies have provided an increasingly encouraging environment for attacks on Black people and other communities of color. The acquittal of yet another police officer accused of murdering a Black man in St. Louis, the raging battle across the country over whether symbols of slavery should be removed from public spaces, and the formation of a "Commission on Election Integrity" to further suppress voting by people of color are just a few of the recent reminders that racism is as American as apple pie.

In moments like these, it's worth remembering a time in U.S. history when Black lives mattered. Reconstruction, the era immediately following the Civil War and emancipation, is full of stories that help us see the possibility of a future defined by racial equity. Though often overlooked in classrooms across the country, Reconstruction was a period where the impossible suddenly became possible.

For example, shortly after hearing in 1865 that she and others on her Florida plantation were no longer enslaved, a woman named Frances told a friend what she thought their future might look like: "This time next year all the white folks will be at work in the fields, and the plantations and the houses, and everything in them will be turned over to us to do with as we please." While her fantasy didn't come true, something remarkable did. Without saying anything to their former owner, on New Year's Day 1866, every freed slave on the plantation left.

The ability of newly freed people to imagine their former owners serving them, or to walk off a plantation in a society that had heavily policed Black movement, reveals the possibilities of a period where something that had only a few years prior seemed unthinkable was now a fact of life. As historian David Roediger writes in his book *Seizing Freedom*, "If anything seemed impossible in the 1850s political universe, it was the immediate, unplanned, and uncompensated emancipation of 4 million slaves."

When this once seemingly impossible fate became a reality, it democratized and revolutionized U.S. society. It was a moment in which people who had been enslaved became congressmen. It was a moment where a Black-majority legislature in South Carolina could tax the rich to pay for public schools. It was a moment that spawned the first experiments in Black self-determination in the Georgia Sea Islands, where 400 freedmen and women divided up land, planted crops, started schools, and created a democratic system with their own constitution, congress, supreme court, and armed militia. It was a moment where thousands of Blacks and poor whites organized together across the South in the Union Leagues, engaging in strikes, boycotts, demonstrations, and educational

LIBRARY OF CONGRESS

THE FIRST COLORED SENATOR AND REPRESENTATIVES.
In the 41st and 42nd Congress of the United States.

U.S. Senator H.R.REVELS, of Mississippi   BENJ.S TURNER, M.C. of Alabama.   ROBERT C. DE LARGE, M.C. of S.Carolina.   JOSIAH T WALLS, M.C. of Florida.   JEFFERSON H.LONG, M.C. of Georgia   JOSEPH H.RAINY, M.C. of S.Carolina.   R. BROWN ELLIOT, M.C. of S.Carolina.

NEW YORK, PUBLISHED BY CURRIER & IVES, 123 NASSAU STREET

campaigns. And it was a moment where other social movements — in particular, the labor movement and the feminist movement — drew strength from the inspiring actions of African Americans to secure and define their own freedom. In sum, the Reconstruction era was a moment when Black lives, Black actions, and Black ideas mattered.

Yet the possibilities and achievements of this era are too often overshadowed by the violent white supremacist backlash. Too often the story of this grand experiment in interracial democracy is skipped or rushed through in classrooms across the country. This reflects the textbook treatment of the era. For example, in the chapter on Reconstruction in *History Alive! The United States*, the only time the textbook explicitly discusses the monumental accomplishments of Black Americans is in one paragraph titled "African Americans in Office." Yet there are two paragraphs devoted to "White Terrorism" and *five pages* — nearly half the entire chapter — discussing Reconstruction's demise. Although it is crucial to teach the counter-revolution that led to the establishment of Jim Crow, it's also important that teachers don't make the backlash the only story — once again putting whites at the center of U.S. history. To ignore or minimize the successes of Reconstruction reinforces the narrative of slow American racial progress — a historical myth in which our country gradually evolved from slavery to Jim Crow to a post-racial society. This is a fable that ignores the actions of millions of people who fought to end systems of white supremacy and prevent new ones from taking hold.

The story of Reconstruction, told in nearly every major American history textbook, highlights the ideas and actions of those at the top — the debates between the president and Congress. For example, the popular textbook *The American Journey* spends about 15 of the 21 pages it devotes to Reconstruction explaining the actions of Congress and the president. The book dedicates most of the remaining pages to white resistance to Reconstruction in the South. The message communicated through textbooks like *The American Journey* is clear: It's the actions of those at the top that matter most. Yet, as Howard Zinn, author of *A People's History of the United States*, wrote:

> An education that focuses on elites, ignores an important part of the historical record. . . . As a result of omitting, or downplaying, the importance of social movements of the people in our history . . . a fundamental principle of democracy is undermined: the principle that it is the citizenry, rather than the government, that is the ultimate source of power and the locomotive that pulls the train of government in the direction of equality and justice.

The Reconstruction era is precisely one where the government was pulled "in the direction of equality and justice" by the actions of citizens — many of whom had only recently won that designation. This is why in January 2017 the Zinn Education Project published our Reconstruction-era lesson "Reconstructing the South" (see p. 99). Together, students discuss who should have owned the plantation land — and what that land would be used for; the fate of Confederate leaders; voting rights; self-defense; and conditions placed on the former Confederate states prior to being allowed to return to the Union. By having students confront the questions that shaped the Reconstruction era from the perspective of freedmen and women, they achieve some understanding of the sense of power and historical possibility of the era.

Today — in a moment where activists are struggling to make Black lives matter — every student should probe the relevance of Reconstruction. If anything, the Reconstruction period teaches us that when it comes to justice and equality, what may seem impossible is indeed possible — but depends on us, not simply the president or Congress. That's why, to mark the 150th anniversary of the 14th Amendment, the Zinn Education Project launched our "Teach Reconstruction" campaign. It's time to make Reconstruction an essential part of the U.S. history curriculum. ∎

Adam Sanchez (asanchez@zinnedproject.org) is an editor of Rethinking Schools *magazine. Sanchez teaches at Harvest Collegiate High School in New York City and works as curriculum writer and organizer with the Zinn Education Project. This article first appeared in* The Nation.

Reconstructing the South
A role play

By Bill Bigelow

What kind of country is this going to be? This was the urgent question posed in the period immediately following the U.S. Civil War. When students learn about Reconstruction, if they learn about this period at all, too often they learn how the presidents and Congress battled over the answer to this question. Textbooks and curricula emphasize what was done to or for newly freed people, but usually not how they acted to define their own freedom. This role play asks students to imagine themselves as people who were formerly enslaved and to wrestle with a number of issues about what they needed to ensure genuine "freedom": ownership of land — and what the land would be used for; the fate of Confederate leaders; voting rights; self-defense; and conditions placed on the former Confederate states prior to being allowed to return to the Union. The role play's premise is that the end of the war presented people in our country with a key turning point, that there existed at this moment an opportunity to create a society with much greater equality and justice.

The students' role begins: "And now the war is over. This is a joyous time. The horrors of slavery have ended. In millions of gestures, large and small, Black people in America resisted slavery from its very beginning in 1619. You won your freedom and the 13th Amendment to the Constitution ended slavery once and for all. All through the summer of 1865 there have been parades and celebrations. It's a time of unbelievable excitement, but also apprehension. What exactly does freedom mean? What kind of lives will you have now?"

Knowing how deeply segregated and unequal our country is today can make it seem that this was our destiny. As Howard Zinn often said, when we look only at what happened, it can make history seem inevitable. But history is full of choice points; there are always alternatives. Looking carefully at Reconstruction can alert students to some of the most significant could-have-beens in our country's history.

Materials Needed
- Copies of "Freedmen and Women" role for every student (see p. 103).
- Copies of "Reconstructing the South: Problems" for every student (see p. 104).
- For digital copies of these materials, go to teachingforblacklives.org.

Suggested Procedure
1. Of course, the more background on slavery and the Civil War students have, the better. Ask students, "Now that the Civil War is over and the Confederate leaders have sur-

rendered, and the 13th Amendment has ended slavery, what do you think will happen to the people who had until just recently been enslaved?" Pause for students to think about and respond to this question, but don't turn this into a full discussion, as it's meant simply to get them thinking about the issues they will explore in more depth in the role play.

2. Distribute the "Freedmen and Women" role to every student in the class. Read it aloud with the class, pausing to make sure everyone understands the circumstances in which people find themselves. Depending on how much writing on slavery students have already done, one way to help students enter their role is by asking them to create a persona as a formerly enslaved individual and to write an interior monologue from this person's perspective. (See "Promoting Social Imagination Through Interior Monologues" at the Zinn Education Project for examples of how to help students write interior monologues.) If you choose to do this, brainstorm possible interior monologue perspectives with students and list these for students to see. Allow students to write for 10 minutes or so. The aim is not to complete a finished piece, but to get them to quickly enter another persona and to imagine this individual's hopes and concerns. Once students have finished writing — and it's fine if they stop mid-thought — ask students to pair up and to read their monologues to one another. Afterward, ask for volunteers to share a few interior monologues aloud with the rest of the class. Ask students to comment on what they appreciate about these pieces, and about which themes emerge from students' writing.

3. Distribute a copy of "Reconstructing the South: Problems" to all students (see p. 104). Over the years, I have handled this in a number of different ways. If students are accustomed to doing homework, you can give these questions to students in advance of the class period in which they will be discussed, and ask students to read and decide what they think is best, keeping in mind that they are attempting to consider these as people who were recently enslaved. Another option is to put students into small groups and have them attempt to reach agreement on each of the questions, and then to meet as a large group to talk through these problems. This has the advantage of students having thought about and discussed these prior to the large-group meeting. The small-group work makes it more likely that once the large group convenes, every student will have something to say. The disadvantage is that it makes this a longer activity, and may feel repetitive, as each question gets discussed twice, once in the small group and once in the large group. I've also simply given these questions to the full class to discuss and decide. Instructions from here on out presume this last option.

4. The structure of this role play is simple. All students are in the same role — attempting to represent people who have been recently freed from slavery. The premise of the role play is described in the student handout: "You are part of a delegation of African Americans who, up until recently, were enslaved. You are traveling to Washington, D.C., to demand legislation that will make sure that freedmen and women become truly free and are able to advance socially, politically, educationally, and economically. Before you leave, there are a number of key questions that you must agree upon. These are difficult questions, and your answers to them could determine whether your future is one of progress or misery."

Tell students that you will not be leading them in this activity — that, just as in the real historical moment, it was the people themselves, newly freed from slavery, who had to confront these difficult choices. Students will need not only to figure out what they think are the best answers to the questions posed in the handout, but they will also need to decide how they will discuss and resolve these. Review with students some of the ways that they might handle their conversations about these issues. They might choose one student to chair the entire proceedings. They might choose one student per question to chair the discussion. They might decide to have a system where one student raises a hand to speak and then calls on the next student who calls on the next student. Through the years, this last choice has been the one that has seemed to work best with a whole-group role play like this, but I still remember one class several years ago that selected a trusted student to call on people and lead the deliberations, and this student was magnificent. The important thing is that students feel that the process belongs to them. At the outset, I emphasize that they should discuss and decide on a process for decision-making prior to beginning their conversations. On occasion, these can become chaotic when students have not agreed on the process. Also, remind them to speak in the "I" or "we" voice, as people formerly held in slavery.

As students deliberate, my job is to take notes on their conversations. I will be able to review these to plan teaching from this point forward but also I use these to read excerpts aloud to students so that they can appreciate themselves as intellectuals, struggling with big ideas. The first question focuses on the ownership of land. It's key, of course. Here's a sampling from one year's 2nd-period class at Franklin High School in Portland, Oregon:

> Julia: We did all the work. We worked so everyone else could live.
>
> Miguel: We need a new beginning. Somehow we need to grow as people. I think that we should own all the plantations. Well, not all. But it would bring a new wave of power to us.
>
> Christy: We should be given the plantations. What would whites do with them? Where else would we live if we didn't have the plantations?
>
> Andrew: I don't think we should get the land. They've owned the land a long time. If there are 50 of us on a plantation, which one gets it? We should work for wages.
>
> Lakeesha: It's their land. They owned it. During the time they held us as slaves, it was legal. They didn't do anything illegal.
>
> Nicole: They paid for them in money, but we paid for them in work. We took care of them. We bought that land with our labor. It ought to be ours.
>
> Marci: I think we should think about what we would do if the roles were reversed. Think about what happened to the Indians, getting kicked off their land. Do we want to do that to the plantation owners? We have to think about this from their point of view.

Ultimately, in an 18 to 11 vote, this class decided not to demand ownership of the plantations. It's not the decision that I would have argued for had I been a participant in their deliberations, but that's not the point. No matter what decisions students reach, their discussions — and these are sometimes heated — lend themselves to rich follow-up, exploring fundamental questions about legality, ownership, justice, and race.

And students' comments allow me to see where there are misunderstandings, as in Marci's false equivalence of taking land from Native Americans and from plantation owners. (*Freedom's Unfinished Revolution* includes an excellent chapter exploring land ownership following the Civil War, "The Promised Land"; this is included at the Zinn Education Project.)

5. Depending on how students' conversation goes for the six questions, you might simply let them continue these until they have finished. Another alternative is to pause after each question to discuss students' arguments and to draw them back to their charge to demand policies that will advance them "socially, politically, educationally, and economically."

6. Following their deliberations, I ask students to choose at least three of the issues they discussed and to write about what they think happened in real life and why. I also ask students to reflect on the process of making decisions together: What difficulties did you have making decisions that freedmen and women might also have had? When were you successful in overcoming these difficulties? Carmen concluded her response paper: "These questions were hard to answer according to our role. You felt like you had to be realistic and honest about what could happen, but at the same time you wanted to think big, and stand up for your full rights. I'll be interested to find out what really happened. . . . [The role play] gave us a better understanding for other people and a sense of empathy."

And that's where we want to leave students with this activity: eager to learn about "what really happened," how the actual human beings resolved these questions. I return to my notes on students' conversations about the six questions to plan my follow-up discussion on the role play. There are always gems deserving to be explored further, like Miguel's comment while discussing the fifth question that asks, "How will the Black freedmen and women be protected from the revenge of the defeated soldiers and from the plantation owners?" Miguel said: "We need to fight the system of our country. If we can't change that then there is no way to protect ourselves — we have to completely change the South."

Through engaging students in some of the essential questions that confronted people freed from slavery, students can begin to grasp how these questions are interrelated. It gives them a framework to evaluate different proposals for how the South would be "reconstructed" after the war. And as the "opening act" in students' study of Reconstruction, it establishes that the interests of freedmen and women should be seen as paramount. ∎

Bill Bigelow is curriculum editor of Rethinking Schools *and co-director of the Zinn Education Project. He co-edited* A People's Curriculum for the Earth: Teaching Climate Change and the Environmental Crisis. *This lesson was first published at the Zinn Education Project.*

RESOURCES

For digital copies of the teaching materials that accompany this article, go to teachingforblacklives.org

Freedmen and Women

1865/1866: And now the war is over. This is a joyous time. The horrors of slavery have ended. In millions of gestures, large and small, Black people in America resisted slavery from its very beginning in 1619. You won your freedom and the 13th Amendment to the Constitution ended slavery once and for all. All through the summer of 1865 there have been parades and celebrations. It's a time of unbelievable excitement, but also apprehension. What exactly does freedom mean? What kind of lives will you have now? True, you are free to leave the plantation. You are free to go North. Free to travel. Free to seek out lost family members who had been sold off. But you're also free to starve, free to be attacked by angry whites seeking revenge, free to be kicked out of your homes by defeated plantation owners.

Consider all the problems you face: Even though you have lived your entire lives in the South working to make white people rich, you yourselves own nothing. The shack you live in is owned by your former owner. Same with all the tools, work animals, and seed. Even the clothes you have on are owned by your ex-master. Most important, you own no land. For the last 250 years, enslaved Black people were robbed of their labor and their knowledge in order to make white people rich and now in "freedom" you own absolutely nothing. Without land you will always be dependent, always forced to serve the property owners. You want to farm your own land, and grow food for your family.

And there are other problems: At least 90 percent of you are illiterate. Under slavery it was a crime to teach enslaved people to read or write. Some learned anyway, but most had no opportunity. Most of you own no guns. Almost all firearms are owned by your former masters and the whites who fought for the Confederacy. (Remember, however, that the Union Army still occupies much of the South, and some Union soldiers used to be held in slavery, like you.) Also you have no political rights: You can't vote or hold office.

Long ago, your people were kidnapped in Africa, stuffed into the bellies of stinking slave ships, stripped of your language, dumped in a strange land, punished for practicing your religion, frequently separated from your family members, and forced to labor with a whip at your back. The wealth of this country, both South and North, is because of *your* labor, *your* skills, *your* knowledge. You've suffered too much — and whites have profited too much — for you to be forced to wander the countryside as beggars. This is not your idea of freedom.

Reconstructing the South
Problems

You are part of a delegation of African Americans who, up until recently, were enslaved. You are traveling to Washington, D.C., to demand legislation that will make sure that freedmen and women become truly free and are able to advance socially, politically, educationally, and economically. Before you leave, there are a number of key questions that you must agree upon. These are difficult questions, and your answers to them could determine whether your future is one of progress or misery.

1. SITUATION: Right now, almost no formerly enslaved people in the South own any land. Legally, most of you don't even own the clothes you are wearing. All your lives you have lived and worked on plantations owned by wealthy whites. Some people argue that the legitimate owners of the Southern plantations are you, the freed slaves. They say that for almost 250 years, your people are the ones who did all the work and made the plantations profitable — and that because of your sacrifices, rightfully the plantations should belong to you. And, remember, these white plantation owners are traitors. They began a war that killed more than 600,000 people. Why should they get to keep the land that you worked on all those years? Others say that this might be the moral thing to demand, but it would be politically unwise. Ultimately, it will be Northern politicians who will be deciding your fate. Remember, like Abraham Lincoln, most of these people were never abolitionists. And now that you are free, they will be reluctant to take away the property of other white people to give it to Black people. For one thing, they may worry that this would set an example for poor whites in the North to take over the property of rich whites. They, too, could say that the factories were built with their labor and they should own them. Northern politicians may also worry that if you owned the land, you might want to grow food instead of cotton, and this could have a negative impact on the Northern economy.

QUESTION: Now that the war is ended, who should own and control these plantations?

2. QUESTION: Would you be willing to promise the Northern politicians that if they gave you land, that you would continue to grow cotton?

ARGUMENTS: Some of you argue that, of course, you have to give politicians this assurance, otherwise you'll get nothing from them. They argue: Look, we may not want to grow cotton, and we may not want to make promises to anyone, but we have to be realistic; these people care about Northern industries maintaining their supply of cheap cotton more than they care about your desires. It's better to get something than to get nothing. Others of you argue that to offer this promise is just to trade in one kind of slavery for another. What kind of freedom is it when you are forced to grow a crop you don't

Freed slaves on the way to New Bern, North Carolina. *Harper's Weekly*, Feb. 21, 1863.

want to grow? Cotton is a "sorrow" crop, associated with slavery. You can't eat cotton and growing it makes you dependent on cotton dealers — all white — to market your product. And it makes you vulnerable to prices of cotton going up and down, something you have no control over. If it's your land, you should be able to grow what you want.

3. SITUATION: There are still lots of Confederate (Southern) military officers and political leaders at large in the South. True, the war is over. But these are the people who actively led the slave owners' fight to keep slavery.

QUESTION: What do you propose should happen to these Confederate leaders?

ARGUMENTS: Some of you argue that the top leaders should be executed or at least imprisoned for the rest of their lives. They argue that these ex-Confederate leaders are guilty of mass murder because they led an illegal war — a war that killed more than 600,000 human beings and caused great suffering. These people also argue that not only do Confederate leaders deserve to be executed because of their role in the war, but more importantly they also pose the greatest danger to your freedom. These are the people who will be desperate to return to slavery days and they have the money and leadership capabilities to organize secret armies to push you back into slavery. Others argue that if you appear to want revenge, and go after the most popular white leaders in the South that it will poison relations between Blacks and whites, and damage the long-term possibility for racial harmony. They argue that the best way to get white Southerners to rise up against you is to kill or imprison their leaders. They say that we need to put the war behind us, and that so long as you have rights and resources, you don't need to hurt anyone else.

4. SITUATION: Before the war, enslaved Blacks counted as ⅗ of a person in determining how many U.S. representatives a state was entitled to — even though, of course, Blacks held in slavery had no vote. Now that slavery has ended, Blacks will be counted as full people whether or not they are allowed to vote. Ironically, if formerly enslaved people don't vote, this could mean that the white-controlled South could become even more powerful.

QUESTION: Who should be allowed to vote in the new South? Everyone? Only former slaves? Only those who were loyal to the United States during the war? Women?

ARGUMENTS: This is a controversial and complicated issue: Some people say only those with land should vote, because they are the ones who have the most stake in society and they are the most stable people. Some argue that only people who can read should be able to vote, because otherwise people will not vote intelligently. Others say this sounds good, but if landownership or literacy were qualifications for voters, then people who would be able to vote would be mostly rich white people with educations. Some argue that any Southerner who picked up arms against the U.S. government should not be allowed to vote — that these people proved that they were disloyal to the United States and should not now be rewarded with the vote. Besides, anyone who supported the Confederacy and slavery will now use their vote to work against your freedom. Others believe that if you try to deny the vote to all those who supported the Confederacy that would mean taking it away from most white Southerners, and this would make it seem like you were trying to impose a Black government on the South. Denied the vote, whites might turn to rebellion or terrorism and begin murdering Blacks. As you know, many of those who made up the abolition movement in the North were white women. They argue that now is the time to demand a constitutional amendment that would give everyone the vote: white men, white women, Black men, Black women. Freedom and democracy is in the air, and this is the time to create a whole new society based on equality. Others say that if you demand the right for women to vote, this will make you look radical and foolish and no one will take you seriously. It will be seen as radical enough just demanding the vote for Black men, but to add women to the mix will doom your movement.

5. SITUATION: Most of the guns in the South are owned by whites. Many people who fought with the Confederacy still have their weapons from the war. Temporarily, the South is occupied by the Union Army. Many white Southerners, probably most of them, would like nothing better than to return Blacks to slavery. There has been talk of a new organization, called the Ku Klux Klan, designed to terrorize Blacks and their white supporters, and to return the South to slavery.

QUESTION: How will the Black freedmen and women be protected from the revenge of the defeated soldiers and from the plantation owners?

ARGUMENTS: One proposal would be to keep the Union Army in the South, and perhaps to even bring in more troops. Some people argue that the Confederate Army might not have been able to defeat the Union Army, but it would be able to defeat the newly freed Black people. Therefore the Union Army will be needed for years. Others argue that the presence of Union soldiers will continue to anger white Southerners and some other solution must be found. Some argue that no Confederates should be allowed to own guns. Others counter that this would not be a solution and would continue to anger white Southerners. Some suggest that the Union Army should arm Blacks, so that they can defend themselves from possible attacks from whites. Others say that more guns in the South will just lead to more violence.

6. QUESTION: What conditions should be put on the Southern states before they are allowed to return to the Union?

ARGUMENTS: Some Northerners say that the Southern states never actually left the Union, so these states should be allowed back into the United States immediately. After all, didn't Lincoln wage the war based on the belief that secession was illegal? Others say this is ridiculous, the Southern states would just re-elect the rich racists who led the country to Civil War — the Southern states left the Union and organized a separate country, with a new constitution and president. The 13th Amendment to the U.S. Constitution ended slavery forever. However, if the South is allowed to re-enter the Union without any changes, what would stop them from passing laws that would bring back slavery under a different name? Here are some possibilities you might consider: Southern states can rejoin the Union after they ratify (approve) the 13th Amendment abolishing slavery. Others say this isn't enough, that the Southern states need to create new state governments that are democratically elected by the people, including now-freed Black people. Others say that this is not the business of the federal (U.S.) government, that it's up to each state to decide who gets to vote or not. Some Northerners say that the South should be ruled as conquered territory for several more years. It's too early to even raise the question of allowing the former Confederate states back into the Union. What do you think?

Medical Apartheid
Teaching the Tuskegee Syphilis Study

By Gretchen Kraig-Turner

When I think of Black Lives Matter, what comes to mind first is police brutality and the resulting lost lives of young men and women in recent times. But as a science teacher, I know that racism in the United States also has roots that extend deep into the history of medical research. Medical apartheid, the systematic oppression and exclusion of African Americans in our healthcare systems, has existed since the time of slavery and continues today in medical offices and research universities. What care people receive, what diseases are studied, and who is included in research groups are still delineated by race.

The term medical apartheid is explained in Harriet Washington's 2007 work, *Medical Apartheid: The Dark History of Medical Experimentation on Black Americans from Colonial Times to the Present*. Washington documents how "diverse forms of racial discrimination have shaped both the relationship between white physicians and Black patients and the attitude of the latter towards modern medicine in general."

Medical apartheid is a reality that many of my students and their families face. I teach in the only predominantly African American high school in Oregon. My students report being talked down to by doctors as a common experience, as is leaving the doctor's office without receiving adequate care. One of my students told us that her uncle's treatment for a heart condition was so substandard, her family sued the hospital for discrimination. Critically examining the history of medical research is a way to bring the experiences of my students and their families into the classroom, and a way to connect our study of bioethics to the often hidden history of African American men and women who fought for their dignity and rights against a medical system that treated them like lab rats.

So I begin my Research and Medicine course, a senior-level course in our Health Sciences and Biotechnology Program, with an exploration of bioethics, a theme that continues throughout all of the units. We focus on the Tuskegee Syphilis Study (TSS), a chapter of scientific and medical history rarely discussed in high school. Particularly as a white educator, I am conscious that leading the school year with a unit on a deeply painful example of Black oppression needs to be done with care. This is the capstone course of the program, and I already know the students when the class starts. Without a level of trust and mutual respect already established, this unit would not be as successful. If I did not know my students well, I would wait until later in the year, after a safe space had been created. Another reason to wait is that the TSS leads to discussions about cell types (particularly types of bacteria) and epidemiology, which are typically covered later in the year.

Day one of the unit starts with me asking a simple question: "In what ways are you in control of your health and in what ways are you not in control?" I list a couple examples:

"I'm in control of how often I exercise but I'm not in control of air pollution in my neighborhood." The students do a think-pair-share with the question, scribbling down answers and then sharing with their lab bench partner.

As we start to answer the question as a whole class, I write their answers on the whiteboard under the headers "In Control" and "Not in Control." Pretty quickly, someone disagrees about the appropriate header.

"One way I'm in control of my health is what food I eat," Robert says. I write "foods" under In Control.

Charene asks, "What if good food isn't available?"

Kia yells out, "Our school lunch is terrible but it's free. Is that a choice? I don't eat that junk!"

After more examples are generated, I ask: "Who does have a choice about what food they eat? Why do some people have different levels of access to doctors? How come some neighborhoods have better air quality? Why can't some people go running safely at night?"

Soon nothing in the In Control column is safe from my kids' scrutiny. We talk about each item through a social justice lens. For example, going to the doctor regularly is tied to insurance — which is tied to job and education level — and access to transportation. Exercising is linked to living in a safe neighborhood, childcare, money for gyms, air quality, and concern about what police see when a middle-aged white woman is running vs. a Black or Brown youth. The class inevitably concludes that health and healthcare are a complex mix of choice and circumstance, and that those with more social and economic power have a different level of choice.

Sade sums it up: "None of this is a choice for poor people, just for people who can buy whatever they choose, and who has that kind of money isn't always fair."

The Tuskegee Mixer

My students' insights on these intersections in our healthcare system lead into a mixer on the TSS. The TSS exemplifies how race, class, and healthcare have intersected in this country, all themes the students raised during our warm-up.

The "Tuskegee Study of Untreated Syphilis in the Negro Male" (now formally known as the "U.S. Public Health Service Syphilis Study at Tuskegee"), which began in 1932 in rural Alabama, spanned most of the 20th century. African American men with syphilis (the sexually transmitted disease or a different strain of the bacteria known as yaws) were observed, yet received no treatment. They were denied standard treatment — heavy metal treatments at first, and later penicillin — and forbidden to seek medical treatment elsewhere. The architects of the study went as far as barring the men from the World War II draft, where they would have been treated with penicillin. The study continued into the early 1970s, when a whistle-blower, fed up with trying to get the attention of his superiors, took the story to a journalist. After the article appeared, Congress held hearings that suspended the study and led to passage of the National Research Act, which includes a mandated code of ethics for research on human subjects.

"We're going to look at a time in medical history when informed consent didn't exist," I tell the students as I introduce the mixer. I give each student the role of a study subject, a doctor, a public health official, a widow, or a journalist. There are roles that show the damage inflicted, and also roles that show the resistance and whistle-blowing that ultimately exposed and ended the study. For example:

Charles Pollard was a participant who later became an activist:

> I am a Macon County farmer, and I started in the Tuskegee Study in the early 1930s. I recall the day in 1932 when some men came by and told me I would receive a free physical examination if I came by the one-room school near my house. So I went on over and they told me I had bad blood. . . . And that's what they've been telling me ever since.
>
> I was at a stockyard in Montgomery, and a newspaper woman started talking to me about the study in Tuskegee. She asked me if I knew Nurse Rivers. That's how I discovered I was one of the men in the study. Once I found out how those doctors at Tuskegee used the African American men of Macon County in their study, I went to see Fred Gray. He was Rosa Parks' and Martin Luther King Jr.'s attorney. He took our case and sued the federal government for using us as guinea pigs without our consent.
>
> Being in this study violated my rights. After I found out about the real purpose of the study, I told reporters, "All I knew was that [the doctors and nurses] just kept saying I had the bad blood — they never mentioned syphilis to me, not even once."

Other roles include Nurse Eunice Rivers and Dr. Eugene Dibble, both African Americans who worked as researchers in the study, supporting the study perhaps as a way to bring both money and prestige to Tuskegee. Roles of the white doctors who designed and orchestrated the study include upsetting quotes. For example, Dr. Thomas Murrell, an advisor to the study's leaders, said:

> So the scourge sweeps among them. Those that are treated are only half cured, and the effort to assimilate into a complex civilization drives their diseased minds until the results are criminal records. Perhaps here, in conjunction with tuberculosis, will be the end of the Negro problem. Disease will accomplish what man cannot.

Once the students read, understand, and are prepared to play the person in their role sheet, I ask everyone to walk around the room, telling people who they are and learning about other participants in the drama.

Their initial curiosity quickly changes to disbelief for some and hardening anger for others. They fill out a question sheet as they meet the other characters, and then spend a few minutes reflecting on questions raised by the mixer, and what surprised, angered, or left them hopeful.

"Why did they do this? What did they learn?"

"Why didn't they give the men penicillin?"

"How long did this last?"

Students start to make the connections between the study and the pre-World War II eugenics movement they studied previously. As David points out, "This is a lot like what the Nazi doctors did in Auschwitz."

Whistle-Blowers

Then we transition into reading the article that brought national attention to the study. In 1966, Peter Buxtun, a U.S. Public Health Service (PHS) venereal disease investigator, tried to alert his superiors about the immorality and lack of scientific ethics of the study, but they would not listen. In 1968, William Carter Jenkins, an African American statistician at PHS, called for an end to the study in a small anti-racist newsletter he founded. Nothing changed. Finally, Buxtun went to the mainstream press, and Associated Press journalist Jean Heller broke the story in the *Washington Evening Star*. She begins:

> Washington, July 25 [1972] — For 40 years the United States Public Health Service has conducted a study in which human beings with syphilis, who were induced to serve as guinea pigs, have gone without medical treatment for the disease and a few have died of its late effects, even though an effective therapy was eventually discovered.
>
> Officials of the health service who initiated the experiment have long since retired. Current officials, who say they have serious doubts about the morality of the study, also say that it is too late to treat the syphilis in any surviving participants.

The students also read the Centers for Disease Control and Prevention's description of syphilis, including the progression of the disease and recommended treatment, and a summary I created of other relevant information.

Then I assign some writing: Using these resources and what you learned from meeting everyone in the mixer, write a first-person testimony that could have been used at the congressional hearings that followed Heller's story. You can be the same person you portrayed in the mixer, or someone else. Explain why you think the study happened, your understanding of the disease itself, and if reparations are appropriate or not. Explain your reasons.

These are quick-writes, not final pieces, but aimed at getting students to understand the human lives behind the medical facts. Lejay writes from the perspective of a widow of one of the men in the study:

I am Ruth Fields and I became a widow during the Tuskegee Syphilis Study. My husband passed away from the effects of syphilis. . . . In the early 1920s, syphilis was a major health issue and concern. In 1932, a study was conducted of 399 men with syphilis and 201 without. The men were given occasional assessments, and were told they were being treated. In 1936, local physicians were asked to help with the study, but not treat the men, and to follow the men until death. Penicillin became a treatment option for syphilis but the men in the study couldn't receive it. . . .

I endured so much hurt, pain, and loss because of this study, and I just want everyone who was involved to be punished for their actions, because they hurt and killed and destroyed so many lives.

Shirene writes from the point of view of one of the men in the study:

I am Roy Douglas. Poor, uneducated African American men like myself experienced an outbreak of syphilis. We were sent to hospitals for having "bad blood." Doctors didn't know how the STD worked, the side effects, or the symptoms. To get the information that they needed, they used us as test dummies. More than 400 of us were denied help, medicine, and the proper treatment for years. Some men suffered from mild symptoms like rashes, then spots appeared on the surface of their skin. With time, their nerves, brains, and more shut down. . . . In 1945, penicillin was finally accepted as a treatment for syphilis.

After more than 30 years of researching, the study finally ended in 1972. I personally feel like the study was a small version of a genocide. . . . It was unnecessary and wrong to use poor, Black men as guinea pigs for experiments. Out of the whole dehumanizing study, the only positive outcome was the cure. There should have been more rules or procedures set up to maintain the health of the sick men. No one deserves to die when there is some type of medicine to cure them. I believe who every person that lent a hand in the study should have gone to prison.

Where Do We Go from Here?

There is so much of the TSS that is hard to swallow. The sheer length — more than 40 years — is astounding for any longitudinal study, let alone one that watched men die from a brutal infection that attacks the nervous system. The fact that researchers went to great lengths to keep the men from finding out that there was a simple cure shows the purpose was not to find treatment. That the study continued throughout and after the Civil Rights Movement is perplexing and contrary to a narrative of racial equity so often spun in history books. But my students' anger is often more personal.

The students are not paranoid. The United States has a history of funding unethical studies on vulnerable populations. We read articles about similar cases in which U.S. doctors and scientists took advantage of vulnerable populations — from sterilizing female prisoners in California to infecting prisoners in Guatemala with syphilis.

It's at this point that I ask students to write up their own code for bioethical human research: If you were in charge of how and what research could be conducted, what limitations would you place? How would you define informed consent? How would you guarantee informed consent? Is anyone off limits? If not, how do you guarantee that they are not being taken advantage of by unscrupulous researchers?

After writing their own codes, I distribute copies of the Nuremberg Code and the Belmont Report. The students then write a reflection on how their codes differ and what might be missing from each of the lists: How is your code similar to the Nuremberg Code and the Belmont Report? How is it different? What did you mention that should be added to those codes?

With their bioethical codes hung in the hallway leading to my classroom and armed with the knowledge that science isn't always ethical, I give students their first major assignment of the year: a research paper on a bioethics topic of their choice.

Before we began this course with a study of the TSS, I read papers about artificially extending life or genetically modified creatures that sounded more like science fiction than real issues affecting my students and their families. But now that we begin with an exploration of bioethics rooted in the history of the TSS, the papers have become more interesting and personal. I still give the students a list of bioethics topics from the CDC website, but through conversations in class and students opening up about their own experiences, the topics have increased in relevance and student engagement. Now students write about why mortality rates of cancers are different for people of different races. They explore how U.S. scientists have engineered studies taking place in Latin America. One young woman wrote a history of gynecology in the United States, from unanesthetized surgeries of women who were enslaved through much more recent forced sterilizations of women of color. Another student wrote about medical experiments by Japanese doctors in Chinese prisoner of war camps during World War II. They now write about subjects that tomorrow's doctors and researchers need to understand in order to combat the idea that the health and healthcare of some do not matter as much as that of others. ∎

Gretchen Kraig-Turner teaches at Burlington-Edison High School in Burlington, Washington, and formerly taught at Jefferson High School in Portland, Oregon.

RESOURCES

Materials for the Tuskegee Syphilis Study mixer are available at teachingforblacklives.org

Centers for Disease Control and Prevention. 2016. *Sexually Transmitted Diseases (STDs): Syphilis.cdc.gov/std/syphilis*

Centers for Disease Control and Prevention. 2016. *U.S. Public Health Service Syphilis Study at Tuskegee: The Tuskegee Timeline.* cdc.gov/tuskegee/timeline.htm

Tuskegee University. 2016. *About the USPHS Syphilis Study.* tuskegee.edu/about_us/centers_of_excellence/bioethics_center/about_the_usphs_syphilis_study.aspx

Washington, Harriet. 2006. *Medical Apartheid: The Dark History of Medical Experimentation on Black Americans from Colonial Times to the Present.* First Anchor Books.

KEITH HENRY BROWN

Beyond Just a Cells Unit

What my science students learned from the story of Henrietta Lacks

By Gretchen Kraig-Turner

Every year when I distribute *The Immortal Life of Henrietta Lacks* by Rebecca Skloot to my biotechnology class, I am greeted with "Turner, this isn't English class!" And every year I tell my students, "I promise you: This book is going to change the way you think about science. Give it a chance."

I make this promise to my students because I know the beginning of the story will pique their interest. Skloot brilliantly describes the beginnings of both Henrietta Lacks, the woman, and HeLa, the first immortal cell line, in a way that gains the interest of a wide swath of students. Henrietta's daughter, Deborah, is quoted on the first page: "When I go to the doctor for checkups I always say my mother was HeLa. They get all excited, tell me stuff like how her cells helped make my blood pressure medicines and anti-depression pills . . . but they don't never explain more than just sayin, Yeah, your mother was on the moon, she been in nuclear bombs, and made that polio vaccine. . . . But I always thought it was strange, if our mother's cells done so much for medicine, how come her family can't afford to see no doctors? I used to get so mad. . . . But I don't got it in me no more to fight. I just want to know who my mother was."

Students who take my class out of a pure interest in science get what they came for in the descriptions of lab science and discoveries about cells and cancer. And students who take my class because a family member or teacher said they should be in the biotech program get drawn in by family stories, the tales of Henrietta being shuffled around amongst family members and her children growing up without a mother — all with the ease of reading a well-told, captivating story. And students who have not seen themselves in science history hear the voices and stories of Black women front and center — sometimes for the first time — from the very beginning of this book.

When students come back the second day after getting the book, they are excited, saying: "OK, this book is alright" and "I didn't think I'd like it this much" and "She's Black?" and "Wait, her cells are still alive?"

Rebecca Skloot was a high school student at an alternative school in Portland, Oregon, when she first heard a story about a Black woman whose cells have immeasurably changed our understanding of the very basics of biology. Skloot was taking a community college course when an instructor mentioned Henrietta Lacks during a lecture on cell division. He told the class that Henrietta's cells had led to great discoveries, that her cells continued to live decades after her death in labs around the world, that her cells were the first to do this, to be immortal, and he told the class she was Black. At that point, this was about all that the scientific community really knew of Henrietta Lacks, the woman whose cancer cells, which grow and divide very quickly and remain a laboratory staple today, would be used to add volumes to our understanding of cells, genetics, and a host of other fundamental areas of science. Skloot remained curious about Ms. Lacks as a person, and went on to write a book that told the story of Henrietta, her family, and how the cells came into the hands of doctors, scientists, and Johns Hopkins Hospital in 1951.

Skloot's book on Henrietta Lacks is a fascinating account of her previously hidden story. The writing expertly weaves the journey of the Lacks family's tireless work to uncover the story of Henrietta's cells with both scientific and African American history. The basic narrative is that Henrietta Lacks, a Black woman from Baltimore, sought care for cervical cancer in a segregated hospital, and in the process of doing so, white doctors and scientists took her cancer cells with dubious consent, believing that the patients of the "colored ward" were essentially trading being research subjects for healthcare. The impacts of this incident specifically, and inequalities in healthcare more generally, affected Henrietta's children and grandchildren immensely. The importance of her cells to the scientific community cannot be overstated, and yet the Lacks family never saw any of the money generated from the innumerable discoveries from the cells. Henrietta's descendants struggled with poverty, including battles with getting proper healthcare, and were left in the dark — the consent forms then were rudimentary at best — about what doctors and scientists both took and found. One can infer that had Henrietta been white with more resources, either her cells would never have been taken in the first place or her family would have received recognition for their mother's profound contribution to science.

> **"I promise you: This book is going to change the way you think about science. Give it a chance."**

The book combines the science behind why her cells are so important with personal narrative in a unique way. As a science teacher in the only majority African American high school in Oregon, I thought my students would find the story an engaging way to learn about cells (particularly cell growth and cancer), how research protocols have evolved over the last 100 years, and about the intersections of institutionalized racism and biomedical history. We typically spend about six weeks on the book, and the richness of the story, both in science content and my students' ability to relate to the Lacks family, make this relatively long unit worthwhile.

Reading the Book to Teach the Book

Before reading *The Immortal Life of Henrietta Lacks*, I had never considered using a book that more resembles a novel than an academic science text in my classes. I initially thought we could maybe read a section of the book before doing some more serious work on how cells grow. The story would be a small feature of a cell unit, not cells being a section of a book unit. But, after reading the book, I couldn't pick out just one section or one passage and contain the powerful story to a mere sidenote to a cell unit.

As a science teacher, I had no idea how to teach books — this wasn't ever addressed in our pedagogy courses, nor did I have examples from other science teachers of how to do this. I wanted the process to be familiar to my students, so I worked with English teachers at my school to learn how they taught books. I learned how to do dialogue journals and teach students to take notes with a final paper in mind. When I read the book, I thought about what I would do if I were asked to write a paper on the story, and I picked several themes: Medical Apartheid (a term coined by Harriet Washington to describe racial inequity in healthcare), Informed Consent, Lab Science, and Scientific Discoveries. Then I re-read the book, this time keeping a dialogue journal with quotes on one side and my comments on the other. I divided my notebook into five sections with the themes listed above and a fifth one titled "Family." I created discussion questions for each chapter and found supplemental readings about cell culturing, cancer growth, and rights to one's own tissues and genetic codes (in subsequent years, the amount of supplemental articles on Henrietta exploded and this became easier). I also kept an eye out for when I could do labs alongside the reading to bring to life what the scientists did in the book.

As the unit developed over the years, more research has come out about Henrietta's cells, including bioethical violations such as publishing the genetic code of HeLa (which was a violation of her family's rights to their own genetic codes). Continuing to monitor the *New York Times* science section (where Rebecca Skloot has published updates to the initial narrative, including "The Immortal Life of Henrietta Lacks, the Sequel" in 2013) helps tremendously with making sure the supplemental readings I give my students are current.

Other supplemental materials stemmed from students wanting to know more about the examples of medical apartheid discussed in the book. The Tuskegee Syphilis Study, a long-term study conducted by the U.S. Public Health Service on untreated syphilis in Black men that went on decades after the cure was found, is referenced several times throughout the book, but the most chilling descriptions of how African American people were treated comes in a chapter called "Night Doctors." This chapter outlines much of why African American people have reasons to distrust the medical establishment and includes stories of enslaved people being used for "gruesome research," Black people being kidnapped off the streets to be used in medical studies and as cadavers, and more recent studies looking for genes that could predict criminal behavior by studying Black families. Harriet Washington's book *Medical Apartheid* is an excellent resource for students wishing to learn more, as is the Centers for Disease Control and Prevention's website on the Tuskegee Syphilis Study.

Cell Culture

Cell culturing is central to the beginning of the book. Scientists tried for decades to grow human cells outside of the human body before finding Henrietta's immortal cells. While we obviously can't grow human cells in the classroom, the process of even much more basic cell culturing was new to my students. I designed a lab on yeast culturing, a eukaryotic cell often used in genetics experiments, that we did as we read about the first ventures of human cell culture. The lab was a simple exploration into how to maximize growth and minimize contamination. And the supplies to do such labs are actually relatively inexpensive. I used baker's yeast from the grocery store for my cell source, and ordered basic petri dishes and a yeast-peptone-dextrose (YPD) media. Students made a media with 25g of YPD and 10–15g of agar per liter of distilled water and poured this into the petri dishes, which then sat overnight to solidify. We mixed a small amount of the yeast with table sugar in warm water (just as you'd do when baking bread) and then poured that mixture onto the plates. We grew the yeast at both room temperature (25 C) and in an incubator at 37 C (human body temperature). When growth didn't occur or contamination from bacteria took over the yeast growth, I tell my students, "These issues are the same as what the scientists in the book faced. This is real science." We work to problem-solve the issues and compare growth at different temperatures. We also discuss how contamination occurs and why sterile environments are so important. I ask, "Why do you think contamination can occur if we keep the lid open too long?" or "How come yeast grows best at body temperature instead of room temperature?"

Teaching About Cancer

As we continued to read the book, I found that students needed to know more about cancer and what happens when the mechanisms of the cell cycle go awry. My students had a lot of questions: "Why can't the scientists use any of her cells? Why only the cancer ones?" I answer that "Only the cancer ones have the mutation that causes the cells to divide uncontrollably." Another student, Ny'osha, wanted to know "If Deborah (her daughter) gets cancer, will those cells be immortal too?" "Not necessarily," I responded. "This could depend on if her cancer was purely genetic or due to viruses." And Marti, somewhat indignantly, wanted to know "If her husband hadn't been messing around, would Henrietta have even gotten that cancer?" "Probably not!" I answered. "Let's talk about oncoviruses!"

The first year I taught this unit I did a review on mitosis and then directed my students to the National Institutes of Health's websites on cancer. Each student did a worksheet on mitosis and wrote a generalized summary of how cancer works. Henrietta's cancer was more robust than most cancers, the vast majority of which would not survive outside the human body. The disruptions to the cell cycle that her cancer caused are representative of many cancers and it's important for the students to understand how cancer cells generally differ from healthy cells. For the last few years of teaching this unit, I also use an article titled "UW Researchers Report on Genome of Aggressive Cervical Cancer that Killed Henrietta Lacks" and show a PowerPoint on HPV and cervical cancer by Lydia Breen and Rebecca Veilleux from an MIT/HHMI Summer Teacher Institute.

My students write short responses to questions such as: What was the "perfect storm" that went wrong in Henrietta's cervical cells? What is a haplotype and what unique information does it give scientists? Why was publishing Henrietta's genome problematic for her family? Why must participants give materials (like cells) for research to occur? Explain the relationship between telomeres and cancer cells' immortality.

Bioethical Issues

The cell culturing and cancer portions take up about the first four of the six-week unit. I teach these as short units that cover basic reviews of cell function and division. As well as diving deeper into those subjects, we set aside time to have discussions around the bioethical questions raised in the book. Discussions take place as a whole class and in small reading groups that I establish when we first start the book. The reading groups meet weekly and discuss a set of questions (some of which are from the Random House Teacher's Guide) for each section. I write out the questions and give them to the students before they read the corresponding chapter. In these groups, the students are able to relate the science they learned in class to the Lacks family story. The book details Henrietta's life, from being raised, along with her cousins, by her grandfather after losing her mother at age 4, to having five children with one of these cousins. Her life started on a tobacco farm in rural Virginia and ended in Baltimore.

While Henrietta is most famous for her immortal cells, my students relate to her on a human level. One student, Asianique Savage, opened her final essay with: "A woman with brown skin as smooth as the back of a chocolate bar, thick long hair as strong as rope, who made sure her nails were always done, painted with bright red nail polish, was brought into the world Aug. 1, 1920." This sentence is not what one typically thinks of as "science writing," and yet it captures how my students see Henrietta.

> My students understand this at a personal level: "They would never take the cells from a white woman like that," claims Ty.

Deborah Lacks, Henrietta's youngest daughter, is a central character in the book. Her anger at losing her mother and not fully understanding the science behind why her mom is so famous creates some tension throughout the book. In response to the question "What does Deborah mean when she says, 'I do want to go see them cells, but I'm not ready yet'?" Keisha said that she sees "why Deborah is always so mad and she's stressed all the time. She doesn't have her mom, the doctors disrespect her and her family, and they're poor while all those people make money off of drug patents. She didn't even really know what a cell was, let alone why her mother's were still alive. It's complicated for her."

Through the story of the Lacks family, my students are also able to explore the deeper questions of how race intersects with medical history as a whole. Questions like: "Describe HL's medical history. Why do you think she canceled appointments, stopped treatments, and refused tests?" "How were HL's tissues obtained? Did she consent? Does it matter?" and "Why did the doctors in the '50s use patients from public wards for research?" were designed to get students to think about how Henrietta, as a Black woman, could have been fearful of going to the hospital. Henrietta's distrust in medical institutions is still seen today in Black culture as described by Vann R. Newkirk II in a 2016 article in the *Atlantic* titled "A Generation of Bad Blood":

> Research has long suggested that the ill effects of the Tuskegee Study extend beyond those men and their families to the greater whole of Black culture. Black patients consistently express less trust in their physicians and the medical system than white patients, are more likely to believe medical conspiracies, and are much less likely to have common, positive experiences in healthcare settings. These have all been connected to misgivings among Black patients about Tuskegee and America's long history of real medical exploitation of Black people.

My students understand this at a personal level: "They would never take the cells from a white woman like that," claims Ty. "But look at what was accomplished with them. They shoulda asked her and gotten her permission though," adds Aliyah. Near the end of the book, I ask my students, "Do the scientists owe the Lacks family anything? Does the lack of consent impact your thoughts on reparations to the family?" Many of my students wrestled with this question as part of their final paper.

The Culminating Paper

Once we are about two-thirds through the book, I have the students start to work on their final papers. The students' composition books were divided into the same categories that are choices for their final papers: Medical Apartheid, Informed Consent, Lab Science, Scientific Discoveries, and a fifth category, Family, as this theme is so critical to the story that my students could not write any paper without including the story of the Lacks family. As they read the book they jotted down their notes in these five sections, and for most students, one of the categories eventually emerged as the one they are most interested in. This category was then the students' focus as they finished the book. We use class time for writing the five- to 10-page final paper, and I encourage students to utilize their reading groups — and me — to go through outlines and drafts.

Many students pick one of the first two themes: Informed Consent and Medical Apartheid. This speaks to how my students related and were interested in the parts of the book that spoke directly to racial biases in medical care and research.

The criteria for these themes are prescribed in my directions to the students. Each section has four to five content-based criteria. Many of my students are not used to writing papers that blend both academic and conversational voices, and I have noticed that without content-specific criteria, my students tend to leave the science out of the science papers!

I have found students are much more comfortable deeply explaining the family issues and generalizing the science content. But the papers that are written using the content-based criteria sheets reflect the understanding of the undeniable contributions to science from using Henrietta Lacks' cells with the perspective and acknowledgement that the matriarch of an African American family is at the very center of these scientific advances and discussions.

Here is an excerpt from Desiree' DuBoise's paper:

> The misuse of Henrietta Lacks' cells, as well as the mistreatment of her family, was unethical. A big reason for the lack of information given to the Lacks family about the use of Henrietta's cells was the fact that there was no precedent for how to go about using and profiting from cell research; it hadn't been done before. The fact that the cells came from a poor Black woman only heightened the unlikelihood of doctors and researchers taking time out to meet the needs of the family (Johns Hopkins). The name of the owner of the cells went unknown for decades. The HeLa cells were thought to belong to either Henrietta Lacks, Helen Lane, or Helen Larson (Skloot, 1). Many have wondered why none of Henrietta's family recognized her picture in articles written or knew about the studies using her cells. The Lacks family was poor and Black and living in the South; most of them had no more than a middle school education, so they wouldn't have had access to articles and journals that were talking about the use of Henrietta's cells.

Giving the cells a name and a story validated my students in a way that is not often seen in our science classrooms. Black students are frequently pushed out of classrooms in a multitude of ways; we need to seek ways to bring Black students' voices into every subject, and particularly into STEM classes where Black students are underrepresented. Terri Watson, in an *Education Week* web series on "Black Girls and School Discipline," said, "I think Black girls are seen as either invisible or they're problematized." Henrietta Lacks and the story of her cells exemplifies both. As a Black woman, Henrietta was separated into the "colored ward" of the hospital where her cells were seen as payment for her healthcare, and her cells were identified as hers only after decades of invisibility. Dedicating significant time to learn the story of a Black woman to whom biomedical research owes a great deal was time well spent. What we learned was more than the sum of Henrietta's story and the science content of the book. ∎

> **Black students are frequently pushed out of classrooms in a multitude of ways; we need to seek ways to bring Black students' voices into every subject, and particularly into STEM classes where Black students are underrepresented.**

Gretchen Kraig-Turner teaches at Burlington-Edison High School in Burlington, Washington, and formerly taught at Jefferson High School in Portland, Oregon.

Teaching SNCC

The organization at the heart of the civil rights revolution

By Adam Sanchez

"That's the problem with Black Lives Matter! We need a strong leader like Martin Luther King!" Tyriq shouted as I wrote King's name on the board.

I started my unit on the Civil Rights Movement by asking my high school students to list every person or organization they knew was involved. They replied with several familiar names: Martin Luther King Jr., Rosa Parks, Malcolm X, Emmett Till. Occasionally a student knew an organization: the NAACP or the Black Panther Party.

"Has anyone ever heard of the Student Nonviolent Coordinating Committee?" I asked while writing the acronym on the board.

"S-N-C-C?" students sounded out as my black Expo marker moved across the whiteboard.

"Have you ever heard of the sit-ins?" I prodded.

"Yeah, weren't they in Alabama?" Matt answered.

"No, Mississippi! Four students sat down at a lunch counter, right?" Kadiatou proudly declared.

This is usually the extent of my students' prior knowledge of SNCC, one of the organizations most responsible for pushing the Civil Rights Movement forward. Without the history of SNCC at their disposal, students think of the Civil Rights Movement as one that was dominated by charismatic leaders and not one that involved thousands of young people like themselves. Learning the history of how young students risked their lives to build a multigenerational movement against racism and for political and economic power allows students to draw new conclusions about the lessons of the Civil Rights Movement and how to apply them to today.

You Are Members of SNCC

Pedagogically based on *Rethinking Schools* editor Bill Bigelow's abolitionist role play, and drawing content from the voices of SNCC veterans and the scholarship of Howard Zinn, Clayborne Carson, and other historians, I created a series of role plays where students imagined themselves as SNCC members. In their roles, students debated key questions the organization faced while battling Jim Crow. My hope was that by role-playing the moments in SNCC's history where activists made important decisions, students would gain a deeper understanding of how the movement evolved, what difficulties it

It was common for Southern segregationists to display the Confederate flag and target protesters who carried the U.S. flag. In this context, displaying the U.S. flag was seen as an act of resistance. This photo was taken during the Selma-to-Montgomery March in 1965.

MATT HERRON | TAKE STOCK

faced, and most importantly, an understanding that social movements involve ordinary people taking action, but also discussing and debating a way forward.

I taught the role play in my U.S. history class at Madison High School in Portland, Oregon, and more recently in a course about the Civil Rights Movement at Harvest Collegiate High School in New York City. Both schools serve a diverse mix of Black, Latinx, Asian, and white students — unusual examples of diversity for both public school districts. They also house a large population of students who come from low-income families.

To introduce the role play, I created a handout that situates students in the role of a SNCC member through providing background on what led up to the formation of SNCC. Before reading the handout out loud as a class, I told students they would be writing from the role of a SNCC member and should highlight any information — particularly about historical events — they might want to include. The role begins with historical background:

> In *Brown v. Board of Education of Topeka*, *Boynton v. Virginia*, and several other court cases, the U.S. Supreme Court has ruled Jim Crow segregation unconstitutional. But from movie theaters to swimming pools, parks to restaurants, buses to schools, almost every aspect of public life in the South remains segregated.
>
> In 1955, 50,000 African Americans in Montgomery (Alabama's second-largest city) participated in a boycott to end segregation of the city buses. . . . But after the Montgomery Bus Boycott, the movement struggled to move forward. Segre-

gationists launched a massive campaign of terror that prevented further gains. . . . While the protests of the 1950s gave you a sense of pride and power, it increasingly became clear that larger, more dramatic actions would be necessary to break the back of Jim Crow. You were prepared to act and you were not alone.

The handout continues by discussing the initial sit-ins that spread quickly across the South and led to the formation of SNCC. After reading about the sit-ins and SNCC's founding conference in April of 1960, we quickly moved on to another crucial event that shaped SNCC's early history: the Freedom Rides.

Freedom Rider Letter

To introduce the Freedom Rides, I edited together two clips from the PBS documentary *Freedom Riders*. The first part introduces students to the concept of the Freedom Rides, a series of bus trips organized by the Congress of Racial Equality (CORE) through the South to protest segregation in interstate travel facilities. The clip also takes students through the burning of one Greyhound bus in Anniston, Alabama, and the attack on the Freedom Riders in a second bus by a white mob in Birmingham.

The second part reveals that after the violence in Birmingham, the first round of Freedom Riders decided to fly to New Orleans and head home. It then turns to the Nashville students in SNCC who decided they couldn't let the Freedom Rides end in failure. As SNCC leader Diane Nash explains in the video:

> If we allowed the Freedom Ride to stop at that point, just after so much violence had been inflicted, the message would have been sent that all you have to do to stop a nonviolent campaign is inflict massive violence. It was critical that the Freedom Ride not stop, and that it be continued immediately.

After the clip, I tell students that to get in the role of a SNCC member, they will be writing letters to their parents as if they were planning to join the Freedom Rides. Together we read a short assignment that reiterates some of the basic facts about the Freedom Rides and gives them more information about what to write: "Describe for your parents the experiences that led you to risk your life in order to end segregation in the South. You can choose your gender, your race, your age, your social class, and the region where you grew up. Give yourself a name and a history. Be imaginative. In vivid detail, tell the story of the events that made you who you are now: a Freedom Rider." While in reality, many Freedom Riders chose not to tell their parents, this activity allows students

WISCONSIN HISTORICAL SOCIETY WHS 38509

to think through what makes someone willing to take great risks for a just cause.

Whether giving this assignment as homework or giving students in-class time to work on it, I often get back incredible letters. Marquandre wrote passionately about why he felt the need to join:

> Dear Mom and Dad,
>
> I have made the decision to join the Freedom Riders. I know it's a big risk, but I feel I need to do this. I'm sure you've heard about the bus that was burned in Anniston and the attack on the Freedom Riders in Birmingham. We can't let this violence be the end. We need to show them that their violence can't stop our fight.
>
> Now I know you'll be angry with me for dropping out of school to join the Freedom Rides. I really appreciate all you have done for me, and how hard you worked to get me to college. But seeing you work so hard for so little is why I'm doing this. I remember how you worked 10 or 12 hours a day just to pay the bills and put food on the table for me and my sisters.
>
> I know you wanted a better future for me. But I've heard that nearly all of last year's graduates fell short of their dreams to be doctors, lawyers, journalists, and so on. They say "knowledge is power," but what's the point of an education when I'm still going to end up in a low-wage job because I'm Black? I want Lily and Diana to know that their brother fought for their future. I want my children to grow up in a country where segregation doesn't exist. . . . If not now, when? This is our time.

> **Without the history of SNCC at their disposal, students think of the Civil Rights Movement as one that was dominated by charismatic leaders and not one that involved thousands of young people like themselves.**

After students finished working, I had them read their letters to each other in pairs or small groups. Sometimes I asked the class to form a circle and read each letter aloud one by one. I was never disappointed when I took the time to do this. It helps students gain a deeper connection to their roles and creates a rich aural portrait of a social movement.

Organizing Mississippi

When students finished sharing their letters, we watched the movie *Freedom Song*. *Freedom Song* is an indispensable film that gives a gripping narrative based on SNCC's first voter registration project in McComb, Mississippi. I've found that the film helps give students a deep visual understanding of SNCC's organizing efforts that grounds the role play that follows. While watching *Freedom Song*, I asked students to pay attention to what leadership looks like in SNCC and how SNCC makes decisions. I also point out that in the last scenes of the film, some of the students from the local community where SNCC was organizing join SNCC and move to organize other parts of the state, while others stay behind and maintain the voter registration classes that SNCC began. In other words, as the best organizers do, SNCC organized themselves out of a job — they built a local movement that not only could sustain itself once they left, but could also help spread the movement to other parts of the state.

Next I distributed a handout containing three key questions that SNCC debated during their fight for racial justice in Mississippi:

1. Should SNCC focus its efforts on voter registration or direct action?
2. Should SNCC bring a thousand mostly white volunteers to Mississippi? If so, should SNCC limit the role of white volunteers?
3. Should SNCC workers carry guns? If not, should SNCC allow or seek out local people to defend its organizers with guns?

Each question is accompanied with some historical context that helps students understand why this has become a debated question within SNCC, as well as short arguments for both sides. Here's an example from the handout:

> **Situation:** While SNCC has always been a Black-led, majority Black organization, there has always been a small number of white SNCC members. But Northern white students have been increasingly getting involved. At SNCC's 1963 conference, one-third of the participants were white. Some staff members are now proposing to bring 1,000 mostly white students from all around the United States to Mississippi in the summer of 1964 to help with voter registration efforts. This plan has sparked discussion in SNCC on the role of whites in the movement.
>
> **Question:** Should SNCC bring 1,000 mostly white volunteers to Mississippi? If so, should SNCC limit the role of white volunteers?
>
> **Arguments:** Some Black SNCC members are concerned that instead of Black volunteers helping to build local leadership to organize their own communities, whites tend to take over leadership roles in the movement, preventing Southern Blacks from getting the support they need to lead. Many Northern whites enter SNCC with skills and an education that allow them to dominate discussions. If SNCC does decide to bring down white volunteers, these organizers insist that white activists should focus on organizing the Southern white community. After all, isn't it the racism in white communities that is the biggest barrier to Black progress? Other SNCC members argue that too many local activists have been murdered for trying to organize and vote and the majority of the nation will only care when their white sons and daughters are in harm's way. Bringing student volunteers from all around the country will mean increased attention on Mississippi's racist practices from the family and friends of the volunteers, as well as the media. This spotlight might force the federal government to protect civil rights workers and Blacks in Mississippi trying to register to vote. In addition, some local organizers argue that if we're trying to break down the barrier of segregation,

we can't segregate ourselves. Moreover, Black people are a minority in the United States and can't change things alone.

I gave students the handout the class period before the actual role play and asked them to jot down initial answers to each question for homework. This is especially helpful for students who don't feel as comfortable speaking in class discussion or who take longer to process their thoughts.

I explained to students that we would run our meetings in the same manner that SNCC ran meetings. We would choose a chair to call on other students and try to reach informal consensus. I echoed what I was told by SNCC veteran Judy Richardson: "Each one of us is putting our lives on the line, so we want to try to make sure that we come to a decision that we all feel comfortable with." Once we chose a facilitator (or one for each question), I concluded with another insight I learned from Richardson: "Now the last thing you need to know about how SNCC ran meetings is that if things got really heated, someone would start singing and then others would join in to remind everyone what they meant to each other and all they'd been through together. So, I'm going to teach you a song that they might have sung, and if our discussion at any point gets really contentious, we can sing to remind us that we are all in this together." I sang for students "Ain't Gonna Let Nobody Turn Me Around," and encouraged them to sing with me the second and third round. This was a little out of my comfort zone as a teacher, and singing in a social studies class can be out of students' comfort zone, but it became an essential and beautiful part of the role play. In addition to when the debate got heated, we sang the song to refocus after a lockdown drill, and I even heard a few students singing it in the hallways after class.

Students Run Their Own Meeting

To start the role play, students sat in a circle. I encouraged them to read the entire question out loud — including the situation and the arguments — before jumping into each debate. This way, students who weren't present when I gave out the questions or who didn't have a chance to read them for homework could still participate in the discussions. Students ran the debate, though occasionally I did jump in to the discussion to play devil's advocate, ensure they were taking all sides seriously, or re-emphasize the historical context that had provoked the question they were debating. When I did jump in, I always did so as an equal — raising my hand and waiting to be called on by the student facilitator. In general, I've been blown away by the seriousness and passion students bring to these discussions. Here's a sample from our class debate on the first question: Should SNCC focus its efforts on voter registration or direct action?

> Dwell: I think we should focus on voter registration because if we had some sort of political power we could take out the racist politicians.
>
> Jade: I disagree. I think direct action is more useful. We've seen that the *Brown v. Board* decision didn't actually desegregate schools. It took direct action. Action moves things forward faster and we want change now.

Giorgio: I agree with Dwell, focusing on voter registration is going to create a permanent change that will come from the government, not just changes in a few small places.

Rachel: But at the end of the day, it was the protests that pushed the government to make new laws. And isn't it suspicious that the Kennedys are saying they will help us secure funds if we focus on voter registration? Whose side are they on? Do they just want these new voters to vote for them?

Shona: I see voter registration as direct action. As we saw in *Freedom Song*, SNCC members get beaten up whether they are doing sit-ins or voter registration. Both are forms of nonviolent disobedience. Why can't we focus on both?

The time frame for the debates has varied depending on the pacing of class discussions and how much wiggle room I had built into the unit, but it has always taken at least one or two class periods. As we go, I have students jot down the decisions the class made, whether they agreed or disagreed with those decisions, and why.

When students finished debating the last question, I gave them a short reading adapted from several sources that explains how these debates played out in reality. Naturally, after debating the questions themselves, students were eager to know what really happened. Either for homework or as a debrief in class, I asked students to compare the decisions we made in class with SNCC's ultimate decisions on those topics, write about what decision they found most interesting or surprising, and think about how SNCC's experience in Mississippi changed the organization. While most students tended to agree with the decisions SNCC made, debating these questions as a class allowed them to look at the decisions more critically and not see them as inevitable. Imari wrote: "While SNCC chose not to limit the role of white volunteers I disagree with this decision. In class we discussed how white college students would tend to dominate discussions and reinforce Southern Blacks' sense of inferiority. While I agree with SNCC that they shouldn't segregate Black and white SNCC members, I think they could have placed some limits on white volunteers."

Adeola's comments about how organizing in Mississippi transformed SNCC were particularly insightful: "I think SNCC members felt like they couldn't be safe without being armed. They would get violently attacked by whites for trying to get the most basic things like the right to vote. They probably began to see nonviolence as more of a tactic than a policy."

After debriefing the role play, we watched part of an *Eyes on the Prize* episode that covers Freedom Summer [season 1, episode 5, "Mississippi: Is This America?"], when more than 1,000 volunteers joined SNCC organizers to dramatically increase voter registration in Mississippi. We also learned how during the summer, activists formed the Mississippi Freedom Democratic Party to challenge the all-white Mississippi Democratic Party at the Democratic National Convention of 1964. The organizing involved in creating the MFDP was tremendous, full of valuable lessons, and worth spending time on in the classroom. I've often used Teaching for Change's phenomenal lesson "Sharecroppers Challenge U.S. Apartheid" to cover this complicated effort with students.

Members of SNCC during
a sit-in at a Toddle House
in Atlanta in 1963.

© DANNY LYON | MAGNUM PHOTOS

Case Studies in Organizing Alabama

After learning about Freedom Summer, we return to the role play. Students are again seated in a circle and run their own meeting. This time, however, I split the class into three circles — groups large enough to still have a diverse group of vocal peers and small enough that they could get through questions a bit quicker. Armed with background about SNCC's work in Mississippi, I wanted to move student discussions away from SNCC's internal and more philosophical debates and toward more concrete problem-solving that happens during an organizing campaign.

I chose two "case studies" that further draw out SNCC's history and unique contributions to the Civil Rights Movement. The first case study looks at the famous 1965 voting rights campaign in Selma, Alabama, from the perspective of SNCC. Several of my students

> **Probably the most important part of SNCC's legacy is not its nonviolent direct action tactics, but its base-building through community organizing.**

had seen the movie *Selma*, but even for them, looking at the campaign through the eyes of SNCC was a new experience. I started with a short reading that gave students background about SNCC's long work in Selma and the new campaign launched by Martin Luther King Jr.'s Southern Christian Leadership Conference. The reading explains the difference between the two organizations' organizing methods: "SNCC projects emphasize the development of grassroots organizations headed by local people. SNCC organizers work, eat, and sleep in a community — for years, if necessary — and attempt to slowly develop a large local leadership that can carry on the struggle eventually without SNCC field staff. . . . The SCLC led local communities into nonviolent confrontations with segregationists and the brutal cops and state police who backed up Jim Crow laws. They hoped to bring national media attention to local struggles and force the federal government to intervene to support civil rights activists."

I explained to students why I've put them in multiple circles, have each circle pick their own facilitator, and hand out five "problem-solving" questions SNCC faced during the Selma campaign. In their circles, students debate and decide on answers to the five questions. Some of the questions ask students to decide whether they should support the efforts of the SCLC, while others are more open-ended and require students to come up with creative solutions. Here's a short excerpt from one student discussion on whether SNCC should support the 50-mile nonviolent march from Selma to Montgomery that will go through some of the most violent areas of Alabama:

> Aris: No, no, no! First, it's a 50-mile march! Then King's going to take them through these violent racist places. And he's nonviolent, so that means that if they want to snatch our people up, we're gonna have to let them!
>
> Nakiyah: But King brings a lot of publicity with him. You think they are going to attack us while the cameras are on us?
>
> Aris: It's a 50-mile march. The cameras can't be on us all the time.
>
> Elian: But the troopers just shot a protester, we have to respond in some way and we're stronger if we respond with King.

After students finish debating the questions, we read what really happened in a short excerpt I adapted from Clayborne Carson's *In Struggle: SNCC and the Black Awakening of the 1960s.* Students often leave this case study a little frustrated with King's actions in Selma — a stark difference to how students feel after watching the movie *Selma.* Aris commented, "The first march he wasn't there. The second march he's there, but turns it around. What's up with this guy?" In our debrief discussion, we return to the philosophical differences between SNCC and SCLC to try and answer this. I point out to students that at least in this instance, the SCLC's strategy worked and the Voting Rights Act was introduced out of the crisis in Selma. But my student Francisco would not let the SCLC off the hook: "But they came in after SNCC had been working in Selma for two years. So who's to say SNCC's strategy didn't work?" The point of this case study is not to answer these questions for students — but to get them to grapple with different organizing models for social change.

The next day we started on the second case study, which takes students through the SNCC organizing campaign in Lowndes County, Alabama. The format is identical to the previous day's, so students come ready to dive in. One question asks students how SNCC will respond to increasing white terror. Another question, set after the Voting Rights Act, asks students now that most official barriers to Blacks voting have come down, should people vote for the Democratic Party? Especially given that Alabama's

Democrats have a slogan that touts "white supremacy?"

In addition to the voting rights campaign in Lowndes, the debrief reading for this case study takes students through the birth of the original Black Panther Party, the Lowndes County Freedom Organization (LCFO), and their impressive showing in the 1966 elections. In less than two years, Lowndes County went from a place that had not one registered Black voter to a model of independent Black organizing that others aimed to emulate across the country.

Why Learn SNCC?

Probably the most important part of SNCC's legacy is not its nonviolent direct action tactics, but its base-building through community organizing. SNCC was influenced by the communities in which they organized, just as SNCC influenced them. The debates throughout SNCC's various organizing campaigns reflect this relationship with the communities in which they organized. Playing out these debates in the classroom shows students that social movements aren't only about protest — but also about tactics, strategy, and the ability to hold a debate and move forward together. Tracking SNCC's ideological transformation can also help highlight how social movements can quickly radicalize, as what seemed impossible only a few years before is made possible through protest and organization.

Too often, the experience of SNCC is ignored when we teach the history of the Civil Rights Movement. Instead, the movement is often taught with a focus on prominent movement leaders. The "Rosa sat and Martin dreamed" narrative not only trivializes the role of these activists, it robs us of the deeper history of the Civil Rights Movement. It's not enough for students to simply learn about the sit-ins or Freedom Rides. SNCC's organizing campaigns need to be at the center of civil rights curriculum. In today's racist world, students need to grasp that social change does not simply occur by finding the right tactic to implement — or waiting around for a strong leader to emerge — but through slow, patient organizing that empowers oppressed communities. This crucial lesson of the Civil Rights Movement will help us plot a course for our movements today — and may help students imagine playing a role in those movements. As my student Nakiyah wrote me in her final course evaluation, "Learning about SNCC was so interesting because SNCC was so effective. Knowing that the racism they experienced still exists in a similar but different way today made me want to make a change and gather my generation to fight." ∎

Adam Sanchez (asanchez@zinnedproject.org) is an editor of Rethinking Schools. *Sanchez teaches at Harvest Collegiate High School in New York City and works as curriculum writer and organizer with the Zinn Education Project. He wants to offer special thanks to SNCC veterans Judy Richardson and Betty Garman Robinson for reading and commenting on multiple drafts of the article.*

RESOURCES

For Adam Sanchez's SNCC teaching materials and role play, go to teachingforblacklives.org

Claiming and Teaching the 1963 March on Washington

By Bill Fletcher Jr.

A ugust 28, 2013 will mark the 50th anniversary of the historic March on Washington for Jobs and Freedom. Publicly associated with Dr. King's famous "I Have a Dream" speech, this march brought more than 250,000 people to the nation's capital. The day went down in history as a powerful show of force against Jim Crow segregation. Over time this great event has risen to levels of near mythology. The powerful speech by Dr. King, replayed, in part, for us every January on Martin Luther King Day, has eclipsed all else — so much so that too many people believe that the March on Washington was entirely the work of Dr. King. It is also barely remembered that the March on Washington was for freedom *and jobs.*

In fact, *The Americans*, a high school history text by publishing giant Houghton Mifflin Harcourt, tells students that the march was called simply "to persuade Congress to pass the [1963 civil rights] bill." In reality, the demand for jobs was not a throwaway line designed to get trade union support. Instead, it reflected the growing economic crisis affecting Black workers.

Indeed, while Dr. King was a major player, the March on Washington did not begin as a classic civil rights march and was not initiated by him. There is one constituency that can legitimately claim the legacy of the march — one that has been eclipsed in both history as well as in much of the lead-up to the August 2013 commemorations: *Black labor.*

Initiated by A. Philip Randolph, president of the Brotherhood of Sleeping Car Porters, the march became a joint project with the Southern Christian Leadership Conference. Randolph and other Black labor leaders, particularly those grouped around the Negro American Labor Council, were responding to the fact that the Black worker was largely being ignored in the discussions about civil rights. In addition, the economic situation was becoming complicated terrain for Black workers.

As historian Nancy MacLean has pointed out, the elements of what came to be known as deindustrialization — which was really part of a reorganization of global capitalism — were beginning to have an effect in the United States, even in 1963. As with most other disasters, it started with a particular and stark impact on Black America.

It is also barely remembered that the Student Nonviolent Coordinating Committee played a key role in the event. The civil rights leadership insisted that the militant rhetoric of the original speech by SNCC's then-chairman John Lewis — now Congressman John Lewis — be toned down. Reading U.S. history textbooks, students are seldom even introduced to the words of Lewis or other speakers. Here is Pearson's U.S. history textbook coverage:

Many people, including Christian and Jewish religious leaders, gave speeches that day, but none moved the crowd as did King. His voice rang as he proclaimed, "I have a dream that my four little children will one day live in a nation where they will not be judged by the color of their skins but the content of their character."

Bayard Rustin (left) was the principal organizer of the march. Shown here with Cleveland Robinson.

LIBRARY OF CONGRESS, PRINTS & PHOTOGRAPHS DIVISION, NYWT&S COLLECTION

Teaching about the March on Washington presents a series of challenges precisely because it involves counteracting sanitized textbooks and demythologizing not only the march, but also the Black Freedom Struggle — the Civil Rights Movement, as it became known. As such, there are a few points that cannot be overlooked if we want to honor the march's true story:

1. The context.

The idea for the march in 1963 did not appear out of nowhere, and the fact that A. Philip Randolph originated it was no accident. The notion of the March on Washington in 1963 was, in certain respects, the revival of an idea from 1941 when Randolph convened a group to plan a march on Washington, D.C., to protest the segregation of the growing war industry. That march, which was planned as a Black march on Washington, never happened because the mere threat of 100,000 African Americans marching forced President Franklin Roosevelt to give in to the demand for an executive order bringing about formal desegregation of the war industry.

2. The actual march was the result of work that began in the 1950s.

Although conceptualized by Randolph, the march was actually the result of the increasing tempo of a social movement. It could not have been organized in a little more than six months — as it was — if it had not been connected to local organizing that had gone on for decades in NAACP youth councils, churches, unions, women's groups, and more. It was not individuals who chartered buses from all over the country — it was organizations.

3. The march's principal organizer was Bayard Rustin.

In 2013, President Obama will posthumously award Bayard Rustin the Medal of Freedom, but teaching about Rustin complicates the simplistic Civil Rights narrative offered to students by corporate history textbooks. Rustin was a gay pacifist with a long history

THE NATIONAL ARCHIVES AND RECORDS ADMINISTRATION

of organizing, but despite his record of achievements, homophobia led to him being denied the title of national director of the march — technically, he served under Randolph.

Rustin closed the march with a list of demands and had everyone pledge "that I will not relax until victory is won." He was a complicated character who remained in organized labor and became a mentor to many, especially to younger activists in the burgeoning gay rights movement. At the same time, he refused to later condemn the Vietnam War and was critical of the Black Power Movement.

Teaching about Rustin complicates the simplistic Civil Rights narrative offered to students by corporate history textbooks. Homophobia led to him being denied the title of national director of the march.

4. The march was controversial on many levels *within* the Black Freedom Movement.

Individuals, such as Malcolm X, were critical of it, albeit in a contradictory manner, claiming that it would not amount to anything. And there were those within the march who, like then-SNCC chairman John Lewis, wanted a more militant posture.

5. The economic situation for African Americans was not addressed in any fundamental manner in the aftermath of the march.

There were periodic improvements, but the crisis that Randolph and the NALC saw brewing in the early 1960s took on the features of a catastrophe by the mid to late 1970s, a fact that we have been living with ever since. Divorcing "civil rights" from economic justice is a feature common to mainstream approaches to history, including those found in school curricula.

6. The entirety of Dr. King's Aug. 28, 1963, address should be read.

What comes across is something very different from the morally righteous and tame "I Have a Dream!" clips and textbook soundbites usually offered around the time of Dr. King's birthday. In fact, the speech is a militant and audacious indictment of Jim Crow segregation and the situation facing African Americans.

To truly honor the legacy of this anniversary, teachers should have students compare the King of the actual speech with the King from the clips. It would also be useful to have students read and discuss some of the day's other speeches. For example, in Randolph's opening speech he proclaimed that those gathered before him represented "the advance guard of a massive moral revolution" aimed at creating a society where "the sanctity of private property takes second place to the sanctity of the human personality." This is a sentiment that we never hear about that day.

This 50th anniversary of the March on Washington also offers an opportunity to connect the issues and experiences of 1963 with current realities. In 2013, Black workers have been largely abandoned in most discussions about race and civil rights. As National Black Worker Center Project founder Steven Pitts has repeatedly pointed out, with the economic restructuring that has destroyed key centers of the Black working class, such as Detroit and St. Louis, much of the economic development that has emerged has either avoided the Black worker altogether or limited the role of Black workers to the most menial positions. Thus, unemployment for Blacks remains more than double that of whites and hovers around Depression levels in many communities.

We can all do justice to this anniversary by asking the right questions and providing the actual historical context in which the 1963 March unfolded. More so, we can also offer, as Rustin asked the marchers in 1963, our "personal commitment to the struggle for jobs and freedom for Americans . . . and the achievement of social peace through social justice. How do you pledge?" ∎

Bill Fletcher Jr. is a longtime labor, racial justice, and international activist. Fletcher is an editorial board member and columnist for BlackCommentator.com *and a senior scholar for the Institute for Policy Studies in Washington, D.C. Fletcher is the co-author (with Fernando Gapasin) of* Solidarity Divided: The Crisis in Organized Labor and a New Path Toward Social Justice *(University of California Press) and* "They're Bankrupting Us!" And 20 Other Myths About Unions *(Beacon Press). This article is part of the Zinn Education Project's* If We Knew Our History *series.*

Reflections of a "Deseg Baby"

By Linda Mizell

KATHERINE STREETER

grew up in the segregated South, and came of age as a "deseg baby." My friends and I began our school lives in modern buildings constructed in our segregated neighborhoods in the late 1950s and early 1960s, some of them during periods of budget reductions.

In 1955, with the decision known as *Brown II*, the Supreme Court decreed that public schools be desegregated "with all deliberate speed," though it would be another 16 years before any real effort was made to carry out that decree on a large scale. Predictably, the responses of the 21 states directly affected by the *Brown* decision ranged from "ready compliance" to hostile, aggressive legal challenge and evasion. A number of Southern states chose the path that Florida did: While attempting to legally challenge the ruling, the state also tried to forestall counter challenges from the Black community by making our separate schools "equal" through a rash of new construction and renovation and unprecedented purchases of new instructional supplies.

It was too little, too late, but it added fuel to a debate that had been carried on for more than a century — whether "separate schools with equal facilities are more advantageous than mixed schools with prejudice" — a question posed by ardent desegregationist Charles H. Thompson, the first dean of Howard University's school of education and founding editor of the influential *Journal of Negro Education.*

There is considerable evidence that until early in the 20th century significant numbers of African Americans, if not the majority, supported the existence of separate schools. Many viewed them as "symbols of racial achievement [that] provided about the only avenue of opportunity for Black professionals," wrote historian Daniel Crofts.

Prior to the 1930s, African American schools were not necessarily considered academically inferior; nor were "mixed" (integrated) schools equated with "equal" (or superior) education. It was not uncommon in the 1930s to be opposed to the evils of segregation and still support separate schools, though it seems paradoxical. This debate was one of the hottest topics in the African American press.

Yet, with few exceptions, supporters of African American schools were denounced as "accommodationists" and/or "self-serving fools" intent on little more than preserving patronage positions. A. Philip Randolph even called them "Jim Crow niggers." Today, if we remember these folks at all, this is pretty much how we remember them.

Judge Robert L. Carter (who served as NAACP General Counsel and was a lead attorney in the *Brown* cases) noted in retrospect that the legal team had not sought the advice of professional educators in shaping its collective ideology, saying "[W]e felt no need for such guidance because of our conviction that equal education meant integrated education." As sociologist Sara Lawrence-Lightfoot noted, "Although the *Brown* decision focused on schooling, it disregarded the development of children and the perspectives of families and communities."

Between 1935, when the NAACP began implementing its school strategy, and 1954, when the Supreme Court handed down the *Brown* decision, the goal of equal educational opportunity and the strategy of desegregation were conflated in such a way as to make it difficult to publicly oppose — or even to question — the ideology of integration. The debate among African Americans didn't end, though; it simply became a private rather than a public conversation.

I grew up hearing those "in-house" conversations. Many times I've wished that I had the opportunity to talk with the folks we dismissed as "Toms," to explore with them the perspectives they gained by simultaneously supporting Black institutions and challenging Jim Crow education. Can "separate but equal" schools really work? We don't know: We've never really had them. Does integration work? Haven't had much experience with that, either.

While much has been written on the challenges, limitations, and miscalculations of desegregation policy as an effective vehicle for guaranteeing equality of access to educational opportunity, the prevailing viewpoint attributes contemporary wisdom to historical hindsight. It would have been difficult to accurately predict the complicated mix of social, political, legal, and economic factors that have led to school resegregation in the United States. Yet academic tracking, discriminatory disciplinary practices, the radical decline in the number of Black teachers and administrators, rising dropout rates, and other challenges that define 21st-century educational apartheid were real and imminent threats to parents and educators in the 1930s — just as real as the inferior facilities and other manifestations of institutional neglect that galvanized their opposition to segregation.

By the time I graduated from high school, the county system had been fully desegregated, but it seemed that we had slipped even further away from the goal of access to quality education. Decades later, hometown debate over the continued failure of our public schools to educate African American children has been deflected by a new proliferation of "neighborhood" schools and a revived emphasis on "choice" as an alternative to court-ordered busing.

Vanessa Siddle Walker, Gloria Ladson-Billings, and others have documented how segregation forced Black communities to develop strategies and structures that allowed effective schools under the worst of circumstances. Yet they are clear that there is nothing to be gained from romanticizing the nonexistent "good old days" of segregation.

It seems to me we're still missing the point that W. E. B. Du Bois made in 1935: "The Negro needs neither segregated schools nor mixed schools. What he needs is Education. What he must remember is that there is no magic, either in mixed schools or in segregated schools."

It's the same point that parents and educators have been making for the last 150 years. Would we now be better prepared to respond to the challenges of desegregation if we'd been able to have a more honest public debate on its potential risks and benefits all along? ■

Linda Mizell is an educational historian, teacher educator, author, and education consultant whose professional interests center on the creation of multicultural, anti-racist, inclusive communities, in pursuit of which she has worked extensively with schools, colleges, and community organizations. Her research focuses on the intersection of social and political activism with education activism in Florida's Progressive Era African American communities.

RESOURCES

Balkin, Jack, ed. 2001. *What Brown v. Board of Education Should Have Said*. New York University Press.

Bell, Derrick A, ed. 1980. *Shades of Brown: New Perspectives on School Desegregation*. Teachers College Press.

Cruse, Harold. 1988. *Plural but Equal: Blacks and Minorities in America's Plural Society*. William Morrow.

Foster, Michele. 1998. *Black Teachers on Teaching*. The New Press.

Ladson-Billings, Gloria. 2009. *The Dreamkeepers: Successful Teachers of African American Children*, 2nd Edition. Jossey-Bass.

Morris, Jerome E. 2009. *Troubling the Waters: Fulfilling the Promise of Quality Public Schooling for Black Children*. Teachers College Press.

Morris, Vivian Gunn and Curtis Morris. 2002. *The Price They Paid: Desegregation in an African American Community*. Teachers College Press.

Shujaa, Mwalimu J., ed. 1994. *Too Much Schooling: A Paradox of Black Life in White Societies*. Africa World Press.

Siddle Walker, Vanessa. 1996. *Their Highest Potential: An African American School Community in the Segregated South*. University of North Carolina.

What We Don't Learn About the Black Panther Party — but Should

By Adam Sanchez and Jesse Hagopian

Textbooks generally omit the role the Panthers played in organizing local communities, including founding liberation schools for Black youth.

BETTMANN | GETTY IMAGES

O n Monday April 1, 1967, "George Dowell and several neighbors from North Richmond, California . . . heard 10 gunshots. Sometime after 5 a.m., George came upon his older brother Denzil Dowell lying in the street, shot in the back and head. Police from the county sheriff's department were there, but no ambulance had been called. . . . [The] sheriff's office reported that deputy sheriffs Mel Brunkhorst and Kenneth Gibson had arrived at the scene at 4:50 a.m. on a tip from an unidentified caller about a burglary in progress. They claimed that when they arrived, Denzil Dowell and another man ran from the back of a liquor store and refused to stop when ordered to halt. Brunkhorst fired one blast from a shotgun, striking Dowell and killing him. . . .

For the Dowells, the official explanation did not add up, and community members helped the family investigate. The Dowells knew Mel Brunkhorst. He had issued citations to Denzil in the past, and on occasion, Brunkhorst had threatened to kill Dowell. . . . There was no sign of entry, forced or otherwise, at Bill's Liquors, the store that Dowell had allegedly been robbing. Further, the police had reported that Dowell had not only run but also jumped two fences to get away before being shot down. But Dowell had a bad hip, a limp, and the family claimed that he could not run, let alone jump fences. . . . A doctor who worked on the case told the family that judging from the way the bullets had entered Dowell's body, Dowell had been shot with his hands raised. . . . Mrs. Dowell publicly announced, 'I believe the police murdered my son.' . . . A white jury took little time deciding that the killing of unarmed Dowell was 'justifiable homicide' because the police officers on the scene had suspected that he was in the act of committing a felony. Outraged, the Black community demanded justice."
—Joshua Bloom and Waldo E. Martin, Jr. Black Against Empire: The History and Politics of the Black Panther Party

Helping North Richmond's Black community demand justice for the killing of Denzil Dowell was one of the first major organizing campaigns of the Black Panther Party, and the first issue of *The Black Panther* newspaper, which at its height around 1970 had a circulation of 140,000 copies per week, asked, "WHY WAS DENZIL DOWELL KILLED?" Anyone reading the story of Dowell today can't help but draw parallels to the unarmed Black men and women regularly murdered by police. The disparity between the police's story and the victim's family's, the police harassment Dowell endured before his murder, the jury letting Dowell's killer off without punishment, even the reports that Dowell had his hands raised while he was gunned down, eerily echo the police killings today that have led to the explosion of the movement for Black lives.

Yet when we learn about the early years of the Panthers, the organizing they did in Richmond — conducting their own investigation into Dowell's death, confronting police who harassed Dowell's family, helping mothers in the community organize against abuse at the local school, organizing armed street rallies in which hundreds filled out applications to join the party — is almost always absent. Born just over 50 years ago, the history of the Black Panther Party holds vital lessons for today's movement to confront racism and police violence — yet textbooks either misrepresent or minimize the significance of the Panthers. Armed with a revolutionary socialist ideology, they fought in Black communities across the nation for giving the poor access to decent housing, healthcare, education, and much more. And as the Panthers grew, so did the issues they organized around.

> Born just over 50 years ago, the history of the Black Panther Party holds vital lessons for today's movement to confront racism and police violence — yet textbooks either misrepresent or minimize the significance of the Panthers.

This local organizing that the Panthers engaged in has been largely erased, yet it is precisely what won them such widespread support. By 1970, a Market Dynamics/ABC poll found that Black people judged the Panthers to be the organization "most likely" to increase the effectiveness of the Black liberation struggle, and two-thirds showed admiration for the party. Coming in the midst of an all-out assault on the Panthers from the white press and law enforcement — including FBI Director J. Edgar Hoover's claim that the Panthers were "the greatest threat to the internal security of the country" — this support was remarkable.

The Textbook Version of the BPP

A few of the major textbooks don't even mention the Black Panthers, while most spend only a sentence or two on the organization. Even the small number that do devote a few paragraphs to the party give little context for their actions and greatly distort their ideology.

Textbooks often associate the Panthers with violence and racial separatism. For example, according to Teachers' Curriculum Institute's *History Alive! The United States Through Modern Times,* "Black Power groups formed that embraced militant strategies and the use of violence. Organizations such as the Black Panthers rejected all things white and talked of building a separate Black nation." While ignoring that the Panthers believed in using violence only in self-defense, this passage also attempts to divide the Panthers from "nonviolent" civil rights groups. The Panthers didn't develop out of thin air but evolved from their relationships with other civil rights organizations, especially

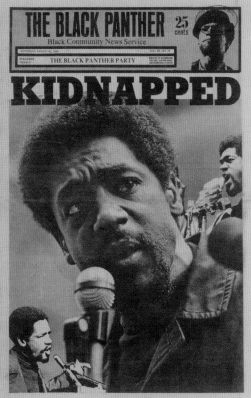

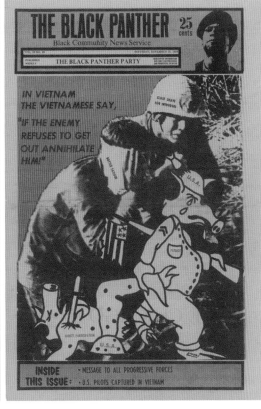

© 2018 EMORY DOUGLAS | ARTISTS RIGHTS SOCIETY (ARS), NEW YORK

The *Black Panther* had a weekly circulation of 140,000 at its height
and was generally designed by artist Emory Douglas.

the Student Nonviolent Coordinating Committee (SNCC). The name and symbol of the Panthers were adopted from the Lowndes County Freedom Organization (LCFO), an independent political organization SNCC helped organize in Alabama, which was also called the "Black Panther Party." Furthermore, SNCC allied with the Panthers in 1968 and although the alliance lasted only five months, it was a crucial time for the growth of the Panthers.

The passage from *History Alive!* also incorrectly paints the Panthers as anti-white, erasing their important work building multiracial coalitions. Most famously, Chicago Panther leader Fred Hampton organized the Rainbow Coalition that included the Puerto Rican Young Lords and the Young Patriots — a group of poor, Southern, white migrants. The Black Panthers helped the Patriots set up their own community service programs. In California, the Panthers made an important alliance with the mostly white Peace and Freedom Party, which in 1968 ran Eldridge Cleaver for president in an attempt to provide an antiwar, anti-racist alternative to the Democratic Party. An editorial in *The Black Panther* explained: "The increasing isolation of the Black radical movement from the white radical movement was a dangerous thing, playing into the power structure's game of divide and conquer."

> **More clearly than any other national civil rights organization, the Panthers linked the fight against racism with the fight against capitalism.**

Other textbooks also erase the socialist character of the Black Panther Party. Holt McDougal's *The Americans* reads, "Huey Newton and Bobby Seale founded a political party known as the Black Panthers to fight police brutality in the ghetto." While the textbook later acknowledges other things the Panthers advocated, by reducing the reason for their founding to fighting police brutality, *The Americans* profoundly diminishes the important ideological basis of the party. More clearly than any other national civil rights organization, the Panthers linked the fight against racism with the fight against capitalism. As Panther Huey Newton explained, "We realize that this country became very rich upon slavery and that slavery is capitalism in the extreme. We have two evils to fight, capitalism and racism. We must destroy both." The Panthers understood that Black people could not achieve socialism on their own and their work building multiracial anti-capitalist coalitions flowed from that analysis. The Panthers developed an education requirement for joining the party that consisted of reading 10 books relating to Black liberation and socialism.

Several textbooks also blame the Panthers for the end of the Civil Rights Movement, while simultaneously ignoring or downplaying the role the FBI played in destroying the party. In a later section in *The Americans*, the authors write, "Public support for the Civil Rights Movement declined because some whites were frightened by the urban riots and the Black Panthers." What textbooks like this fail to mention is that the decline in public support was a result of the counterintelligence program (COINTELPRO) of the FBI. According to scholar Ward Churchill:

The Black Panther Party was savaged by a campaign of political repression, which in terms of its sheer viciousness has few parallels in American history. Coordinated by the Federal Bureau of Investigation . . . and enlisting dozens of local police departments around the country, the assault left at least 30 Panthers dead, scores of others imprisoned after dubious convictions, and hundreds more suffering permanent physical or psychological damage. Simultaneously, the party was infiltrated at every level by agents provocateurs, all of them harnessed to the task of disrupting its internal functioning. Completing the package was a torrent of "disinformation" planted in the media to discredit the Panthers before the public, both personally and organizationally, thus isolating them from potential support.

With minimal and problematic coverage in the history textbooks, there is little curriculum for teachers hoping to provide students with the crucial history of the Black Panther Party. This is why we were excited last year to hear that PBS began distributing Stanley Nelson's new documentary *Black Panthers: Vanguard of the Revolution.* The documentary is an essential tool for the classroom and gives high school teachers an incomparable visual companion to teaching the Panthers. Like any documentary, the film has some oversights that teachers should be aware of. Although it discusses the Panthers' 10-Point Program, it doesn't do a great job of explaining the Panthers' Marxist ideology. It also doesn't provide enough historical context for the Panthers' activities, making it difficult for students to fully understand both the rise and fall of the party. And in its attempt to tell the national story of the Panthers, it sometimes skips over important local organizing efforts. But chunked into sections and coupled with readings that help flesh out the documentary's omissions, it is a crucial addition to any social justice teacher's tool chest.

Teaching the Panthers Through Role Play

To introduce the film and to try to give students a fuller picture of the party's history, we developed a mixer activity in which each student takes on a role of someone who was in, or connected to, the Black Panthers. Students are given a role with a thumbnail sketch of that person's biography along with details that help illuminate aspects of the party. In many roles, we tried to emphasize why people joined the Black Panther Party. For example, the role of Kathleen Cleaver begins:

As a young Black woman growing up in Alabama in the 1950s, you wanted to challenge injustice. You were inspired by powerful women leaders of the Student Nonviolent Coordinating Committee (SNCC). . . . These women were creating a social revolution in the Deep South and all worked with SNCC. . . . In 1966, you went to organize in SNCC's New York office and then to Atlanta. You had joined SNCC at the time it took up the slogan "Black Power," and you saw the Black Panther Party as taking the positions SNCC was headed toward. . . . You decided to move to San Francisco and join the Panthers.

Among the other roles is Ruby Dowell, Denzil Dowell's sister who joined the party after the organizing the Panthers did in Richmond.

We also tried to highlight the repression the Panthers faced along with some of the lesser known but important stories of Panther community organizing. The role for Lumumba Shakur, founder of the New York Black Panther Party chapter, explains how the entire New York Panther leadership was arrested on flimsy evidence. The role then continues:

> You spent two years in prison while the trial proceeded. You organized prisoners to fight for better living conditions and at one point took control of the jail from the prison guards. You demanded and received bail hearings for every prisoner. Hundreds of prisoners were released as a result of the new hearings.

Students also encounter Panther allies like William "Preacherman" Fesperman of the Young Patriots, Madonna Thunder Hawk of the American Indian Movement, Gloria Arellanes of the Brown Berets, and Jose "Cha-Cha" Jimenez of the Young Lords. They also meet Panther "enemies" like FBI Director J. Edgar Hoover and Los Angeles Police Officer Pat McKinley.

One of the most overlooked aspects of the Panthers we tried to highlight was their role in the struggle for anti-racist education. Historian Donna Murch details how the Panthers had their origins in "agitation for Black Studies courses and debates about the 'relevance' of education," and describes the membership of Panthers as "composed largely of Southern migrants under 25, including many students recruited from local high schools and community colleges . . ." The Panthers were originally formed out of a study group at Oakland's Merritt community college. The Panthers' belief in the need for an education beyond what was being taught in the school system led them to develop a network of liberation schools for youth.

The Panthers were originally formed out of a study group at Oakland's Merritt community college. The Panthers' belief in the need for an education beyond what was being taught in the school system led them to develop a network of liberation schools for youth.

In the mixer, the role of Ericka Huggins highlights the Panthers' flagship liberation school in Oakland. Other roles highlight the Panthers' fight for ethnic studies and their free breakfast program that fed hundreds of hungry children before school and was eventually adopted by the U.S. education system — one of the party's most meaningful and lasting reforms.

Lastly, we tried to include criticisms of the Panthers in the roles — not just from the police and conservative politicians, but from Black Panthers themselves. Often students can glorify the Black Panther Party, especially students of color who are reg-

The Panthers offer sickle cell anemia testing at the 1972 Black Community Survival Conference.

SICKLE CELL ANEMIA TESTING
BLACK COMMUNITY SURVIVAL CONFERENCE

BOB FITCH | THE BOB FITCH PHOTOGRAPHY ARCHIVE

ularly harassed by police and are justifiably impressed with the Panthers' bold defiance against what they called "the pig power structure." But the Black Panther Party existed as a national organization for only a short period, and while a large responsibility for their destruction should be put on the FBI and police efforts to destroy the party, it's also important for students to ask whether the Panthers could have done anything differently. Whether it is the sexism some female Panthers experienced, or the ideological debate that caused an eventual split in the party, we wanted to provide students with tools to critically assess this complex history.

To start the activity, we distribute roles to students and ask them to read them several times, underline important information, and list out three or four crucial facts on the back of the role. Students are often blown away by the stories presented. "My character's a badass!" one student exclaimed after reading about Bobby Seale's acts of defiance in the courtroom when he was put on trial after participating in the 1968 antiwar demonstration at the Democratic National Convention.

When students finish reading, we give out eight questions that guide them as they circulate around the room, meeting others and finding a different person to answer each of the questions. For example, "Find someone who has an opinion on the role of women in the Black Panther Party. Who is this person and what is their opinion?" We encourage students to take their time — the point of the mixer is not to race through and get all the answers to the questions, but to learn from the various stories in the room to get a fuller picture of the Black Panther Party. As teachers, we participate in the mixer as well. It's helpful to take a role with a more complex critique that might be hard for students to explain, like Stokely Carmichael or Luke Tripp of the Dodge Revolutionary Union Movement. Students are often eager to learn the stories in the room and a buzz fills the air as they grab one another and share their roles.

At the end of class — with at least 20 minutes left, we ask students to head back to their seats and silently write on four questions:

1. What were some of the things you learned about the Black Panthers that you didn't know before the mixer?
2. Whose story did you find most interesting or surprising?
3. What did you think of the critiques of the Black Panthers you encountered?
4. What would you like to know more about?

We've always been impressed by the rich discussion these four questions produce. Students are often surprised to learn the story of Richard Aoki. "I thought they'd only allow Black people into their group, but Aoki was Japanese American," Maya wrote. For many students this is the first time they learn about Latinx or Asian American radicals.

> **"It was cool to learn about Gloria [Arellanes] and Cha-Cha Jimenez. I didn't know that Mexicans and Puerto Ricans were fighting in the same ways as the Panthers."**

Aliyah exclaimed, "It was cool to learn about Gloria [Arellanes] and Cha-Cha Jimenez. I didn't know that Mexicans and Puerto Ricans were fighting in the same ways as the Panthers." "Yeah, my mom told me about the Brown Berets," Ayanna stated, "but I didn't know that they were connected to the Panthers."

Students are often shocked at the level of violence the Panthers faced at the hands of the FBI. "It was sad to hear the story of Lil' Bobby Hutton," Brandon wrote. "He was trying to help his people and was shot more than 12 times with his hands up. He was only 16!" David added, "I found it interesting the way the FBI set up the BPP. It's clear the government did not want them to succeed." More specifically, James noticed, "The FBI sent fake letters to the Oakland and New York Panthers to create tensions between them. I didn't realize the FBI was so involved in breaking them up."

We've found that students can often be impressively articulate when evaluating the critiques they come in contact with during the mixer. Keisha wrote, "I thought Luke Tripp's ideas made sense when thinking about how to fight capitalism. He founded the Dodge Revolutionary Union Movement in Detroit and was focused on helping working-class Blacks. He thought the confrontations with police would just get Panthers thrown in jail and that they should focus on organizing strikes." Melanie disagreed: "I actually think the confrontations with police were important because it showed people the Panthers weren't scared." Madison grappled with the differing views of sexism in the party that she encountered: "It was interesting that Roberta Alexander called out sexism in the BPP and thought they didn't give women equal rights. Other Panther women I met disagreed. People still have sexist attitudes toward women and women don't have equal rights so that was interesting to think about." Other students defended the Panthers against critiques from the right and left. "[California State Assemblyman] Donald Mulford said that he wanted to protect society from Black people with guns. But I feel like society needs to be protected from white people with guns," declared JT. "I really like Stokely Carmichael," Gregory began, "but I disagree with his critique of the Panthers for making alliances with white people. I get where he's coming from, but you can't fight racism with racism." Without realizing it, Gregory's words echoed Chicago Black Panther leader Fred Hampton's.

> **Students are often shocked at the level of violence the Panthers faced at the hands of the FBI. "It was sad to hear the story of Lil' Bobby Hutton," Brandon wrote. "He was trying to help his people and was shot more than 12 times with his hands up. He was only 16!"**

We hope the mixer we wrote, Stanley Nelson's new documentary, Wayne Au's lesson on the Panthers' 10-Point Program, and Ursula Wolfe-Rocca's lesson on COINTEL-PRO can be starting points for educators who hope to arm a new generation with the story of the Panthers. As the 50th anniversary of the founding of the Black Panther Party passes by, these lessons should be just a few of many to come that help teachers and students explore this rich — and too often ignored — history. ∎

Adam Sanchez (asanchez@zinnedproject.org) and Jesse Hagopian (jesse@rethinking-schools.org) are editors of Rethinking Schools. *Sanchez teaches at Harvest Collegiate High School in New York City and works as curriculum writer and organizer with the Zinn Education Project. Hagopian teaches at Garfield High School in Seattle and is editor of* More Than a Score: The New Uprising Against High-Stakes Testing *(Haymarket).*

RESOURCES
For the Black Panther Party mixer, go to teachingforblacklives.org

COINTELPRO
Teaching the FBI's war on the
Black freedom movement

By Ursula Wolfe-Rocca

RICHIE POPE

Student-selected and student-run current events discussions are a daily ingredient of my high school social studies classes. The first 20 minutes of every 90-minute class period, we read an excerpt from a recent newspaper article and discuss its significance. In the last few years, the discussions have been dominated by names that have piled up with sickening frequency: Trayvon Martin, Eric Garner, Michael Brown, Walter Scott, Freddie Gray, Tamir Rice, Sandra Bland. My students, mostly Asian American and white, live in Lake Oswego, one of the wealthiest cities in Oregon and a community that benefits from mostly positive relationships with police. They struggle to understand a society that continues to allow Black lives to die at the hands of law enforcement.

This year, student attention has turned to how activists are responding to the racism in the criminal justice system, particularly the Black Lives Matter movement. In November 2015, a student brought in an *Oregonian* article, "Black Lives Matter: Oregon Justice Department Searched Social Media Hashtags." The article detailed the department's digital surveillance of people solely on the basis of their use of the #BlackLivesMatter hashtag. My students thoughtfully discussed and debated whether tying #BlackLivesMatter to potential threats to police (the premise of the surveillance program) was justifiable, with most students agreeing with the Urban League and the American Civil Liberties Union that the U.S. Department of Justice acted improperly and potentially unlawfully.

> **My students have grown up in a world that glorifies and mythologizes King; they cannot make sense of the notion that U.S. security agencies viewed him as a threat.**

But what was not noted in the *Oregonian* article was the historical resonance of this story, which recalls the ugly, often illegal, treatment of Black activists by the U.S. justice system during an earlier era of our history.

My students had little way of knowing about this story behind the story because mainstream textbooks almost entirely ignore COINTELPRO, the FBI's counterintelligence program of the 1960s and '70s that targeted a wide range of activists, including the Black freedom movement.

COINTELPRO offers me, as a teacher of classes on government, a treasure trove of opportunities to illustrate key concepts, including the rule of law, civil liberties, social protest, and due process, yet it is completely absent from my school's government book, *Magruder's American Government* (Pearson).

One of the options for U.S. history teachers in my school district is *American Odyssey* (McGraw-Hill). In a section titled "The Movement Appraised," the book sums up the end of the Civil Rights Movement:

> Without strong leadership in the years following King's death, the Civil Rights Movement floundered. Middle-class Americans, both African American and white, tired of the violence and the struggle. The war in Vietnam and crime in the streets at home became the new issue at the forefront of the nation's consciousness.

Here we find a slew of problematic assertions about the Civil Rights Movement, plus a notable absence. Nowhere does *American Odyssey* note that, in addition to King's death and Vietnam, the Civil Rights Movement also had to contend with a declaration of war made against it by agencies of its own government.

American Odyssey is not alone in its omission. *American Journey* (Pearson), another U.S. history textbook used in my school, also ignores COINTELPRO.

The only textbook in my district that does mention COINTELPRO is *America: A Concise History* (St. Martin's), a college-level text used to teach AP history classes. Its summary and analysis takes exactly one sentence: "In the late 1960s SDS and other antiwar groups fell victim to police harassment, and Federal Bureau of Investigation (FBI) and CIA agents infiltrated and disrupted radical organizations." Without context, without emphasis, without a real-life illustration of what "harassment," "infiltrated," and "disrupted" actually meant in the lives of those targeted, this sentence is suffocated into meaninglessness.

Why do textbook writers and publishers leave out this crucial episode in U.S. history? Perhaps they take their cues from the FBI itself. According to the FBI website:

> The FBI began COINTELPRO — short for Counterintelligence Program — in 1956 to disrupt the activities of the Communist Party of the United States. In the 1960s, it was expanded to include a number of other domestic groups, such as the Ku Klux Klan, the Socialist Workers Party, and the Black Panther Party. All COINTELPRO operations were ended in 1971. Although limited in scope (about two-tenths of 1 percent of the FBI's workload over a 15-year period), COINTELPRO was later rightfully criticized by Congress and the American people for abridging First Amendment rights and for other reasons.

Apparently, mainstream textbooks have accepted — hook, line, and sinker — the FBI's whitewash of COINTELPRO as "limited in scope" and applying to only a few organizations. But COINTELPRO was neither "limited in scope" nor applied only to the organizations listed in the FBI's description. Under then-FBI Director J. Edgar Hoover, COINTELPRO included legal harassment, intimidation, wiretapping, infiltration, smear campaigns, and blackmail, and resulted in countless prison sentences and, in the case of Black Panther Fred Hampton and others, murder. This scope of operations can hardly be described as "limited." Moreover, these tactics were employed against every national civil rights organization, the antiwar movement (particularly on college campuses), Students for a Democratic Society, the American Indian Movement, the Puerto Rican Young Lords, and others.

> Why do textbook writers and publishers leave out this crucial episode in U.S. history? Perhaps they take their cues from the FBI itself.

A better way to understand the wide net cast by COINTELPRO is the final report of the Church Committee. In the early 1970s, following a number of allegations in the press about overreaching government intelligence operations, a Senate committee, chaired by Democrat Frank Church of Idaho, began an investigation of U.S. intelligence agencies. Their 1976 report states: "The unexpressed major premise of much of COINTELPRO is that the Bureau [FBI] has a role in maintaining the existing social order, and that its efforts should be aimed toward combating those who threaten that order." In other words, anyone who challenged the status quo of racism, militarism, and capitalism in American society was fair game for surveillance and harassment. Rather than "limited," the FBI's scope potentially included all social and political activists, an alarming and outrageous revelation in a country purportedly governed by the protections of free speech and assembly in the First Amendment.

Bringing COINTELPRO into the Classroom

I post a recent headline on the overhead screen: "Top Officer in Iraq: 'We must neutralize this enemy.'" I ask my 11th-grade U.S. history students, "So what does the word *neutralize* mean in this headline?" Well-schooled in the popular culture of war and violence, they have no trouble with this task.

"Kill."

"Destroy."

"Eliminate."

"Get rid of."

I write their definitions on the board and explain we will come back to them in a bit. I say that in this lesson we are going to look at a bunch of old documents from the FBI. I try to build excitement by telling students that these documents were classified top secret and not meant to be seen by everyday folks like us. I continue: "In fact, we only found out about them because a group of peace activists broke into an FBI office in Media, Pennsylvania, and stuffed suitcases full of documents — selecting the night of a much-anticipated Muhammad Ali-Joe Frazier fight so the security guard would be distracted."

I post the first document on the overhead for the class to analyze together. It's a memo sent by Hoover in 1967 to FBI field offices throughout the country: "Black Nationalist — Hate Groups" (see Resources). In it, Hoover instructs his agency "to assign responsibility for following and coordinating this new counterintelligence program to an experienced and imaginative special agent well-versed in investigations relating to Black nationalist, hate-type organizations."

At this point in the unit, students have compared the activism of the Southern Christian Leadership Conference, the Student Nonviolent Coordinating Committee, the Congress of Racial Equality, Malcolm X, and the Black Panther Party, analyzing the tactics and social critiques brought to bear by different strands of the movement. Students draw on this background when I ask them to predict which organizations will be targeted under Hoover's counterintelligence program. "So guys, who are the 'hate-type organizations' referred to in this document?"

A number of hands shoot up — students think they've got this one. Invariably, their first guess is that the FBI must have targeted the Black Panthers. They explain that the

Panthers advocated Black Power and self-defense, and encouraged members to own firearms. Students plausibly predict that if the FBI were to treat any Black activist groups as a potential threat, those with the most revolutionary rhetoric and those bearing arms would have been first in line.

"Well, you're right," I say. "So, were the Black Panthers a threat to American security? Did the FBI have a justifiable reason to be tracking them?"

There are always some students who bristle at the militancy of groups like the Black Panthers. Whether it is the Panthers' use of the term "pig" to describe law enforcement, or Malcolm X's reference to "white devils," or the philosophy of self-defense, my students struggle with a discomfort they do not feel when we are talking about SNCC's sit-ins. I try to help students separate their discomfort about the group's rhetoric from the question of whether the threat they posed to the U.S. government was a security threat or a political one.

> **COINTELPRO is not just a surveillance story. It is a story about a duplicitous and destructive government-sponsored war against Black and other activists.**

I remind students of prior lessons — the Panthers' 10-Point Program, their careful adherence to state gun laws to protect them from being charged on weapons infractions, their street patrols to monitor police violence, their breakfast for children programs, their freedom schools.

I continue: "But the Black Panthers were not the only ones targeted. Let's take a look at the other groups on the FBI's list."

I reveal the next page of the document, which states the groups to which "intensified attention under this program will be afforded," and I ask students to call out other organizations they see listed that we have studied in this unit.

"SNCC!"

"SCLC!"

"CORE!"

I add some humor by acting confused: "Wait a second, can you guys help me out here? Remind me again, who was the head of the Southern Christian Leadership Conference?"

Before I am even done with my act of feigned ignorance, students are shouting, "King! King was the leader of SCLC!"

"Oh yes, that's right! Now help me again because I can't seem to remember: Was he a member of a 'hate-type' organization?"

Students roll their eyes at my poor acting and adamantly confirm: "No! He was all about nonviolence!"

Now I get serious and pause for some analysis and questioning: "OK, folks, what is going on here? Why would the FBI target activist organizations, including those that were explicitly nonviolent, like SCLC and CORE?"

Students offer a few suggestions:

"Maybe Hoover was really racist and didn't want the Civil Rights Movement to succeed."

"Maybe the FBI worried that the nonviolent organizations were going to become more militant."

But this discussion usually ends soon after it begins. Students are flummoxed. They have grown up in a world that glorifies and mythologizes King; they cannot make sense of the notion that U.S. security agencies viewed him as a threat.

In spite of its brevity, this discussion is important. It frames the inquiry to come by cultivating students' curiosity and confusion.

Now I present to students the final part of the document. This is where Hoover reveals the goal of COINTELPRO:

> The purpose of this new counterintelligence endeavor is to expose, disrupt, misdirect, discredit, or otherwise neutralize the activities of Black nationalist, hate-type organizations and groupings, their leadership, spokesmen, membership, and supporters, and to counter their propensity for violence and civil disorder.

I ask a student to read this quote aloud since hearing the words *disrupt*, *misdirect*, *discredit*, and *neutralize* underscores their sinister meaning.

I remind the class of the earlier definitions of neutralize on the board. I ask, "So what is the FBI saying it wants to do to SCLC, SNCC, CORE, and the Black Panthers?"

Students look at the board, but they can't quite believe what is written there, so they add question marks.

"Kill?"

"Destroy?"

"Eliminate?"

"Get rid of?"

Most years, there will be a student who interjects at this point to suggest that maybe neutralize means something different in this context; surely it can't be as bad as I make it sound. This disbelief is the perfect tone to set for the next step of the lesson, when students delve into the documents and see for themselves what the FBI meant by *neutralize*.

The Documents

I arrange the desks into groups of four. I provide students packets of declassified memos (see Resources) from the COINTELPRO era. These documents are a representative sample of the scope and tactics of the program, and reveal the FBI's use of infiltration, psychological warfare, legal harassment, and media manipulation against activists and organizations.

I give students a worksheet with some guiding questions to complete as they read and discuss. For the memo dated 9/27/68, about the Black Panther Party, the worksheet asks, "How does the FBI characterize the Black Panther Party?" Students skim the memo and locate this sentence: "It is the most violence-prone organization of all the extremist groups now operating in the United States." This is a simple retrieval question. But then I ask, "What activities by the Panthers are not mentioned anywhere in these documents?" Here I urge students to go back to earlier lessons on the social dimensions of the Panthers and recall the breadth of community programs offered by the Panthers, from health clinics to nutrition classes to free breakfasts for children.

Students tackle the documents together, reading aloud, talking, deciphering, and questioning as they go.

COINTELPRO and Martin Luther King Jr.

Midway through the packet, students read about the FBI's program of harassment against Martin Luther King Jr. When they arrive at these documents, I always know, because I start to hear a lot of this:

"Wait, what is this?"

"I am totally confused — this letter was sent to King?"

"Ms. Wolfe, we don't understand this document at all."

This is my cue to stop the group work and read the King documents together as a class, documents that reveal that through illegal wiretapping, the FBI collected evidence of King's extramarital affairs and used this evidence to try (unsuccessfully) to blackmail him. The documents show that the FBI not only attempted to discredit King, but also to get him to commit suicide.

It is hard to overstate how dumbfounded the students are by these revelations. How could the U.S. government participate in this level of harassment of a man they have been taught to embrace as a near-deity?

This is a perfect teaching opportunity to help establish the truth about King: He was not the watered-down, Hallmark-holiday caricature that has come to dominate our culture; in the eyes of people like Hoover, he was a dangerous radical.

The FBI and Hoover saw the King who, in his "Letter from Birmingham Jail," called out racial moderates for their gradualist approach to injustices that required immediate action; the King whose opposition to the Vietnam War, famously expressed at Riverside Church, led him to describe the U.S. government as "the greatest purveyor of violence in the world today"; and the King who warned Americans, "When machines and computers, profit motives, and property rights are considered more important than people, the giant triplets of racism, extreme materialism, and militarism are incapable of being conquered."

When students honestly explore the breadth and depth of King's critique of U.S. society, it isn't hard to see why the FBI might see him as a threat and a target of COINTELPRO.

King Was Human

At this moment in the lesson, students want to talk about King's infidelity.

"Ms. Wolfe, please tell me it is not true that King cheated on his wife!"

"Wait, the FBI made that up, right? To make him look bad?"

I try to limit the length of this conversation, since it is obviously not directly related to the goals of my lesson, but I think it would be a mistake to shut down these heartfelt student questions.

"Yes," I say. "It's true, King did cheat on his wife."

Most students seem saddened by this news and sometimes question whether King's infidelity discredits and undermines his heroic status. I challenge kids to move beyond this all-or-nothing moral position: "Look, humans are multidimensional. We can be fantastic in one situation, but miserable in another. Imagine if your entire life's accomplishments were ignored and you were judged only on the basis of the worst thing you ever did. Would that be fair?"

Students begrudgingly take my point but are still sad, as though they have just learned a dark secret about a close family member.

I wonder if there may be a hidden lesson in critical thinking when we reveal King's moral imperfection to students. If we insist that our activist heroes demonstrate moral perfection — or if we hide their blemishes — do we not in some way transmit the message to young people that heroic action is something for a small elect, the untarnished few, not for imperfect people like you and me?

The Murder of Fred Hampton

We've clarified the goals of COINTELPRO and learned about the actual strategies, methods, and targets of the program. But, so far, COINTELPRO has been revealed only on paper. Now it is time to show students how the program damaged and destroyed people's lives.

I show students an excerpt of the documentary *Eyes on the Prize* — part of the episode "A Nation of Law?" that details the story of Fred Hampton. Hampton was a former NAACP youth organizer who became the chair of the Illinois chapter of the Black Panther Party in 1968. Hampton embodied what was powerful and promising about the Panthers. At just 20 years of age, he helped the Panthers establish a breakfast for children program and a free medical clinic on the South Side of Chicago. He taught political education classes and was working to create a multiracial "rainbow coalition" of Chicago youth groups that included the Blackstone Rangers (a street gang), the Young Lords, and the Young Patriots, an organization of working-class white youth, often migrants from Appalachia. Howard Saffold, a member of the Chicago Police Department at the time, eloquently sums up law enforcement's concerns about Hampton's coalition-building:

> **When students honestly explore the breadth and depth of King's critique of U.S. society, it isn't hard to see why the FBI might see him as a threat and a target of COINTELPRO.**

The Panthers were pursuing an ideology that said we need to take these young minds, this young energy, and turn it into part of our movement in terms of Black liberation and the rest of it. And I saw a very purposeful, intentional effort on the part of the police department to keep that head from hooking up to that body. It was like, you know, do not let this thing become a part of what could ultimately be a political movement, because that's exactly what it was.

Like most of the leaders of the Black freedom movement, Hampton drew the interest of the FBI and COINTELPRO. In 1969, following months of harassment, Hampton was shot and killed as he slept in his bed, his pregnant partner beside him, during a police raid on his home. He was 21 years old.

As they watch the documentary, students take notes and I help them tease out the COINTELPRO dimension of the story: An FBI informant infiltrated the Chicago chapter of the Panthers and earned Hampton's trust. He proceeded to provide a floor plan of Hampton's apartment, noting which room he slept in. This information was used by the raiding officers who killed him.

Following the film, students complete a viewer response journal to talk back to the film, a way to process the horror, shock, and grief many of them feel after watching the deadly consequences of COINTELPRO. Darian grapples with Hampton's innocence: "The police had no reason to come to Hampton's house like that and open fire. He wasn't hurting anyone and he hadn't done anything wrong." Sarah echoes an elderly woman quoted in the film: "The tragic death of Fred Hampton was 'nothing but a Northern lynching.'" Maya writes: "A mob of people came into Fred's home, for no reason, and murdered him. The fact that these were police officers only made it more unbelievably awful."

The Hampton murder also serves as a moment to bring students back to our earlier discussion of the word *neutralize*. Did the FBI target Hampton for murder? Although FBI agents did not pull the trigger on the weapons that killed Hampton, they provided critical information to those who did.

Final Thoughts

When I first started teaching about COINTELPRO back in the early 2000s, I ended the unit with a discussion of then-President George W. Bush's NSA surveillance program, which had recently been exposed and was being hotly debated; more recently, I have drawn connections to the Edward Snowden revelations. This year I will address government tracking of Black Lives Matter activists and the use of social media platforms to gather intelligence on protest movements and protest leaders. It seems that the questions of surveillance and government overreach are never out of date.

COINTELPRO is not just a surveillance story. It is a story about a duplicitous and destructive government-sponsored war against Black and other activists. And though the COINTELPRO documents have long been made public, it is a story history textbooks continue to ignore.

Textbook publishers' disregard for the history of COINTELPRO is one more example of the crucial importance of the Black Lives Matter movement, which lays bare the systemic dangers faced by Black people in the United States while simultaneously affirming and celebrating Black life. When activists use social media to show the nation the brutal strangulation of Eric Garner or the mowing down of Tamir Rice or the deadly harassment of Sandra Bland, we cannot fail to recognize the injustice and racism of the criminal justice system. When that same social media shows us Garner's wife pleading, "He should be here celebrating Christmas and Thanksgiving and everything else with his children and grandchildren"; or a photo gone viral of Rice as a shy, smiling boy; or a Facebook post of Bland looking joyful about a new job — we feel the human potential lost as a consequence of these injustices.

What I attempt in my classroom is a Black Lives Matter treatment of COINTEL-PRO, where we reveal the injustice of the program while simultaneously affirming and celebrating the promise of the activists it sought to silence. Just as Black Lives Matter activists use video footage to convince a disbelieving wider public of what African Americans have long known about police brutality, we teachers can use our classrooms to shine a light on history that has been available, but systematically ignored, by our textbooks and in our curricula, a history that emphatically communicates: Black history matters. ■

Ursula Wolfe-Rocca (ursulawolfe@gmail.com) teaches at Lake Oswego High School in Oregon and is a frequent contributor to Rethinking Schools.

RESOURCES

The COINTERPRO documents below and other materials related to this article are available at teachingforblacklives.org

Goldfield, David, et al. 2005. *The American Journey: A History of the United States.* 3rd ed. Vol. 2. Pearson.

Henretta, James A., David Brody, and Lynn Dumenil. 2006. *America: A Concise History.* St. Martin's.

McClenaghan, William. 2005. *Magruder's American Government.* Pearson.

Nash, Gary. 2004. *American Odyssey: The 20th Century and Beyond.* McGraw-Hill.

PBS. 1990. "A Nation of Law?" *Eyes on the Prize.* Produced by Henry Hampton. Blackside.

COINTELPRO DOCUMENTS

Unless otherwise indicated, the following documents can be found in Churchill, Ward, and Jim Vander Wall. 2001. The *COINTELPRO Papers: Documents from the FBI's Secret War Against Dissent in the United States.* 2nd ed. South End Press.

Dec. 1, 1964. FBI memo about "taking steps to remove King from the national picture." The memo suggests sending Martin Luther King Jr. an anonymous letter encouraging him to commit suicide. p. 98. A clean, unredacted version of the letter to King and be found at nytimes.com/2014/11/16/magazine/what-an-uncensored-letter-to-mlk-reveals.html?_r=1

Aug. 25, 1967. Memo from FBI Director J. Edgar Hoover initiating COINTELPRO against civil rights organizations. vault.fbi.gov/cointel-pro/cointel-pro-black-extremists/cointelpro-black-extremists-part-01-of/view

March 8, 1968. FBI memo suggesting misinformation leaflets be distributed in Baltimore to combat the influence of new SCLC offices opening there. vault.fbi.gov/cointel-pro/cointel-pro-black-extremists/cointelpro-black-extremists-part-01-of/view, p. 78-79.

July 10, 1968. FBI memo proposing false information be used to "convey the impression that [Stokely] Carmichael is a CIA informant." p. 128.

Sept. 27, 1968. FBI memo describing the Black Panther Party as the "most violence prone organization . . . now operating in the United States," with FBI plans to create factionalism within the party. p. 124.

Oct. 10, 1968. FBI memo in which a "media source" is sought "to help neutralize extremist Black Panthers and foster a split between them and the Student Nonviolent Coordinating Committee." p. 127.

December 1969. Floor plan of Fred Hampton's apartment, as drawn by an FBI informant. p. 139.

3

GENTRIFICATION, DISPLACEMENT, AND ANTI-BLACKNESS

Burned out of Homes and History

Unearthing the silenced voices of the Tulsa Race Riot

By Linda Christensen

EVERETT COLLECTION INC. | ALAMY STOCK PHOTO

I teach language arts, so why would I teach my students about the 1921 Tulsa Race Riot? In language arts circles, we discuss reading as a window to the world, but in a country plagued with foreclosures and homelessness, we need to question the world we're gazing at: How are contemporary evictions a historical reach from the past? What has happened to Black and Brown communities? Why do people of color have less inherited wealth than whites? The untold history — the buried stories — reveals patterns that affect our students' current lives, from eviction notices to the hunger of deep poverty. I can wax poetic about the importance of story in students' lives, but reading literature of poverty and despair without offering a historical explanation leaves students with little understanding about how things came to be the way they are. And that's worth reading and writing about.

Jefferson High School, where I co-teach a junior language arts class with Dianne Leahy — a wonderful teacher who allows me to keep my teaching chops alive by creating and teaching curriculum with her — is located in a gentrifying neighborhood that once was the heart of the African American community in Portland. Families were pushed out of their homes because of urban renewal beginning in the 1960s and again, more recently, because of gentrification. As the prices of homes rise in what is now called the "Alberta Arts Neighborhood," most of our students' families can no longer afford to live in our school's neighborhood. They live in apartments on the outskirts of the city, and a number ride buses or the commuter train to come to school at Jefferson.

For me, learning about the history of the Tulsa Race Riot coincided with the current economic crisis that has led to epic foreclosures and evictions. I realized that, like many people, the majority of my family's "wealth" is tied up in our home. We drew on that wealth to send our daughters to college. They will inherit the house, and the wealth it represents, when my husband and I pass on.

The story of Tulsa may be an extreme instance of violent dispossession, but it highlights a pattern of historical expulsions and exclusions that explains the lack of inherited wealth in Black and Brown communities. According to historian Hannibal B. Johnson, "The Tulsa Race Riot of 1921 was set against a backdrop of a multitude of race riots in America. 1919 was known as 'red summer' because blood was flowing in the streets. There were more than 25 major riots in 1919 in America." (See Elliot Jaspin's book *Buried in the Bitter Waters: The Hidden History of Racial Cleansing in America* for more on this topic.) The complicit silence of textbooks about the history of race riots and racial exclusions that pushed Black people off their lands and out of their homes keeps our students ignorant about the reasons for the lack of economic resources in the Black community. Instead, students must imagine why their people lack wealth: unwise spending? Laziness? Ignorance?

The term "race riot" does not adequately describe the events of May 31–June 1, 1921, in Tulsa, Oklahoma. Though some sources labeled the episode a "race riot" or a "race war," implying that both Black and white citizens might be equally to blame for lawlessness and violence, the historical record documents that what occurred was a sustained and murderous assault on Black lives and property. This assault was met by a brave but unsuccessful armed defense of their community by some Black World War I veterans and others. During the night and day of the riot, deputized whites killed more than 300 African Americans; they looted and burned to the ground 40 square blocks, including 1,265 African American homes, hospitals, schools, churches, and 150 businesses. White deputies and members of the National Guard arrested and detained 6,000 Black Tulsans who were released only upon being vouched for by a white employer or other white citizen; 9,000 African Americans were left homeless and living in tents well into the winter of 1921.

Building Background Knowledge and Interest

In class, before we began the unit, I briefly discussed the arc of our upcoming study. "We are starting this unit because I want you to think about wealth in this country. Who has it? Who doesn't? An important study just discovered that whites have 20 times the wealth of Blacks. Why is that? When there's a question that puzzles you, you have to investigate. For many people, including me, our wealth is tied up in our homes. So what happens when you lose your home?"

> "We are starting this unit because I want you to think about wealth in this country. Who has it? Who doesn't? An important study just discovered that whites have 20 times the wealth of Blacks. Why is that? When there's a question that puzzles you, you have to investigate. For many people, including me, our wealth is tied up in our homes. So what happens when you lose your home?"

Students frequently bring up the gentrification of the neighborhood, which has rapidly transformed from mom-and-pop grocery stores to chic restaurants and upscale boutiques. Rather than describe the problem of gentrification at this early stage of the study, I move them into the history, keeping the question of homes and wealth in front of them as we move forward.

To stimulate our students' interest in resurrecting this silenced history of Tulsa, I created a tea party/mixer about the night of the invasion of Greenwood, the African American section of Tulsa. (For more on the tea party activity, go to teachingforblacklives.org.) Using sources from historians John Hope Franklin, Scott Ellsworth, and others, I wrote roles for students that gave them each a slice of what happened that night: the arrest of Dick Rowland, a young African American shoe shiner who allegedly raped Sarah Page, a white elevator operator, in broad daylight (later, students learn that authorities dropped all charges); the newspaper article that incited whites and Blacks to gather at the courthouse; the gathering of armed Black World War I veterans to prevent a lynching; the deputizing and arming of whites, many of whom were in the Ku Klux Klan; the internment of Blacks; the deaths of more than 300 African American men, women, and children; the burning and looting of their homes and businesses.

Destruction in Tulsa's Greenwood neighborhood, 1921.

COURTESY OF THE RESEARCH DIVISION OF THE OKLAHOMA HISTORICAL SOCIETY

Because not all white Tulsans shared the racial views of the white rioters, I included roles of a few whites and a recent immigrant from Mexico who provided safety in the midst of death and chaos. These roles allowed students to understand that even in moments of violence, people stood up and reached across race and class borders to help. I invented one role, Thelma Booker, as a compilation of people I'd read about; the others were individuals whose stories I found in Ellsworth's book, *Death in a Promised Land: The Tulsa Race Riot of 1921*, and other materials. (Visit teachingforblacklives.org for a full list of tea party/ mixer roles.)

I briefly discussed the event before launching into the tea party. "You are going to become people who were involved in what is called the Tulsa Race Riot on the night of May 31, 1921." I told them that Tulsa was divided into two sections — the white section and Greenwood, where most African Americans lived. We had studied Jim Crow, so they understood segregation. "I want you to figure out what happened that night. First, read over your role. Underline or highlight key pieces of information. You will need to be able to tell others about what happened to you and what you witnessed. Once you have read your role, turn over your paper and write down the key events, so you can retell them to your classmates."

After students read their roles, I handed out a series of questions to help them elicit information from each other's roles. We read over the questions, which included: "Find someone who suffered a loss during the riot. What did they lose? What happened?"

ALL THAT WAS LEFT OF HIS HOME AFTER TULSA RACE RIOT – 6-1-1921

DEGOLYER LIBRARY, SOUTHERN METHODIST UNIVERSITY

Students found one or more questions that they could answer based on their role. Before I turned them loose, I added, "You are entering the roles of people whose lives may have been shattered on that night. Take their lives seriously. Give them the dignity they deserve."

Students circulated through the room, talking in pairs, finding out bits and pieces of what happened that night. Because this was an introduction to the unit, not the full story, they ended the activity with information, but also with questions. I asked them to write down key facts they learned about the Tulsa Race Riot and what they still wanted to know. Their questions filled the class: What really started the riot? Did Black people rebuild their houses? Why didn't we learn about this before? (When I guest-taught this lesson in a history class at Jefferson a few years ago, a couple of students spontaneously pulled out their history textbooks and searched for an entry on Tulsa, but didn't find one.)

History and Poetry

Rather than answer their questions in a lecture, I discovered several accessible readings and YouTube clips (The Night Tulsa Burned, Parts 1–4). Four short related videos, narrated by Ellsworth and Johnson and Tulsa Historical Society director Robert Powers, tell the story using historical photographs from the night of the massacre. These clips also feature interviews with three survivors: Juanita Burnett Arnold, George Monroe, and Ernestine Alpha Gibbs. I asked students to take notes that answer the questions they raised in class, but also to record details and stories that resonated for them. "You will write a poem, a piece of historical fiction, and an essay about this time period. I want you to absorb the era as well as the facts. Write down the names of people, buildings, streets, parks. Grab people's stories, their faces, and their lives. I want you to know what happened, but I also want you to try to understand how people felt about that night. As you learn about this history, make connections to what's happening today. How does this history echo in your life?"

After watching each 10-minute video clip, we stopped and debriefed: "What questions got answered for you? What images stuck with you? Whose stories will you carry with you?"

Then I asked: "When we began this unit, I said that we were going to ask about wealth in our country: Who has it, who doesn't, and why? How does the history of Tulsa help us begin to answer these questions? How does what happened in Tulsa connect to the question of Black wealth?" As students talked, I listed their observations on the board as a reference they could return to during our writing.

Once we had images and names, I discussed two ways to write poems about the event — as a persona poem or an image poem: "For a persona poem, write from the point of view of a person or object. Use the word 'I.' For an image poem, describe what you see. Form a picture for the reader with your words." Christina wrote a persona poem from the perspective of a burned wall; she called it "The Last One Standing":

> I am just a memory of what this
> town was before the riot. [...]
>
> I saw the glowing flames in the midst
> of this dark night and the leftover embers
> of the morning.

Reading and Writing Historical Fiction

As we pursued an overall "Stealing Home" unit, Dianne and I discovered *If We Must Die: A Novel of Tulsa's 1921 Greenwood Riot* by Pat Carr. We wanted students to tap into the ways that literature can deepen history by bringing to life the mind-numbing numbers of loss through the stories of individuals. The novel tells the story of 1921 Tulsa through the character of Berneen O'Brien, a woman of "Black Irish" descent, who accepts a job at a Black school in Greenwood. She "passes" for Black during the day and returns home to her uncle, who is a member of the Ku Klux Klan. The reader discovers the racial tensions and the eruption of the massacre from Berneen's perspective.

Students kept track of historical events in their dialogue journal, but they also took notes on the author's craft: the way Pat Carr showed how characters felt through the use of interior monologue, actions, and dialogue, as well as the strategies she used to mix historical fact and fiction. After students read a chunk of the book, they gathered in groups and created posters about the difference between history and fiction by using notes from their dialogue journals. The poster had three sections:

1. Quotes that referenced history.
2. Quotes that illustrated the qualities of fiction.
3. Their analysis of the differences.

For the third section, one group wrote:

> In the novel, fiction is often very detailed and elaborated, for example, "The shoulder of his white shirt suddenly blossomed red as if he'd run headlong into a sack of crimson paint." Fact is usually subtle, using the names of people and places and events — Greenwood Avenue, Dreamland Theatre, the Drexel Building. Most events in the novel were factual — the shooting, the looting, the internment — but most of the characters and their personalities were fabricated. There are things that the author says to describe a character that couldn't be known — their body language, their speech patterns, their interior monologue.

As I teach social justice lessons, I am also teaching students how to read and write with greater clarity. We don't have to parse out the language arts skills and teach them as stand-alone lessons; they are part of the daily classroom work.

We asked students to write a piece of fiction based on their knowledge of the events, modeled on Carr's work. Writing historical fiction pushes students to learn more about the past and to more fully understand the events and the time period. Students had to go back to the documents and videos to get down the sequence of events; they had to get inside people's heads to understand why the African American World War I veterans stood up for Dick Rowland, why they were adamant that there would be no more lynchings. But they also had to learn about people's daily lives — where they lived, where they shopped, where they worked, and details like the fact that no one watched television in 1921.

To prime students for the assignment, we distributed a newspaper article written in 2009 that describes interviews with three survivors of the Tulsa riot — Beulah Smith, Ruth Avery, and Kenny Booker. The article reviews the events and contains quotes from the survivors:

> Beulah Smith was 14 years old the night of the riot. A neighbor named Frenchie came pounding on her family's door in a Tulsa neighborhood known as "Little Africa" that also went up in flames.
>
> "Get your families out of here because they're killing [Black people] uptown," she remembers Frenchie saying. "We hid in the weeds in the hog pen," Smith told CNN. [...]
>
> Booker, then a teenager, hid with his family in their attic until the home was torched. "When we got downstairs, things were burning. My sister asked me, 'Kenny, is the world on fire?' I said, 'I don't know, but we're in a heck of a lot of trouble, baby.'"

Many students used these specific incidents in their stories. Some even used the dialogue from the article, then invented the rest of the story.

Dianne and I developed a graphic organizer for students to get them started. Then we spent part of a period listing potential characters and scenes that students could use in their stories: Kenny Booker, Sarah Page, Beulah Smith, NAACP journalist Walter White, Ruth Phelps. I also encouraged them to use pieces of their own lives in their stories. I told them, "In the novel I'm writing about women organizing for change on the Mexican border, I have the main character bake desserts when she's stressed. I also tap into my own desire for justice and my organizing work. I found that when I use pieces of my life, the characters come to life." Students who have experienced homelessness or evictions used their feelings of loss as they wrote. Desiree', who is biracial, wrote her story from the points of view of two characters — an African American boy caught with his younger sister in the riot and fire, and the white girl who loves him. Jalean recreated his family — an older brother who lives with his mother and two younger siblings he adores. He also created a character modeled on the security guard at Jefferson, who has been a wise elder in Jalean's life.

> These roles allowed students to understand that even in moments of violence, people stood up and reached across race and class borders to help.

The student writing was stunning. Students invented backstories to help readers understand their characters' histories and motivation. They used the tools of fiction writers — character development, dialogue, interior monologue, setting descriptions.

Desiree' DuBoise's story illustrates how students used the scenes from the photos of the city's destruction, the voices of the people we studied, and the history of the time period to create their stories:

> The sky rained down rivers of flame. I had always been the man of the house, but now Mama was probably long gone, too. She had gone into Greenwood to her floral shop that morning and never came back home. I was alone in the attic except for Billy Mae. I looked down into her round brown eyes and saw fear that reflected my own. Her thick black lashes were coated with tears, and the only noise that came from her was a soft keening. She was so young, younger than I had been when the Klan took Pop away. I watched as they strung him up like an animal and beat him 'til every inch of his tall frame was coated with crimson blood. That was years ago. Now my sister had to watch her own city burn, the only place she'd ever known. She could hear the screams coming up from the streets just as well as I could. The floorboards of the attic creaked as I shifted my weight. My sister looked at me then. "Kenny?" she said my name quietly. "Is the world on fire?"

Dianne and I took our students to the band room, the only room big enough to comfortably accommodate all 42 of us, and students read their stories from the podium. The read-around took two days. As students read, those who were stuck or who couldn't get started figured out a storyline; others were prompted to revise after hearing their peers' details, flashbacks, and interior monologues. Although the students didn't directly address the loss of economic wealth through their stories, they wrote about the impact of the devastation: the deaths, the loss of photos, pianos, houses, neighborhoods. Jalean said, "I felt proud to know that there were thriving African American communities. I feel cheated that I never got to live in one."

Reparations Role Play

To inject hope and justice into the unit, Dianne and I created a role play about the efforts to obtain restitution for the deaths and damages suffered by the Black population of Greenwood. We needed to return more directly to our theme of wealth inequality, to reinforce the idea that the injustices of the past affect the present, and that it's never too late for justice — even many years after an event like the Tulsa Race Riot.

> Jalean said, "I felt proud to know that there were thriving African American communities. I feel cheated that I never got to live in one."

In 1997, the Oklahoma State Legislature authorized a commission to study the riot. After three and a half years of research, the commission delivered its report. Rather than just reading about the results of those proceedings — and a 2003 lawsuit initiated on behalf of the survivors and their descendants — we wanted students to think about what "fair" compensation for the loss might mean. We put students in the position of commission members. We asked them to determine what reparations, if any, should be made to the survivors of the Tulsa Race Riot and their descendants.

Before we started the activity, we reviewed the losses from that night — the deaths and the number of homes, schools, and businesses burned and looted. We gave students three choices to initiate their conversations:

1. Do nothing.
2. Repay individuals and their descendants for their losses.
3. Create reparations for the Greenwood community.

Students had passionate arguments about what should happen. Students' understanding of the long-term impact of the loss of inherited wealth through the destruction of homes and community echoed throughout their discussions. A number of students repeated Aaron's statement: "We can't change what happened in the past, but we can compensate the offspring for the loss of their property and inheritance. At least give the descendants scholarships." Some students felt that wasn't enough. Desiree' said, "Who suffered the most? Which was worse — death or property loss? The entire community suffered. We should choose a mixture of compensations: There should be scholarships as well as compensation for the survivors and their descendants. There should be a memorial day and a reburial of the mass graves."

Sarah was afraid that bringing up the past would open old wounds and restart the racism that initiated the riot. Skylar said, "Who cares if it makes people uncomfortable? They are going to have to deal with it. These things happened, and we have to address them." Vince and many others agreed. "This is not just the past. Racial inequality is still a problem. Forgetting about what happened and burying it without dealing with it is why we still have problems today."

And this was exactly what we wanted kids to see: The past is not dead. We didn't want to get lost in the history of Tulsa, though it needs to be remembered; we wanted students to recognize the historical patterns of stolen wealth in Black, Brown, and poor communities. We wanted them to connect the current economic struggle of people of color to dynamics from the past. We wanted them to see that in many ways Tulsa and other historically Black communities are still burning, still being looted. We wanted to bring that story home. ∎

> **And this was exactly what we wanted kids to see: The past is not dead. We didn't want to get lost in the history of Tulsa, though it needs to be remembered; we wanted students to recognize the historical patterns of stolen wealth in Black, Brown, and poor communities.**

Linda Christensen (lmc@lclark.edu) is director of the Oregon Writing Project at Lewis & Clark College in Portland, Oregon, and a Rethinking Schools *editor. She is author, most recently, of* Reading, Writing, and Rising Up: Teaching About Social Justice and the Power of the Written Word (*2nd edition*).

AUTHOR'S NOTE: *Thanks to my National Writing Project colleagues Deshawn Dickens and Shanedra Nowell and historian Scott Ellsworth for their collaboration and wisdom on this topic.*

RESOURCES

For the Tulsa Race Riot tea party and other teaching materials related to this article, go to teachingforblacklives.org

Carr, Pat. 2002. *If We Must Die: A Novel of Tulsa's 1921 Greenwood Riot.* Texas Christian University Press.

Ellsworth, Scott. 1982. *Death in a Promised Land: The Tulsa Race Riot of 1921.* Louisiana State University Press.

In Search of History: The Night Tulsa Burned. The History Channel. 1999. Weller/Grossman Productions. Available on YouTube.

Jaspin, Elliot. 2007. *Buried in the Bitter Waters: The Hidden History of Racial Cleansing in America.* Basic Books.

Oklahoma State Legislature. "Tulsa Race Riot: A Report by the Oklahoma Commission to Study the Tulsa Race Riot of 1921," Feb. 28, 2001. Available: okhistory.org/research/forms/freport.pdf

White, Walter F. and *The Nation* editors. Aug. 23, 2001. "Tulsa, 1921," *The Nation.*

"The Most Gentrified City of the Century"

By Becky HenkleBerry
and Jeff Waters

Boise-Eliot/Humboldt School is a special place. It stands, 90-year-old red brick and mortar, amongst newly constructed condos, craft breweries, and combination laundromat-bars, just a block off historic Mississippi Avenue in the Albina area of North Portland, Oregon. It is an obstinate place that, despite its decreasing enrollment and "level one" Oregon State School Report Card status, has survived two separate school closures and simply refused to yield to the forces of gentrification.

A recent article in *Governing* magazine described Portland as "the most gentrified city of the century," and the vast majority of the gentrified tracts are in North and Northeast Portland. Although North Portland's demographics have drastically changed over the last two decades, from predominantly African American to predominantly white, Boise-Eliot/Humboldt's student population hasn't. In a neighborhood that is mostly white, we serve the largest volume of African American students in the state. Less than half of the students who live within our district boundary attend our school, and less than half of our student population lives in our neighborhood.

As gentrification has forced out many working-class families of color, affluent white families, who often choose to opt out of the neighborhood's "failing" public schools, have moved in. Many of the students we teach at Boise-Eliot/Humboldt travel long distances, riding public transportation from far in East Portland, to attend our historically

CHRIS KINDRED

Black school. Families often use the addresses of aunties, grandmas, and friends to ensure that their sons and daughters will continue a legacy that sometimes dates back to the flood of 1948, which destroyed the World War II shipyard-worker city of Vanport and pushed its largely African American population into the Albina area.

The mechanisms of segregated housing — unfair lending practices, exclusionary laws, eminent domain, urban renewal, and gentrification — are not distinct to Portland. These racist laws and practices continue to affect communities nationally. Our school, our neighborhood, and our students are part of a larger story, a larger conversation. Because this history is so relevant to our students' lives and is often ignored by traditional curriculum, we decided to co-teach an integrated language arts/social studies unit on gentrification and neighborhood history to our 8th graders.

We hoped this unit would say: "Yes, you've lived this. You are living this. Your experiences are important. And, in the face of a changing community, you have something to share that is irreplaceable. You have the opportunity to educate our community and neighborhood about a destructive process that we've all been part of."

We wanted to help students wade through Oregon's often ignored racial history, and to help them feel empowered to go beyond the facts and into the messiness of evaluation and activism. What resulted was a yearlong process that included facilitating structured student discussions; interviewing families; lots of reading and writing; self-publishing a digital multimedia book about the history of race in our state, city, and neighborhood (see Resources); and a student-driven community activism project.

"Those Fancy Apartments Are Going Up All Over"

We decided to launch our unit with a general overview of gentrification — What is it? How has our neighborhood changed? — and students' personal narratives. We wanted to show students that this unit was deeply rooted in their own experiences. Moreover, we hoped to encourage students to find their own voices to talk back to discriminatory practices.

In his social studies class, Jeff began with a simple definition: "Gentrification is a change in a neighborhood," he said, writing the sentence as a bullet point on a note sheet beneath the document camera. The students dutifully copied the sentence in the notes section of their social studies notebooks. "Our neighborhood has gone through gentrification. A lot of you grew up here. How have you seen it change?" Jeff asked the class.

> **These racist laws and practices continue to affect communities nationally. Our school, our neighborhood, and our students are part of a larger story, a larger conversation.**

The students looked up from their notes, and a few hands went halfway up. "The New Seasons [a high-end grocery store] is new. Does that count?" asked Jada.

"Absolutely, that's a change. Let's write it down." Jeff wrote a second bullet in the notes: "How has our neighborhood changed?" and beneath it he put a dash and wrote "New Seasons Market."

A few more hands shot up. "There are a lot more white people," stated Jayla. "I'm not trying to be racist, but I was walking down Mississippi and I didn't see any Black people at all, and it didn't used to be like that."

"They tore down that one bar; what was it called?" asked Aaliyah.

"LV's 22? Wasn't that it?" offered Jayla, leaning forward in her seat.

"That's interesting. What are they building in its place?" Jeff prodded.

"Probably some of those fancy new apartments. They're going up all over, down Mississippi and Vancouver and Williams," said Jayla.

Jeff added "a lot of new buildings" to the list as students named more changes they had seen in the neighborhood. MyKayla talked about her family moving. Jordan said the butcher shop no longer carried certain items, like oxtails, that her grandma wanted. Hailey mentioned that Self-Enhancement Inc. (a Black community-focused charter school and community resource) had moved its services out to East Portland — or, as our students call it, "the Numbers" (a reference to street names like 157th Avenue). Aaliyah talked about the new bike lanes on Vancouver and Williams, major thoroughfares a few blocks from the school. It just kept coming. After a substantial list was created, we organized our experiences into three categories: people, physical structures, and community services.

"But gentrification isn't any old change," Jeff said. "It impacts certain people more than others, doesn't it? Jayla, what did you notice about race in our neighborhood? Can you connect that to gentrification?"

"Well," Jayla began, "it seems like the people who were already here, Black people, have been hurt more."

Later, we would discuss specific aspects of Portland's development, like using eminent domain to force people of color and low-income families out of their homes. But the students seemed ready to write, and Jeff introduced the first assignment of our unit — the personal narrative: "We've all seen or experienced at least one aspect of gentrification, but many of our families have been here for generations."

"My great-grandma went here!" shouted a student.

"Over the weekend you are going to interview your parents, grandma, auntie, someone you live with, about your family's experiences with gentrification. You can ask them whatever you want, but there are a few questions that you have to ask. Turn your notebooks to your writing section and let's get them written down. What section?"

"Writing!" came a chorus of voices.

Leaving half a page for each question, students wrote down the following:

- Why do we live where we live?
- Why do I attend Boise-Eliot/Humboldt?
- How have the changes in our neighborhood affected our family?
- Do you think these changes are good or bad?
- What are your hopes for me, my education, and our school?

Students seemed excited about the activity, and we hoped that this excitement would bring families and their stories into the curriculum. Almost immediately, we started hearing from family members and school staff about the impact the project was having on students. One parent commented, "This project is important because it's about what is really going on in our kids' lives." Our students were talking about gentrification in the halls and other classes, on the bus ride home to East Portland, and around their kitchen tables.

When they returned to social studies class on Monday, many came with stories to share. "Did you know my great-grandpa owned the Desert Motel and the Rose City Cab Company? And those are the oldest African American businesses in the city?" Jada exclaimed when given the opportunity to share her research with the class.

Happy to build on the enthusiasm generated by students' discussions with their families, Jeff introduced the narrative through a prompt: "As a member of this school community, you have experienced gentrification in some capacity. Use your family interviews to craft a personal narrative that explores your family's experience."

Over the next two weeks we used our school's computers to draft, edit, and revise the narratives. As the students wrote, Jeff furiously read, responded, and asked questions. What emerged was a complex portrait of family history and a changing community.

For example, Cayden wrote: "On holidays like Thanksgiving, 4th of July, and birthdays, it is harder to get my whole family all in one house because my uncle and cousins live out in the Numbers." She also tried to make sense of the relationship between the changing demographics of North Portland, where the school is, and East Portland, the Numbers, where her family now lives:

> The only kind of people we see in East Portland are Hispanic and African American people. Finally, one day I asked my uncle, "Why don't you ever see Caucasian people in this neighborhood?"
>
> "A few years back if we would have lived out here you would have seen a lot of white people, but now you mostly see African American people because the prices of the houses in North and Northeast have raised, and I would not be able to afford the houses closer, near my job," he replied.

Many students expressed a frustration that likely mirrored that of their family members. Hailey, our 8th-grade vice president, wrote:

> I don't think white folks get it. You are making things more expensive for us people in a place where we still are struggling to survive. We don't wanna be a part of it anymore because we know that it's going to be too expensive, and what we want the neighborhood to be will not be considered.

"He Was Even a Doctor"

Students recognized and could describe the changes that were taking place in North Portland. They saw the unfairness of having to move due to rent hikes and the decline of Section 8 (subsidized) housing in the neighborhood. However, students were left wondering why and how this had happened. What were the explicit and intentional policies whitewashing the neighborhood? The purpose of the subsequent reading lessons was to help students understand the mechanisms and policies behind the changes. We wanted to give them specific people, places, and policies so that they could analyze the marginalization many were experiencing and take on the role of activist.

When students entered language arts class on Monday, each table had a manila envelope with five copies of the same article. Becky explained: "Today we are going to build on what you've learned in Mr. Waters' class by reading parts of a research project, *The History of Portland's African American Community, 1805 to the Present*. We're doing this for three reasons: to learn more about the history of our neighborhood, to practice reading tricky text by chunking and paraphrasing, and to see what good nonfiction writing looks like." Becky instructed students to read through the article once independently and to underline what confused or surprised them.

As Becky circulated through the room, she began to notice patterns in what students were highlighting. After 10 minutes, she asked students to share out what they were wondering and uncovering.

Elijah raised his hand. "Did you know that Dr. Unthank, the one from Unthank Park, had a dead cat thrown at his house because he moved into a white neighborhood down by Grant High School?"

"Yeah, and they broke his windows and threw garbage all over the place. And someone wanted to give him $1,500 if he would move out," Jacob added.

"He was even a doctor, and they did that."

As we continued reading, chunking, paraphrasing, and discussing, students kept a chart in their notebooks that was split into three categories: people, places, and policies. They continued to record names: DeNorval Unthank; the Dude Ranch, the center of the Portland jazz and arts scene in the 1940s; and the Hill Block Building, the center of Black-owned business in Northeast Portland.

New vocabulary surfaced. We took time to define and discuss important terms: Oregon Exclusion Laws (the legal exclusion of people of color from the state), redlining (the purposeful and legal confinement of people of color within specific neighborhoods), and eminent domain (the city's ability to oust residents based on a justification that the property could be better used to serve the public) all created a climate that has encouraged the exploitation of the city's citizens of color.

> One parent commented, "This project is important because it's about what is really going on in our kids' lives." Our students were talking about gentrification in the halls and other classes, on the bus ride home to East Portland, and around their kitchen tables.

We wanted the students to see how the terms connected and interacted. We used the history of the Hill Block Building and Legacy Emanuel Hospital to illustrate this.

The iconic metal dome of the Hill Block Building, all that's left of the historic building, now sits atop a gazebo in a neighborhood park a handful of blocks from the school, something the students were quick to point out.

"What do we know about why that building was torn down?" Becky asked. "And how Legacy Emanuel was developed?"

Hailey raised her hand, her eyes on the article on her desk. "This article says that 188 houses were torn down to expand the hospital."

"Didn't the hospital apologize for that?" came a voice from the back.

"How could they just tear down houses?" came a surprised and angry response.

"Well, they were 'blighted,'" Hailey explained, looking through her graphic organizer, "and so the city said they could. But the article also says that the city was purposefully ignoring neighborhood requests for help, and we know that the city used" — she looked down at her paper again — "they used redlining to make sure that the neighborhood was mostly Black people in the first place. So basically, they forced people to live there, ignored them, and then forced them to move by using eminent domain."

"And the Hill Block Building?" Becky asked, returning to the original question.

"That building was torn down, too," Hailey stated flatly.

As our notebook charts filled with names and ideas, students began to connect the current changes with what they had learned.

Emiliano commented: "Places getting expensive here is like opposite redlining. It's keeping people out of the neighborhood now."

Students had begun to see the current changes in the neighborhood as the most recent iteration of a long history of purposeful disenfranchisement and systematic racism.

"What Can We Do About This?"

As the group settled into Jeff's class, sharpening pencils and scraping chairs, he typed the starter question into a PowerPoint: "Why are we learning about this?"

"Well," Hailey began, "we are learning about this because it's important."

"But why does it matter?" Cayden quipped.

The students looked at one another. "It matters because people have been hurt," Hailey said, a little unsure of herself. "Most of my family has had to move out to the Numbers, and a lot of these people moving into the neighborhood, they don't even know that." Many students nodded.

> **Students had begun to see the current changes in the neighborhood as the most recent iteration of a long history of purposeful disenfranchisement and systematic racism.**

"What can we do about this? Should we do anything?" Jeff asked.

"Should we tell them?" asked Malik, often one of the most soft-spoken boys in the room.

The students settled on an answer: Yes, we should tell them. We should tell the stories of urban renewal, of Legacy Emanuel Hospital, of a vibrant Black middle class. We should tell the stories of Vanport. We should tell them that exclusion laws, codified by Chief Justice Reuben P. Boise, our school's namesake, required beatings for African Americans caught living in the state. The students wanted to tell it all.

After class, we reflected on Hailey's candor and Malik's question. This was an opportunity to make it about something bigger than the essay, or the test, or the assignments, or the grade. Percolating in Becky's mind was an iBook project she had learned about a few months previously during a workshop with Peter Pappas, a faculty member at the University of Portland. With his graduate students, Pappas had edited an iBook about Portland's Japantown in the 1950s. The iBook platform included widgets, scrolling sidebars, and wipe-away images to showcase student writing. More importantly, it was possible to make a compendium of class articles available to the broader community as a free download.

It seemed simple enough: Students would need to write and revise their pieces, Becky would compile the articles, and then together we would find a way to actually get people in the neighborhood to read it.

In language arts, students began by choosing their topics. If we wanted a book that told the truth and sang justice, we knew kids were going to have to love their topics. To prepare, Becky pulled out all of the readings, images, and classwork from the past two months, and then asked students to do the same as they entered class.

"What histories live in our neighborhood that shouldn't be forgotten?" she asked. "What do we want new people in the neighborhood to know about how gentrification has happened in our neighborhood?" She asked students to reflect on their own as they looked through their body of work. After a few minutes, she broke the quiet of the room and asked students to begin writing names of people, places, or events that were possible chapters for our book.

She circulated, noticing what students were scribbling.

Jayla wrote: Aunt Vera, Williams Avenue

Jada wrote: jazz, Cotton Club, Vanport, Dr. Unthank

Zion wrote: I-5 freeway project, the Rose Garden

Malena wrote: eminent domain, Legacy Emanuel Hospital

When most students had finished, Becky directed them: "In a moment, I would like you to get up and move around the room. Read your lists with a few different people and then decide on the story you really want to write."

Chairs scraped and the room got loud. Students shared their lists and began to discuss their topics. To encourage students to say more about their topics and stay focused, Becky wrote two sentence starters on the board:

> I want readers to know. . .
> This topic is important to tell because. . .

"I want to write about Vanport because so many people died," Michael told a friend.

"I want readers to know that only white men got free land from the government in the Donation Land Act," Zion decided.

Eventually, discussions petered out and students returned to their seats. Becky projected a document titled "Albina Research Topics" and instructed students: "When you're ready, raise your hand and I'll write your topic on the board." What emerged was the rough draft of the table of contents of our book, *Albina Stories*. It was fairly even-

> **"What histories live in our neighborhood that shouldn't be forgotten?" she asked. "What do we want new people in the neighborhood to know about how gentrification has happened in our neighborhood?"**

ly divided between important historical places that showed the historic culture of the neighborhood, racist and unfair policies that paved the way for our neighborhood's destruction, and biographies of people who worked for change. Students were curating the story of who had been left out and who benefited.

As we dug into the nitty-gritty of research and writing, Becky encouraged a few students to craft a foreword and an afterword to our historical compilation. These students had stepped up to the plate as leaders in this conversation and appeared ready to help guide their peers. Becky asked them to read the foreword and afterword of *The History of Portland's African American Community*, and to think about the purpose of these parts of a book. What do authors try to get across to their readers and how do they reflect on their own research?

A few days later, Becky sat down to read what Cayden had written:

> This book was written to enlighten people of the history of Portland and explicitly the Albina neighborhood. It goes back to before Oregon was a state and ends in 2014. Our research has come from a wide array of sources, from articles and essays to images and journals. This book isn't just informative, it has the views of the writers and their feelings about the topic. Whether it's gentrification or eminent domain, our views of right and wrong are expressed.
>
> Prejudice and discrimination against the minorities in Portland started before Oregon was even a state. Whites who wanted nothing to do with African Americans moved out west. . . . One of them remarked that he had come to Oregon to get rid of "saucy free Negroes." When Oregon became a state, the legislative committee created exclusion laws to keep African Americans from living in Oregon. Although these laws are no longer a part of the state constitution, we still feel the effects of this unequal treatment.

Cayden's writing was reflective of what powerful research does: It makes us question our assumptions by voicing truth, not just facts. Classroom research is about how teachers and students relate to the world, about developing an informed voice and working together to question, to challenge, to talk back, and to encourage change.

"Know Your History"

The final product was a sleek multimedia project that included video interviews, short narratives, informational articles, and an abundance of pictures. Fifty-eight different projects filled the "pages" of the digital book. But months slipped by, and we realized we had never actually sent it out into the world or asked students to turn their knowledge, opinions, and emotions into action.

"We're going to circle back to something we did a little while ago," Jeff said, as he pointed to the iPad cart in the corner. "Get a partner. Send one student per group to the cart to grab an iPad."

He handed each student a graphic organizer with instructions for how to access the *Albina Stories* iBook. The plan was to reacquaint students with the contents of the book, get them to draw connections between a few articles, and ask them how they would get someone else excited about the articles. The students had other ideas.

"Tiana! Read mine!" MyKayla shouted across the room.

"I can't believe I wrote that! Are we going to get to work on these?" asked Tiana.

"Sure, if that's what you decide to do," Jeff responded.

"My name is spelled wrong!" complained Malik.

"This looks really nice," said Alexis.

After fighting the momentum and trying to pull students back to the graphic organizer, Jeff decided to step back and watch. The classroom was loud, it was buzzing, the students were on task, and the graphic organizers were getting done, slowly.

What was supposed to be a half-hour lesson turned into 50 minutes, and Jeff wrapped up by bringing the class back together and assigning a task to keep the project on track: "This is a remarkable book. You all did incredible work. How do we get people to read it? Throw out some ideas, and let's make a list. You can do anything you want, as long as it is focused, and as long as it promotes *Albina Stories*."

It felt risky giving students so much freedom, but the ideas that came back were solid. Yes, there were a few student groups that decided to "make a poster," but the vast majority took divergent and exciting paths — a letter to President Obama and our district superintendent, social media promotion, T-shirts and hats promoting the book and expressing opinions on gentrification. For some groups, the poster turned into an opportunity to canvass the neighborhood, staple fliers to telephone poles, and hand them out on the street. "Gentrification destroys communities!" exclaimed Jasmine's poster.

> The students settled on an answer: Yes, we should tell them. We should tell the stories of urban renewal, of Legacy Emanuel Hospital, of a vibrant Black middle class. We should tell the stories of Vanport. We should tell them that exclusion laws, codified by Chief Justice Reuben P. Boise, our school's namesake, required beatings for African Americans caught living in the state. The students wanted to tell it all.

Alexis decided on letter writing. In a letter to President Obama, she wrote about our school, the negative impact of gentrification, and *Albina Stories*. Then she hammered it home with specific policy requests, advocating for fair housing laws and rent control. In another letter, to the Portland superintendent of schools, she requested that the school district use our book to teach the history of race in our city.

One group decided to use the opportunity to fundraise for our school's end-of-the-year activities. They baked a ton of cookies, made 50 fliers advertising *Albina Stories*, and based themselves outside Jada's mom's beauty shop, located a handful of blocks from the school. They raised more money in an hour and a half than any of our in-school fundraisers.

The students returned to school buzzing about the conversations and connections they had experienced.

"Mr. Waters, come look at this," Chris called from across the computer lab. Chris, Kareem, Malik, and Michael were huddled around the screen.

"What is it?" Jeff asked.

"It's our Facebook page for the book. We have more than 100 likes."

"How many of those are students at our school?"

"Not very many. Some are from other schools. Some are people we don't even know," said Kareem. Even the local neighborhood association expressed an interest in sharing the book on their website.

At our spring open house and 5th-grade night, Becky set up her classroom with computers so students could share *Albina Stories* with parents and families. Families hovered over the devices, flipping through pages, as students explained the interviews, pictures, and essays.

Throughout the unit, we had struggled to answer the question "To what end?" Through the community action project, this came into focus. We had helped students understand the history of racism in our city, brought their families into the process, given them space to reflect on their own experiences, and helped them take responsibility and feel empowered.

The quality of student work argues against the narrative of a failing school and disengaged students of color. As students and their families continue to be forced to move miles away from the historical Black center of Portland, our students joined their voices with many other local activists and community members to expose the policies that support the rich and white in our community, and punish people of color. Our middle schoolers became community changemakers. ∎

Becky HenkleBerry taught both elementary and middle grades for 10 years. She currently serves as an assistant principal with Portland Public Schools. Jeff Waters is an educator, organizer, and community justice advocate. He focuses on engaging school communities in democratic dialogue.

RESOURCES

Boise-Eliot/Humboldt School. 2015. *Albina Stories*. goo.gl/9pFWaO. This is the student publication referenced in the article.

Gibson, Karen J. 2007. "Bleeding Albina: A History of Community Disinvestment, 1940–2000," *Transforming Anthropology*. kingneighborhood. goo.gl/1137KV

Pappas, Peter. 2014. *Portland's Japantown Revealed*. itunes.apple.com/us/book/portlands-japantown-revealed/id887076348?mt=13

Oregon Public Broadcasting. 1999. *Local Color*. goo.gl/PVX8B

Parks, Casey. 2012. "Fifty years later, Legacy Emanuel Medical Center attempts to make amends for razing neighborhood." *Oregon Live*. oregonlive.com/portland/index.ssf/2012/09/post_273.html

Portland Bureau of Planning. 1993. *The History of Portland's African American Community, 1805 to the Present*. multco.us/file/15283/download

What Do You Mean When You Say Urban?

Speaking honestly about race and students

By Dyan Watson

SHANNON WRIGHT

Ethnic, inner city, urban. What do these terms mean in education? I am a teacher educator who studies how people use language to talk about race. One word that I've examined over the years is *urban*. A quick look in the dictionary, and there is no surprise: Urban means related to the city, characteristic of a city or city life. So what does that mean when we say urban education? What is unique about city schools or city education? That depends on the city you're talking about. In large, densely populated cities, such as Boston, New York, and Los Angeles, city schools are often characterized by large, diverse populations, many poor students, budget shortfalls, and bureaucracy. So why, then, do we use the term *urban* when what we really mean are schools with majority Black and Latinx populations?

Take for example my city: Portland, Oregon. Downtown there is a high school named Lincoln. It is less than a mile from the Pearl District, a hip place that boasts unique food, shops, new condos, and the best of urban renewal. It is a stone's throw from a soccer stadium and surrounded by tall buildings, people biking to work in suits, panhandlers, and the hub of the public transit system.

Across the river in North Portland, there is a high school named Jefferson. It is surrounded by family dwellings, mom-and-pop shops, and wide streets for biking, walking, and playing. There is a community college across the street.

Which one of these schools is urban? Lincoln? Jefferson? Both?

Before you decide, let me give you a bit more information. At Lincoln, the downtown school, the population is more than 75 percent white, 4.5 percent of the students are Black, 8.6 percent are Asian, and 6.6 percent are Latinx; 10.5 percent are on free/reduced lunch; and the school does not receive Title 1 funding. At Jefferson, the school across the river, 59 percent of the students are Black, 8 percent are Asian/Pacific Islanders, and 17 percent are Latinx; 70 percent are on free/reduced lunch; and the school does receive Title 1 funding.

Made up your mind yet?

A few years ago I interviewed 17 teachers who attended an "urban education" program. I asked them what was the difference, if any, between urban teaching and non-urban teaching. Ruth remarked: "To me, urban students come from an environment where they can't see the value of education. They can't see why it matters, because everyone who they know, everything that they do, has nothing to do with having an education."

> So why, then, do we use the term urban when what we really mean are schools with majority Black and Latinix populations?

Thinking about the definition of urban — related to the city — I can't help but wonder: What is it about city kids that makes this teacher think they don't value education? It wasn't until after three interviews of each teacher that the whole picture emerged, one in which urban was constructed as a code word for race — specifically Black and Latinx — and often for poor. Teachers equated urban with students of color and the characteristics they perceived as belonging to students of color.

At one point I asked these teachers what *urban* meant and the most often cited response was "racially diverse students." Now taken as is, this would mean students of a multitude of races — including whites. But it was clear from these interviews that "racially diverse" excluded white students and often left Asian Americans and Native Americans on the side as well.

As Molly noted: "My teacher education program definitely prepared me to be a teacher. I think my school placement prepared me to be an urban teacher. Had I been in the exact same university classes, but had a school placement in Lake Genesis [a majority white high school], I wouldn't have been prepared to be an urban teacher."

I wonder, which parts of good teaching translate into all types of schools and which parts don't? What's urban about urban teaching?

Some years ago I presented this research to preservice teachers. One of them challenged me. "But that is how they act. Urban kids don't want to learn as much as the other students in class. Their parents don't care as much, they don't arrive at school on time, and they don't get their homework done. So these teachers are just responding to reality. I see it at North High School all the time."

Reflecting on this, I thought about how he separated his students — all of whom were from the local neighborhood — into two categories: urban and normal. Then I thought, oh yeah, urban means *less than*. The kids who are doing well, the kids who know how to do school, are normal. And the kids who don't know how to do school are urban.

Does it matter what language we use? It only matters if you are going to use it to mask your feelings — overly positive or negative — about a certain race or economic group. This is no time for euphemisms and unexamined beliefs about race. Our schools are deeply divided along racial and class lines. We need teachers who will examine themselves as racial beings who teach other racial beings and figure out what they are doing wrong and what they are doing right.

What would it look like to use race words (e.g., African American, European American, Korean American) when thinking about your classroom and curriculum? You might test yourself by starting to use "Black" when you really mean it instead of low achieving, underserved, at-risk, our kids, those kids, inner city — or urban.

So what do you mean when you say urban? ∎

> We need teachers who will examine themselves as racial beings who teach other racial beings and figure out what they are doing wrong and what they are doing right.

Dyan Watson, an editor for Rethinking Schools, *is an associate professor in teacher education at the Lewis & Clark Graduate School of Education and Counseling. She is also one of the co-editors of the popular book for teachers,* Rhythm and Resistance: Teaching Poetry for Social Justice.

Vacancies to Fill

Considering desire in the past and future of Chicago's vacant schools

By Eve L. Ewing

The late afternoon light coming west on 51st Street lends a gilded edge to the leaves scattered along the sidewalk, reminding me that we are approaching the time photographers refer to as the "golden hour" — when the sun sits in a way that makes even the most unadorned landscapes appear a little bit special, a little bit magical. Everything glows. In this light, the marquee sign posted in front of Crispus Attucks Community Academy seems fitting: "EVERY CHILD IS A PROMISE," it reads in bold, black capital letters. "EVERY CHILD IS A STAR." The day is unseasonably warm for autumn in Chicago, and it's around 4 o'clock in the afternoon, when one might expect to see parents and children coming and going for after-school activities. But the windows are all obscured — some with blinds, others with what looks like taped-up white butcher paper or tarp. A flagpole stands at attention in front of the door, bereft of a flag.

> Is this Crispus Attucks Community Academy? Is it John Farren Public School? Or is it a vacant building? The somewhat paradoxical answer is that it is all three.

The opposite side of the marquee reads "CONGRATULATIONS 2015" and below that "LOVE ALL." And on the southwest face of the building, just above the stone marking the date the building was constructed — 1960 — is a large sign reading "For Sale" in white and emerald green, with the names and contact information for a realtor. The building is vacant. The "For Sale" sign is bolted into the brick, but peeking out from underneath it is the gray cement surface of another sign. That sign identifies the building as John Farren Public School.

Taken together, these signifiers seem to tell conflicting stories. Is this Crispus Attucks Community Academy? Is it John Farren Public School? Or is it a vacant building? The somewhat paradoxical answer is that it is all three. And the present state of the building — a vacant structure abutted on two corners by vacant lots — gestures toward a troubling past, one marked by segregation and rapid change in a city marked by one of the most disturbingly racist histories in America.

Spaces of Possibility

In 2013, parents, teachers, students, and community members across the city of Chicago received some shocking news. Chicago Public Schools (CPS), the third-largest district in the country, was planning on closing 50 schools at the end of the academic year. The stated reason was that the school buildings were "underutilized" — they had been constructed to serve far more children than were now enrolled.[1] The city has experienced tremendous depopulation associated with decreased in-migration, political woes, violence and safety concerns, and the demolition of public housing. District officials claimed that by closing and repurposing the schools, they could save millions of dollars — no small feat given CPS's budget deficit of more than a billion dollars.[2] Critics said that such estimates were flawed, and, perhaps more importantly, that school closures would disrupt the lives of thousands of children. But despite vehement protests and recommendations from independent judges tasked with reviewing the proposed closures that several of the schools remain open, the closings proceeded. Almost 11,000 students, 88 percent of them Black, were reassigned to attend another school, deemed a "welcoming" school by the district even though in many cases there were tensions and even hostilities between the old school and the new.[3]

> **Given that the closed schools are situated almost exclusively in economically depressed areas, any of these reuses could be of potentially tremendous benefit to Chicagoans in need.**
>
> **But in order for these possibilities to come to fruition, someone would actually have to buy the buildings.**

And what would become of the vacant schools? Mayor Rahm Emanuel appointed an Advisory Committee for School Repurposing and Community Development, charged with devising a process and set of standards for determining the future of the buildings. They were to be sold on the private market to anyone who wanted them — if they could meet a set of basic criteria, including demonstrated experience in implementing similar projects, and demonstrated support from the community surrounding the building. Further, any proposals to repurpose an empty building should offer a benefit to the community, "such as employment opportunities, healthcare, housing, access to fresh produce, etc."[4] The committee went so far as to name potential reuses that had already been discussed by unspecified "interested parties," including urban farming, tutoring and mentoring, affordable housing, a health clinic, or a community arts center. Given that the closed schools are situated almost exclusively in economically depressed areas, any of these reuses could be of potentially tremendous benefit to Chicagoans in need.

But in order for these possibilities to come to fruition, someone would actually have to buy the buildings.

Socioeconomic Characteristics of Communities Housing Vacant Schools

School[a]	Community Area	Per Capita Income[b]	Unemployment Rate[b]	Percent Black[c]
Buckingham	Calumet Heights	$28,887	20	93
Burnham	South Deering	$14,685	16.3	62.4
Earle	West Englewood	$11,317	35.9	94
Emmet	Austin	$15,957	22.6	84.2
Fiske	Woodlawn	$18,672	23.4	84.8
Goldblatt	West Garfield Park	$10,934	25.8	95.7
Henson	North Lawndale	$12,034	21.2	90
Key	Austin	$15,957	22.6	84.2
King	Near West Side	$44,689	10.7	30.2
Kohn	Roseland	$17,949	20.3	96.7
Mays	Englewood	$11,888	28	95.4
Melody	West Garfield Park	$10,934	25.8	95.7
Morgan	Auburn Gresham	$15,528	28.3	97
Paderewski	South Lawndale	$10,402	15.8	11.8
Parkman	Fuller Park	$10,432	33.9	87.5
Pershing	Douglas	$23,791	18.2	71.1
Ross	Washington Park	$13,785	28.6	95
Songhai	West Pullman	$16,563	19.4	93.4
Woods	West Englewood	$11,317	35.9	94
City of Chicago	-	$28,202	12.9	31.5

a: Building vacant as of June 2017 (Belsha & Kiefer, 2017). b: Based on 2008–2012 Census data (City of Chicago, 2011). c: Chicago Metropolitan Agency for Planning, 2016

Persistent Vacancies

As of this writing, four years after the closures, only five of the 43 available buildings have been successfully repurposed.[5] Buyers with the adequate capital to purchase and repurpose a building are, it seems, not interested in investing in the communities where the vacant schools are located. And with maintenance costs averaging from $100,000 to $300,000 a year, the buildings may be out of reach for the kind of community-facing organizations described by the Advisory Committee.

This challenge should not come as a surprise. In 2011, the Pew Charitable Trusts released a report analyzing the process and outcomes of school closures in six urban centers in an effort to provide guidance to the city of Philadelphia, which was considering its own potential school closures. The authors of the report highlighted the difficulties of selling vacant schools as a major finding, noting that "a lot of closed school buildings are tough sells, even in the best of times," and "districts have struggled to balance community desires with market realities."[6] In Chicago, the buildings are almost all located in Black communities, and the average per capita income in the community areas surrounding the vacant buildings is $16,650, with an average unemployment rate of 23.8 percent — about 1.8 times the city average.

But years have passed, and as the vacant buildings remain unsold, they have become an additional burden on communities that are already vulnerable. Residents have complained, filed police reports, and captured footage in response to vandalism, stolen copper pipes and wiring, broken windows, stolen fixtures, and pipes that have burst in response to brutal winters.[7] Such physical distress makes it hard to imagine them as fruitful spaces for potential real estate investment, and adds blight to landscapes that in many cases are already beset with vacant lots and boarded-up homes.

Who could want such buildings? The challenge of selling the schools reveals something fascinating, and perhaps also saddening, about the nature of *desire* when it comes to urban landscapes, and how we might understand desire in relation to something like market value. In a sense, the empty buildings hold two distinct levels of value, which are wildly disparate: their [low] value in a private market largely dominated by hegemonic streams of capital and investment, and their [high] value in the eyes of the communities that surround them — communities that have imbued the buildings with tremendous symbolic value as vessels of tradition and memory, as well as practical value as potential venues for desperately needed resources. The notion of a building in an urban space as *desirable* or not, and the consideration of *whose* desires we mean, thus becomes a contested question.

Behind the Boarded-Up Windows

On the Near West Side, about eight miles northeast of Attucks, father of two Demetrius Amparan walks with me around what was once King Elementary. Plywood, looking darkened and worn by the harsh Chicago weather, blocks the doors and the windows. "The school was so ingrained in the community," Amparan tells me. We continue down the block. "The old houses, these people have been there for 50 years. You talk to some of them, and they're in denial about what was going on around them. When the schools were closing, it was a shock. They were like, 'damn, we didn't think this could actually happen! No one finna come on our block!' . . . The parents were freaking out."

As early as 1930, Black people in Chicago "led the way" in spatial isolation among American cities, hemmed into specific regions of the city by redlining and threats of physical violence.

This formulation, of the block as *our block* and the specter of outsiders invading to commandeer homes or schools, makes a certain kind of sense given the history of the area surrounding King Elementary. The school is neighbored on the north by the Eisenhower Expressway, on the northeast by the United Center (the largest indoor sports arena in the United States) and on the east by the University of Illinois at Chicago campus. Each of these developments, in its time, has played a role in threatening Near West Side residents with displacement. The Eisenhower, known locally as the "Ike," displaced 13,000 people and 400 businesses by the time it was completed in 1961.[8] Throughout the 1960s, government agencies purchased 238 acres of land in the area, of which then-mayor Richard J. Daley secretly committed 100 acres to the construction of the university, while publicly denying any such plans.

"This is an area that has really been battered by waves of redevelopment. And it was the historic gateway to a thriving African American neighborhood. Mostly working class, but along Madison Street you had a lot of independently owned stores," said Rachel Weber of the Great Cities Institute in a 2011 interview.[9] Now, the neighborhood is just one-third Black, making it an outlier among the areas that are home to vacant schools.

As countless scholars and activists have documented, racism and segregation have cemented years of compounded immobility, neglect, and disadvantage onto Chicago's Black neighborhoods, and maintained fierce social boundaries between those neighborhoods and the areas surrounding them. As early as 1930, Black people in Chicago "led the way" in spatial isolation among American cities, hemmed into specific regions of the city by redlining and threats of physical violence against those who dared venture beyond their prescribed borders.[10]

Realtors also took advantage of the fact that banks would refuse to provide mortgages to would-be Black homeowners by offering loans with extremely high down payments and interest rates, taking a cash advance, encouraging families to buy homes beyond their means, then evicting them summarily when they were unable to pay. And long after restrictive covenants were struck down by the courts in 1948, realtors continued to use various methods to keep from selling to Black people looking to move into white neighborhoods; one study using surveys and interviews with realtors identified 26 different methods realtors used, including flat-out refusing to show a property or lying and saying it was no longer available. By 1970, the dissimilarity index (the proportion of people who would have to move in order to achieve desegregation in an area) in Chicago was 91.9, the highest among America's 30 metropolitan areas with the highest Black populations.[11]

While many would consider redlining and restrictive covenants to be relics of a forgotten past, housing discrimination against Black Chicagoans has persisted into eras that we might like to consider more "civilized." Studies in the 1980s found that Black homebuyers were less likely than white homebuyers to be shown available homes, and that they were offered financial information at half the rate of white homebuyers. Today, more insidious forms of housing discrimination exist, such as the widespread practice of landlords illegally refusing to accept housing assistance vouchers as a form of rental payment. This contributes to the trend of Black residents remaining clustered in highly segregated neighborhoods, regardless of their income; even when accounting for socioeconomic status, Black families live in neighborhoods with the highest prevalence of violence and the lowest income levels, and tend to remain in such neighborhoods over intergenerational periods. Sociologist Patrick Sharkey refers to this pattern as the *inherited ghetto*: "the neighborhood environment structures the experiences and opportunities of children in ways that alter their trajectories, with consequences that persist over the individual life course and across generations."[12]

Despite these histories, one might think that the vacant school buildings would be desirable on the private market for other reasons. They are spacious, many are situated close to parks or busy thoroughfares, and many are architecturally impressive. However, there is evidence that when it comes to Black communities, such considerations are immaterial. In a study tracing gentrification in Chicago neighborhoods over time, researchers found that Black and Latinx neighborhoods were less likely to gentrify — and that after the concentration of Black residents in a neighborhood passed a certain threshold, the likelihood of gentrification dropped off sharply. When the proportion of Black residents in the population of a certain area surpassed about 40 percent, it seems that "residents, developers, and institutions may make neighborhood selection decisions using neighborhood stereotyping based simply on a neighborhood having a relatively high proportion of Blacks, believing they have sufficient 'evidence' to make judgments about the neighborhood," the authors explain.[13]

In other words, it should come as no surprise that these school buildings would remain vacant so long after entering the private market. They are situated in neighborhoods that have long been marked by segregation and disinvestment, neighborhoods that constantly receive the message *we do not want you* — marked with a scarlet letter of anti-Black racism that makes them persistently unappealing to many would-be investors.

Visions of the Possible

Nevertheless, for many of the residents who share space with these schools, they are sites of intense desire, imbued in equal parts with the bonds of history and the promise of possibility. Consider King Elementary, for instance. Amparan, who taught a poetry program in the school for a time, gets a faraway look when he talks about it, one that belies the current desolate state of the building. "It was one of the prettiest elementary schools I have ever seen," he says. "King is beautiful. The murals were so beautiful. . . . The principal was so nice, everything was so great, and they had so much pride in their school." When he muses about what the building could become in its post-closure life, Amparan takes on another dreamlike look. "It could be a community haven," he says, "maybe with workshops to teach kids and parents about things like healthy eating, or job training. All the things communities of color are deprived of could be run through there."

While longtime activist Valerie Leonard of the North Lawndale community on the West Side shares Amparan's vision of the vacant school buildings serving the community, she still mourns the loss of the schools themselves. "They were built to be *schools*," she says. "I would love for one of those schools to be open as a high-quality public school. But I know that that won't happen. The politics of that just won't work. So in the absence of that, I would like to see a community center . . . something that would serve multiple buildings for arts and cultural activities, and provide a safe space. Having cultural activities, educational enrichment activities, athletic activities . . . some health facilities as well. We've got a dearth of access to healthcare. I would like to see those types of activities under one roof."

The amenities Leonard dreams of would go to good use in North Lawndale. A half-century ago, Martin Luther King made the West Side community a physical and symbolic headquarters for what would be called the Chicago Freedom Movement. "In the South," said King, "we always had segregationists to help make issues clear. . . . This ghetto Negro [in Northern cities] has been invisible so long and has become visible through violence."[14] King moved himself and his family into a North Lawndale apartment with a broken refrigerator and the persistent smell of urine, for which he paid $90 a month, and he worked with local activists to clean and renovate a nearby building that housed a family living with rats and no heat. While this tradition of community activism continues in the

North Lawndale of today, the neighborhood faces many struggles. The neighborhood has a per capita income of about $12,000, and one in five North Lawndale residents is unemployed. Thirty percent of North Lawndale residents have no high school diploma, and the area has one of the highest incidences of violent crime in the city.[15]

Leonard, whose parents were both public school teachers, has seen North Lawndale's history unfold firsthand. "Growing up, I felt like the school communities were part of our families," she says. "We had great schools right in North Lawndale. And to see where children are now compared to where we were then hurts my heart." In Leonard's view, the set of recommendations the mayor's committee prepared for repurposing schools is a "beautiful document," one that would serve as a helpful guide in making sure the vacant buildings found appropriate new uses — if it were adhered to. Leonard has found the repurposing process "disappointing," and places blame in the city's history of valuing patronage and nepotism over transparency and democracy. "It's the Chicago Way," she says. "It's the way it's always been done. . . . And we are a low capacity, low-income community. But people like to feel like they're part of the process." Instead, says Leonard, North Lawndale residents have the sense that decisions are being made behind closed doors, without their input being heard.

> "Growing up, I felt like the school communities were part of our families," she says. "We had great schools right in North Lawndale. And to see where children are now compared to where we were then hurts my heart."

Another North Lawndale resident, engineer Frank Bergh, is still relatively new to Chicago. Bergh, one of the 2 percent of North Lawndale residents who are white, moved to the community in 2012 because of an interest in the neighborhood's role in fair housing struggles. But he has been here long enough that, like Leonard, he has come to see the management of the school closures as more than carelessness, but as a symptom of a deeper corruption. Bergh's back door looks out onto Pope Elementary. Nearby are the Albany Park townhomes — the only gated community in North Lawndale, where Alderman Michael Scott Jr. lives. "This entire block is nothing but a closed school and a gated community next to Douglas Park," Bergh says. "Which, to me, is like . . . that's why you closed the school." Bergh believes that the closure was part of a broader plan to displace low-income Black residents from the neighborhood and develop it as a hub for new housing and activities directed primarily at white people — activities like Riot Fest, the punk rock music festival that moved to Douglas Park in 2015 and brought mostly white concertgoers who residents said "turned their noses up" at North Lawndale.[16]

One day, Bergh was riding his bicycle by Pope and was amazed to see something new and unfamiliar: a bevy of children chattering as they lined up to enter the building, and signs touting course subjects like chemistry and ethics. He was thrilled, thinking that perhaps the school building had been re-engaged for some sort of educational program

— until he realized it was all a façade. The building was being contracted for the day to shoot a school scene in an episode of a television show. It felt like a cruel joke.

"I've fantasized about cutting the lock [on the fence] and installing some basketball hoops," he laughs. "I often ask myself, *what if*? What would it be like to see children coming and going here? To see school buses lined up every day? The block can feel very desolate." He refers to these feelings of sadness and frustration as the real "carnage of closed schools" — the consternation of seeing a potential community hub unused in a community that truly needs it.

The Cost of Dreams

For generations, schools and school buildings have held tremendous symbolic value that transcends their ostensible purpose. Schools are community centers, markers of identity, pathways to participation in the project of democracy. In schools, we vote, we cheer on *our* team, we shelter from tornadoes and hurricanes. And in this era of their lives, the buildings that once served as schools all over Chicago's South and West Sides are at once sites of foreclosure and infinite possibility. With their primary function stripped away, in the absence of a clear purpose, the buildings have arguably the most promise that they have ever had. As Amparan frames it, there is imaginative space for "all the things" to take up residence. In this way, the vacant buildings represent at once a manifestation of everything wrong with the schools and the city — "the Chicago Way," as Leonard notes — and vessels for community desire. They are catalysts for community members to reflect on all the years of malfeasance, and all the resources worth dreaming of.

However, the very people for whom the schools have the most value are also the people for whom the material capital to invest is least likely to manifest. As schools, King and Pope had annual maintenance costs of $234,233 and $277,500 respectively.[17] Potential buyers would need to be able to not only establish a winning bid for the cost of the building itself, but have some assurance that they would be able to maintain the building in addition to programming costs for whatever its reuse might be. Furthermore, the buildings require various degrees of renovation to even make them habitable after four years of sitting, unused, through heat waves and blizzards, as well as theft of major appliances, pipes, and wiring.

> For generations, schools and school buildings have held tremendous symbolic value that transcends their ostensible purpose.

Now that CPS has opened the building bidding process to nationwide investors, Alderman Chris Taliaferro, a city legislator whose ward includes the Austin neighborhood, is worried that community organizations with a true vision for accountable repurposing will be outbid by out-of-towners who have the capital to buy a building, but not the commitment to community desires — or that local leaders will be able to purchase a building, but unable to keep it up. "It would be great for people within the community to be able to buy the buildings, but people may not be able to do so because of limited resources," he says.

Nakisha Hobbs, principal and co-founder of the independent Village Leadership Academy, has experienced this challenge firsthand. Village Leadership Academy is a social justice-focused school serving Black youth from the South and West Sides, and Hobbs thought there might be a good opportunity to move the school closer to where most of her students live. Hobbs herself grew up in Austin, and now lives in North Lawndale; she says she and her students were "devastated" to see schools in these communities closing and the impact of the closures on Black children. But Hobbs also thought that repurposing one of the buildings as a new home for VLA could be good for both the school and the community. She reached out to the alderman, and then the private company that manages the school bidding process, with the hopes of bidding on the Drake Elementary building on the South Side. But despite the fact that the bidding is supposed to be an open process, Hobbs feels that "it was very evident that there was some behind-the-scenes dealing" between then-alderman Will Burns and the electricians' union, which ultimately won the bid for the building. Hobbs says that in doing research for her own bid, a local contractor told her the union already had a deal with the alderman to acquire Drake. "I feel like the whole damn thing is rigged," Hobbs says. "They had an open meeting, and the co-founder of [VLA] went to that meeting. And at that meeting there were other folks there who know how things work, and they said 'all these buildings are earmarked for people,' except for the ones further west." Like Leonard and Bergh, Hobbs is disillusioned with this way of doing things — the "Chicago Way," where some people "know how things work" and those people have an inside track into making decisions with people in power while those who are impacted are excluded from the process. "I think there are people who have stronger relationships with the mayor, and he is figuring out ways to get the more prime real estate properties into the hands of those folks."

"No one is willing to invest in these communities. These are forgotten communities. Forgotten spaces . . . forgotten people."

Aside from the outcome on the Drake bidding process, Hobbs' frustration is rooted in a deeper concern about the communities she calls home, and how vacant school buildings are affecting the people who live there. "I was in Austin, driving through my old community, and there is a building right at the corner of Central and Madison. It's a huge school building [Goldblatt Elementary] that is literally boarded up. And seeing a school building on the corner boarded up moved me to tears. It got me thinking, what kind of message does it send to the children? To the residents of this community? That a space or place that should be open for learning or activities is not even open or available to us anymore. Seeing those empty buildings is just kind of devastating to the psyche of the community." Hobbs worries that the presence of these buildings is like the physical manifestation of a dream deferred — a daily reminder of all the ways the struggles of Chicago's poor Black communities can seem insurmountable. "People feel like they have less agency. There are folks who engaged in struggle to keep those buildings open, and they lost. And those are the same communities where there is the most violence. . . . No one is willing to invest in these communities. These are forgotten communities. Forgotten spaces . . . forgotten people."

Living in Ruins: Maintaining Space for Desire

As we consider the histories of cities like Chicago, histories mired with racism and inequality, the question of *desire* is a critical one if we are to retain any hope in the possibility of social transformation. In "Suspending Damage: A Letter to Communities," scholar Eve Tuck calls on us to consider not only the ways in which communities have been "broken and conquered," but also their desires: "the hope, the visions, the wisdom of lived lives and communities."[18] Desire, Tuck writes, "is about longing, about a present that is enriched by both the past and the future. It is integral to our humanness." While it is clear that school closure and the aftermath of vacancies have enacted immense damage on communities, it is also integral that we understand the desire of those who have been harmed — a desire that remains resilient in the face of continued dismissal. In a sense, for residents of these communities, the buildings are not "vacant" at all. Rather, they are endowed with the ghostly recollections of the past, which in turn offer the foundation for a richer future. As I have written elsewhere,[19] such desire transcends the boundaries of linear time; when residents see a closed school, they see it not just as it is — a boarded-up building — but as it was. And they see the buildings as they could be. In this way, to view the buildings is to look across time and space, across harms done and lingering hope for a remedy.

For these citizens, led by their desires, the imaginative possibilities are as endless as the list of transgressions that have come before. In the book *Architecture After Revolution*, authors Alessandro Petti, Eyal Weizman, and Sandi Hilal consider the ways in which Palestinians engaged in a struggle for resistance and freedom must engage the physical landscape, which is marked with the artifices of the military. Such structures, they write, "are not only the dead matter of past power, but could be thought of as material for reappropriations and strategic activism within the politics of the present. The question is how people might live with and in ruins."[20] As Black Chicagoans live with vacant school buildings as a sort of ruin, the very emptiness itself — in other words, a void, a space, an opening — poses an invitation for something new to emerge from the misuses of past power.

Until then, they remain vacant. ■

Eve L. Ewing is a sociologist of education and a writer from Chicago. She is the author of Electric Arches *and* Ghosts in the Schoolyard: Racism and School Closings on Chicago's South Side *and the co-author of* No Blue Memories: The Life of Gwendolyn Brooks. *She is a scholar at the University of Chicago School of Social Service Administration. Her work has been published in the* New Yorker, *the* Atlantic, *the* New York Times, *and many other venues.*

ENDNOTES

[1] Karp, Sarah. 2012. "Under-Utilized Schools Continue to Shed Students: Map." *The Chicago Reporter*. Dec. 5. chicagoreporter.com/under-utilized-schools-continue-shed-students-map/

[2] Strauss, Valerie. 2013. "Chicago Closing 54 Schools; Union Leader Blasts 'Outrageous' Plan." *Washington Post*. March 21. washingtonpost.com/news/answer-sheet/wp/2013/03/21/chicago-closing-54-schools-union-leader-blasts-outrageous-plan/?utm_term=.dd3f6a1e39b9

[3] Kelleher, James B., and Mary Wisniewski. March 21, 2013. "Chicago Announces Mass Closing of Elementary Schools," *Reuters*. reuters.com/article/us-usa-education-chicago/chicago-announces-mass-closing-of-elementary-schools-idUSBRE92K1CI20130322

[4] Chicago Public Schools. 2014. "Proposal Requirements." Aug. 20. cps.edu/Pages/proposalrequirements.aspx

[5] Belsha, Kalyn, and Matt Kiefer. 2017. "What Happened to the Closed School in Your Neighborhood?" *The Chicago Reporter*. Sept. 19. chicagoreporter.com/what-happened-to-the-closed-school-in-your-neighborhood/

[6] Pew Charitable Trusts. 2013. *Shuttered Public Schools: The Struggle to Bring Old Buildings New Life*. Feb. 11. pewtrusts.org/~/media/assets/2013/02/11/philadelphia_school_closings_report.pdf ?la=en

[7] Nitkin, Alex, and Lorraine Forte. 2015. "Vacant Schools Still Waiting for a Second Life," *The Chicago Reporter*. March 30. chicagoreporter.com/vacant-schools-still-waiting-for-a-second-life/

[8] Loerzel, Robert. 2016. "Displaced: When the Eisenhower Expressway Moved In, Who Was Forced Out?" *WBEZ.org*. Aug. 28. interactive.wbez.org/curiouscity/eisenhower/

[9] Rachel Weber, interview by Alison Cuddy. 2011. "Examining How the United Center Has Impacted Chicago's Near West Side." *Eight Forty-Eight*. WBEZ Chicago. May 9. wbez.org/shows/eight-fortyeight/examining-how-the-united-center-has-impacted-chicagos-near-west-side/1bcb28b4-893c-4682-86e6-a480e2c825c6

[10] Ewing, Eve L. 2015. "'We Shall Not Be Moved': A Hunger Strike, Education, and Housing in Chicago." *The New Yorker*. Sept. 21. newyorker.com/news/news-desk/we-shall-not-be-moved-a-hunger-strike-education-and-housing-in-chicago

[11] Massey, Douglas S., and Nancy A. Denton. 1993. *American Apartheid*. Cambridge, MA: Harvard University Press.

[12] Sharkey, Patrick. 2003. *Stuck in Place: Urban Neighborhoods and the End of Progress Toward Racial Equality*. Chicago: University of Chicago Press.

[13] Hwang, Jackelyn, and Robert J. Sampson. 2014. "Divergent Pathways of Gentrification: Racial Inequality and the Social Order of Renewal in Chicago Neighborhoods." *American Sociological Review* 79, no. 4: 726–751. doi: 10.1177/0003122414535774.

[14] "Chicago Campaign (1996)." 2018. *King Encyclopedia*. Accessed Jan. 19. kingencyclopedia.stanford.edu/encyclopedia/encyclopedia/enc_chicago_campaign/

[15] "Crime in Chicago." 2018. *The Chicago Tribune*. Last modified Jan. 9. chicagotribune.com/ct-crime-in-chicago-20171114-storygallery.html

[16] Moore, Evan F. 2016. "Douglas Park Neighbors Have Mixed Emotions on Riot Fest After Year Two." Sept. 19. *DNAinfo*. dnainfo.com/chicago/20160919/north-lawndale/douglas-park-neighbors-have-mixed-emotion-on-riot-fest-after-year-two

[17] "2013 School Actions Building Repurposing and Sale Process." 2017. *Chicago Public Schools*. Last modified Aug. 22. cps.edu/Pages/schoolrepurposing.aspx

[18] Tuck, Eve. 2009. "Suspending Damage: A Letter to Communities." *Harvard Educational Review* 79, no. 3. hepg.org/her-home/issues/harvard-educational-review-volume-79-issue-3/herarticle/a-letter-to-communities_739

[19] Ewing, Eve L. 2015. "Phantoms Playing Double-Dutch: Why the Fight for Dyett Is Bigger than One Chicago School Closing." *Seven Scribes*. Aug. 26. sevenscribes.com/phantoms-playing-double-dutch-why-the-fight-for-dyett-is-bigger-than-one-chicago-school-closing

[20] Petti, Alessandro, Eyal Weizman, and Sandi Hilal. 2013. *Architecture After Revolution*. Berlin: Sternberg Press.

Plotting Inequalities, Building Resistance

By Adam Renner, Bridget Brew, and Crystal Proctor

Media depictions of San Francisco show idyllic images of fog pouring under the Golden Gate Bridge or happy tourists riding cable cars, but rarely the mostly non-white neighborhoods of the east side. San Francisco public schools have a bad track record of mimicking this masquerade, with very low numbers of African American and Latina/o students making it to senior year, and less than a quarter of those who do graduating with the credits to move on to college. Our high school, the June Jordan School for Equity (JJSE), is located on the east side of the city, and was started by a group of teachers and parents who were disturbed by the high numbers of Black and Brown youth being underserved and then dropping out. We are an intentionally small school with a focus on social justice.

Our commitment to send students of color to college means that they need a strong math education. As members of the math department, we believe, like Bob Moses, that math literacy in itself is a civil rights issue for students of color. We have seen too many "math haters" end up in remedial classes in college, short-circuiting their career options.

The teachers who helped found our school were mostly from the humanities departments, and it is easier to imagine getting straight to a student's heart and experiences with a great piece of literature or history told from a non-oppressor perspective than it is to imagine the quadratic formula liberating anyone. Part of our school's mission is to help our students become agents of social change, so making explicit connections to social issues in math class is something that we try to do, though many math standards do not make this easy. Our ongoing goal is to develop important math skills while exploring social justice issues that are central to students' lives.

The Scatter Plot Project

No one took making explicit social justice connections more seriously than Adam Renner, who started as a 9th-grade math teacher at JJSE in fall 2010 after many years as a teacher educator at the university level. In one of his first major projects, he had his students use math skills as a way to dig into a deeper understanding of the chasmic divide between rich and poor in our city. He wanted to shed light on the impact of economics and the structures of racism on education, housing, and job opportunities.

Adam began by introducing his students to Zip Skinny, a user-friendly website for finding and comparing data about local communities. (We originally used Zip Skinny but it appears that site might now be unavailable, but there are other similar demographics websites like ZipWho.com.) Our students live primarily in three San Francisco ZIP

MICHAEL DUFFY

codes: the Excelsior, Visitacion Valley, and Bayview/Hunters Point. Along with mining for data in these ZIP codes, Adam selected four other ZIP codes for comparison: the Mission (an eclectic, centrally located neighborhood), the Presidio (one of San Francisco's wealthiest neighborhoods), and the Outer Sunset and Outer Richmond (two neighborhoods along San Francisco's Pacific coast). He asked the students to record in a table the following data: median neighborhood income, percentage of high school completion or higher, percentage of bachelor's completion and higher, unemployment rate, and percentage of non-white residency.

The freshmen had to find these data independently using Zip Skinny. Then, in carefully constructed groups, they had to graph two different sets of data on the same coordinate plane in order to discover the

Math literacy in itself is a civil rights issue for students of color.

relationship between the sets of data. One example of a scatter plot they created was comparing X = median income vs. Y = high school completion; another was X = college completion vs. Y = percentage of non-white residency. In this way, students could see what it means for two circumstances to be related or correlated, but not necessarily by cause and effect. They also saw the difference between a weak correlation (the points are spread out) and a strong correlation (the points are almost in a line), as well as the idea of positive correlation (one circumstance increases with the other) and negative correlation (one circumstance decreases as the other increases). As they were learning the mathematical terms for data analysis, they began to discover that math can describe and order their world.

Seniors as Mentors

Crystal, who teaches probability and statistics, had a class of JJSE seniors who were completing a similar exercise using spreadsheets and the various graphing and analysis functions of Microsoft Excel. We decided to do a group activity with the seniors and the freshmen that would further develop basic math skills like plotting points as well as data analysis. We brought the three JJSE math teachers, the 60 or so freshmen, and the 12 prob/stats seniors together to engage in some cross-class mentoring and jointly discuss these issues.

The mathematical purpose for the seniors was to establish which data would pair well together and to be able to share that information with the freshmen. The mathematical purpose for the freshmen was to understand the spread of data in order to scale and label each axis and to plot points.

The social purpose for both age groups was to work together as a community in order to have conversations about the implications of the data. The data essentially reveal that people in San Francisco have different life experiences based on the neighborhood where they live, and that neighborhood is strongly correlated with race. We wanted our students to have conversations about the statistics that seem to prove the racism that many of them experience, what that means for their communities, and what they might do about it.

Crystal asked the seniors to prepare a short lesson — based on the data that both classes had discovered and analyzed — that would introduce a new variable and help the freshmen create a scatter plot. Her class prepared for teaching the freshmen by spending time in class talking and doing math before meeting with the younger students. She asked the seniors: "What makes a neighborhood?" The students talked about the kinds of specifics that define the character of a neighborhood. For example, they mentioned the number of payday loan stores as well as the demographics (e.g., age, race, gender, education level). Each senior decided which variables to use and created their scatter plots themselves, both by hand and using Excel. This preparation allowed the seniors to feel comfortable with the math that they were about to teach. Crystal did not spend class time talking about how to interact with freshmen, but we will have that conversation when we do this project again in the future. We paired each senior with five or six 9th graders.

On the first day of the project we met in the cafeteria and the seniors led their groups in discussing the data and creating large scatter plot posters. Although the freshmen had been exposed to plotting points on a coordinate plane, the issue of how to scale each axis — "How might we label the X-axis for unemployment, which ranged from 2.1 to 5 percent, differently from how we would label it for median income, which ranged from $37,000 to $740,000?" — requires sophisticated reasoning skills that the seniors had to demonstrate.

Questions about what the data mean, not only how to plot it, led to some rich conversations. One group's data showed that neighborhoods with more women were correlated with less unemployment. Ninth-grader Kari asked Shauna, her senior leader: "Isn't it more normal for women to stay home with kids while men go to work?" Shauna laughed gently: "Who goes to work where you live?" Kari was relying on a stereotype about gender roles that is simply not true in many households. Shauna had learned in her three years at JJSE how the increasing number of men of color in prison has led to neighborhoods where most families are led by women who are the sole support of the household.

On the second day of the project we all met in the library so that groups could complete their scatter plot posters and so that seniors could lead their groups in a discussion about the data. Some of this discussion centered on the math (e.g., how tight was the correlation and was it positive or negative), but the primary focus was conversations about what the data reveal about our city and what, if anything, we can do to shift some of these trends. During the presentations Mimi, a senior, talked about her group's scatter plot, which showed a negative correlation between non-white residents and resident stability (how long people stay in their homes). She said, "Gentrification might be a reason that more non-white people means more moving." In her small group Mimi discussed new condominiums that are being built in the Bayview district that are prohibitively expensive for many families who have lived in that area for multiple generations. Mimi had one of her freshmen speak after her. Although the freshman did not show a clear understanding of gentrification (yet), she was able to talk about plotting the points, which was a new skill for her.

> She said, "Gentrification might be a reason that more non-white people means more moving." In her small group Mimi discussed new condominiums that are being built in the Bayview district that are prohibitively expensive for many families who have lived in that area for multiple generations.

The 9th graders had to consider what it meant when points were close together in a pattern, and what it meant when they were spread out. Sometimes, the data were confusing. There seemed to be a positive correlation between number of kids and wealth of a family, but upon further inspection the freshmen had not scaled the axes correctly, and what one may expect (that more kids means a family has less wealth, at least in most neighborhoods) turned out to be true.

The freshmen were noticeably rapt while being taught by the seniors in ways that they simply are not with us, their teachers. Suddenly the ability to plot and analyze data points became a tool for freshmen to engage with cooler upperclassmen. The seniors did a post-project reflection in their class, and one student wrote, "The freshmen listened to us because we are role models and they respect us, sometimes more than the adults." Another senior observed, "Students who would not participate during class with teachers and other classmates participated with us, which made teachers feel surprised yet excited at the same time." We were.

Bringing the freshmen into the conversation about the intersection of math and social justice was important, but the unintended result of the project was what it taught the seniors. The senior reflections showed that they felt like math scholars and community leaders during this process, even though as freshmen most of them were intimidated and uninterested in math. The seniors were moved by the sense of responsibility that comes with teaching. Marshall wrote: "I felt like a teacher because everyone was listening to me and everyone was looking up to me to understand how to plot points, how to read a graph, and how to compare categories."

What Does It Mean? What Can We Do About It?

The math was straightforward, but the statistics about our neighborhoods were wrought with emotion. They revealed some upsetting truths about our city. In their final analyses, freshmen had the following to say: "The graphs show us that non-white residents of San Francisco have a difficult time with money and finishing high school and continuing to get their bachelor's degrees like white students." Sage's group worried: "It lets us know how the incomes are, and they are really low. It makes us feel bad because we should be getting a higher income and we have no idea what to do about it." Reactions ranged from "Indifferent" to "We don't care about it" to "The graphs show to us the need to start changing for the better." Regarding what to do, some students were equally fatalistic: "No matter what we do, it's not going to change." Others showed a spark of passion and indignation: "It makes you feel like there is racism in San Francisco. It makes us feel bad there are not equal rights. We should make our own city."

The statistics provided both the freshmen and seniors with a tool for discussion, but did not reveal something completely new. We have students who live in a housing project that frequently does not have running water; they turn on MTV to see people their age celebrating birthdays with celebrity entertainers and new cars. Many of our students' lives are characterized by prevalent violence — whether it be the gangs that operate in the neighborhood where our school resides, the complicated way some of our students must travel to school to avoid specific neighborhoods, and/or the cycle of violence in several of our students' families. They enter high school knowing that their lives are different from the media's depiction of an American teenager, and this math lesson just helps explain those differences.

To some it may seem irresponsible to show these statistics to 9th graders. But we trust that our students, even the youngest, can learn about the real circumstances that surround them. In fact, we feel strongly that it is dangerous not to have discussions with students about race and class. They have seen and lived with the injustices for their entire lives, but are programmed to believe that poverty and violence are natural or that members of their communities and families just make bad decisions that lead to these outcomes. By having conversations based on numbers we are giving them the analytical tools to decipher the deluge of these messages, which is a step toward them being able to change the world around them. Math offers us a chance to analyze our world.

> **Students studying the circumstances of their neighborhoods is an activity in community building, and communities in solidarity may be the strongest antidote to some of these statistics.**

This project gave seniors an opportunity to claim ownership of what they have learned about inequities during their time at JJSE. When asked what we should do about these truths, one senior wrote that city officials should really understand these statistics: "It is possible to look at the ZIP codes on their own and act accordingly in each ZIP code, and not lump them all together. One solution for the whole city couldn't possibly help everyone." Another senior vowed: "I want to go to college and earn a degree and come back and help these low-income communities throughout San Francisco to fight against this environmental racism."

As educators we believe that at least part of the solution is people coming together to learn. Students studying the circumstances of their neighborhoods is an activity in community building, and communities in solidarity may be the strongest antidote to some of these statistics.

The inequality students experience is planned; it is plotted. And, so we, in turn, show them how to plot the(ir) inequality to build resistance. We are learning how to study in a way that puts students at the center of the academic experience. They are the curriculum. ■

Bridget Brew (bridgetbrew@gmail.com) is a PhD candidate in sociology and continues to teach math through the Cornell Prison Education Program. Crystal Proctor (ms_proctor@yahoo.com) teaches math at June Jordan School for Equity.

AUTHOR'S NOTE: *This article would be incomplete without sharing the sad news that one of the authors, Adam Renner, died suddenly and unexpectedly in December 2010 at the age of 40. Before coming to teach math at June Jordan School for Equity in San Francisco, Adam was an education professor at Bellarmine University in Louisville, Kentucky. Adam was a true warrior in the fight for social justice and his loss has been devastating to many people and communities. Though the world was definitely a better place with Adam in it, it is in his honor that we will continue to fight.*

The scene outside the Superdome in the aftermath of Hurricane Katrina on Sept. 3, 2005.

SHANNON STAPLETON

Bearing Witness Through Poetry

By Renée Watson

"This is an oral history lesson
just in case the textbooks neglect the truth:
Natural disaster holocausts
are destroying the poor.
Tens of thousands of bodies lie in Haiti's ditches.
Hundreds of deferred dreams drowned
in Katrina's waters. . ."

My high school students stood on stage performing their collaborative poem at the Schomburg Center for Research in Black Culture in Harlem. How fitting that these budding protest poets would be given the opportunity to have their voices rise in the Langston Hughes Auditorium. DreamYard's annual spoken word poetry festival gave parents, teachers, youth, and even politicians a chance to witness New York City's teen poets speak their truth. I sat in the front row, beaming with pride, not only because their performance went off without a hitch, but also because I knew these students meant every word they were reciting. What started out as a compare-and-contrast assignment for a social issues unit turned into a piece of art. A declaration.

As a teaching artist in public schools, I am paired with classroom teachers to teach poetry and to give students an opportunity to experience their academic curriculum through the arts. At the beginning of the school year, I gave my students the ongoing, yearlong assignment to watch the news, to pay attention. We studied Gwendolyn Brooks, who wrote about Emmett Till, and Langston Hughes, whose poetry is a literary commentary on the Black experience in America. "Great poets listen to their world and speak back," I told my students.

Our poetry class started off with the sharing of works in progress and the reporting of current events students felt passionate about. At that point, headlines and news stories inspired students to write about human trafficking, Chris Brown and Rihanna's public display of domestic violence, and the HIV epidemic in the Bronx — where they live.

Just after winter break, on Jan. 12, 2010, five years after New Orleans' levees broke, Haiti's earth quaked. The next day, every student wanted to talk about it. But how do you talk about something so devastating, so heartbreaking, without repeating clichéd responses like "That's so sad" or "Can you believe what happened?"

I encouraged students to look at the situation with empathy, but also with a critical eye. Knowing many of them were working with their classroom teachers on sharpening their skills for writing compare-and-contrast essays, I asked them to apply what they were learning to our poetry class. I posed the question: How do race and class affect the aftermath and recovery from a natural disaster?

A Study in Contrasts

I gave students the task of investigating the similarities and differences among three natural disasters: Hurricane Katrina — New Orleans, 2005; the San Diego wildfires — California, 2007; and the 7.0 Port-au-Prince earthquake — Haiti, 2010.

Most of my high school students were in elementary or middle school when Katrina swept through New Orleans. They had faint memories of something bad happening in Louisiana, but had no emotional connection to it and knew very few facts about the aftermath of the storm. When I asked how many knew anything about the wildfires in California, no one raised a hand.

The following week, I started class differently. I passed out the lyrics to Jay-Z's rap "Minority Report," a four-minute history lesson about New Orleans. I decided to use Jay-Z's song to help students understand what took place in 2005. Using music in my classroom has given many students who resist writing — especially poetry — a way in. Printing out the lyrics for them helps me show the similarities between verses and stanzas, and students are able to point out literary devices that singers and rappers often use.

> We studied Gwendolyn Brooks, who wrote about Emmett Till, and Langston Hughes, whose poetry is a literary commentary on the Black experience in America. "Great poets listen to their world and speak back," I told my students.

I played the song and instructed students to read along and underline lyrics that stood out to them because they liked the way Jay-Z said it, or because they agreed. "Circle phrases you don't understand," I added.

After students listened to the song, I led a brief discussion. "What is this song about? When did Katrina happen? How does Jay-Z feel about how things were handled in New Orleans?" Students volunteered to share what they underlined and circled.

Many students underlined the lyric "Wouldn't you loot, if you didn't have the loot?/ Baby needed food and you stuck on the roof." Students also underlined phrases that referred to how poor the people in New Orleans were before the hurricane. Several students circled lines about the Superdome and the lack of water and supplies.

After discussing the song, I asked students to turn their handout over. On the other side, a worksheet had a three-column chart with the headers Before, During, and After at the top, and three rows labeled New Orleans, 2005 — Hurricane Katrina; San Diego, 2007 — Wildfires; and Haiti, 2010 — Earthquake.

I showed students a slide show with images of all three places before, during, and after the tragedy. First, we watched the entire slide show without stopping it or talking.

The second time through, I stopped the slide show and gave students time to fill out the worksheet. In the images of life before, I asked, "What do you see?" "What do you notice about the houses?" "How would you describe this community?"

When I showed the slides of San Diego, students blurted out, "I want to live there!" "That house is tight!" Words students wrote in the "Before" column for San Diego included fancy, wealthy, vacation, big.

When we looked at the slides of Haiti, one student pointed to the screen, which held an image of children so thin their bones could be seen, and asked, "Is that really how Haiti looked before the earthquake?"

The next slides showed the devastation that happens when storms come, fires spread, and buildings crumble. Words students wrote in the "During" column were solemn: death, destruction, demolished, memories vanished, helpless, fear, tragic. Whether the house had been flooded, sizzled to ash, or collapsed to dust, it was clear that these three places, which in the previous column had obvious disparities with regard to class, all suffered enormous grief and loss.

The next photographs showed what happened in the immediate aftermath of each natural disaster. "What do you see?" I asked again. For New Orleans, students noted: crowds, handwritten signs pleading for help and for water, sick elderly people, despair. For San Diego, students wrote: buffets, massages, sleeping on cots, pets playing with their owners. And for Haiti: people sleeping outside in the dark, wounded people, sadness, loss, dead bodies thrown on top of each other.

I gave students time to silently write a response to these images. "How do these images make you feel? What are your gut reactions to these images?" Students wrote for about three minutes and then we discussed their findings.

I asked students not to draw any conclusions yet, but rather to share with the class what they wrote on their chart. "Just tell us what you noticed," I said.

The first comment was about the loss. "I noticed that all three places had a lot of damage done to their homes."

Another student saw that the homes in San Diego had cars parked in the driveway and many of the homes in New Orleans didn't.

"I noticed that the people in New Orleans looked hot, frustrated, and stranded, and the people in San Diego looked relaxed and taken care of."

"The people in San Diego looked organized and calm, and the people in New Orleans and Haiti looked chaotic and a lot more stressed out."

Adding Research to Rap

To help students add facts to their observations, we read the Associated Press article "Football Stadium Now a Shelter for Fire Evacuees," dated Oct. 23, 2007. I asked students to add pertinent information to their charts. "This article will give you facts to add to your feelings and observations," I explained. Occasionally, I stopped the class to see if anyone had a question or to make sure students understood the article. By the time I finished reading the second paragraph, students were gasping in disbelief. The article further explained what the images showed:

San Diego — Like Hurricane Katrina evacuees two years earlier in New Orleans, thousands of people rousted by natural disaster have fled to an NFL stadium, waiting out the calamity outside San Diego and worrying about their homes. The similarities ended there, as an almost festive atmosphere reigned at Qualcomm Stadium. Bands belted out rock 'n' roll, lavish buffets served gourmet entrees, and massage therapists helped relieve the stress for those forced to flee their homes because of wildfires. . . .

The New Orleans evacuees had dragged themselves through floodwaters to get to the Louisiana Superdome in 2005, and once there endured horrific conditions without food, sanitation, or law enforcement.

I also read them an article from the *New York Times*, Jason DeParle's "What Happens to a Race Deferred," which I first discovered in Linda Christensen's essay "Hurricane Katrina: Reading Injustice, Celebrating Solidarity." After looking at a graph in the article titled "The Reach of Poverty in New Orleans," which details by race who had cars and who did not, students began to draw conclusions about how race and class play a role in natural disasters.

> I mentioned Jay-Z's song as an example of an artist who lent his pen to a cause. "Write your version of 'Minority Report.'"
>
> "What do you have to say to New Orleans, San Diego, Haiti?" I asked them. "What do you want to say to America?"

It was clear to students that there were many differences in the response, resources, and rebuilding of New Orleans and San Diego. I asked students, "Why do you think there is such disparity? Should anything have been done differently? If so, what? Why or why not?"

Students were full of answers and suggestions. "If the government knew the people of New Orleans didn't have much to begin with, they should have been more prepared to handle something like Hurricane Katrina," Urias answered.

Destiny pointed out that maybe by 2007, two years after Katrina, the government had learned a lesson and that's why Qualcomm Stadium had so many resources. "And besides," she added, "Hurricane Katrina affected everybody in New Orleans. But not everyone in San Diego had to leave their home, so more people were able to volunteer and help out."

Lydia saw her point, but was adamant that more could have been done for Louisiana. "But five days?" she yelled. "They had no water for five days!"

"How is it that we can get stuff to other countries overnight but can't help our own?" Vaughn asked. "I'm not saying California didn't deserve help, I just think that New Orleans deserved it, too."

After comparing the hurricane and the fires, we took a closer look at the earthquake. Students learned that Haiti is the poorest country in the Western Hemisphere, and they quickly drew the conclusion that if, five years later, New Orleans was still rebuilding,

Haiti had a long road ahead. "I think it's good that everyone is donating money to them now, but where were all these donations before the earthquake?" Urias asked.

I didn't want to end the discussion, but I needed to bring our conversation to a close, so I could prepare students for their assignment and end class. I could tell students had lingering questions and I wanted to give them a chance to ask them. I tore pieces of blank scrap paper and handed out colored strips to the students, asking them to write down any question or thoughts that they didn't get to share. They didn't have to put their name on the slip of paper. I explained that we might not be able to answer their question in class, but that they should search out the answer. The slips of paper included the following questions:

- What would happen if a tragedy took place in New York City? Would Times Square be restored before neighborhoods in the Bronx?
- Do the poor know how to save money? Do they have enough money to save for a "rainy day"?
- How does a homeowner choose an insurance policy?
- Are there places that are currently in great need but may never get help unless tragedy strikes them?
- Whose responsibility is it to help the poor?
- Will history books tell the truth about what happened in New Orleans?

Although not the purpose of our class, these questions could lead into units on a variety of issues in many different subjects, including math, economics, and history. Students were beginning to see that what happened in New Orleans and Haiti — and what happens in their neighborhood — is rooted in deep issues that span a variety of aspects of their lives.

"What Do You Have to Say?"

In our next class, students began their poems. I mentioned Jay-Z's song as an example of an artist who lent his pen to a cause. "Write your version of 'Minority Report.'"

"What do you have to say to New Orleans, San Diego, Haiti?" I asked them. "What do you want to say to America?"

I encouraged my students to incorporate phrases from the articles, the rap, their free-write, and their chart into their poems. "You've collected a lot of information and documented your feelings very well. Use the material you've gathered in your piece," I instructed. "If you don't know how to begin, state a fact from the article or a lyric from the song and start from there."

Students got right to work. And so did I.

Whenever possible, I model doing the assignment so that students see and hear a "real writer's" process, and so that I encounter possible frustrations and stumbling blocks before they do. I let them hear my first drafts, revise them, and read them to the class again as an example of how even adult writers revise and edit their work. I also want to show my students that I am willing to take the risks I daily ask them to take. To write their opinions; to express their anger, hurt, and joy; to shout out questions to a world that may not respond with the answer they hoped for is a brave thing. I encourage them to take those risks with me.

After everyone's poem was complete, I took lines from all of our poems and combined them to create a collaborative piece.

Destiny and Vaughn both wrote about the lack of resources in New Orleans:

2005.
New Orleans flooded. . .
they named it
Hurricane Katrina.
And Katrina means Pure.
But the Superdome
had no pure water. . .

New Orleans,
for five days
you drank your salty tears
and there were no medical supplies
for your heartache.

And the ignorant asked: Why didn't
you get out?
Not realizing the poor have no cars to
drive to hotels to wait out a storm. . .

Urias, Lily, and Jazmin created stanzas about the neglect of Haiti:

Haiti's earth quaked
five years after New Orleans' levees broke.

And we are the aftershock. Shocked
that it took a catastrophe to pay attention to the poor.

Why is it that it takes tragedy to unify a world?

Haiti, we never remembered you. We knew your people
stood in line for their only meal of the day — beans and rice —
and we looked away.

Long before buildings barricaded your
children under tons of bricks
we knew you were the poorest country
in the Western Hemisphere.
And we looked away. . .

Denisse, who takes dance classes, volunteered to create an interpretive dance to go along with the poem. She rallied her peers together to rehearse outside of class. Observing them practice, I realized that, just a month before, all they could articulate about Haiti was that what happened was "sad," "a tragedy," "so unfortunate."

Now, they had facts and critical ideas to support them as they expressed their emotions. They took the skills they learned with their classroom teacher and applied them to their art. And instead of keeping silent, instead of hiding their questions, fears, and frustrations, they did what the poets they studied have done: They sounded the alarm. "Every time we say this poem, people will remember," Destiny told me. She understood that her words would not change what happened and her teenaged wallet might not be able to donate funds for recovery, but she could lend her pen.

Her voice.

There was a consensus in the group: "This is a tribute for people everywhere who are struggling. We have to make it special."

And they did.

And what happened on stage, in Langston's beloved Harlem, was more than a poetry recital. My students joined a new generation of poets committed to being recorders, responders, rebukers, rejoicers, and rebuilders.

What happened was the rising of voices:

> Santa Ana winds come again.
> Blow relief to the 9th Ward, to Haiti . . .
> Let the fire of revival spread to Bourbon Street and Port-au-Prince . . .
> Let our words be the rope you hang onto. May they pull you out of the
>   rubble.
> Syllable by syllable let each verb,
> each noun
> build a fortress on your insides. Strengthening the levees of your soul
>
> so you do not break.
> May you never break.
>
> And if the history books forget to add
> a footnote apologizing
> for not being proactive but reactive . . .
> take this account. Take this truth
> and write it in stone. Carve an
> evacuation plan

My students joined a new generation of poets committed to being recorders, responders, rebukers, rejoicers, and rebuilders.

and post it in every poor city, every
desolate nation . . .

there is a way out . . .

tell every child that lives lacking: As long as you can speak you
can survive
because words are seeds and this oral
history will bring a harvest.
We plant your name in the ground
of hope,

Haiti.
New Orleans.
Ethiopia.
Flint, Michigan.
Bronx, New York.
You will not be forgotten. . . . You will rise. You will rise
because we will lift you up.

Renée Watson is an author, educator, and activist. Her young adult novel, Piecing Me Together, *received a Newbery Honor and Coretta Scott King Award. She is the founder of I,
Too Arts Collective, a nonprofit housed in the brownstone where Langston Hughes lived and
created.*

RESOURCES

Associated Press. Oct. 23, 2007. "Football Stadium Now a Shelter for Fire Evacuees." MSNBC.com. msnbc.msn.com/id/21435605/

DeParle, Jason. Sept. 4, 2005. "What Happens to a Race Deferred." *The New York Times*. .nytimes.com/2005/09/04/weekinreview/04depa.html

Jay-Z. 2006. "Minority Report." *Kingdom Come*. Roc-a-Fella Records.

Shock-Doctrine Schooling in Haiti

Neoliberalism off the Richter scale

By Jesse Hagopian

"Why are we having all these people from shithole countries come here? . . .
Why do we need more Haitians?"
—U.S. President Donald Trump

"In addition to providing immediate humanitarian assistance, the U.S. response
to the tragic earthquake in Haiti offers opportunities to reshape Haiti's
long-dysfunctional government and economy as well as to improve the public
image of the United States in the region."
—The Heritage Foundation

Two days before the 2010 earthquake devastated Haiti, my 1-year-old son and I accompanied my wife there for an HIV training course she was going to conduct. And two days after surviving the quake, we drove to the center of Port-au-Prince from the Pétion-Ville district, where we had been staying, and passed a school that had completely collapsed.

As we drove by, I remember successfully convincing myself that not one student or teacher had been struck by the chunks of drab-gray cinderblock that lay scattered in the courtyard. As a teacher, I could not stomach the image of being trapped with my students under the debris.

I had just spent the last two days wrapping dozens of children's bloodied appendages with bed sheets. I had children die while I was working to stop the bleeding. I needed the peace of mind that the students in that school had lived.

When I returned to Seattle and reviewed the statistics — that the earthquake on Jan. 12 displaced 1.3 million people, and injured 300,000, with another estimated 300,000 dead — it seemed certain that my confidence in the well-being of that school community was just a delusional coping mechanism.

The Haitian government estimated at least 38,000 students and more than 1,300 teachers and other education personnel died in the earthquake. As UNICEF reported at the time, "80 percent of schools west of Port-au-Prince were destroyed or severely damaged in the earthquake, and 35 to 40 percent were destroyed in the southeast. This means that as many as 5,000 schools were destroyed and up to 2.9 million children here are being deprived of the right to education."

Haiti's Education Minister Joel Desrosiers Jean-Pierre declared "the total collapse of the Haitian education system."

The buildings may have collapsed, but the truth, however, was that the seismic activity of free-market principles had shattered the education system in Haiti long before Jan. 12, 2010.

In 2010, some 90 percent of schools in Haiti were private schools, and according to U.N. statistics, primary school tuition often represented 40 percent of a poor family's income — forcing parents to make the unthinkable decision about which of their children they would send to school. Only about two-thirds of Haiti's kids were enrolled in primary school before the earthquake, and less than a third reached 6th grade.

> **The Haitian government estimated at least 38,000 students and more than 1,300 teachers and other education personnel died in the earthquake.**

Secondary schools enrolled only one in five eligible-age children, which is one reason why the illiteracy rate in Haiti was more than half in 2010 — 57.24 percent. Poverty and lack of access to education led to mass child servitude, known as the restavèk system, with an estimated 225,000 Haitian youth living in a state of bondage.

For most people, Haiti's broken school system — which was literally buried under tons of rubble — is an incomprehensible horror. But for a few, the rubble looked more like building blocks, and the earthquake created a big break for business.

Meet Paul Vallas.

Vallas was the former CEO of the Chicago and Philadelphia public school systems and was hired in the aftermath of Hurricane Katrina as superintendent of the Recovery School District of Louisiana that oversaw the transformation of the New Orleans school system.

Vallas' legacy in these cities of privatizing schools, reducing public accountability, and undermining unions, made him a shoo-in to take charge of the Inter-American Development Bank's (IDB) education initiative in Haiti.

"There's a real opportunity here, I can taste it. That is why I've flown [to Haiti] so many times," Vallas said.

The comment was clearly cribbed from former U.S. Education Secretary Arne Duncan, who indirectly praised Vallas' work in New Orleans, saying, "I think the best thing that happened to the education system in New Orleans was Hurricane Katrina."

Duncan justified his statement by arguing that the destruction of the storm allowed education reformers to start from scratch and rebuild the school system better than before. However, as Naomi Klein, author of *The Shock Doctrine: The Rise of Disaster Capitalism*, pointed out:

BRIAN STAUFFER

The auctioning off of New Orleans' school system took place with military speed and precision. Within 19 months, with most of the city's poor residents still in exile, New Orleans' public school system had been almost completely replaced by privately run charter schools. . . . New Orleans teachers used to be represented by a strong union; now, the union's contract had been shredded and its 4,700 members had all been fired.

It should be apparent, then, that with Vallas at the helm of redesigning the Haitian school system, no child would be safe from an off-the-Richter-scale neoliberal quake.

Vallas' scheme for Haitian education centered on maintaining a system in which 90 percent of schools are private, with the one modification: That the Haitian government finance these private schools based on the charter school model Vallas delivered to New Orleans.

The IDB's then-proposed five-year, $4.2 billion plan for the remaking of the Haitian education system might best be described as the "Trojan school": Using the promise of the day when there is reduced tuition in the bulk of Haitian schools as a means to permanently enshrine a private schooling system subsidized by the government.

When President Michel Martelly was elected in April of 2011, he made a promise to implement the IDB's plan and the Program for Universal Free and Obligatory Education (Programme de Scolarisation Universelle Gratuite et Obligatoire — PSUGO) was established with the goal of educating "more than a million" students per year for five years.

In 2013, government banners around the capital declared "PSUGO — A victory for students!" But Haiti Grassroots Watch (HGW) conducted a two-month investigation in Port-au-Prince and Léogâne, revealing many problems with the education system.

> For most people, Haiti's broken school system . . . is an incomprehensible horror. But for a few, the rubble looked more like building blocks and the earthquake created a big break for business.

"In addition to suspicions of corruption, the amount paid to the schools is clearly inadequate, the payments don't arrive on time, and the professors are underpaid. Also, most of the schools visited by journalists had not received the promised manuals and school supplies, items crucial for assuring a minimally acceptable standard of education," according to the HGW.

Teachers went on strike, and managed to win salary increases of 30 to 60 percent, but their salaries were already so paltry that the raises were inadequate. And as the Institute for Justice & Democracy in Haiti wrote, "PSUGO pays private schools six times the amount paid to public schools. This formula makes building a viable public school system virtually impossible."

As was clear with the 2010 earthquake and the collapse of the school system — and with Vallas and other U.S. corporate reformers draining public resources — there can be no doubt that Haiti has many severe challenges, and there can also be no doubt that the cesspool of U.S. power, and other dominant nations, are at the root of them.

That's why for those who know their history, President Trump's declaration that Haiti (along with El Salvador and other African nations) is a "shithole" country, was simultaneously both horrifying and absurd.

The urge to dominate Haiti dates back to its very founding in a mass slave revolt. In fact, the United States refused to recognize Haiti as a nation, from its independence in 1804 until 1862, because of the worry that the Black republic, run by former slaves, would send the wrong message to its own slave population. Then from 1915 to 1934, the United States enforced a violent and bloody military occupation on Haiti. As historian Mary Renda wrote, "By official U.S. estimates, more than 3,000 Haitians were killed during this period; a more thorough accounting reveals that the death toll may have reached 11,500."

> With Vallas at the helm of redesigning the Haitian school system, no child would be safe from an off-the-Richter scale neoliberal quake.

Since the 2010 earthquake, the United States and the international community's record on Haiti reveals the same impulse to dominate rather than aid. As the Center for Economic and Policy Research (CEPR) Director Mark Weisbrot said in a January 2014 report, "The lasting legacy of the earthquake is the international community's profound failure to set aside its own interests and respond to the most pressing needs of the Haitian people."

Not much has changed in the years since then, as CEPR's 2018 report reveals foreign aid to Haiti is still primarily being used to enrich U.S. corporations: Overall, just $48.6 million — or just over 2 percent — has gone directly to Haitian organizations or firms. Comparatively, more than $1.2 billion — or 56 percent — has gone to firms located in Washington, D.C., Maryland, or Virginia.

Even more horrifying is the fact that U.N. troops introduced cholera to post-earthquake Haiti by dumping the waste from their portable toilets into a tributary near their base. Instead of Haiti bringing a hot mess to other countries, as Trump would insinuate, it was literally a shithole from the world's most powerful governments that was dumped on Haiti — and it resulted in a cholera epidemic that has killed more than 10,000 people and sickened another 1 million.

This is why Trump's decision in 2018 to end the Temporary Protected Status for the Haitian refugees in the United States who fled after the earthquake isn't only mean — it will actually be a death sentence for many. And far from Haiti being dependent on the United States, the balance ledger of history reveals Haiti has actually contributed far more financially and culturally to the United States. After the French lost the war to Black rebels and Haiti gained its independence, Napoleon Bonaparte was in need of some quick cash to continue his wars in Europe. So Napoleon struck a deal with the United States for 828,800 square miles of land — the Louisiana Purchase — for $219 million in today's dollars. It was Haiti's uprising and eventual defeat of Napoleon that led to the nearly doubling in size of the United States.

Moreover, the history and culture of Haiti and New Orleans are inextricably linked. As historian Carl A. Brasseaux has noted, "During a six-month period in 1809, approximately 10,000 refugees from Saint-Domingue (present-day Haiti) arrived at New Orleans, doubling the Crescent City's population. . . . The vast majority of these refugees established themselves permanently in the Crescent City. [They] had a profound impact upon New Orleans' development. Refugees established the state's first newspaper and introduced opera into the Crescent City. They also appear to have played a role in the development of Creole cuisine and the perpetuation of voodoo practices in the New Orleans area."

> **When the shock doctrine is applied to schooling, it has the effect of both profiteering off children and denying them access to the knowledge that could help them escape subjugation.**

But the nature of the relationship between these two cultures is currently being remade. The United States unmistakably exported its Hurricane Katrina response to Haiti and its schools — in a textbook case of Naomi Klein's concept of the "shock doctrine" in which disaster capitalists seek to profit from calamity.

Most recently, teachers in Puerto Rico are worried the U.S. and other foreign governments will use the widespread destruction of Hurricane Maria to justify widespread privatization.

On Oct. 26, 2017, about a month after Hurricane Maria first hit the mainland, Puerto Rico's Secretary of Education Julia Keleher tweeted photos of school construction in New Orleans with the caption "Sharing info on Katrina as a point of reference; we should not underestimate the damage or the opportunity to create new, better schools."

When the shock doctrine is applied to schooling, it has the effect of both profiteering off children and denying them access to the knowledge that could help them escape subjugation.

Governments the world over owe a debt to Haiti that is long past due — some from a history of direct colonial control or later economic subjugation, and some from failing to honor pledges made in the aftermath of the earthquake. If these debts were repaid, that would be the basis for constructing world-class education and health systems.

But with a white supremacist in the White House, it would be silly to wait for an apology, or for the proper type of funding to come through.

We need nothing less than a new Haitian revolution that connects with the movement for Black lives in the United States and brings down the structures of racism across the African diaspora. ∎

Jesse Hagopian teaches ethnic studies at Seattle's Garfield High School, is a member of Social Equity Educators (SEE), and is an editor of Rethinking Schools. *You can follow him on Twitter @JessedHagopian.*

Lead Poisoning
Bringing social justice to chemistry

By Karen Zaccor

've been reading *Rethinking Schools* for years, wondering "How do these teachers get such great engagement, such profound thinking from their students?" Like many science teachers, I struggle to incorporate social justice topics in my science classes, especially in chemistry. I can't send students off to college unfamiliar with basics like the periodic table, but none of them come to class excited about metals vs. nonmetals or the significance of valence electrons.

And then the catastrophe of lead-contaminated water in Flint, Michigan, hit the media. The stories exposed how, in early 2014, Flint's governor-appointed city manager, in a cost-saving move, decided that the primarily African American city, already reeling from high poverty and unemployment rates, would get its water from the highly corrosive Flint River rather than continuing to use Lake Huron. The health problems this created were compounded by the decision to save an additional $100 a day by not adding anticorrosive agents. City, state, and national officials brushed off residents' complaints for months while the Michigan Department of Environmental Quality falsified data to minimize the lead problem. By the time a newly elected mayor declared a state of emergency, the percent of children under 6 with elevated blood lead levels (BLLs) had doubled; in the most affected neighborhoods, almost 16 percent of young children had been poisoned. The devastating effects of these decisions and the racism behind them were laid bare for all to see.

Because the Flint crisis is shining a light on lead poisoning nationally, it seemed a perfect topic for my chemistry class. Lead poisoning is also a problem in Chicago, where I teach. So I thought it would resonate with my students, many of whom were already interested in social justice issues.

My main objective for the unit was to get my students to see how a science-based issue in their own city was affecting them personally. I wanted them to realize that learning about it could empower them to take action.

> She had just read that Chicago spends more each year on software licensing than it does to eliminate lead poisoning. "The government doesn't care to help because [we're] lower class and African American."

Lead in Water, Lead in Paint

We kicked off the second semester and the new unit with a brainstorm about what students had heard about Flint. The crisis was news to many students, but a few had heard about the lead in the water. Some reflected, as Justin did, that "Flint happened because they don't care about Black people."

"Flint is a scandal that's making news right now," I said, "but we also have a lead poisoning scandal right here in Chicago." I passed out a recent article by *Chicago Tribune* reporter Michael Hawthorne. I wanted to set a context for how my students viewed Chicago policies and actions regarding lead. I agreed with students like Justin who believed that the cost-saving measures taken in Flint occurred out of a profound lack of concern for the health and well-being of the mostly African American, mostly poor population. I wanted my students to ponder whether a similar lack of concern for its poor residents of color lies beneath Chicago's failure to invest in solutions to this most solvable of public health problems.

"Why do I call lead poisoning in Chicago a scandal? As you read and record the ideas that are important to you and your reaction to them, I want you to keep that question in mind. Think about who this is happening to and why." Students began to read quietly, creating a dialogue journal with important information recorded on the left side and their reactions in the form of insights, questions, and connections on the right.

Over and over, my students linked the lack of funding to a lack of concern for their communities. In a city that closed 50 schools "to save money" but somehow has money for bike paths and a new sports stadium, in a city wracked by police killings of youth of color, it's hard to reach any other conclusion.

Hawthorne highlights a family living in public housing. All nine children in the family were eventually found to have lead poisoning. Chicago Housing Authority (CHA) practice was to conduct only a visual inspection (rather than testing surfaces for lead) and they proclaimed the home safe before the family moved in. When the mother sought to move to lead-free housing, she was threatened with loss of her Section 8 (federally subsidized housing) voucher. CHA was also operating under HUD guidelines that were 25 years out of date, using a blood lead standard of 20 µg/dL of lead (200 parts per billion) versus the current CDC standard of 5 µg/dL (50 ppb).

This article and many others we read focused on the problem of lead-based paint. The Flint crisis has exposed the problem of lead in the water due to widespread use of lead pipes. Although most communities use anticorrosives, they are not foolproof, and stories about lead in water are now appearing all over the country. But experts say that, except in the case of babies drinking formula made with lead-contaminated water, water is the source of about 20 percent of the lead in children's blood. And that means identifying and remediating the source of the other 80 percent. In cities like Chicago with many

BORIS SEMÉNIAKO

buildings built before 1978, the main source of lead poisoning is most likely the paint in children's homes.

Poisoning rates can be quite high. In Chicago, the percent of children with elevated BLLs is double the national average. In the poorest neighborhoods, more than 20 percent of the children tested have elevated BLLs.

"Who is in charge of the CHA program? Because they are the real problem," Afia wrote in her reading log, responding to reporting that CHA regulations allow landlords to request indefinite extensions to fix lead paint hazards as they continue to collect taxpayer-financed rent checks. Janesha was angry that the family's rent subsidy was threatened when the mother tried to protect her children from lead. "Why did they treat her like she was nothing when she told them about the lead?"

"They should take action no matter how much lead is found in the blood," observed Krysstal. Current science acknowledges that no level of lead can be considered safe. Perhaps most poignant was Ciera's comment: "I used to live in a house with lead paint when I was in 5th grade." Several other students with younger siblings expressed concerns about the potential for lead in their apartments.

The Science of Lead Poisoning

To understand how lead harms children, we focused in on the biochemistry of lead poisoning. Lead is a poison when ingested in any quantity. As an ion, it mimics calcium and iron in the body. It can replace iron in hemoglobin in someone with an iron-poor diet, increasing the likelihood of anemia. Lead can penetrate the blood-brain barrier and replace calcium in key pathways that are part of the development of neural networks, memory function, and the control of executive function. This is of particular concern in children under 6, whose brains are still developing; brain damage caused is permanent. The students worked in groups to create posters or body models showing the different ways lead can affect a child's growth and development.

We read studies showing that several points of IQ can be lost, even at low levels of lead exposure. An analysis of standardized test scores of Chicago 3rd graders showed a significant increase in failure rates in math and reading for children with low BLLs. The study attributed as much as 25 percent of test failures to lead poisoning. My students have grown up in a school system where standardized test results can result in students being held back a grade. Monique connected the dots for us: "Even a small amount of lead might cause a student to fail the test. They fall behind and don't graduate high school. Then employment becomes difficult."

Indeed, a lifetime of challenges awaits the child with lead poisoning. Since the damage that occurs can be subtle, many families never realize that their children have been poisoned and are losing their full potential.

The Geography of Lead Poisoning

Many students felt a strong connection to this issue, but I wanted to deepen the impact. So I created a "Lead Where We Live" assignment based on an interactive website put up by the *Chicago Tribune*. I found the census tracts with the highest levels of lead poisoning in the city and constructed the assignment to highlight that information, as well as leaving space for students to record citywide averages and averages for their home census tract. The website tracks changes in the incidence of lead poisoning in Chicago between 1995 and 2013. One thing I wanted students to understand was that in the early 1990s, lead poisoning was equally likely to affect any community in the city from the richest to the poorest. By 2013, it was far more likely to affect the poorest communities.

"I want you to explore this site," I told my students. "Look for patterns. How does the pattern of lead poisoning change for the city as a whole from 1995 to 2013? Where is there a drop in the number of cases? Is it the same everywhere? What could explain differences? How does the pattern for your own census tract compare with the pattern for the whole city?"

After gathering data, the students graphed what they found and then answered some analysis questions. I was working to balance reading with other activities that offered a change of pace and developed students' skills at summarizing information or representing data. I also wanted to press them to think about how data can be used — or misused. On one hand, the huge decline in lead poisoning from the mid-1990s is a wonderful thing. On the other hand, that decline can obscure the fact that, in some communities, more than one child in five has a high BLL; that adds up to about 10,000 children per year in the city. Since only about half of the children between 6 months and 6 years old were tested in 2013, the actual number could be much higher.

My students were angry that more is not being done in communities hit hardest by lead poisoning. In their reflections on the data, they were adamant that every child's future should be considered important. They couldn't believe that so few people knew enough about the possible dangers of lead. Over and over, they reported that neither they nor their parents remember them being tested for lead as young children — and their younger siblings are not being tested either.

Each article and activity reinforced the students' realization that lead poisoning is an entirely preventable problem. "They invest in the wrong things," said Keshanna angrily. She had just read that Chicago spends more each year on software licensing than it does to eliminate lead poisoning. "The government doesn't care to help because [we're] lower class and African American," she said.

Over and over, my students linked the lack of funding to a lack of concern for their communities. In a city that closed 50 schools "to save money" but somehow has money for bike paths and a new sports stadium, in a city wracked by police killings of youth of color, it's hard to reach any other conclusion.

What Can Families Do?

Most people's initial response to a health problem is to resort to medicine, but there is no pill or potion to cure lead poisoning. At very high BLLs, chelation therapy, in which a chemical agent binds to lead to remove it from the blood, is often used. But it comes with its own risks and side effects and does not resolve brain damage that has already occurred. The best protection is to prevent exposure to lead in the first place, but the huge drop in funding for lead poisoning, from the national level to the city, means that Chicago's lead inspection program is reactive rather than proactive. Inspection comes after a child has been poisoned and the damage is already done.

> In the early 1990s, lead poisoning was equally likely to affect any community in the city from the richest to the poorest. By 2013, it was far more likely to affect the poorest communities.

"Back in the early 1990s, the BLL that would trigger an inspection was 20 μg/dL," I explained. "Now the standard is 5 — but we learned that HUD and CHA are still using a standard of 20. The city has only 11 inspectors. Do they come quickly when a child is found poisoned or is there a backlog? How long does the landlord get to fix the problem? We don't know the answers to these questions, but what we've read suggests months, even years, can pass.

"We know that our families are not being informed about lead poisoning and its dangers. We know lead is everywhere, thanks to years of lead-based paint and leaded gasoline. The city has to take responsibility and get rid of every bit of lead paint that could hurt a child. But, in the meantime, is there anything families can do themselves?"

We set out to develop a lead poisoning prevention protocol for families. There are certain cleanup methods that make it less likely that children will ingest lead even if it is present in their building. In addition, there are nutrients parents should make sure their children are eating: iron and calcium — essential minerals that compete with lead for absorption — and vitamin C, which makes it easier to digest those minerals. We did a simulation in the lab to demonstrate how consuming more calcium and iron reduces how much lead the body takes up.

Then we went to the library. Working in small groups, students researched foods that are lead-healthy. Other students came up with a list of cleanup guidelines:

- Wipe down windowsills and doorframes with a damp rag daily to minimize dust from open windows and doors.
- Damp mop floors instead of vacuuming, which can spread lead dust.
- Wash toys frequently.
- Shoes that can track in dirt from lead-contaminated soil should be left outside.
- If a family member works at a job involving lead-based products, leave their work clothes outside the house.
- Wash children's hands frequently and definitely before eating.

What Should We Fight For?

These were things families could do, but what about systemwide solutions? My students agreed that inspecting properties before families move in was the single best strategy. It fit perfectly into our discussion when Sheila Sutton from the Metropolitan Tenants Organization (MTO) came to speak to the class. She told us that the MTO was pushing an ordinance called the Chicago Healthy Homes Inspection Program that would require proactive inspection for lead and other common issues prevalent in low-income housing. She invited us to consider ways their work might fit into whatever we decided to do.

Indeed, the time had come to decide what we were going to do for a culminating project. I did not want to lose out on an ideal opportunity for activism. At the same time, I was wary of confusing my own desire for action with my students' needs and interests. So I started a brainstorming session based on these questions:

- What do you feel most interested in/motivated to work on?
- What did we learn that is worth sharing?
- What do you think it is possible for us to have an impact on?

I recorded their ideas. Several students had ideas for information that should go out to the community:

"We could share information on the effects of lead."

"What about how to protect your children?"

Others focused on systemwide changes we should push the city to make. Eventually we agreed on the most important information for a community awareness campaign and five demands to make of city officials:

1. Do citywide outreach about the dangers of lead poisoning and how to prevent it, especially to families in Section 8 and other low-cost housing.
2. Make sure all health providers know and follow the recommended schedule for testing infants and children for lead poisoning.
3. Adopt and fund the Chicago Healthy Homes Inspection Program ordinance.

Ensure that HUD and CHA adequately inspect their buildings, using current CDC standards for lead.

4. Inspect elementary schools and daycare centers for lead-based paint and adequately fund lead abatement.
5. Make sure the Chicago Public Schools (CPS) food program includes the daily requirement of nutrients that protect against lead poisoning.

I went home excited about the great ideas the students had generated. I used their suggestions to design a flexible final assignment. The next day, I let students choose the format for the project they would create. They chose to work on an informational brochure, a PowerPoint presentation, a radio public service announcement (PSA), a TV PSA, and a press packet.

Ideally, students would have gotten a few class periods of work time and then a day to present. They would have had clear guidelines for their work and I would have had time to meet with each group to clarify any confusion. But, as all too often happens, my plans were interrupted by field trips, professional development, and standardized testing. When the time came to present, I realized I should have been more alert to the students who were struggling with what their product should look like and how they could get there.

> **"Flint happened because they don't care about Black people."**

In the end, we had a good brochure, an excellent TV PSA, and some interesting new nuggets of information. One example came from research into our demand to inspect Chicago schools for lead. "CPS's own documents say we should assume any school built before 1978 has lead-based paint," wrote Ayiana. She read articles about a CPS school in which lead paint was found in 2009 but not cleaned up until 2014. "If this school had lead this recently," she argued, "other CPS schools must have lead, too."

In fact, Chicago is now testing for lead in the water at all CPS schools. Former CPS head Forrest Claypool vowed to do "whatever it takes" to eliminate the lead in the water, but no one mentioned the need to inspect schools for lead paint nor vowed to clean that up, although it may be an even more serious problem.

Looking to the Future

Eventually, two groups of students were able to share our findings with real audiences. The PowerPoint group presented at our school's annual Social Justice Expo and got lots of positive feedback. Another group of students presented our demands and the evidence behind them to our local alderman, who was very receptive.

However, once the unit was over it was a challenge to find the time or student motivation to take our demands to another level. We haven't been able to get an audience with other aldermen and attempts to reach a wider audience fizzled as students headed toward the end of the school year.

Looking back, I see a lot of things I would do differently in the future. In particular, I would put the students more in charge of seeking information, rather than doing so much of the work myself. Instead of relying so heavily on articles, I would also ask students to survey classmates, teachers, and families; interview people whose families were affected by lead poisoning; and reach out to local experts. I would also structure the project so students had an opportunity to report our initial findings at an earlier stage. I have observed in the past that, once students realize that others see the information they have to offer as valuable, they become more interested in the work. I think that would have created a stronger commitment to pursue some kind of action.

I'm encouraged, though, as I read students' final reflections and see how many students discussed the lead issues we were studying with others:

- I learned something I never heard of before and I was able to make others aware of it.
- I spoke to my neighbor and explained lead, how we are exposed, and how we can change it.
- I had my sister take my nephews to get tested for lead poisoning.

In the end, the biggest takeaway may be that the students realized that chemistry is important in their everyday lives and can inform struggles for justice in their communities. ■

Karen Zaccor (kzaccor@comcast.net) teaches high school science and has taught in Chicago Public Schools for 20 years.

RESOURCES

For additional materials related to this article, go to teachingforblacklives.org

Epton, Abraham, Alex Bordens, and Geoff Hing. May 1, 2015. "Chicago Lead Poisoning Rates Vary by Location, Time." apps.chicagotribune.com/news/watchdog/chicago-lead-poisoning/index.html

Hawthorne, Michael. May 1, 2015. "Lead Paint Poisons Poor Chicago Kids as City Spends Millions Less on Cleanup." *Chicago Tribune.* chicagotribune.com/news/ct-lead-poisoning-chicago-met-20150501-story.html#page=.

Hawthorne, Michael. Dec. 31, 2015. "Federal Housing Policy Leaves Poor Kids at Risk of Lead Poisoning." *Chicago Tribune.* chicagotribune.com/news/ct-cha-lead-paint-hazards-met-20151231-story.html

Kowalski, Kathiann. July 24, 2015. "To Protect Kids, Get the Lead Out." *Science News for Students.* student.societyforscience.org/article/protect-kids-get-lead-out

Mergel, Maria. Oct. 20, 2010. "Health Effects of Lead." *Toxipedia.* toxipedia.org/display/toxipedia/Health+Effects+of+Lead

4

DISCIPLINE, THE
SCHOOLS-TO-PRISON
PIPELINE, AND MASS
INCARCERATION

Jailing Our Minds

By Abbie Cohen

A crowd of students milled about aimlessly — the doors were locked. Hoods on, shoulders slumped, huddled together to avoid the cold morning wind. They exchanged looks and morning yawns. Every face was Black or Brown. Suddenly, a loud buzz. The doors unlocked. Bodies filed in one by one, feet barely lifting off the cement. At the first set of doors, a petite white woman greeted each person. She stuck out her hand, expecting a firm handshake and eye contact. If anyone did not meet her standards, she sent them to the back of the line to try again.

After passing through the first checkpoint, the students silently climbed a staircase and stripped off their winter clothes. The rules were clear: all jackets, hats, and gloves had to be removed. Everyone had to be in uniform. If anyone failed to complete that task, they were taken into a side room to finish the job.

At the top of the stairs stood another white woman. Everyone also had to give her a firm handshake with satisfactory eye contact. In addition, she offered every person the command: "belt." On cue, each individual raised their shirt to prove that they were, in fact, wearing a belt. If the woman surmised that someone lifted their shirt in a sassy manner or demonstrated "attitude," she directed them into a side room. If a person messed up their uniform in the process of revealing their belt, they too were ushered into the side room to re-tuck their shirt and redo the presentation.

Finally, the group entered a large open area. They sat silently in rows, fidgeting uncomfortably. Many of their bodies were too big for the small space mandated for them. As they awaited instructions, there were two options: read silently or stare off into space. There was no noise. No chatter. No laughter. No fun.

After 10 minutes, another white woman emerged. She dismissed each row individually. The silence remained. If a person made a sound or stood up too soon, the woman ordered the entire row to sit back down and try again. The task had to be performed to her exact specifications. As the room gradually emptied, the bodies trudged off in a variety of directions for other checkpoints.

It felt like some sort of prison. At best, it resembled some kind of Dickensian factory, ruled with an iron — and white — fist. In reality, this is the daily routine at STRIVE Prep-Green Valley Ranch, a Denver public charter school that in 2016–17 housed some 120 6th graders, 120 7th graders, and 120 8th graders.

These children are not inmates, they are middle schoolers.

HANNA BARCZYK

What It Means to STRIVE

The STRIVE Preparatory Schools network of charters was founded about a dozen years ago. It has quickly expanded throughout Denver's educational landscape and as of January 2018 this charter management organization (which according to the Colorado League of Charter Schools is actually a CMO-nonprofit/EMO-for-profit) has opened 11 schools serving students from kindergarten to 12th grade across the city. STRIVE Prep claims, on the homepage of its website, to provide an academic space "where a revolutionary education is commonplace and attending college is expected." This CMO boasts that it provides academically demanding courses and high expectations for students. But in practice, in order to reach these objectives, STRIVE Prep has implemented a regimented, punitive educational experience that eliminates creativity, fun, self-expression, and the joys of being a child or going to school.

The STRIVE Prep network appears to fully embody the "no-excuses" pedagogical approach to teaching and classroom management. The no-excuses movement emerged in the 1990s and was later supported by federal education policies like No Child Left Behind (NCLB) that encouraged market-oriented reformers to solve this country's stubborn opportunity gap. No-excuses schools argue that they can increase the academic performance of Black, Brown, and working-class youth by instituting a rigid and inflexible disciplinary system. Severe punishments like suspension and expulsion are linked to small infractions like talking in the hallway or not wearing appropriate attire. No-excuses schools suggest that ending behavioral issues guarantees academic success. In practice, however, many no-excuses schools have simply over-punished Black and Brown youth, turning public schools into detention centers.

> **No-excuses schools suggest that ending behavioral issues guarantees academic success. In practice, however, many no-excuses schools have simply over-punished Black and Brown youth, turning public schools into detention centers.**

I visited STRIVE Prep-Green Valley Ranch as part of my former job as a member of the administrative team at Breakthrough Kent Denver, an organization that provides opportunities to under-resourced middle and high school students, while also preparing recent high school graduates and college students to enter the field of education. I spent much of my time recruiting 6th graders across the city to apply to our program and checking in with our alumni. During the 2016–17 academic year, I visited nearly 30 middle schools and 20 high schools in Denver. What I witnessed at STRIVE shook me to the core. Their disciplinary procedures highlighted the potential pitfalls of turning over public schools to the free market. This kind of autonomy from the public school district is one of the key reasons that charterization appeals to free-market reformers — and other Denver charters have also adopted punitive regimes that essentially criminalize students' behavior. They seem to take their cues from this country's prison-industrial complex: Students are inmates and deserve to be treated as such.

Certainly, not all charter schools have a disciplinary program as strict, rigid, or problematic as STRIVE Prep. But the fact such a program exists in the first place — and in the public system, no less — presents a grave threat to the future of public education in this city and across the nation.

"No Excuses"

"No-excuses" charter schools suggest that Black and Brown youth can achieve academically only within environments that have a disciplinary code that mirrors that of the carceral state. These schools explicitly critique the cultural norms and rhythms of non-white students. They imply that the only way to learn is by conforming to a prescribed routine and strict rules that dictate what students wear, what it means to pay attention in class, how students should organize their work, and even how they should walk up a flight of stairs or enter a classroom. In many ways, it adheres to a type of "broken windows" reasoning employed by some police departments. If students are slouching, they must be punished. If students are talking in the hall, they must be punished. If students don't have their eyes on the teacher, they must be punished. Research shows that the "no-excuses" model is also built on a profound system of rewards and punishments. If students perform or execute a task well they could receive merits or shout-outs at an all-school assembly. However, if students perform poorly or execute a task not up to "standard" they may be given a range of punishments from detention to all-too-frequent suspensions.

A report published in 2015 by Padres & Jóvenes Unidos — a nonprofit in Denver that, among other things, works to illuminate harsh school discipline, zero-tolerance policies, and the disproportionate impact of those practices on students of color from working-class families — found that from 2013 to 2014 STRIVE Prep-Green Valley Ranch had the fourth highest rate of out-of-school suspensions (OSS) in the city. That year the school had a jaw-dropping rate of 29.5 incidents of out-of-school suspensions for every 100 students. A school that sends kids home so often cannot be effectively educating all of its students.

"No-excuses" discipline is a problem that extends beyond this one school. In Denver's public school district, more than one-fourth of the just over 200 schools are charters. The 2015 Padres & Jóvenes Unidos report illustrates that in 2013–2014, five of the top eight schools with the highest OSS rates were all charters. The most flagrant offender, Sims-Fayola International Academy Charter School, was Denver's first all-boys public charter. It had an OSS rate of 71.3 percent in 2013–2014 and shut down about three years after opening, throwing its students and their families into turmoil. The next seven schools on the Padres & Jóvenes Unidos list all have OSS rates between 25.6 and 32.7 percent. Three of them are in the STRIVE network.

School suspensions traumatize students and families, making teaching and learning more difficult. In 2016, I had the opportunity to discuss disciplinary procedures with students at Breakthrough Kent Denver's monthly "Saturday School" program. One student who attended STRIVE Prep-Green Valley Ranch described to me the fear STRIVE instilled in her. Like many 7th graders she enjoyed experimenting with her newfound sense of maturity and creativity. She had recently dyed her hair red. Only afterward did she panic and realize that this act violated her school's disciplinary code. If an administrator or teacher noticed, she would be subject to an in-school suspension (ISS). She noted that she had already been suspended three times in the 2016–2017 academic year for wearing the wrong shoes to an exam, wearing fake nails, and wearing an out-of-dress-code shirt because her mother could not afford another STRIVE polo. If she received another ISS, she was sure she would receive an out-of-school suspension. This young student is bright, highly motivated, and excited about her future; she wants to be an engineer. However, she has come to hate school because she is unable to express herself and embrace her creative side.

"Got to Go"

This disturbing phenomenon is not unique to Denver. Success Academy Charter Schools, New York City's largest charter network (with more than 40 schools and plans to expand), has made headlines for its punitive measures. In 2015, the *New York Times* published an exposé of Success Academy based on interviews and documents that "suggest that some administrators in the network have singled out children they would like to see leave." The article noted that at Success Academy Fort Greene, a K–4 school, school leaders had a list of 16 students' names:

> The heading on the list was "Got to Go."
>
> Nine of the students on the list later withdrew from the school. Some of their parents said in interviews that while their children attended Success, their lives were upended by repeated suspensions and frequent demands that they pick up their children early or meet with school or network staff members. Four of the parents said that school or network employees told them explicitly that the school, whose oldest students are now in the 3rd grade, was not right for their children and that they should go elsewhere.

Eva Moskowitz, Success Academy's CEO, responded to the list by saying "mistakes are sometimes made." The numbers suggest a different story. Suspensions appear to be endemic to Success Academy and NYC charter schools. According to that same *New York Times* article:

> In the 2012–13 school year, the most recent one for which state data is available, Success schools suspended between 4 percent and 23 percent of their students at least once, with most suspending more than 10 percent. According to the most recent statistics from the city's Education Department, from 2013–14, traditional public schools suspended 3 percent of students that academic year.

Moreover, the 7 percent of students who go to charter schools in New York City made up 42 percent of suspensions, according to an article in the *Atlantic* that cited data from 2014. The article also noted that comparable patterns exist in Washington, D.C., and Boston and that in 2014–2015, 48 of the 50 schools in New York City with the most student suspensions were charters.

It is important to note that Moskowitz is a supporter of controversial Secretary of Education Betsy DeVos. DeVos, an ardent believer in school choice, envisions school systems entirely geared to the free market. DeVos' budget proposal outlined her desire to expand school choice across the nation, while also eliminating programs for our most vulnerable students. Her plan would slash $9 billion in the 2018 fiscal year. This includes a $3.5 billion cut to teacher training and after-school programs, among others.

Meanwhile, DeVos wants the federal government to stimulate more choice options both in the public and private school sector. *Education Week* reported in 2017 that while DeVos was visiting a charter school in Washington, D.C., she explained, "I think the choices that have grown up and have been afforded to families here are very, very strong and encouraging. I think there's continued room for more choices and improvements across the board." DeVos' support for choice in D.C. ignores the larger context. Charter schools in D.C. suspend and expel at rates substantially higher than the national average. A report from the U.S. Government Accountability Office reveals that Black students in Washington, D.C., and students with disabilities were expelled and suspended at disproportionate rates in the 2013–2014 school year.

HANNA BARCZYK

The *Washington Post*, citing data from that GAO study, noted that "Black students were 80 percent of charter school students, but 93 percent of those suspended and 92 percent of those expelled during 2013–2014." Moreover, Black boys represent "39 percent of the charter students, but 56 percent of the suspended students and 55 percent of those expelled." Even more appalling evidence from the GAO report points out that "16 of D.C.'s 105 charter schools suspended more than a fifth of their students over the course of the school year 2015–2016." By expanding charterization and choice, DeVos' budget will only exacerbate the problem of no-excuses discipline, widening the opportunity gap in the process.

A national report published by UCLA's Civil Rights Project/Proyecto Derechos Civiles provided the first comprehensive nationwide description and comparison of school discipline in both charter and non-charter public schools in 2011–12. Of all 95,000 schools across the country included in the Civil Rights Project's report, more than 500 charters suspended Black youth at a rate that was at least 10 percentage points higher than the rate for white students. Clearly, the racialized impact of these policies is a national phenomenon. This intensive policing of students of color has bleak consequences for our young students and our democracy.

> **This intensive policing of students of color has bleak consequences for our young students and our democracy. Educational research has shown that students who are harshly disciplined in school are more likely to end up in the juvenile justice system.**

Educational research has shown that students who are harshly disciplined in school are more likely to end up in the juvenile justice system. A report published in 2011 by the Council of State Governments Justice Center and Texas A&M University's Public Policy Research Institute found that more than one in seven students who was suspended or expelled "was in contact with the juvenile justice system (i.e., contact with a county's juvenile probation department) at least once between 7th and 12th grade." According to a *Washington Post* article from 2011 that cited the data, "by comparison, just 2 percent of students with no suspensions or expulsions had juvenile justice involvement." The evidence is clear: No-excuses charter schools only exacerbate this country's racialized criminal justice system.

Denver Public Schools and the city government have publicly expressed that they want to end the school-to-prison pipeline. Local officials will never reach that goal as long as so many schools treat students as inmates. Democracy is healthiest when our educational institutions reflect our best virtues — creativity, joy, and growth. We must strengthen our oversight over no-excuses charter schools, thereby ensuring that no child in that city — or our country — is subjected to policies that could have been culled from one of Denver's neighboring prisons. ■

Abbie Cohen is a master's candidate at Harvard Graduate School of Education studying education policy and management.

Schools and the New Jim Crow
An interview with Michelle Alexander

By Jody Sokolower

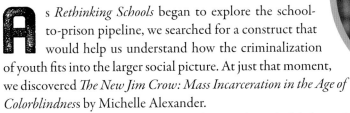

As *Rethinking Schools* began to explore the school-to-prison pipeline, we searched for a construct that would help us understand how the criminalization of youth fits into the larger social picture. At just that moment, we discovered *The New Jim Crow: Mass Incarceration in the Age of Colorblindness* by Michelle Alexander.

Alexander poses a thought-provoking and insightful thesis: Mass incarceration, justified by and organized around the war on drugs, has become the new face of racial discrimination in the United States. Since 1970, the number of people behind bars in this country has increased 600 percent.

What is most striking about these numbers is the racial dimension. The United States imprisons a larger percentage of its Black population than South Africa did at the height of apartheid. In Washington, D.C., for example, it is estimated that 75 percent of young Black men can expect to serve time in prison.

Equally disturbing is Alexander's description of the lifelong civil and human rights implications of being arrested and serving time in prison, and the implications for what many call our "post-racial" society. As she explains in her introduction:

> What has changed since the collapse of Jim Crow has less to do with the basic structure of our society than with the language we use to justify it. In the era of colorblindness, it is no longer socially permissible to use race, explicitly, as a justification for discrimination, exclusion, and social contempt. So we don't. Rather than rely on race, we use our criminal justice system to label people of color "criminals" and then engage in all the practices we supposedly left behind. Today it is perfectly legal to discriminate against criminals in nearly all the ways that it was once legal to discriminate against African Americans. Once you're labeled a felon, the old forms of discrimination — employment discrimination, housing discrimination, denial of the right to vote, denial of educational opportunity, denial of food stamps and other public benefits, and exclusion from jury service — are suddenly legal. As a criminal you have scarcely more rights, and arguably less respect, than a Black man living in Alabama at the height of Jim Crow. We have not ended racial caste in America; we have merely redesigned it.

We asked Alexander to share her thoughts about the implications of her work when applied to education and the lives of children and youth. She spoke with *Rethinking Schools* editor Jody Sokolower on Sept. 1, 2011.

JODY SOKOLOWER: What is the impact of mass incarceration on African American children and youth?

MICHELLE ALEXANDER: There is an extraordinary impact. For African American children, in particular, the odds are extremely high that they will have a parent or loved one, a relative, who has either spent time behind bars or who has acquired a criminal record and thus is part of the under-caste — the group of people who can be legally discriminated against for the rest of their lives. For many African American children, their fathers, and increasingly their mothers, are behind bars. It is very difficult for them to visit. Many people are held hundreds or even thousands of miles away from home. There is a tremendous amount of shame with having a parent or other family member incarcerated. There can be fear of having it revealed to others at school.

But also, for these children, their life chances are greatly diminished. They are more likely to be raised in severe poverty; their parents are unlikely to be able to find work or housing and are often ineligible even for food stamps.

For children, the era of mass incarceration has meant a tremendous amount of family separation, broken homes, poverty, and a far, far greater level of hopelessness as they see so many of their loved ones cycling in and out of prison. Children who have incarcerated parents are far more likely themselves to be incarcerated.

When young Black men reach a certain age — whether or not there is incarceration in their families — they themselves are the target of police stops, interrogations, frisks, often for no reason other than their race. And, of course, this level of harassment sends a message to them, often at an early age: No matter who you are or what you do, you're going to find yourself behind bars one way or the other. This reinforces the sense that prison is part of their destiny, rather than a choice one makes.

A Birdcage as a Metaphor

SOKOLOWER: At one point in *The New Jim Crow*, you refer to the metaphor of a birdcage as a way to describe structural racism and apply that to mass incarceration. How does what is happening to African American youth in our schools fit into that picture?

ALEXANDER: The idea of the metaphor is there can be many bars, wires that keep a person trapped. All of them don't have to have been created for the purpose of harming or caging the bird, but they still serve that function. Certainly youth of color, particularly those in ghetto communities, find themselves born into the cage. They are born into a community in which the rules, laws, policies, structures of their lives virtually guarantee that they will remain trapped for life. It begins at a very early age when their parents themselves are either behind bars or locked in a permanent second-class status and cannot afford them the opportunities they otherwise could. For example, those with felony convictions are denied access to public housing, hundreds of professions that require certification, financial support for education, and often the right to vote. Thousands of people are unable even to get food stamps because they were once caught with drugs.

The cage itself is manifested by the ghetto, which is racially segregated, isolated, cut off from social and economic opportunities. The cage is the unequal educational opportunities these children are provided at a very early age coupled with the constant police surveillance they're likely to encounter, making it very likely that they're going to serve time and be caught for committing the various types of minor crimes — particularly drug crimes — that occur with roughly equal frequency in middle-class white communities but go largely ignored.

So, for many, whether they go to prison or not is far less about the choices they make and far more about what kind of cage they're born into. Middle-class white children, children of privilege, are afforded the opportunity to make a lot of mistakes and still go on to college, still dream big dreams. But for kids who are born in the ghetto in the era of mass incarceration, the system is designed in such a way that it traps them, often for life.

SOKOLOWER: How do you define and analyze the school-to-prison pipeline?

ALEXANDER: It's really part of the large cage or caste that I was describing earlier. The school-to-prison pipeline is another metaphor — a good one for explaining how children are funneled directly from schools into prison. Instead of schools being a pipeline to opportunity, schools are feeding our prisons.

It's important for us to understand how school discipline policies have been influenced by the war on drugs and the "get tough" movement. Many people imagine that zero-tolerance rhetoric emerged within the school environment, but it's not true. In fact, the Advancement Project published a report showing that one of the earliest examples of zero-tolerance language in school discipline manuals was a cut-and-paste job from a U.S. Drug Enforcement Administration manual. The wave of punitiveness that washed over the United States with the rise of the drug war and the "get tough" movement really flooded our schools. Schools, caught up in this maelstrom, began viewing children as criminals or suspects, rather than as young people with an enormous amount of potential struggling in their own ways and their own difficult context to make it and hopefully thrive. We began viewing the youth in schools as potential violators rather than as children needing our guidance.

The Mythology of Colorblindness

SOKOLOWER: In your book, you explain that the policies of mass incarceration are technically "colorblind" but lead to starkly racialized results. How do you see this specifically affecting children and young people of color?

ALEXANDER: The mythology around colorblindness leads people to imagine that if poor kids of color are failing or getting locked up in large numbers, it must be something wrong with them. It leads young kids of color to look around and say: "There must be something wrong with me, there must be something wrong with us. Is there something inherent, something different about me, about us as a people, that leads us to fail so often, that leads us to live in these miserable conditions, that leads us to go in and out of prison?"

The mythology of colorblindness takes the race question off the table. It makes it difficult for people to even formulate the question: Could this be about something more than individual choices? Maybe there is something going on that's linked to the history of race in our country and the way race is reproducing itself in modern times.

I think this mythology — that of course we're all beyond race, of course our police officers aren't racist, of course our politicians don't mean any harm to people of color — this idea that we're beyond all that (so it must be something else) makes it difficult for young people as well as the grown-ups to be able to see clearly and honestly the truth of what's going on. It makes it difficult to see that the backlash against the Civil Rights Movement manifested itself in the form of mass incarceration, in the form of defunding and devaluing schools serving kids of color and all the rest. We have avoided in recent years talking openly and honestly about race out of fear that it will alienate and polarize. In my own view, it's our refusal to deal openly and honestly with race that leads us to keep repeating these cycles of exclusion and division, and rebirthing a caste-like system that we claim we've left behind.

SOKOLOWER: We are in the midst of a huge attack on public education — privatization through charters and vouchers; increased standardization, regimentation, and testing; and the destruction of teacher unions. Much of it is justified by what appears to be anti-racist rhetoric: Schools aren't meeting the needs of inner-city children, so their parents need choices. How do you see this?

ALEXANDER: People who focus solely on what do we do given the current context are avoiding the big why. Why is it that these schools aren't meeting these kids' needs? Why is it that such a large percentage of the African American population today is trapped in these ghettos? What is the bigger picture?

The bigger picture is that over the last 30 years, we have spent $1 trillion waging a drug war that has failed in any meaningful way to reduce drug addiction or abuse, and yet has siphoned an enormous amount of resources away from other public services, especially education. We are in a social and political context in which the norm is to punish poor folks of color rather than to educate and empower them with economic opportunity. It is that political context that leads some people to ask: Don't children need to be able to escape poorly performing schools? Of course, no one should be trapped in bad schools or bad neighborhoods. No one. But I think we need to be asking a larger question: How do we change the norm, the larger context that people seem to accept as a given? Are we so thoroughly resigned to what "is" that we cannot even begin a serious conversation about how to create what ought to be?

The education justice movement and the prison justice movement have been operating separately in many places as though they're in silos. But the reality is we're not going to provide meaningful education opportunities to poor kids, kids of color, until and unless we recognize that we're wasting trillions of dollars on a failed criminal justice system. Kids are growing up in communities in which they see their loved ones cycling in and out of prison and in which they are sent the message in countless ways that they, too, are going to prison one way or another. We cannot build healthy, functioning schools within a context where there is no funding available because it's going to building prisons and police forces.

SOKOLOWER: And fighting wars?

ALEXANDER: Yes, and fighting wars. And where there is so much hopelessness because of the prevalence of mass incarceration.

At the same time, we're foolish if we think we're going to end mass incarceration unless we are willing to deal with the reality that huge percentages of poor people are going to remain jobless, locked out of the mainstream economy, unless and until they have a quality education that prepares them well for the new economy. There has got to be much more collaboration between the two movements and a greater appreciation for the work of the advocates in each community. It's got to be a movement that's about education, not incarceration — about jobs, not jails. A movement that integrates the work in these various camps from, in my view, a human rights perspective.

Fighting Back

SOKOLOWER: What is the role of teachers in responding to this crisis? What should we be doing in our classrooms? What should we be doing as education activists?

ALEXANDER: That is a wonderful question and one I'm wrestling with myself now. I am in the process of working with others trying to develop curriculum and materials that will make it easier to talk to young people about these issues in ways that won't lead to paralysis, fear, or resignation, but instead will enlighten and inspire action and critical thinking in the future. It's very difficult but it must be done.

We have to be willing to take some risks. In my experience, there is a lot of hesitancy to approach these issues in the classroom out of fear that students will become emotional or angry, or that the information will reinforce their sense of futility about their own lives and experience. It's important to teach them about the reality of the system, that it is in fact the case that they are being targeted unfairly, that the rules have been set up in a way that authorizes unfair treatment of them, and how difficult it is to challenge these laws in the courts. We need to teach them how our politics have changed in recent years, how there has been, in fact, a backlash. But we need to couple that information with stories of how people in the past have challenged these kinds of injustices, and the role that youth have played historically in those struggles.

I think it's important to encourage young people to tell their own stories and to speak openly about their own experiences with the criminal justice system and the experiences of their family. We need to ensure that the classroom environment is a supportive one so that the shame and stigma can be dispelled. Then teachers can use those stories of what students have witnessed and experienced as the opportunity to begin asking questions: How did we get here? Why is this happening? How are things different in other communities? How is this linked to what has gone on in prior periods of our nation's history? And what, then, can we do about it?

Just providing information about how bad things are, or the statistics and data on incarceration by themselves, does lead to more depression and resignation and is not empowering. The information has to be presented in a way that's linked to the piece about encouraging students to think critically and creatively about how they might respond to injustice, and how young people have responded to injustice in the past.

SOKOLOWER: What specifically?

ALEXANDER: There's a range of possibilities. I was inspired by what students have done in some schools organizing walkouts protesting the lack of funding and that sort of thing. There are opportunities for students to engage in those types of protests — taking to the streets — but there is also writing poetry, writing music, beginning to express themselves, holding forums, educating each other, the whole range. For example, for a period of time the Ella Baker Center in Oakland, California, was focused on youth engagement and advocacy to challenge mass incarceration. They launched a number of youth campaigns to close youth incarceration facilities in Northern California. They demonstrated that it is really possible to blend hip-hop culture with very creative and specific advocacy and to develop young leaders. Young people today are very creative in using social media and there is a wide range of ways that they can get involved.

The most important thing at this stage is inspiring an awakening. There is a tremendous amount of confusion and denial that exists about mass incarceration today, and that is the biggest barrier to movement building. As long as we remain in denial about this system, movement building will be impossible. Exposing youth in classrooms to the truth about this system and developing their critical capacities will, I believe, open the door to meaningful engagement and collective, inspired action. ∎

Jody Sokolower is a former managing editor of Rethinking Schools, *editor of* Teaching About the Wars, *and co-editor of* Rethinking Sexism, Gender, and Sexuality. *She is currently a teacher educator and coordinator of the Teach Palestine Project at the Middle East Children's Alliance in Berkeley, California.*

AUTHOR'S NOTE: *Alexander's book and this interview were published during the Obama presidency. With Trump in the White House, it is no longer possible to pretend that this is a colorblind or post-racial society. This makes* The New Jim Crow *that much more prophetic and significant.*

Racial Justice Is Not a Choice

White supremacy, high-stakes testing, and the punishment of Black and Brown students

By Wayne Au

> "Education is the great civil rights issue of our time."
> —Former U.S. President George W. Bush (2002)

> "[The educational achievement gap] is the civil rights issues of our time."
> —Former U.S. Secretary of Education Rod Paige (2004)

> "Education is the Civil Rights Movement of our generation."
> —Former U.S. Secretary of Education Arne Duncan (2010)

> "Education is the civil rights issue of our time."
> —Former U.S. President Barack Obama (2011)

> "Education is the civil rights issue of our time."
> —U.S. President Donald Trump (2017)

Starting with the No Child Left Behind Act of 2001, the logic has been this: There are race-based gaps in standardized test scores. Closing those gaps should be the goal for achieving racial equality in education. Connected to clear punishments for failure, we can use those tests to achieve this goal.

Since then, politicians from both parties have repeated the mantra that educational achievement gaps are the "civil rights issue of our time." This is one of the reasons why a number of mainstream civil rights organizations in May 2015 spoke out against the movement to let students and parents opt out of high-stakes testing. Their argument: Without the data, we can't hold schools and teachers accountable for racial inequality.

The problem is that high-stakes standardized testing has not only failed at achieving racial equality, its proliferation has only exacerbated racial inequality and worsened the education for students of color.

But we are in a moment of profound resistance and change as the movements to bring Ethnic Studies to classrooms across the country and make Black students' lives matter in schools are gaining traction. And it is critical we understand that high-stakes standardized tests do not serve students of color. They support white supremacy.

The Faulty (Bio)logics of Testing for Racial Justice

The logic of high-stakes testing for racial justice is simple. Standardized tests produce data that we can look at and identify "achievement gaps." Then, if we don't see the scores of low performing racial groups increase to close these gaps, teachers, schools, and students are held "accountable" to punishments like funding cuts, charter school conversion, or withholding diplomas, among other consequences. The idea is that these threats will lead to higher test scores for students from low-income families and students of color.

The arguments for using high-stakes testing for racial equality all assume that our standardized tests provide accurate measurements of teaching and learning. This presumption does not hold true. Test scores correlate most strongly with family income, neighborhood, educational levels of parents, and access to resources — all factors that are measures of wealth that exist *outside* of schools.

This is not to say that schools and teachers are not important in student learning and achievement. However, it is to say that while teachers are central to how our children learn and experience education, the tests offer such narrow measures that they miss most of the processes, experiences, and relationships that define teaching and learning. Further, it is also to say that, as we have seen in so many "miracle" schools, a rise in test scores is rarely connected to genuine improvements in student learning and instead has typically been produced by gaming the system, being selective about who is enrolled in a school, or losing low achievers through attrition or expulsion.

It is also important to recognize that high-stakes tests are not race-neutral tools capable of promoting racial equality. At their origins more than 100 years ago, standardized tests were used as weapons against communities of color, immigrants, and the poor. Because they were presumed to be objective, test results were used to "prove" that whites, the rich, and the U.S.-born were biologically more intelligent than non-whites, the poor, and immigrants. In turn the tests provided backing to early concepts of aptitude and IQ, which were then used to justify the race, class, and cultural inequalities of the time.

For instance, in 1916, based on standardized test scores, Stanford Professor Lewis Terman (one of the founding fathers of standardized testing in U.S. schools) argued that certain races inherited "deficient" IQs, saying that "No amount of school instruction will ever make them intelligent voters or capable citizens." He further asserted that "feeblemindedness" was "very, very common among Spanish-Indian and Mexican families of the Southwest and also among negroes [sic]," and suggested that "Children of this group should be segregated in special classes and be given instruction that is practical . . ." Terman reasoned that while these students were unable to "master abstractions" they still could be made into "efficient workers." This testing was then brought en masse into the growing public school system (in large part due to Terman's work), and standardized test scores were used to justify educational tracking for kids of color, immigrants, and the poor.

This kind of test-informed inequality stems in part from the design paradigm of our standardized tests themselves: They were — and are — built on the assumption that human intelligence is based on biological aptitude that is "naturally" distributed across populations on a bell curve. This bell curve logic decrees that, if a test was given to a large population, some would score high, a lot would be in the middle, and some would do very poorly.

The bell curve underlying the construction of high-stakes standardized tests means that they will always produce high scorers and low scorers. Put differently, the assumed unequal distribution of intelligence built into the tests makes it impossible for everyone to pass and be deemed successful. This reality paints all discussion of closing the achievement gap in test scores in a new light. It does not mean everyone succeeds on the tests. Rather, "closing the achievement gap" in test scores means proportionate success and failure between groups, such that we have equal numbers of rich and poor students passing and failing, equal numbers of Black, white, Asian, Native, and Latinx passing and failing, etc. — all neatly and equally distributed along the bell curve.

In addition, the test-and-punish logic of using a high-stakes standardized test to hold schools, teachers, and students "accountable" for race-based score improvement has failed miserably. While it is true that, for instance, according to a National Research Council 2011 report test scores in Math and English/Language Arts for Black and Latina/o students have generally risen since the implementation of No Child Left Behind, the report also points out that the test scores of white students have risen even more in the same time period. So, after more than a decade of the punitive policies, the threats against, and disciplining of, teachers, students, and schools have exacerbated racial test score gaps instead of closing them.

High-Stakes Testing and the Disciplining of Black and Brown Bodies

The idea of discipline is at the heart of policies and practices aimed at holding students, teachers, and schools "accountable" for raising test scores. There is physical discipline: Students are bound by a set amount of testing time. They must remain silent. Their movements are restricted and generally must stay seated. They also are taken out of their regular classrooms and are required to sit in test-specific rooms. They either cannot access resources beyond the assessment or are limited to only using specified resources (e.g., calculators). Testing happens under the disciplinary gaze of an authority (a proctor) watching for transgressions.

There is also the discipline of enduring the stress and physical limits placed on students for hours at a time, as well as the emotional discipline of handling the stress of the high stakes. While this is problematic for all kids, it is especially damaging to young children who are expected to endure testing experiences that are developmentally inappropriate for them.

High-stakes standardized tests also discipline curriculum and learning: they determine what knowledge and content is considered legitimate for teaching in the classroom. They also discipline teachers' pedagogy because they compel teachers to teach to the test and place restrictions on depth and breadth of subject matter. Further, the tests discipline educational resources, as money gets used on test-aligned textbooks, teaching materials, technologies, and professional development.

While high-stakes standardized testing disciplines all students, non-white and low-income students are disciplined with disproportionate intensity because the tests concentrate failure in their schools and communities. This means that low income and kids of color are tested more; experience the greatest loss of time spent on non-tested or less-tested subjects like art, music, science, and social studies; don't have multicultural, anti-racist curriculum made available to them because those areas are not on the tests; and lose opportunities for culturally relevant instruction because the tests tend to inhibit processed-based, student-centered instruction in favor of rote memorization.

Further, because of the increased intensity of testing and more restrictive curriculum and educational environments, high-stakes tests acculturate children of color to a norm of being disciplined by state authorities — they are tested more frequently, have their performance scrutinized more closely by educational officials and policymakers, are punished more often for test performance, and are subjected to more drastic "corrections" in curriculum and pedagogy than their white counterparts.

The disciplining of Black and Brown children by high-stakes standardized testing also manifests in very concrete and material ways. A 2013 study by the Economic Policy Institute found that in one state having a high-stakes graduation exit exam correlated with a 12.5 percent increase in the rate of incarceration. Again, given that these tests fail kids of color disproportionately, this study suggests that high-stakes standardized tests are a conduit for the school-to-prison pipeline.

High-Stakes Testing as Retributive Justice

Ultimately, high-stakes standardized testing, with its focus on surveillance, discipline, and punishment, represents a form of retributive justice. Built around the concept of "retribution" for a crime, *retributive justice* seeks vengeance for a wrongful act, and it is the cornerstone of our entire system of criminal justice in the United States. Howard Zehr, Distinguished Professor of Restorative Justice at Eastern Mennonite University, explains that retributive justice operates along three questions:

- What rule has been broken?
- Who is to blame?
- What punishment do they deserve?

Educational "accountability" based on high-stakes testing is an expression of retributive justice. Our systems of accountability criminalize test failure, and instead of trying to fix the problem, policymakers use the results to punish students, teachers, schools, and communities.

Can we test our way to racial justice? Currently, we cannot. The paradigm of test and punish does not promote justice in any form. Indeed, looking at its impact, high-stakes standardized tests serve to promote injustice and inflict acute damage on kids of color. However, there are other models beyond retributive justice.

Restorative Assessment

Restorative justice has become an increasingly popular alternative to models of disciplinary, retributive justice that are all too common in schools. According to Zehr, models of restorative justice ask a different set of questions:

- Who has been hurt and what are their needs?
- Who is obligated to address these needs?
- Who has a "stake" in this situation and what is the process of involving them in making things right and preventing future occurrences?

Following this, a model of assessment aimed at racial justice would begin by recognizing that students of color have been hurt by institutionalized racism and white supremacy in our schools and that our current assessments have perpetuated this hurt. Further, a restorative assessment model would then need to explicitly name who is obligated to address the institutionalized racism and white supremacy faced by our students in their schools. We would also need to attend to who has voice and power in determining the assessment, as well as their role and responsibility in making things right.

Restorative assessment would also take seriously the idea of healing our kids and communities. Imagine the possibility of an assessment that would be a part of a process of healing the hurt caused by white supremacy and institutionalized racism. Imagine an assessment that was culturally responsive in form and content, one that assessed students for identity development, knowledge of self, cultural knowledge, and confronting internalized oppression/colonization.

Aspects of restorative assessment exist in some places. For instance, much of Linda Christensen's work, which asks students to write powerfully through pain, or to consider race, class, and the power of language in their lives, begins to point the way toward forms of restorative assessment in the classroom. Her lessons often urge students to express their identities through language, in the process humanizing them while opening pathways toward healing. The practices and pedagogy of the formerly banned Mexican American Studies program in Tucson, Arizona, also orient us toward restorative assessment, as they engaged their students in deep learning that sought to decolonize curriculum and their cultural selves.

One example at the elementary level is La Escuela Fratney, a two-way bilingual elementary school in Milwaukee, Wisconsin, where students have used gallery walks and student-led parent conferences to demonstrate knowledge of their own cultures, skills for working in diverse groups, strategies to fight racist experiences, and reading and writing in languages other than English in order to meet district goals and performance indicators for anti-racist and anti-biased attitudes.

Restorative assessment also invites a conversation about the very forms our assessments take. For instance, as opposed to numerical scores generated by the typical high-stakes standardized test, processed-based portfolios and performance assessments allow for more nuanced, human, and complex expressions of student learning, growth, and development that could more accurately embody restoration and healing. It also puts the very idea of A–F and decimal grading systems into question since those singular grades and decimal scores perform the same functions of surveillance and punishment as standardized tests.

The public New York Performance Standards Consortium schools have produced evidence that this kind of restorative assessment is more effective, in particular, with students of color. In the consortium, in order to graduate high school, students are required to produce a series of portfolios across multiple subject areas to demonstrate their skills and learning, and are then also required to defend that portfolio to a panel of teachers, their peers, and community members. The consortium schools have significantly lower dropout rates and higher college attainment rates for their low-income students, students of color, and English Language Learners than other comparable public schools.

Transformative Assessment

However, because restorative justice focuses mainly on individual wrongdoing and individual events, many activists see it as just a small step toward something bigger: transformative justice — which recognizes the conditions that contribute to and shape wrongdoing. According to Zehr, transformative justice asks a set of distinctly different questions from both retributive and restorative models of justice:

- What social circumstances produced the harmful behavior?
- What structures exist between this structure and others like it?
- What measures could prevent further occurrences?

If we applied these to thinking through what transformative assessment might look like, then it suggests a series of skills and a knowledge base that we want to make sure our students are learning. For instance, we might assess students on their understanding of what historical and socioeconomic circumstances produced the institutionalized racism and white supremacy we see in our schools. Given the continued focus on high-stakes testing in education policy and practice, transformative assessment could also check for student understanding of how testing itself reproduces inequalities and maintains white supremacy.

As is implied by the name, transformative assessment could also assess students on their understanding of, and capacities for, institutional and community transformation. This could include assessing their knowledge of strategies for challenging institutional racism in their schools, districts, and communities. From an activist and transformational perspective, there are concrete skills, understandings, and forms of resistance that we want to foster and develop in our students as potentially powerful individuals and collectives. If we want to assess those skills, then we are forced to consider forms of assessment that are not retributive and ways that are not connected to our current norms and assumptions about standardized testing and accountability.

For instance, in May 2016, students at Forest Grove High School outside of Portland, Oregon, protested a Trump-inspired "build a wall" banner that was hung at their school. Hundreds of Forest Grove students walked out and rallied against the act of racism. Soon, as word spread through social media, they were joined by students from six other high schools in the area. In the following days students from Portland high schools and Portland Community College joined for a rally in the city of Portland itself. It was a powerful moment for student organizing in the Portland area that helped sharpen peoples' consciousness about anti-immigrant racism in the region.

The Forest Grove High School students offer just one example, and we're seeing even more effective organizing by young people, for instance, in the wake of the Stoneman Douglas High School shooting that took place in Parkland, Florida. There are basic skill sets for organizing that we could see in student learning through transformative assessment. There are also forms of consciousness and political orientations that are anti-racist (in the case of Forest Grove) and oppositional to structural authority, helping students understand and act on their collective power in transformative ways. Indeed, student activism also points to the important relationship between restorative and transformative assessment: Restorative assessment, with its focus on healing, cultural self-knowledge, and decolonization can help foster the kinds of critical consciousness that can contribute directly to student involvement in mass mobilizations and movements for social justice we might connect with transformative assessment.

Further, student organizing in Forest Grove, Parkland, and elsewhere suggests the possibility that we can create and wield restorative and transformative assessments to foster this kind of activism as a central aspect of public education. Such assessments would have to challenge racism and white supremacy with a focus on cultural and community healing and radical institutional transformation. Such assessments would also have to be constructed to openly challenge hegemonic power and require a complete break from our current system and the faulty logics of high-stakes standardized testing.

Reclaiming Assessment

The possibility of restorative and transformative assessment is a call for educators and students to reclaim the very idea of "assessment" from the high-stakes standardized tests and corporate education reformers using them for profits and privatization. It invites us to see the very act of assessment as both a tool of healing and as a means to fight the white supremacist legacies of public education in this country. Further, this reclaiming of assessment is also critical for activists and educators working to reform the disciplinary practices of schools. The simple fact is that you can't practice restorative and transformative justice in schools that rely on retributive forms of assessment like high-stakes standardized testing. The healing and hopefulness of one is smothered by the punishment and pain of the other.

Right now, there are real fights in the streets about police killings of Black people, about xenophobia, nationalism, white supremacy, native sovereignty, Islamophobia, gentrification, poverty, healthcare, and the protection of the environment. Students are struggling with these issues in their lives and are out protesting in the streets. Our students need restorative understandings to help them make sense of their lives and times, and they need to know about transformative strategies and skills that they can use in these fights. The possibility of restorative and transformative assessment is a call for educators to create forms of schooling and assessment that are liberatory, partisan, and in the interest of justice. ■

Wayne Au, a former public high school teacher, is a professor in the School of Educational Studies at the University of Washington Bothell, and is a longtime editor of Rethinking Schools.

How K–12 Schools Push Out Black Girls

An interview with Monique W. Morris

By Kate Stoltzfus

As a researcher and author working at the intersection of education, civil rights, and juvenile and social justice, Monique W. Morris has long studied the issues women of color face in the United States. She is co-founder and president of the National Black Women's Justice Institute — a Berkeley, California-based nonprofit organization that works to improve racial and gender disparities in the criminal justice system for Black women. Morris previously served as a vice president for economic programs, advocacy, and research at the NAACP. She and Rebecca Epstein, executive director of the Georgetown Center on Poverty and Inequality, partnered in a two-year project to improve the relationships between girls of color and school resource officers.

Her latest research sheds a light on the treatment of Black girls in K–12 schools. In her fourth book, Pushout: The Criminalization of Black Girls in Schools *(New Press, 2016), Morris takes a closer look at the educational policies, practices, and conditions in U.S. schools that marginalize Black girls both academically and socially as early, she argues, as pre-K. In the book, Morris unpacks the racial and gendered stereotypes that affect how schools respond to Black girls on a daily basis.*

Recent studies from the U.S. Department of Education's office for civil rights show that many current disciplinary measures end up barring these young students from schools at higher rates than those for any other female student group and most male groups, which puts them at greater risk of entering the juvenile justice system. Morris frames this research around the stories of girls she spoke with across the country who experienced "pushout" — defined as the practices that foster criminalization in schools and how this criminalization leads to imprisonment — to expose what she says are the untold stories of the conditions that remain a barrier to Black girls' education and well-being.

Education Week's Commentary Associate Kate Stoltzfus *interviewed Morris by phone to discuss why young Black girls are disproportionately pushed out of schools and how educators and policymakers can join forces with their communities to create school environments that allow all Black girls to thrive in the classroom.*

KATE STOLTZFUS: Black girls are 16 percent of the female student population in public schools in the United States but more than one-third of all female school-based arrests, according to 2011–12 data from the U.S. Department of Education's Office for Civil

Rights. The disparities between how schools discipline Black female students and all other female student groups, as well as many male groups, start as early as preschool. How do we begin to make sense of this polarizing gap?

MONIQUE MORRIS: One of the things I've been sharing in this conversation about school pushout and Black girls is that Black girls are the only group of girls who are disproportionately overrepresented in all categories for which discipline data are collected by the U.S. Department of Education. When we look at this continuum of discipline in partnership with the community conditions, the ways in which our society has misunderstood and misrepresented elements of Black femininity, and the other issues that contribute to school pushout like academic marginalization or underperformance in school, we start to understand that this is not about girls just being bad. We start to see a set of conditions that presents a unique opportunity for there to be a vulnerability to contact with the criminal legal system and contact with school disciplinarians or policies and practices. What we're talking about is the convergence of multiple factors. These are girls who are dealing with multiple forms of victimization, abuse, and oppression, and their response to that oppression is often misread as combative, angry behavior. Sometimes it is angry, and that doesn't make it any less victimizing. So when we're talking about contact with the disciplinary authorities in schools and Black girls, it's important for us to understand the centrality of trauma and to also explore the cultural conditions that have facilitated a consciousness that renders Black girls uniquely vulnerable to having their behaviors being read as loud and aggressive and dangerous to the school environment when they may not necessarily be so.

STOLTZFUS: In the process of writing *Pushout*, you talked with Black girls in elementary through high schools across the country about their experiences in education. What did those conversations reveal to you that statistics or formal research couldn't?

MORRIS: I worked backward and talked to girls who had experienced school pushout, who had been removed from school, who were being educated in juvenile detention facilities. I talked to them about what their education story was, and in almost all of those cases, these Black girls understood that education was important to them. At the same time, while they valued education in theory, they had gone to schools and had engagement with educators that was telling them something different. Almost all of the girls had been suspended or expelled early on in their lives, having their first experiences with suspension in kindergarten and 1st grade. They had experience with racial and gendered bias from the educators in their lives as well as with the other caring adults on campus. They also described being repeatedly victimized in community and in schools, and having that victimization either rendered secondary to the pain and victimization of their male counterparts, or not believed in their spaces of learning and in their homes. What has happened in their lives is that they express the way children do when they have been exposed to trauma and victimization; they have acted out in ways that adults have deemed disruptive. Their narratives represent an opportunity to hear from the viewpoint of girls who have experienced school pushout what their stories are and how they believe the community of caring adults could better understand these conditions.

STOLTZFUS: You described seeing a "raw, uncultivated version" of yourself in the girls you spoke with. How do your own past experiences in school inform your exploration of the criminalization of Black girls in education?

MORRIS: I was always a high performer in school, but that didn't mean I was not subjected to differential treatment from some educators or to some of the thoughts and comments that triggered me in other ways to question my own behavior and my own body. I am a survivor of sexual assault, and this early victimization in my life has shaped how I read and respond to girls who also risk sexual victimization and who are in schools where now there are dress code policies that allow for adults to continuously police the bodies of girls and to police the bodies of Black girls in ways that they perceive to be different from the way in which their white or Asian counterparts have their bodies policed. My very first job was as a student teacher in the Summer Bridge Program in San Francisco. I have always understood that education is an important factor in the development and healthy well-being of our communities. I establish in the book the critical role that education has played in the lives of Black women and Black girls historically. What we've got to do as the community of caring adults, as educators, as those who are committed to educational equity, is to continue to interrogate and center the narratives of girls in ways that allow for us to establish more robust and critical engagements. My personal background and training as a researcher in the criminal and juvenile legal field contributes to that. Having the opportunity to engage with girls who had been in contact with the justice system and were trying to get back into school, or who had been commercially sexually exploited and out of school for a long time, their narratives were not engaged the way that I felt they could be, especially when they overlapped with the oppressions that are faced by girls uniquely as a function of their race and gender. That's where I started to ask a series of questions: Why aren't they in school? What is happening in school that makes them feel like they can't be there?

STOLTZFUS: As you note in your book, in a nationwide culture of increased surveillance and zero-tolerance behavior policies in schools, unconscious bias created by racial and gendered stereotypes in America increases the exclusion of Black girls from learning spaces, which has the potential to push girls who are already struggling into the criminal justice system. What do you believe are the biggest issues facing K–12 Black female students?

MORRIS: What we're dealing with are a series of issues that are tied to harsh punishment in response to problematic student behavior. You get cases like a 6-year-old girl having a tantrum in her kindergarten class and instead of her being engaged with love or responded to with some degree of caring, she is placed in handcuffs in the backseat of a police car. There are a host of ways in which Black girls are uniquely feeling that their presence in school is not consistent with who the school believes should be there. For Black girls who tend to attend these hyper-segregated schools that are high-poverty and often low-performing, they are in schools where there is the belief among administrators that zero-tolerance responses to negative student behavior is the way to curb negative student behavior. This is rather than the development of a continuum of responses or restorative practices that allow for young people to come to terms with how they have created harm and who will be responsible for resolving the harm together — co-constructing discipline and other policies that impact them. What's happening here is the presence of biased learning environments and the absence of resources and other college and career pathways that can facilitate healing in response to much of the problematic behavior and the underlying causes of the problematic behavior.

STOLTZFUS: You say that one of the biggest causes of the discipline disparity is that Black girls do not fit into society's narrow definition of femininity. You note in your book that Black girls are subject to more scrutiny and put into two categories: either "good" girls or "ghetto" girls, both of which reinforce historical and current stereotypes about Black femininity. How can educators combat their unconscious bias and help to recast the negative images of young female Black students often perpetuated by American culture?

MORRIS: I believe most educators are in the field because they love children and believe in the promise of education. I also believe that we are all living with unconscious bias that informs how we read behaviors, what decisions we make, and how we interpret language, volume, and presentation. Whether it aligns with our professed beliefs or not, we are still impacted by negative stereotypes about individuals and identity. In order for us to come to terms with that, we have to engage in the development of other tools, training, and decision-making instruments that serve as a guide for us to engage in a much more equitable way when we're talking about how we respond to children. I don't think that society's narrow definition of femininity, which aligns most closely to what is normed for white, middle-class families, serves anyone particularly well. It has a particular impact on girls who are perceived as the opposite of that. If girls are loud rather than quiet or present in ways that are typically perceived as more masculine than wearing a skirt, that's a problem. When we don't have a particularly diverse teaching force, then we have a greater likelihood that the individuals engaging with youth from various backgrounds are not necessarily going to understand, at least innately, what is happening. What needs to happen is a much more robust discussion in teachers' preparation and training opportunities about implicit bias, decision-making matrices, and the ways in which youth can be brought into establishing both a school and classroom culture that honors their norms as well as those that are typically enforced by schools. I'm also of that mind that while dress codes are increasing in popularity among schools — especially when we're talking about the codes that most directly impact girls — they have little to do with how girls learn. There is an opportunity for us to think about dress codes, to examine them, and to, at a very minimum, remove language that has a disproportionate impact on Black girls and girls of color in a way that is negative in order for us to really move forward with supporting them as critical thinkers and learners in schools.

STOLTZFUS: You offer solutions to cultivate quality learning environments for young Black female students, including protection from victimization; fostering discussions about healthy, intimate relationships; quality student-teacher relationships; creating school wraparound services; providing more focus on learning and less focus on discipline; and establishing school credit recovery between alternative schools (such as those in detention centers) and district schools. What might putting these solutions into practice look like — both at the policy and classroom level?

MORRIS: Schools can either reinforce dominant ideas that are present in society, or they can actively work to develop skill sets among young people to be critical participants in the process of developing the society they want to be a part of and live in. There need to be particular conditions in place: developing healing-informed responses to problematic student behavior and healing-informed classrooms in schools (in recognition of trauma that is alive in many ways among girls who are most at-risk of school pushout), establishing college and career pathways for girls, and developing de-biased learning (which includes culturally competent, gender-responsive curriculum; integrating the arts; and directly addressing the issue of implicit bias). It's important for us to think about how we engage young people in co-constructing with adults the kind of learning environment that we want to facilitate and have in place.

STOLTZFUS: In continuing to seek solutions, you are traveling the country with Rebecca Epstein, executive director of the Georgetown Center on Poverty and Inequality, to speak with girls of color and school police officers. Can you explain what this work is and talk about what these conversations have revealed? Where you would like the larger conversation about the involvement of law enforcement in school discipline to go?

MORRIS: The project that the National Black Women's Justice Institute and the Georgetown Center on Poverty and Inequality are involved in is broader than just Black girls. It's looking at girls of color and their relationship to school resource officers. The policies and practices that have been put in place in response to these elevated discipline rates for girls of color were not constructed with girls in mind. There's been very little that explores the actions that officers are called to enforce in schools. The only time we hear about engagement with law enforcement and girls of color is if there has been an arrest on campus and it makes the news in some way. What we wanted to do was engage law enforcement officers in an opportunity to talk about how they see their role as school resource officers and what engagement and training they've had on working specifically with girls of color. School resource officers have become part of the school climate, so it's very important to talk to them too, about the implicit biases that they are engaging when they interface with girls of color and what kinds of training they're receiving to help reduce the use of harmful tactics when talking to and working with girls of color. ■

Kate Stoltzfus is a writer and editor in Washington, D.C. Her work has appeared in Education Week, *the* Chronicle of Higher Education, *the* DCist, *and the* Journal of Feminist Studies in Religion, *among other places. This interview was originally published by* Education Week *and has been edited for length and clarity.*

Haniyah's Story

By Haniyah Muhammad

Haniyah wrote this article as a 17-year-old participant in Project WHAT!, a program of Community Works West, based in Berkeley, California. The young people in Project WHAT! all have family members who are or have been incarcerated. After an intense summer training, they lead presentations and trainings for teachers, social workers, and criminal justice system staff to create awareness of the problems faced by young people in their situation. Their Resource Guide for Teens with a Parent in Prison or Jail can be downloaded at communityworkswest.org.

My baby pictures are of my dad holding me, getting ready to kiss me, in the visiting area of a juvenile facility. In the photos you can see my dad is wearing a jail suit. I have another photo of me when I was 2 or 3, sitting outside after a visit. At that point my dad was in adult jail. I am now 17 and at age 35, my dad has spent most of my life incarcerated.

It's been so hard for me having a parent in and out of my life since I was born. Whenever my father is fresh out he always looks so beautiful. My dad is darker skinned than me but we have the same calm, slow walk and smooth vibe. We talk similar and have the same facial expressions. My dad is a political rapper, Askari X, and I rap, too. If I'm rapping in the mirror I see movements that I've seen him do even though it's not conscious, I'm just being myself. When my dad is out, he teaches me so much in just a few hours that he spends with me. My dad is so smart. Everyone who knows him says there isn't any subject he doesn't know about. They used to call him Professor X. When he's out we plan fun things to do for holidays or for my birthday and get so excited. But he always seems to get arrested before those things can happen. A month before my 16th birthday my mother told me my father got locked up for not going to court. All I could think about was the red Cadillac he said he was going to buy me. It felt like he reached for my heart in my body and just ripped it out. I had nothing to say.

One of the hardest things about having my dad incarcerated has been the lack of information about what was going on. As a little kid, I knew the police had taken my father away, but I didn't really know what that meant. When I was 4 years old I learned that 911 was the number to call the police, so I dialed 911 and asked to speak to my father. A police officer came to my house and said I was playing on the phone. He told my mother to watch me and make sure I didn't call again.

Growing up, nobody in my family would tell me what my dad was in jail for. I wondered if they didn't want to tell me because he did something really bad and they thought I was going to look at my father differently. But I feel people should tell a child if they want to know why their parent went to jail. Whatever I found out wouldn't change my opinion or love for my father. But not knowing anything causes me hurt and worry.

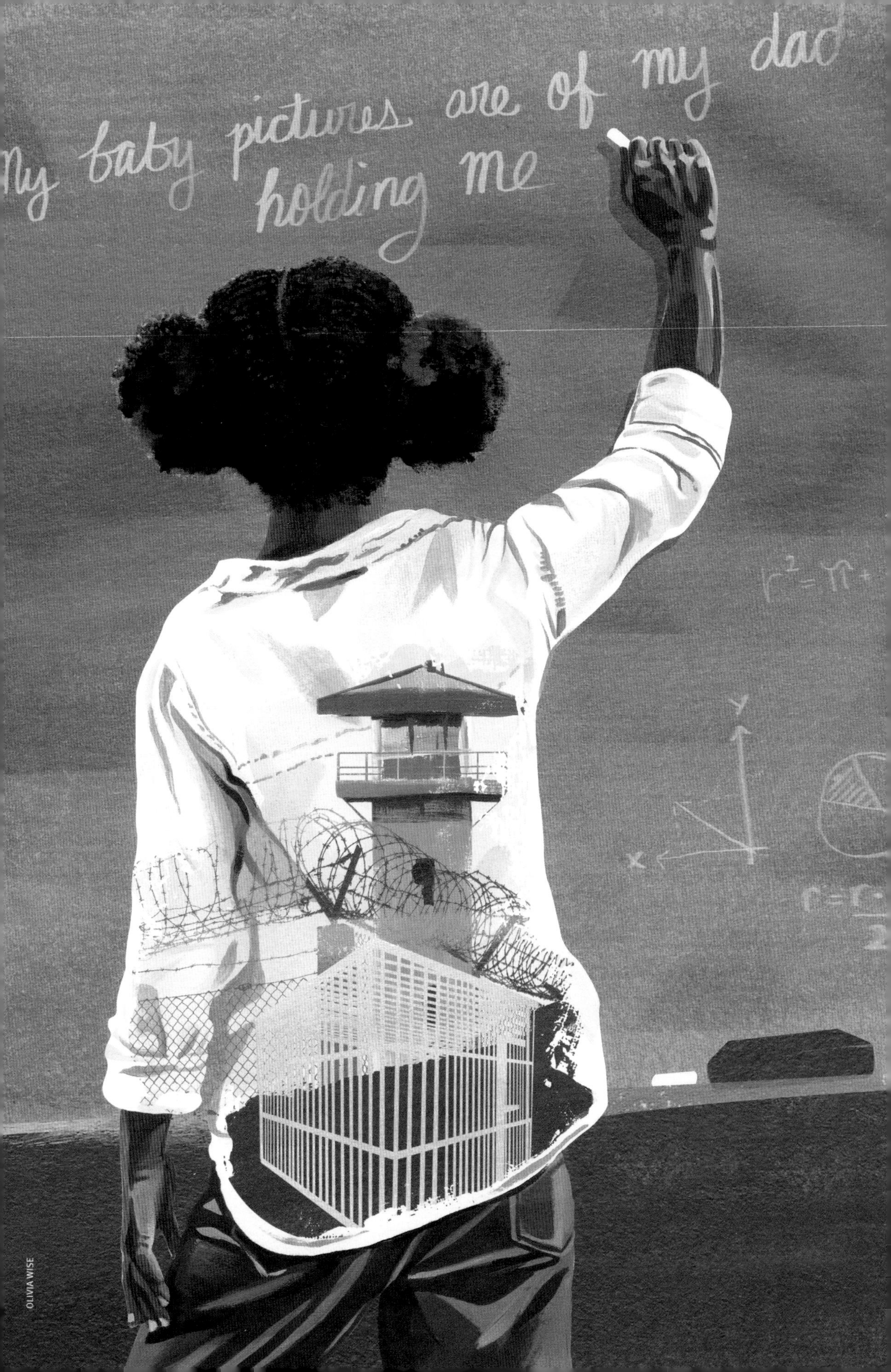

OLIVIA WISE

Right now my father is in jail and no one will tell me what is going on with his situation or when he might get out. I've overheard family members and friends of my father say he has three strikes. I don't know if that means he would get life or a long time locked up. It's sad to know those are his options. But I would feel stronger knowing one way or the other what's going on.

I think my family members are hesitant to tell me information about my dad because they want to protect me. My auntie writes him letters, but when I ask what the situation is she won't say anything, she just says to write him myself. So I wrote my dad a letter recently. I told him how much I missed him. I told him about a school assignment where we had to write a children's story and I wrote mine about my dream of going to the studio and rapping with him, showing him what I can do. In real life I'm always shy to rap in front of him, smiling too much to even start. I told him about the documentary I'm in, about my music with the Oakland youth program Beats Rhymes and Life. They filmed me at my house rapping in front of a poster of my dad and talking about him. I told my dad about that in the letter. I asked my dad how he was doing in there and if he knew when he would be released.

I received a letter from my dad the following week. He told me how much he loved me and how proud he was that I was doing something positive. But he didn't mention anything about when he might get out. I don't know if it's because he doesn't know when he'll be released or if he's just not telling me. I think if I visited I could ask him and look in his eyes to see the truth. But it's been hard for me to visit for a while because I was on an ankle monitor myself.

I got arrested for the first time after my friends got in a fight with a woman on an AC Transit bus. The police arrested me right from school, two months after the incident, saying they had me on video camera on the bus. They put me in an unmarked car alone with three big guys. I was scared, thinking they might hit me or rape me. They didn't have uniforms so I wasn't even sure they were really police. The police told my mother I didn't do anything but I was considered an accessory because I was with the girls who got in the fight. They were trying to charge us as a gang because we got on the bus together coming from school and we got off at the same place. I was taken to juvenile hall for three days. I never want to go back now that I see how they treat the youth in there. Luckily I had the support of my mom and Tomás, my Beats Rhymes and Life teacher, who wrote a letter to the court vouching for me. When I left I told the probation officer and the staff on the unit, "I'm not coming back," and they said: "Yeah right, everyone comes back. We'll see you again." Doesn't it make it more likely that you will come back if they say that, putting that negativity out in the atmosphere?

Sometimes my future seems doomed because I've had similar obstacles in my young life to my father and others in my community. In my father's family, all of his siblings except one have been in and out of jail. Sometimes I feel sick to my stomach trying to figure out how to reverse the curse.

Sometimes it feels like the education system is designed to set you up for failure and grooms you for a life of incarceration. I started my early education in Oakland public schools. I had a hard time focusing on my schoolwork because the kids were so hostile, everyone had to prove they were tough, and I had to defend myself most of the school year. The teachers and staff saw what was going on and they did nothing to stop it. I was outspoken, and I didn't show a lot of emotions like smiling or getting excited when they felt like I should have, so I was told I couldn't go to recess with the other children, would be escorted to lunch alone by an adult, and that they were going to order a psychiatric evaluation for me. I was only 6 years old. My mom fought for me but the treatment continued until she placed me in Berkeley public schools. My schools in Berkeley were not as hostile or as violent as Oakland. I didn't have any fights. However, all the kids talked about how they treated the Black students differently.

My father had trouble in school too, but he didn't have anyone to look out for him because both his parents used crack cocaine. He had problems at home from not being fed properly and abuse. Child Protective Services got involved but they kept placing him back in the home. At school, instead of supporting him, they labeled him and isolated him, saying he was a threat to other kids at only 6 or 7 years old. Eventually, he ran away from home and school. He started running the streets, stealing food from stores to get by. At age 10 he was in Alameda County Juvenile Hall. His life in and out of jail began. By 16 he had released his first album. It was called *Ward of the State*.

Sometimes my future seems doomed because I've had similar obstacles in my young life to my father and others in my community. In my father's family, all of his siblings except one have been in and out of jail.

My dad started using alcohol and weed at an early age to ease his pain. That just contributed to the cycle of incarceration. When he's in jail, he's sober, but once he's out it's all too easy for him to drink or get high. Seeing my dad out of his mind makes me want to hurl. His eyes are red, he looks terrible, and he's not his normal self, the one with eyes wide open, smiling and making jokes. It's hard for me to know that people in power allow drugs and alcohol in our communities and then profit from locking people up for making mistakes influenced by those poisons. Instead of incarceration, people should be able to go to some kind of program to deal with their trauma and addictions.

My dad is a messenger who uses his music to share knowledge with young people in a way that makes them really want to listen. He tells them not to call each other nigger, not to get trapped in the system, not to get addicted. But since he didn't get support in his youth, it's hard for him to stay out of those traps himself.

As for me, I plan to do everything I can to stay out of jail. Jail is not tight like I used to think when I was real young. I don't want to follow in my dad's footsteps in that way. But I do want to follow in his footsteps with his music and what he raps about, teaching people to do right. ■

Haniyah "Askara X" Muhammad is a teaching artist with the organization Beats Rhymes and Life.

Teaching Haniyah

By Jody Sokolower

Several years ago, I taught a unit on power in my 9th-grade social studies classes at Berkeley High School in California's Bay Area. It's a diverse school — rich folks from the hills, middle- and working-class from the flats; about one-third each of African American and white students; the other third a combination of Latina/o, multi-ethnic, South Asian, and others.

For our initial activity, I asked students to interview someone — a relative, neighbor, or themselves — about an encounter with the police. I emphasized that it could be any kind of contact, positive or negative. The questions were basic: Where were you and what were you doing when the encounter began? What did the police do and say? What was the result? How did it make you feel?

The next day, I had the students tell their stories in small groups. Then we rotated the groups so each student ended up hearing everyone else's story. After we returned our desks to a large circle, I asked the students: "What did you hear? What does it make you think?"

The results were stark. As Valerie, a Filipina student, said: "At least in terms of the cops, there are two realities happening in the same city, one for white kids, one for everyone else." To be sure, some white students told stories of being hassled for skateboarding or followed in stores, but there were also stories of lost children reunited with their families and of petting police horses in the park. Among the African American, Latina/o, and Muslim students, the stories piled up of being stopped while walking down the street, thrown against walls, and frisked; immigration agents breaking into apartments; visits to older brothers and other relatives in prison. I was stunned by how sharp the differences were. I was also surprised by the level of openness in the room. The students with painful stories were eager to share them, and the other students were interested and supportive.

One student wrote in a reflection on the activity: "My brother is in jail, and it makes everyone in my family upset. But I never talk about it at school or with my friends. That makes it even worse." Like Haniyah, many of my students of color were describing the impact of the criminal justice system on their families and communities. They were also describing their own fears and vulnerability to getting trapped in the school-to-prison pipeline, and their need to have school be a place to share, analyze, and put their experience in a broader context.

As Haniyah so clearly describes, having a parent or loved one caught up in the criminal justice system is an ongoing crisis that affects every aspect of family life. In many communities, we are in essence teaching in war zones. In California, for example, as you travel through the Central Valley, virtually every freeway exit accesses an institution where people are locked up. Some of us have spent way too much time in or visiting prisons; others have no idea that we are surrounded by people who are incarcerated. Nationally, more than 7 million children have a parent caught up in the criminal justice system.

As teachers we need to understand what is happening so we can provide support. One source of information is programs like the one that Haniyah participated in. Project WHAT! provides leadership development and paid jobs to youth with incarcerated family members. The young people connect their own experiences to the skills and information they need to lead workshops for teachers, social workers, probation and parole officers. They hope to raise awareness and improve services and policies that affect children with incarcerated parents.

"It's enormously helpful if teachers look for context, if they realize that a child might be acting out because of something big that happened at home," according to former director of Project WHAT! Anna Wong. "Maybe they witnessed someone in their family getting arrested. Maybe they went to visit a sibling in jail and were denied a visit. You never know if you don't ask."

Mailee Wang is the current program and policy director. Both of her parents were arrested and incarcerated when she was a teenager. "In my case, it was in the newspapers, so everyone knew, but no one talked to me about it. I felt like an outcast. The teachers were judging me, but no one acknowledged that I was going through really tough times." She ended up being expelled from school. But, Wang says, supportive teachers and other adults can make an enormous difference. Participant Brynesha Williams explains:

> Like Haniyah, many of my students of color were describing the impact of the criminal justice system on their families and communities. They were also describing their own fears and vulnerability to getting trapped in the school-to-prison pipeline, and their need to have school be a place to share, analyze, and put their experience in a broader context.

I was at school talking to a friend in the lunchroom about how I found out my mom went back to jail. I started crying and right then a lady who was walking by noticed me and stopped. Most teachers wouldn't stop if they saw a student crying, but she did. I didn't know her at all. I just saw a very tall, light-skinned woman in her 40s with a kind face. "Why are you crying?" she said. I told her, "My mom's back in jail." She introduced herself as Ms. Boone, the health coordinator, and asked if I wanted to come talk to her. I could tell she had a good spirit, so I went and told her about the whole situation.

Ms. Boone made herself available to talk whenever Brynesha was upset, found her a girls' group and tutoring, and eventually helped her re-establish contact with her mother inside.

"Felon" Is Not an Identity

The relationship to loved ones in prison is a central and vulnerable issue for many of these students. One of the most important lessons Haniyah teaches us lies in her description of her father. He emerges as a complex person — someone with enormous strengths and gifts as well as weaknesses, someone whose own initial contact with the criminal justice system happened when he was far too young and far too vulnerable.

Haniyah loves and admires her father while recognizing how his mistakes have affected her life. The same is true for many of our students whose parents are incarcerated. They need our support in recognizing the significance of their parents in their lives. The mass incarceration that is destroying the fabric of our society rests on stereotyping those in prison as worthless, as if "felon" were a full-blown character description. This puts children with incarcerated parents or siblings in a terrible psychological bind. That bind is exacerbated by the silence, even in the most affected communities, about how many people are locked up. Michelle Alexander explains:

> As Haniyah so clearly describes, having a parent or loved one caught up in the criminal justice system is an ongoing crisis that affects every aspect of family life. In many communities, we are in essence teaching in war zones.

Mass incarceration, far from reducing the stigma associated with criminality, actually creates a deep silence in communities of color, one rooted in shame. Imprisonment is considered so shameful that many people avoid talking about it, even within their own families. . . . Even in communities devastated by mass incarceration, many people struggling to cope with the stigma of imprisonment have no idea that their neighbors are struggling with the same grief, shame, and isolation. . . . Even in church, a place where many people seek solace in times of grief and sorrow, families of prisoners often keep secret the imprisonment of their children or relatives. As one woman responded when asked if she could turn to church members for support, "Church? I wouldn't dare tell anyone at church."

What Can Teachers Do?

When my daughter was in elementary school, a friend of ours, Donna Willmott, was in federal prison for several years, and her daughter Zoe and husband lived with us. When Zoe's teacher, Marilyn Garcia, found out that Donna was at a prison an hour away, she applied to be on Donna's visiting list. Then she went to the prison to have a parent/teacher conference in person. She corresponded with Donna, sending her a class photo and examples of Zoe's work. Not everyone has the time, resources, and generosity of spirit to do all of that, but the impact on both Donna and Zoe was immeasurable.

The first step is to break the silence. Each fall I teach, I look for a way to mention that people I love have been in prison for many years, and that I visit them regularly. Other teachers will have different ways of opening up the subject, using poetry, fiction, news articles, or videos.

Wang offers some guidelines for teachers:

- Don't judge, blame, or label the child because their family member is incarcerated.
- Don't treat the child as though their parent's incarceration is a reflection on them.
- Don't project any feelings you have about incarcerated people onto the child.
- Don't ask why their family member is incarcerated. The details aren't important.
- Don't assume that the child thinks poorly of their incarcerated parent.
- Treat them as you do every other student, believe in them, and let them know they are worthy of success.

The next step is to develop and teach curriculum about the criminal justice system that supports all our students in thinking critically and deeply. In the same way that there are developmentally appropriate ways to engage even young children in discussions of war, immigration, and other critical current issues, we need to create the context and support for our students to grapple with the realities of "law and order." Mass incarceration is affecting many, many of our students, and we need to shine the light of social justice teaching and critical thinking on the issues.

The final and most important step is to fight — in our schools, neighborhoods, states, and nation — to stop the criminalization and incarceration of our students and their families. ■

Jody Sokolower is a former managing editor of Rethinking Schools*, editor of* Teaching About the War*s, and co-editor of* Rethinking Sexism, Gender, and Sexuality*. She is currently a teacher educator and coordinator of the Teach Palestine Project at the Middle East Children's Alliance in Berkeley.*

RESOURCES

Alexander, Michelle. 2010. *The New Jim Crow: Mass Incarceration in the Age of Colorblindness*. The New Press.

Project WHAT! 2008. *Resource Guide for Teens with a Parent in Prison or Jail*. Communityworks.

Teaching the Prison-Industrial Complex

By Aparna Lakshmi

"Harm comes from prior harm." As Deandra says this, I am sitting in the back of my classroom, taking notes. My students are sitting in a circle in the middle of the room, talking to each other about the questions on the board: "What is the purpose of prison? Do prisons work?" In front of them are annotated readings, lecture notes, and typed response papers. They seem to have forgotten that I am there.

Deandra and Lee are discussing what would happen if there were no prisons. Deandra has just finished telling the story of a boy who, fearful of his abusive father, suffocates a girl rather than get in trouble for having a guest over when he is not supposed to. In this case, who should be punished? The boy who is clearly old enough to know his actions are wrong? The father who has instilled such tremendous fear in his son?

If there were no prisons, how would human beings respond to harm like this? Deandra and Lee wrestle with what Deandra has raised: "Harm comes from prior harm." People harm others when they have been harmed themselves — by abuse, poverty, trauma — but prison does not address this prior harm. According to Deandra, it only adds a new layer of trauma to that individual, their family, and their community. As Roberto points out, "When you hurt a person, you hurt a bunch of people connected to that person." Therefore, prison not only harms inmates, but their families and communities as well. But what response to harm is fair to victim, perpetrator, and community? What can stop the cycle of violence?

Conversations like these happened roughly once a week in my senior humanities class. I was teaching in an alternative school in Boston Public Schools and working with students who had dropped out, transferred, or been expelled from their previous schools. Many of my students struggled with reading complex texts and had never learned how to make and defend an argument through their writing. I was determined that they would leave my class confident about their research, reading, and writing skills, and the proud possessors of a portfolio that demonstrated those skills. But I was worried about how to engage students when their school careers had been marked by serious academic challenges.

Therefore, I decided to begin the year with a Freirean exercise I had read about in an article by a former teacher at El Puente Academy in Brooklyn, New York. On the first

day of class, my students walked in to see a large "problem tree" drawn on the board. We spent the whole period filling in the leaves of the tree with the problems we saw in our local communities, nation, and world. After an hour, the leaves were filled with words like racism, probation system, rape, and standardized testing. I explained to students that we would spend the year studying something on this tree and that what we studied was up to them.

For the next two weeks, the students and I worked to choose one problem to study together. First, I gave them cards that represented each of the tree leaves. In pairs, they organized these problems into categories, and soon we had filled in the branches of our tree with broader topics: education, poverty, government, violence, and prison. To give students a glimpse of what the year would be like if we studied any of these topics, I taught a mini-lesson about each one. Next, students interviewed someone in their family or community about the most serious problem that person faced. Most talked about the economy or violence in the community.

Finally, the students voted to study the U.S. prison system. At the end of the year, during a feedback circle, Shanell said: "The best thing about this class was we got to choose what we wanted to learn about. I did the reading and wrote the papers because I was interested in this topic."

Relevance in the classroom is a tricky thing. We may deeply believe that what we teach is relevant to students' lives, but they often experience school as disconnected from their daily realities. The things that students do experience may be outside of our interests, expertise, or comfort zone. When I first started teaching in Boston, I couldn't have imagined spending a year studying the prison-industrial complex. I needed to listen deeply to students' voices about what was relevant to their lived experience before I began to make connections between what I thought was important to study and what they thought mattered. High student interest in a theme they had chosen themselves allowed us to delve into historical content more deeply and facilitated engagement in the academic writing process.

"Neither Slavery nor Involuntary Servitude, Except as a Punishment for Crime . . ."

During the first half of the year, our class looked at the origins of today's skyrocketing incarceration rate. We began by looking at slavery and emancipation and closely analyzing the text of the 13th Amendment: "Neither slavery nor involuntary servitude, *except as a punishment for crime whereof the party shall have been duly convicted*, shall exist within the United States, or any place subject to their jurisdiction" (emphasis added). We investigated the Slave Codes and Black Codes, as well as the convict lease system and the county chain gang.

This historical context enabled students to engage with an excerpt from Angela Davis' *Are Prisons Obsolete?* Davis makes the argument that today's prison system is a reincarnation of slavery, and she calls for the abolition of prisons as necessary in order to truly bring about the final abolition of slavery.

Are Prisons Obsolete? is a dense text and one that challenges even highly skilled readers.

Interest alone will not support students' understanding of a text that is well above their reading level, and many of my students struggled with even grade-level reading comprehension. Therefore, I modeled how to actively read a text using simple reading strategies: pre-reading, annotation, and re-reading. As we read Davis' words aloud, we paused frequently to highlight questions such as "Are prisons racist institutions?" and "Is racism so deeply entrenched in the institution of the prison that it is not possible to eliminate one without eliminating the other?" Students wrote notes in the margin when we read that both chattel slavery and the penitentiary "subordinated their subjects to the will of others." Many students were shocked when they read that officials who enforced the Mississippi Black Codes often prescribed the convict lease system or county chain gang as punishment for the crime of "vagrancy." The Black Codes "declared vagrant anyone who was guilty of theft, had run away [from a job], was drunk, was wanton in conduct or speech, had neglected job or family and . . . all other idle and disorderly persons."

When students were assigned to finish the excerpt for homework, I supported their reading by including vocabulary, background on Davis, and two questions to consider:

What is the connection between slavery and prison?

Who benefits from slavery? Who benefits from prison?

Over the year, I scaffolded access to a variety of texts. Students read memoirs (the autobiography of Assata Shakur), newspaper articles ("A Mother's Day Plea for Justice" by Johnna Paradis), and comics (*The Real Cost of Prisons Comix*), as well as academic texts. I invited students to come after school every Monday to actively read that week's text, and many students would join me to do that week's reading together.

Over the course of the first half of the year, we explored a variety of topics: the legacy of slavery, prison economics, wealth inequality in the United States, the war on drugs, motives for incarceration, inmate rights, resistance movements, and alternatives to incarceration. Every week we explored two open-ended questions together. For example, when studying the war on drugs, we considered:

Are prisons racist institutions? If yes, how so? If not, why not?

From 1970 to 2010, the number of people incarcerated in the United States went from about 325,000 to more than 2 million. How and why did this happen?

The structure of each week reflected my philosophy that it is important for students to have a balance of receptive and expressive experiences. Receptive experiences included listening and reading, while expressive experiences included speaking and writing. For example, when we studied the war on drugs, students took notes on a lecture that included information on Nixon's declaration of war on drugs in 1971, Reagan's decision to fund this "war" with $1.7 billion, and the wave of legal changes that swept the country (including New York's Rockefeller Drug Laws, California's three strikes laws, and the increases in mandatory minimum sentences).

Then we played a game that helped students understand that race and class are key determinants in what happens when someone is arrested for drug use. Each student received an index card stating a defendant's race, class, occupation, drug possession charge, offense number (first, second, or third), and whether the defendant had representation from a private lawyer or a public defender. Students stood in a straight line and listened to the statements I read out loud: "Take one step back if your defendant is represented by a private lawyer." "Take one step forward if your defendant is below the poverty line." The closer you were to the front of the room, the closer your defendant was to prison.

At the end, students were shocked. The game revealed that race and class were much stronger determinants in sentencing than the substance the defendant was using or selling. Students learned that African American, Native American, Latina/o, Southeast Asian, and poor and working-class communities are dramatically overrepresented in prison. In Rafael's words, it was "just crazy" to see that middle-class college students could use heroin and receive community service, but people with less privilege could receive a lengthy prison sentence for the same offense. Students linked the game to the reading they had done that week and noted that, according to "Prisoners of the War on Drugs," one of the comics in *The Real Cost of Prisons Comix*, although African Americans are 13 percent of the U.S. population and 13 percent of drug users, they comprise "35 percent of drug arrests, 55 percent of drug convictions, [and] 74 percent of those sentenced to prison for drugs."

Moving Toward Research and Writing

At the beginning of every year, I survey students about their experiences with reading and writing. Based on their responses, I learned that many of my students had never learned how to craft an argumentative thesis, defend an argument in depth using cited sources, or create a bibliography. Some were used to handwriting all of their assignments. Walking into my class, they were shocked to hear that they had to write eight two-page papers and a 10- to 12-page research thesis.

Writing is a creative act, an act of communication that can be both deeply personal and deeply public. I hoped that my students' engagement in the ideas we were discussing would result in a commitment to working on their writing about those ideas. However, as with reading, high student interest is not a guarantor of clear and thoughtful writing, nor is it a substitute for direct and explicit writing instruction or structures such as writers' workshops, teacher and peer feedback, and public forums to exhibit work.

To scaffold students' research and writing skills, the requirements for writing a paper progressed from simple responses to more structured response papers. Students began the year by choosing quotations to respond to and free-writing their responses. Once students had chosen three quotations and briefly written about them, I asked them to craft three arguments — each based on the evidence (quotation) from the text they had selected. We used the metaphor of a detective who makes an argument about what occurred based on the evidence that she finds. This metaphor helped my students make *arguments*, which we defined as debatable, defendable statements that are not facts and not opinions, but assertions that can be proven using evidence and analysis. The structure of argument, evidence, and analysis helped students craft well-organized paragraphs that communicated something meaningful to their readers.

For example, here is a paragraph from one of Crystal's early papers responding to *Are Prisons Obsolete?*:

> Prisoners back then were not treated like they were human beings. "The prisoners ate and slept on bare ground, without blankets or mattresses, and often without clothes" (33). Although they were in jail they were not provided the proper shelter. They also would get whipped if they would try to run away. If these examples don't scream out slavery then I don't know what does. Slavery was abolished but the prisoners were still being treated as if they were slaves. I think that it was unfair that the prison guards got to break the law when it comes down to prisoners.

Once students had mastered finding evidence and making an argument based on that evidence, I gradually pushed them to start proving their arguments. For each paper students wrote, I gave them extensive feedback on the strength of their arguments ("This is a fact, not an argument"), the strength of their evidence ("Why did you choose this quotation? I don't see how it helps prove your assertion"), and the strength of their analysis ("This is very convincing writing. The examples you use really work to prove your point"). After writing eight short papers in the first term, most students were able to write a cohesive, well-structured short response paper. Most importantly, they were able to make an argument in their writing and defend that argument through evidence and analysis. They were now ready to tackle the challenge of researching and writing a thesis.

> **Angela Davis makes the argument that today's prison system is a reincarnation of slavery, and she calls for the abolition of prisons as necessary in order to truly bring about the final abolition of slavery.**

I gave the students a list of 40 topics that connected in some way to the U.S. criminal justice system, and they brainstormed more on their own. We took a trip to the Copley branch of the Boston Public Library, where students were able to see which topics they had chosen had the strongest sources available. Some of their final topics included U.S. practices of extraordinary rendition, the constitutionality of the death penalty, responses to drug trafficking, and the experiences of women in prison. After choosing a final topic and selecting six sources, students began actively reading their sources in preparation for their thesis. They typed 25 quotations from their sources to build a body of evidence for their paper and organized their arguments and evidence into an outline.

When students were ready to construct their thesis statements, I invited guest teachers into the classroom for a writing workshop so that each student was able to spend 20 minutes with a teacher developing a strong, clear thesis statement. By then the students had significant experience in crafting arguments, so they were able to construct strong thesis statements by developing and refining the larger argument they wanted to make in their papers based on the smaller, more specific arguments they were making in each section. Examples of students' thesis statements included:

> Prison harms women, manipulates them, and makes them less healthy.

> In theory, the Stanford Prison Experiment was ethical, but the real things that happened during the experiment were unethical.

> The U.S. government targeted Puerto Rican independence movements with surveillance and violence because the government sees the movement as a threat to U.S. colonialism.

After five weeks of outlining, drafting, revising, and editing, students turned in their final papers and exhibited them in small peer review circles that were observed by other students as well as outside teachers and guests.

Here is an excerpt from Crystal's thesis, comparing prison labor in the 19th-century Deep South and prison labor in U.S. prisons today:

> Between the late 1800s and the early 1900s, prison labor was used as a replacement for slavery. Prisoners worked on state-operated chain gangs, and they were also leased to private companies and plantations. Under this new convict lease system, "Blacks suffered far more than whites, who rarely left the penitentiary walls. In 1882, for example, 126 of 735 Black state convicts perished, as opposed to 2 of 83 whites" (Oshinsky 46). "The leasing act was designed for Black, not white convicts" (Oshinsky 41). This act was designed to keep Blacks enslaved even though slavery was abolished. The prison system back then was a racialized system, just as slavery had been. The white men in the prisons rarely left the prison, so they never had to do the type of labor that the African Americans were doing.

It is clear from these two excerpts of her writing that Crystal grew significantly over the course of the year in her ability to make an argument, use evidence, and analyze her evidence to prove her assertions. When I spoke with her on the day she turned her thesis in, she couldn't quite believe she had written it.

At the end of the year, most students agreed that researching and writing the thesis was their most rewarding experience in the class, and all of them felt a keen sense of accomplishment. For me, the most powerful moment of the year came during one of the peer review circles.

Five students and I were sitting around a table in the middle of the classroom, while other students and guests watched from an outer circle. Each of the five had written a paper about the experiences of incarcerated women or incarcerated parents. Some had chosen to focus on the perspective of the incarcerated adults ("Moms in Orange Jumpsuits"), while others had chosen to focus on the perspectives of children whose parents are incarcerated ("One Child at a Time"). Shauntae was speaking about the experiences of these children, and her sources included *Children with Parents in Prison*, edited by Cynthia Seymour and Creasie Finney Hairston; "Prisoners of a Hard Life," one of the comics in *The Real Cost of Prisons Comix*; and *Tenacious*, a publication by women in prison for women. Shauntae explained that children of incarcerated parents "may have lower levels of self-esteem and [may] be more likely to believe what others say about them and their parents. They are also more likely to live with a nonparent caregiver and are therefore at higher risk for abuse or neglect." She suggested possible solutions for the care and well-being of these children, proposing increased contact between incarcerated parents and their children, as well as increased contact between these parents and the adults in their children's lives, such as teachers, caregivers, and social workers.

Finally, Shauntae shared that she herself had experienced the incarceration of a parent: "From my personal experience, having an incarcerated parent . . . has not been easy, and while [my father] was gone I have never seen such change in my little brother and myself. . . . However, I do know that if we had gotten the help and support we needed, it would have been much easier than what it was for all of us during that time."

I was moved that she felt comfortable enough to share this very personal experience in the context of our classroom, and I was even more moved that the process of writing something for school had served as an opportunity to process and respond to her own experience. Moments like these taught me that studying the prison-industrial complex was valuable for students on a personal, political, and academic level. The class offered students the opportunity to move beyond pathologizing their own lives, families, and communities by helping them put their experiences in a broader social context — an experience that was deeply strengthening for both the students and myself. ∎

Aparna Lakshmi is a Boston Public Schools history teacher and a member of the Boston Teachers Union.

RESOURCES

For additional materials related to this article, go to teachingforblacklives.org

13th. 2016. Directed by Ava DuVernay, Kandoo Films.

Ahrens, Lois, ed. 2008. *The Real Cost of Prisons Comix*. PM Press.

Alexander, Michelle. 2010. *The New Jim Crow: Mass Incarceration in the Age of Colorblindness*. The New Press.

Barber II, Rev. Dr. William J. and Jonathan Wilson-Hartgrove. 2016. *The Third Reconstruction: How a Moral Movement Is Overcoming the Politics of Division and Fear*. Beacon Press.

Benko, Jessica. March 26, 2015. "The Radical Humaneness of Norway's Halden Prison." *New York Times Magazine*.

Davis, Angela. 2003. *Are Prisons Obsolete?* Seven Stories Press.

Gilmore, Ruth Wilson. 2007. *Golden Gulag: Prisons, Surplus, Crisis, and Opposition in Globalizing California*. University of California Press.

Restorative Justice
What it is and is not

By the editors of *Rethinking Schools*

Misbehave, get punished. That pretty much sums up the approach to "disciplining" students that educators through the decades have taken in schools and classrooms. The most extreme form of this law-and-order strategy is zero tolerance, described in *Rethinking Schools* by Bill Ayers and Bernardine Dohrn back in 2000, as these policies gained popularity:

> Schools everywhere — public, private, urban, suburban, rural, and parochial — are turning into fortresses where electronic searches, locked doors, armed police, surveillance cameras, patrolled cafeterias, and weighty rule books define the landscape.

In schools today, educators still respond to what they perceive as student misbehavior with punishment. However, schools and school districts appear to be abandoning the language of zero tolerance and in many places are introducing what is often called "restorative justice." This represents an enormous victory for the activists and organizations that for years have fought the school-to-prison pipeline. Zero tolerance puts school resources toward policing and push out instead of toward teaching and support. The number of youth — overwhelmingly youth of color — out of school and incarcerated has skyrocketed; LGBTQ and disabled youth are also targeted.

So we welcome the abandonment of zero tolerance.

But simply announcing a commitment to "restorative justice" doesn't make it so. Restorative justice doesn't work as an add-on. It requires us to address the roots of student "misbehavior" and a willingness to rethink and rework our classrooms, schools, and school districts. Meaningful alternatives to punitive approaches take time and trust. They must be built on schoolwide and districtwide participation. They are collaborative and creative, empowering students, teachers, and parents. They rely on social justice curriculum, strong ties among teachers and with families, continuity of leadership, and progress toward building genuine communities of learning.

Too often, this is not what we see in places that tout a focus on restorative justice.

ERIK RUIN

At far too many schools, commitments to implement restorative justice occur amid relentless high-stakes "test-and-punish" regimens — amid scripted curriculum, numbing test-prep drills, budget cutbacks, school closures, the constant shuffling from school to school of students, teachers, and principals.

Meaningful restorative justice also requires robust funding. It can't mean a high school teacher released for one class period to "run the program" or a mandated once-a-year day of staff development training. Under these circumstances, announcing one's embrace of "restorative justice" is hypocritical window dressing.

What Is Restorative Justice?

The concepts of restorative justice are based largely on Indigenous approaches. The Navajo system is a good place to start, described by Robert Yazzie in "Life Comes from It: Navajo Justice Concepts":

Navajo justice is a sophisticated system of egalitarian relationships, where group solidarity takes the place of force and coercion. In it, humans are not in ranks or status classifications from top to bottom. Instead, all humans are equals and make decisions as a group. . . .

There is no precise term for "guilty" in the Navajo language. The word "guilt" implies a moral fault that commands retribution. It is a nonsense word in Navajo law due to the focus on healing, integration with the group, and the end goal of nourishing ongoing relationships with the immediate and extended family, relatives, neighbors, and community.

So what might this look like in public schools? Cedric, a thin African American teenager in a red shirt, sits in a circle with his parents, other students, teachers, counselors, the principal — about two dozen people. Cedric is returning to Ralph J. Bunche High School in Oakland, California, after being incarcerated, and this is his welcome and re-entry circle.

Eric Butler, from Restorative Justice for Oakland Youth (RJOY), explains the goal: to provide support for Cedric's return to school. The circle starts with a relationship-building round: Everyone says what they, as children, hoped for in adulthood.

> **Meaningful alternatives to punitive approaches take time and trust. They must be built on schoolwide and districtwide participation. They are collaborative and creative, empowering students, teachers, and parents.**

The next round is on values necessary to have the discussion: speak your truth, compassion, commitment. Then a round on what everyone commits to doing for Cedric. The principal says, "I am the person who will ensure you get your high school diploma and get on with your life."

"You're making me blush," Cedric says, covering his face with his hands. Later he explains: "That touched me. . . . At first I couldn't trust them, but then they all looked me in the eye and told me what they could do to help me, so I felt like I could give them a chance."

Butler asks Cedric's mom what kind of help she needs from the group. "I need you to support my son," she says.

After repeated times around the circle, they make a concrete plan, decide who will do what, and agree to meet in 30 days. At the end, everyone shakes Cedric's hand or gives him a hug.

The circle for Cedric (made into a short video by RJOY) highlights what restorative justice can offer — healing harm rather than continuing a cycle of crime and punishment. There are a number of models of restorative practices, but they always start with building community. Then, when a problem arises, everyone involved is part of the process. As in Cedric's healing circle, shared values are agreed on. Then questions like these are asked: What is the harm caused and to whom? What are the needs and obligations that have arisen? How can everyone present contribute to addressing the needs, repairing the harm, and restoring relationships? Additional questions can probe the roots of the conflict and make broader connections: What social circumstances promoted the harm? What similarities can we see with other incidents? What structures need to change?

A commitment to restorative justice has to be built over time; it can't be mandated or compelled. For example, Rita Renjitham Alfred was hired in 2005 as case manager in a pilot program to reduce expulsions, suspensions, and fights at Cole Middle School in Oakland. She started with a support group for teachers. The next year, Alfred and a colleague offered five days of training in restorative justice spread out over the year. They also got a commitment from the principal to conduct one staff meeting a month on restorative justice principles.

Soon the teachers suggested that the students get involved. Alfred went class to class, explaining restorative practices and starting discussions. The following year there was an elective in restorative justice and it became an accepted approach for dealing with school problems. By the program's third year, suspensions had dropped 87 percent.

Alfred tells a story that illuminates the program's impact and how it reaches into the school curriculum:

> One day, two middle school students at Cole came to me in tears. "We need an RJ circle on teaching slavery," they said. They asked for my help talking to their teacher, a wonderful teacher who had been an active participant in our RJ trainings, about how she was teaching a unit on slavery in U.S. history. She agreed and we set up the circle.
>
> "We love you," the students said, "but we have to tell you what this unit is doing to us. This is our identity, and the way you're teaching slavery is making us feel terrible." After a long discussion, with tears on all sides, the teacher suggested a strategy: She would reconstruct the unit, putting it in the context of African history overall, and as an international struggle over power, resources, and economic systems — looking at slavery in the context of conquest and resistance all over the world rather than isolating a specific group as victims. She still teaches the unit that way.

What Isn't Restorative Justice?

Given the strengths of restorative justice, doesn't it make sense to charge full steam ahead? Of course, but restorative justice depends on building community, rooting it in social justice curriculum, and integrating classroom practices with schoolwide practices.

Restorative justice is not a set of prompts. The switch from seeing offenders and victims to looking for harm (when everyone involved may well have been harmed) is an enormous one. It's also not a quick fix to change suspension statistics.

Kathy Evans, from Eastern Mennonite University, worries that in our haste to implement RJ in schools, we don't lose our way. Not all programs that call themselves restorative are indeed restorative. Many are restorative-ish; others have been completely co-opted so that restorative terminology is used to rename the detrimental programs they are meant to replace. For example, having kids wash the cafeteria tables in lieu of suspension may be a better option, but it isn't necessarily restorative. . . . Implementing restorative justice to address behavior without critically reflecting on how curriculum content or pedagogy perpetuates aggression is limiting.

Restorative Justice as the Finger in the Dike

Several years ago, at a workshop on restorative practices at the national Free Minds, Free People conference, teachers spoke up during the discussion period. "We spent three years getting buy-in from the administration and the staff for restorative justice, and we were starting to work with the kids. Then our school got 'turned around,' and we lost our principal and most of our staff. Now we're starting over." "I've started over three times," one New York teacher said. "I can't do it again."

Restorative justice won't work as a Band-Aid when schools are being torn to shreds. Look at Philadelphia. The schools have faced years of devastating cuts. Last year at Bartram High School, there were two counselors for more than 1,000 students, 91 percent low-income. Bartram has lost more than a third of its total staff over the last three years, including its only librarian, assistant principals, aides, and a third of its teachers. Dozens of new students came to Bartram as a result of 24 city school closings in 2013. Violence increased, including an assault on a conflict resolution specialist. The administrative response: four more police officers, stricter enforcement of the uniform policy, and rules against cell phones and tardiness — and "a commitment to restorative practices." Under such circumstances, what real meaning does that commitment have?

And, as the students at Cole understood, there is a strong relationship among curriculum, pedagogy, and restorative practices. Restorative justice can't grow in the margins of scripted, test-driven curriculum; it's based on teachers hearing, understanding, and responding to the academic, social, and emotional needs of students.

Don't get us wrong. Rejecting zero tolerance is huge. "Restorative-ish" programs are a vast improvement over zero tolerance. But we need to advocate the essential values of restorative practices. That includes fighting for schools that meet the needs of all our students and the communities they serve. The healing that lies at the heart of restorative practices must include healing the wounds from the kinds of miseducation that oppress children and teachers alike. ■

RESOURCES

Ayers, Bill, and Bernardine Dohrn. 2000. "Resisting Zero Tolerance." *Rethinking Schools*, Vol. 14, No. 3.

Evans, Kathy. June 26, 2014. "Restorative Justice in Education — Possibilities, but Also Concerns." Zehr Institute for Restorative Justice Blog. zehr-institute.org/resource/restorative-justice-in-education-possibilities-but-also-concerns/

Restorative Justice for Oakland Youth and Oakland Unified School District. 2013. "Restorative Welcome and Re-Entry Circle." Filmed by Cassidy Friedman. youtube.com/watch?v=uSJ2GPiptvc&list=UUsMtgGtRkytVLIn7dFfeeaQ

Yazzie, Robert. 2005. "Life Comes from It: Navajo Justice Concepts," in Nielsen, Marianne and James Zion, eds. *Navajo Nation Peacemaking: Living Traditional Justice*. University of Arizona Press.

Baby Steps Toward Restorative Justice

By Linea King

One afternoon last October, I looked up from my notes just in time to see Adolfo push his chest into Abdi's, then bam — he punched Abdi in the face and Abdi punched back. "Shit," I thought, "they're going to be suspended." Since the beginning of the year, I had been talking to my students about our classroom community and how important it is that everyone be present: When one person is gone, it breaks the circle and makes each of us incomplete. Now, because of our district's strict no-fighting policy, both boys would be gone for at least two days.

Adolfo and Abdi were in my class of Latina/o and Somali intermediate and early advanced English language learners (ELLs). Many of my students were also in Spanish dual immersion and/or special education classes, so they had no non-academic electives; in other words, no gym, no art, no music, no alternative ways to express themselves. This was the last class of the day, and many of us were tired and often frustrated.

The year before had been my first year back at the K–8 school in Portland, Oregon, after two years of being a teacher on special assignment. Despite the fact that I had taught ELL at this school for more than 10 years before I left, I felt like a first-year teacher all over again. After two years of writing curriculum and planning professional development, I could talk a good talk about the importance of building community, but I couldn't remember how to walk the walk, and my classroom was a train wreck. Students would start chatting with each other as soon as they arrived, and I would spend the next 45 minutes trying to get their attention so we could learn. I tried keeping students in for lunch recess the next day, writing referrals, teaching to the few who were listening. Almost every day I ended up sending kids out for time-outs. The majority of my 20 students got F's for the year; my most common report card comment was "grade does not reflect ability."

> When one person is gone, it breaks the circle and makes each of us incomplete. Now, because of our district's strict no-fighting policy, both boys would be gone for at least two days.

Theory Is Easier than Practice

Ironically, at the same time I was using time-outs as the go-to disciplinary tool in my classroom, in my off hours I was working with the Portland Parent Union fighting

SIMONE SHIN

the school-to-prison pipeline and other exclusionary practices. The Portland Parent Union is a grassroots parent advocacy group founded by Sheila Warren, an African American woman who struggled with the school district about her own children and grandchildren. The organization primarily supports parents of color and parents of children with special needs in navigating the school system, which often involves pushing back on exclusionary disciplinary practices. We held forums on the school-to-prison pipeline at the teacher union hall, we conducted restorative listening circles between families and teachers, we joined Dignity in Schools' Solutions Not Suspensions national campaign.

I was functioning in a haze of cognitive dissonance, knowing in my heart that sending kids out was wrong, but telling myself: "This kid is making it impossible for me to teach, so he is the sacrificial lamb for the greater good. At least I'm not having him suspended."

That summer I attended a workshop, Echoes of the Past, Voices of Today: The American Indian Student Experience. The facilitator spoke of our classrooms as circles; when one child is gone, the circle is broken. I was deeply affected by his words. Although I had probably said similar things to my class, it somehow resonated in a deeper way. I made a commitment to myself and to my kids that I would not be the one who broke our circle.

But there I was, a month into the school year, with a fistfight in my class. "Hey!" I shouted in my deepest, sternest voice. I ran to the back of the room and tugged on elbows and shirts — to no effect. The boys fell onto the ground and rolled behind my desk, throwing and blocking punches, gasping and grunting. I stepped over their squirming feet and tried calling the office, but there was no answer. "Wendy, go down to the office and get someone — don't worry about a pass!" The student closest to the door rushed out. Finally, the boys bumped my bookshelf one too many times and a ceramic mug fell to the ground and shattered. Abdi, who was on top, jumped up and moved away. They both sat at separate tables breathing hard, looking chagrined. Wendy came back with a male teacher close behind who bellowed, "Come with me — now!" They skulked after him and out the door.

"I'm so sorry that happened," I said to my wide-eyed and silent class. Adrenaline was pumping through my system. "But, you know, part of the reason it happened is because of the negativity in the room. People were putting each other down and that just makes a negative environment."

Issa said that shouldn't make a difference. People should just feel good about themselves. I told them that I joke with my friends about having a perfect ego — I generally feel pretty good about myself, but even with my perfect ego, I am affected by the people around me and negativity in the air. I said, "Right now, after this fight, I feel very uncomfortable. I feel like a bad teacher because it happened in my room. I don't know if anyone else is feeling uncomfortable or scared, but I know I am."

> **Paulo Freire said that teachers need to "live a part of their dreams within their educational space." Referrals aren't a part of my dreams.**

I saw some emphatic nods; others shifted in their seats.

"What's the big deal?" asked Natalia. "People get in fights all the time."

"Well, now they will both be gone for a few days — and our community will not be intact. Is everyone OK?"

"Yeah, we're OK," they murmured, and the bell rang. It was the end of the day.

I was shaken up as I went to our middle school teachers' meeting. I told a colleague about the fight and he said, "Good!" My heart fell. When another teacher joked about disciplining with a baseball bat, I jumped down his throat, yelling that violent talk poisons the air. Later he came into my room to apologize. "I'm so sorry," he said. "That was stupid of me to say. I used to teach in Chicago Public Schools and I remember how awful it is to have a fight in my room."

No administrator came to talk to me. A few days later, I got an email from our assistant principal asking for written details of the fight for her records.

Starting with Compliments

As I reflected on the day and how I might turn the experience into something positive for our class community, I thought back through the work I'd done with the Portland Parent Union and wondered how it might be applicable to this situation. And I remembered a story I had read about a South African community that believes that when someone does something bad, it is because they have forgotten about their own goodness and worth. A community member who transgresses is brought to the center of the village, and everyone who knows them surrounds the individual and tells about all the good things they have done in their life. I decided that, after their suspensions, that is how we would welcome the boys back.

The next day we got into a community circle and I explained my thinking: "So, there was a fight in here yesterday. It was upsetting and we need to heal from it. We know that Abdi and Adolfo are good people — they were born good and they are still good, and when they come back we need to remind them of that." I told my students about the South African community's approach and explained we were going to try it out. First, we would brainstorm all of the good qualities of each of the boys, then we would go around and everyone would give their compliment to an empty chair so students could practice. We started with Abdi.

"He's like a brother to me," said Natalia.

"How so?" I asked. "Can you say something specific about what he does to make you feel that way?"

"He listens to me and helps me with my problems."

"He's funny," said Jose.

"He helps me with my work sometimes."

"He has a great smile."

After everyone had a chance to say something, we went around the circle again and they directed their comments to Abdi in the empty chair.

"Abdi, you're like a brother to me. You listen to me and help me solve my problems."

"Abdi, you're funny."

We continued around the circle and then repeated the process for Adolfo.

Facing the Harm

Two days later, it was Friday and only Adolfo had returned to school. Before class, I began to worry that if we just gave compliments, I might be sending the message that if someone is feeling a little fragile all they need to do is something bad, then they will be guaranteed a bunch of compliments. I realized that we needed to make space in our meeting to acknowledge the harm and how each boy could repair it. At recess I talked to a few kids and asked them to describe the harm that resulted from the fight.

"It broke our community circle because they were suspended."

"It made me scared in class."

"It interrupted the lesson, so we didn't learn as much."

I asked those kids if they would be willing to share their ideas during our circle. I hoped that would get the conversation rolling. I gave Adolfo a heads-up before class that we were going to talk about the fight.

Once we got into our circle, we started the meeting talking about the harm. Besides the students I had already talked to, a few more students shared that they were uncomfortable and one said that property was destroyed.

Adolfo listened closely with his eyes down, nodding. I asked if he had anything to say. "I'm very sorry and will not do anything like that again."

I then explained to him about the community in South Africa and their philosophy of reminding people of their goodness. I asked for a volunteer to start and we went around the circle.

"Adolfo, you are a good friend."

"You make me laugh."

"You have a fresh style."

After each person gave a compliment, Adolfo looked at them and said "thank you." When we had gone around the circle, he asked if he could give some compliments. "Sure," I said. After he appreciated a few people for being his friend or letting him come over to their house, we opened it up and had a big compliment fest, with everyone in the circle getting complimented.

The following Monday Abdi returned and we got into our circle again. "Oh my God, why?" Natalia protested as I told the class to circle up. "It was just a fight. Everyone does it."

"Well, it is something we need to heal from. It harmed us all and we need to deal with it. Plus we need to give Abdi some love."

We started with the compliments. Abdi and Adolfo were able to give each other compliments.

"That was stupid of me, man. I'm sorry. You're a good friend."

"You too, man."

We then went on to identify the harm. By then, the reading I had done about restorative justice was seeping back into my brain — I remembered that not only do all the parties come together to identify harm, they also figure out how to repair the harm. "OK, so what can these two young men do now to repair the harm they caused?" The students made a list of actions that the two boys could take:

> **I remembered a story I had read about a South African community that believes that when someone does something bad, it is because they have forgotten about their own goodness and worth. A community member who transgresses is brought to the center of the village, and everyone who knows them surrounds the individual and tells about all the good things they have done in their life. I decided that, after their suspensions, that is how we would welcome the boys back.**

- Be friendly
- Work hard
- Stay quiet
- Be teachers/role models
- Help people
- Sing a song and/or do a dance for the class together
- Write a letter

Abdi and Adolfo agreed that they could do all of these things, but were particularly excited about the dance.

About a month after the fight, the boys performed their dance for an enthusiastic and supportive audience. They took turns B-boying with acrobatic moves that they had worked on together. Afterward, I passed out a half sheet of paper with these reflection questions:

After the fight I felt _____ because _____.
Now I feel _____ because _____.
I thought the process in the community meeting was _____ because_____.
Ms. King, I really want you to know _____.

"Are you kidding, Ms. King? It happened forever ago! Are we ever going to stop talking about this?"

"Natalia, I promise: This is the last thing — I just need to find out how everyone felt about the process."

Many of the responses conveyed that students were uncomfortable, sad, or worried after the fight; now they were happy that the boys were still friends. Students thought the process was good because everyone got a chance to talk. A few of them wrote: Ms. King, I really want you to know we are a community.

I still struggled with this class. A lot of time was wasted with interruptions, cross talk, chatter. But I didn't send kids out of the class anymore. And instead of the majority of the students getting F's like the previous year, the majority had C's or better.

My assistant principal has told me I need to be writing referrals for disruptive behavior. But I don't think so. Paulo Freire said that teachers need to "live a part of their dreams within their educational space." Referrals aren't a part of my dreams. I think we are due for another compliment fest — it shouldn't take a fight to bring in the love. ∎

Linea King (linea@teleport.com) has been teaching English language learners in Portland, Oregon, public schools for two decades.

5

TEACHING BLACKNESS, LOVING BLACKNESS, AND EXPLORING IDENTITY

"IGNORANCE ALLIED w/ POWER IS THE MOST FEROCIOUS ENEMY JUSTICE CAN HAVE"

~ JAMES BALDWIN

MOLLY CRABAPPLE

A Talk to Teachers

By James Baldwin

Let's begin by saying that we are living through a very dangerous time. Everyone in this room is in one way or another aware of that. We are in a revolutionary situation, no matter how unpopular that word has become in this country. The society in which we live is desperately menaced, not by Khrushchev, but from within. To any citizen of this country who figures himself as responsible — and particularly those of you who deal with the minds and hearts of young people — must be prepared to "go for broke." Or to put it another way, you must understand that in the attempt to correct so many generations of bad faith and cruelty, when it is operating not only in the classroom but in society, you will meet the most fantastic, the most brutal, and the most determined resistance. There is no point in pretending that this won't happen.

Now, since I am talking to schoolteachers and I am not a teacher myself, and in some ways am fairly easily intimidated, I beg you to let me leave that and go back to what I think to be the entire purpose of education in the first place. It would seem to me that when a child is born, if I'm the child's parent, it is my obligation and my high duty to civilize that child. Man is a social animal. He cannot exist without a society. A society, in turn, depends on certain things which everyone within that society takes for granted. Now, the crucial paradox which confronts us here is that the whole process of education occurs within a social framework and is designed to perpetuate the aims of society. Thus, for example, the boys and girls who were born during the era of the Third Reich, when educated to the purposes of the Third Reich, became barbarians. The paradox of education is precisely this — that as one begins to become conscious one begins to examine the society in which he is being educated. The purpose of education, finally, is to create in a person the ability to look at the world for himself, to make his own decisions, to say to himself this is black or this is white, to decide for himself whether there is a God in heaven or not. To ask questions of the universe, and then learn to live with those questions, is the way he achieves his own identity. But no society is really anxious to have that kind of person around. What societies really, ideally, want is a citizenry which will simply obey the rules of society. If a society succeeds in this, that society is about to perish. The obligation of anyone who thinks of himself as responsible is to examine society and try to change it and to fight it — at no matter what risk. This is the only hope society has. This is the only way societies change.

Now, if what I have tried to sketch has any validity, it becomes thoroughly clear, at least to me, that any Negro who is born in this country and undergoes the American educational system runs the risk of becoming schizophrenic. On the one hand he is born in the shadow of the stars and stripes and he is assured it represents a nation which has never lost a war. He pledges allegiance to that flag which guarantees "liberty and justice for all." He is part of a country in which anyone can become president, and so forth. But on the other hand he is also assured by his country and his countrymen that he has never contributed anything to civilization — that his past is nothing more than a record of humiliations gladly endured. He is assured by the republic that he, his father, his mother, and his ancestors were happy, shiftless, watermelon-eating darkies who loved Mr. Charlie and Miss Ann, that the value he has as a Black man is proven by one thing only — his devotion to white people. If you think I am exaggerating, examine the myths which proliferate in this country about Negroes.

Now, all this enters the child's consciousness much sooner than we as adults would like to think it does. As adults, we are easily fooled because we are so anxious to be fooled. But children are very different. Children, not yet aware that it is dangerous to look too deeply at anything, look at everything, look at each other, and draw their own conclusions. They don't have the vocabulary to express what they see, and we, their elders, know how to intimidate them very easily and very soon. But a Black child, looking at the world around him, though he cannot know quite what to make of it, is aware that there is a reason why his mother works so hard, why his father is always on edge. He is aware that there is some reason why, if he sits down in the front of the bus, his father or mother slaps him and drags him to the back of the bus. He is aware that there is some terrible weight on his parents' shoulders which menaces him. And it isn't long — in fact it begins when he is in school — before he discovers the shape of his oppression. Let us say that the child is 7 years old and I am his father, and I decide to take him to the zoo, or to Madison Square Garden, or to the U.N. Building, or to any of the tremendous monuments we find all over New York. We get into a bus and we go from where I live on 131st Street and Seventh Avenue downtown through the park and we get in New York City, which is not Harlem. Now, where the boy lives — even if it is a housing project — is in an undesirable neighborhood. If he lives in one of those housing projects of which everyone in New York is so proud, he has at the front door, if not closer, the pimps, the whores, the junkies — in a word, the danger of life in the ghetto. And the

> **The purpose of education, finally, is to create in a person the ability to look at the world for himself, to make his own decisions, to say to himself this is black or this is white, to decide for himself whether there is a God in heaven or not. To ask questions of the universe, and then learn to live with those questions, is the way he achieves his own identity. But no society is really anxious to have that kind of person around.**

child knows this, though he doesn't know why.

I still remember my first sight of New York. It was really another city when I was born — where I was born. We looked down over the Park Avenue streetcar tracks. It was Park Avenue, but I didn't know what Park Avenue meant *downtown*. The Park Avenue I grew up on, which is still standing, is dark and dirty. No one would dream of opening a Tiffany's on that Park Avenue, and when you go downtown you discover that you are literally in the white world. It is rich — or at least it looks rich. It is clean — because they collect garbage downtown. There are doormen. People walk about as though they owned where they were — and indeed they do. And it's a great shock. It's very hard to relate yourself to this. You don't know what it means. You know — you know instinctively — that none of this is for you. You know this before you are told. And who is it for and who is paying for it? And why isn't it for you?

Later on when you become a grocery boy or messenger and you try to enter one of those buildings a man says, "Go to the back door." Still later, if you happen by some odd chance to have a friend in one of those buildings, the man says, "Where's your package?" Now this by no means is the core of the matter. What I'm trying to get at is that by the time the Negro child has had, effectively, almost all the doors of opportunity slammed in his face, and there are very few things he can do about it. He can more or less accept it with an absolutely inarticulate and dangerous rage inside — all the more dangerous because it is never expressed. It is precisely those silent people whom white people see every day of their lives — I mean your porter and your maid, who never say anything more than "Yes Sir" and "No, Ma'am." They will tell you it's raining if that is what you want to hear, and they will tell you the sun is shining if *that* is what you want to hear. They really hate you — really hate you because in their eyes (and they're right) you stand between them and life. I want to come back to that in a moment. It is the most sinister of the facts, I think, which we now face.

> As adults, we are easily fooled because we are so anxious to be fooled. But children are very different. Children, not yet aware that it is dangerous to look too deeply at anything, look at everything, look at each other, and draw their own conclusions.

There is something else the Negro child can do, too. Every street boy — and I was a street boy, so I know — looking at the society which has produced him, looking at the standards of that society which are not honored by anybody, looking at your churches and the government and the politicians, understand that this structure is operated for someone else's benefit — not for his. And there's no reason in it for him. If he is really cunning, really ruthless, really strong — and many of us are — he becomes a kind of criminal. He becomes a kind of criminal because that's the only way he can live. Harlem and every ghetto in this city — every ghetto in this country — is full of people who live outside the law. They wouldn't dream of calling a policeman. They wouldn't, for a moment, listen to any of those professions of which we are so proud on the Fourth of July. They have turned away from this country forever and totally. They live by their wits and really long to see the day when the entire structure comes down.

The point of all this is that Black men were brought here as a source of cheap labor. They were indispensable to the economy. In order to justify the fact that men were treated as though they were animals, the white republic had to brainwash itself into believing that they were, indeed, animals and *deserved* to be treated like animals. Therefore it is almost impossible for any Negro child to discover anything about his actual history. The reason is that this "animal," once he suspects his own worth, once he starts believing that he is a man, has begun to attack the entire power structure. This is why America has spent such a long time keeping the Negro in his place. What I am trying to suggest to you is that it was not an accident, it was not an act of God, it was not done by well-meaning people muddling into something which they didn't understand. It was a deliberate policy hammered into place in order to make money from black flesh. And now, in 1963, because we have never faced this fact, we are in intolerable trouble.

> Even today, so brainwashed is this republic that people seriously ask in what they suppose to be good faith, "What does the Negro want?" I've heard a great many asinine questions in my life, but that is perhaps the most asinine and perhaps the most insulting.

The Reconstruction, as I read the evidence, was a bargain between the North and South to this effect: "We've liberated them from the land — and delivered them to the bosses." When we left Mississippi to come North we did not come to freedom. We came to the bottom of the labor market, and we are still there. Even the Depression of the 1930s failed to make a dent in Negroes' relationship to white workers in the labor unions. Even today, so brainwashed is this republic that people seriously ask in what they suppose to be good faith, "What does the Negro want?" I've heard a great many asinine questions in my life, but that is perhaps the most asinine and perhaps the most insulting. But the point here is that people who ask that question, thinking that they ask it in good faith, are really the victims of this conspiracy to make Negroes believe they are less than human.

In order for me to live, I decided very early that some mistake had been made somewhere. I was not a "nigger" even though you called me one. But if I was a "nigger" in your eyes, there was something about *you* — there was something *you* needed. I had to realize when I was very young that I was none of those things I was told I was. I was not, for example, happy. I never touched a watermelon for all kinds of reasons. I had been invented by white people, and I knew enough about life by this time to understand that whatever you invent, whatever you project, is you! So where we are now is that a whole country of people believe I'm a "nigger," and I *don't*, and the battle's on! Because if I am not what

I've been told I am, then it means that *you're* not what *you* thought you were *either*! And that is the crisis.

It is not really a "Negro revolution" that is upsetting the country. What is upsetting the country is a sense of its own identity. If, for example, one managed to change the curriculum in all the schools so that Negroes learned more about themselves and their real contributions to this culture, you would be liberating not only Negroes, you'd be liberating white people who know nothing about their own history. And the reason is that if you are compelled to lie about one aspect of anybody's history, you must lie about it all. If you have to lie about my real role here, if you have to pretend that I hoed all that cotton just because I loved you, then you have done something to yourself. You are mad.

Now let's go back a minute. I talked earlier about those silent people — the porter and the maid — who, as I said, don't look up at the sky if you ask them if it is raining, but look into your face. My ancestors and I were very well trained. We understood very early that this was not a Christian nation. It didn't matter what you said or how often you went to church. My father and my mother and my grandfather and my grandmother knew that Christians didn't act this way. It was a simple as that. And if that was so there was no point in dealing with white people in terms of their own moral professions, for they were not going to honor them. What one did was to turn away, smiling all the time, and tell white people what they wanted to hear. But people always accuse you of reckless talk when you say this.

All this means that there are in this country tremendous reservoirs of bitterness which have never been able to find an outlet, but may find an outlet soon. It means that well-meaning white liberals place themselves in great danger when they try to deal with Negroes as though they were missionaries. It means, in brief, that a great price is demanded to liberate all those silent people so that they can breathe for the first time and *tell* you what they think of you. And a price is demanded to liberate all those white children — some of them near 40 — who have never grown up, and who never will grow up, because they have no sense of their identity.

> If, for example, one managed to change the curriculum in all the schools so that Negroes learned more about themselves and their real contributions to this culture, you would be liberating not only Negroes, you'd be liberating white people who know nothing about their own history.

What passes for identity in America is a series of myths about one's heroic ancestors. It's astounding to me, for example, that so many people really appear to believe that the country was founded by a band of heroes who wanted to be free. That happens not to be true. What happened was that some people left Europe because they couldn't stay there any longer and had to go someplace else to make it. That's all. They were hungry, they were poor, they were convicts. Those who were making it in England, for example, did not get on the *May-flower*. That's how the country was settled. Not by Gary Cooper. Yet we have a whole race of people, a whole republic, who believe the myths to the point where even today they select political representatives, as far as I can tell, by how closely they resemble Gary Cooper. Now this is dangerously infantile, and it shows in every level of national life. When I was living in Europe, for example, one of the worst revelations to me was the way Americans walked around Europe buying this and buying that and insulting everybody — not even out of malice, just because they didn't know any better. Well, that is the way they have always treated me. They weren't cruel, they just didn't know you were alive. They didn't know you had any feelings.

What I am trying to suggest here is that in the doing of all this for 100 years or more, it is the American white man who has long since lost his grip on reality. In some peculiar way, having created this myth about Negroes, and the myth about his own history, he created myths about the world so that, for example, he was astounded that some people could prefer Castro, astounded that there are people in the world who don't go into hiding when they hear the word "Communism," astounded that Communism is one of the realities of the 20th century which we will not overcome by pretending that it does not exist. The political level in this country now, on the part of people who should know better, is abysmal.

The Bible says somewhere that where there is no vision the people perish. I don't think anyone can doubt that in this country today we are menaced — intolerably menaced — by a lack of vision.

It is inconceivable that a sovereign people should continue, as we do so abjectly, to say, "I can't do anything about it. It's the government." The government is the creation of the people. It is responsible to the people. And the people are responsible for it. No American has the right to allow the present government to say, when Negro children are being bombed and hosed and shot and beaten all over the Deep South, that there is nothing we can do about it. There must have been a day in this country's life when the bombing of the children in Sunday School would have created a public uproar and endangered the life of a Governor Wallace. It happened here and there was no public uproar.

I began by saying that one of the paradoxes of education was that precisely at the point when you begin to develop a conscience, you must find yourself at war with your society. It is your responsibility to change society if you think of yourself as an educated person. And on the basis of the evidence — the moral and political evidence — one is compelled to say that this is a backward society. Now if I were a teacher in this school, or any Negro school, and I was dealing with Negro children, who were in my care only a few hours of every day and would then return to their homes and to the streets, children who have an apprehension of their future which with every hour grows grimmer and darker, I would try to teach them — I would try to make them know — that those streets, those houses, those dangers, those agonies by which they are surrounded, are criminal. I would try to make each child know that these things are the result of a criminal conspiracy to destroy him. I would teach him that if he intends to get to be a man, he must at once decide that he is stronger than this conspiracy and that he must never make his peace with it. And that one of his weapons for refusing to make his peace with it and for destroying it depends on what he decides he is worth. I would teach him that there are currently very few standards in this country which are worth a man's respect. That it is up to him to change these standards for the sake of the life and the health of the country. I would suggest to him that the popular culture — as represented, for example, on television and in comic books and in movies — is based on fantasies created by very ill people, and he must be aware that these are fantasies that have nothing to do with reality. I would teach him that the press he reads is not as free as it says it is — and that he can do something about that, too. I would try to make him know that just as American history is longer, larger, more various, more beautiful and more terrible than anything anyone has ever said about it, so is the world larger, more daring, more beautiful and more terrible, but principally larger — and that it belongs to him. I would teach him that he doesn't have to be bound by the expediencies of any given administration, any given policy, any given time — that he has the right and the necessity to examine everything. I would try to show him that one has not learned anything about Castro when one says, "He is a Communist." This is a way of *not* learning something about Castro, something about Cuba, something, in fact, about the world. I would suggest to him that he is living, at the moment, in an enormous province. America is not the world and if America is going to become a nation, she must find a way — and this child must help her to find a way — to use the tremendous potential and tremendous energy which this child represents. If this country does not find a way to use that energy, it will be destroyed by that energy. ■

> I began by saying that one of the paradoxes of education was that precisely at the point when you begin to develop a conscience, you must find yourself at war with your society. It is your responsibility to change society if you think of yourself as an educated person. And on the basis of the evidence — the moral and political evidence — one is compelled to say that this is a backward society.

James Baldwin (Aug. 2, 1924–Dec. 1, 1987) was a novelist, essayist, playwright, poet, and social critic. "A Talk to Teachers" © 1963 by James Baldwin was originally delivered as "The Negro Child — His Self-Image." Originally published in the Saturday Review. *Collected in* JAMES BALDWIN: Collected Essays, *published by Library of America. Copyright renewed. Used by arrangement with the James Baldwin Estate.*

Black Like Me

By Renée Watson

**Being seen —
truly seen — is to
feel that all parts
of who I am are
recognized not as
compartmentalized
pieces of myself,
but blended truths
of my identity.**

When I was in middle school, I was bused to the other side of town for my education. Portland Public Schools wanted to integrate middle schools in Southeast Portland. This meant that a handful of Black students — most of us from Northeast Portland who had attended elementary school together — boarded a yellow school bus before sunrise to ride across town. We sat at the back of the bus laughing at the boys stinging on each other with yo momma jokes. My best friend and I shared the headphones to her Walkman so that we both could sing along to Bell Biv DeVoe and Mariah Carey. For the 30-minute ride we were ourselves and there was no shame in the way we talked or related to each other. No one made a big deal about seeing my hair in braids one day and straightened the next. We bragged about how well our mommas cooked and shared our leftovers with each other at lunchtime, even though one day a white girl loudly whispered to her friend that "Black food smells bad."

We had pride and there was a care we took with each other. Though there were normal middle school cliques and dramas, there was also a strength and loyalty among us. On that bus, we were family. I felt like I belonged.

But when I got to school, I felt invisible. Which is ironic because I was a plump dark-skinned girl with hair that would kink and curl at one drop of rain.

I stood out.

So how is it that I felt no one saw me?

Being seen — truly seen — is to feel that all parts of who I am are recognized not as compartmentalized pieces of myself, but blended truths of my identity. So when my white friends told me they didn't see me as a Black girl that meant they didn't see me. When white teachers seemed shocked to hear me speak Black vernacular in the hall-

way with my friends when I "spoke so well in class," what they didn't understand is that code-switching came natural to me — I talked both ways and I wasn't trying to fit in with my friends or impress my teachers. I was being myself.

One day, on our way to a field trip to see the Oregon Symphony, a teacher tried to assure me that if I "gave the music a try" I might really find that I liked it. I told her that I loved classical music. That I loved jazz, too. Her smile told me that she thought this was a good thing. When she said, "Well, that's good because that rap stuff is not music," I told her that I loved hip-hop and R&B and gospel and country, too. My family was a musical family. We had a collection of records that included Tennessee Ernie Ford, Mahalia Jackson, Marvin Gaye, and the Jackson 5. My sister played in a jazz ensemble that traveled to Europe. My grandfather played the piano at church.

> **In middle school I learned that some adults saw me as an "exception to the rule." To be called confident for an overweight, dark-skinned Black girl was to say that overweight, dark-skinned Black girls had low self-esteem. If I was smart for a Black girl that meant the rule was Black children weren't normally smart.**

She didn't seem to value the variety of music I enjoyed. There was clearly one that was better than the others and I took this to mean that the Black parts of me were better off hidden. There was a shame that came with owning up to the parts of me that fit the stereotypes and assumptions of what people expected Black children to be like.

In middle school I learned that some adults saw me as an "exception to the rule." To be called confident for an overweight, dark-skinned Black girl was to say that overweight, dark-skinned Black girls had low self-esteem. If I was smart for a Black girl that meant the rule was Black children weren't normally smart.

It was one thing to feel different, to be different. It was another thing to be judged on those differences. To realize that people had expectations of me because of what I looked like or the neighborhood I was from.

I often excused racist or insensitive remarks and actions, and instead blamed myself or thought that maybe I was taking it the wrong way.

But there was no excusing away what my 7th-grade science teacher said the day she passed out the tests we had taken a few days before. She walked to the front of the room and yelled, "I am so disappointed in all of you!" She paced the floor, walking between our desks. "None of you passed the test. You will be taking it again. Right. Now."

I looked down at my paper. Saw the capital A scribbled in red ink across the top of the page.

"I will give you a chance to look through your notes and then you will retake the test."

I looked back at my paper. "But I have an A," I said. First to myself and then out loud when I raised my hand and asked, "Do I have to retake the test?"

"Oh, that's right," my teacher said. "You got an A." She turned her back to me and addressed the rest of the class. "And this is why I am so disappointed in all of you. You let Renée Watson come all the way over here from Northeast Portland and get a better grade than you in science!"

I have often replayed that day in my mind. I have thought of new endings where I stand up for myself and walk out of class refusing to be humiliated. I have wondered what would have happened if she asked me to be a tutor for the other students in class. What if she taught me — and the rest of the class — about Black scientists and their revolutionary discoveries? What if she had allowed space in her narrative for Black children from Northeast Portland to be capable of meeting high expectations, of achieving academic success?

What if she really saw me?

As an educator, I try to see my students. I encourage them to embrace all parts of their culture — where they come from, what they eat, the music they enjoy, the joyous and disastrous parts of their neighborhoods and families. I strive to learn their individual and collective histories. I share my stories with them, and we grow and heal together. We laugh at ourselves for sometimes being the stereotype. We proudly proclaim that we are more than the stereotype. We mourn and rejoice over our ancestors — their struggles and victories, their shortcomings and strengths. We commit to sharing our true selves. We commit to seeing each other. ∎

> As an educator, I try to see my students. I encourage them to embrace all parts of their culture — where they come from, what they eat, the music they enjoy, the joyous and disastrous parts of their neighborhoods and families.

Renée Watson is an author, educator, and activist. Her young adult novel, Piecing Me Together, *received a Newbery Honor and Coretta Scott King Award. She is the founder of I, Too Arts Collective, a nonprofit housed in the brownstone where Langston Hughes lived and created.*

black like me
By Renée Watson

black like me

and suddenly everyone will see

how black i am.

black like collard greens & salted meat
    simmering on a stove.
black like hot water cornbread & iron
    skillets, like juke joints & fish frys
black like soul train lines & the electric
    slide at weddings and birthdays
black like vaseline on ashy knees, like beads
    decorating braids
black like cotton fields & soul-cried
    spirituals.

my skin is black

like red kool-aid, red soda, the red blood
of the lynched and assassinated and the
    ethiopian man
those skinheads killed with a baseball bat
    when i was in the fifth grade.

i am as black as he was.
my science teacher knows this. she sees
my black and is blind to my brilliance.
can't believe i passed the test with an a
when all the white kids failed.

and when she says to the white students,
"you ought to be ashamed of yourselves. . ."
what she really wants to say is,
    "i can't believe this black girl is smarter
        than you."

all the white kids look at me
and this is when we learn that the color
    of our shells
come with expectations.

i stop being good
at science and math.

my english teacher gives me books and
    journals
and i read and write the world
as it is, as i want it to be.
i read past my black blues, discover that
    i am black
like benjamin banneker and george
    washington carver
black like margaret walker and fannie
    lou hamer

i am not just slave and despair.
i am struggle and triumph. i learn
to live my life in the searching,
    in the quest:

can i be black and brilliant?
can i be jazz and gospel, hip-hop
    and classical?
can i be christian and accepting?
can i be big and beautiful?

can i be black like me?
can anyone see me?

Dear White Teacher

By Chrysanthius Lathan

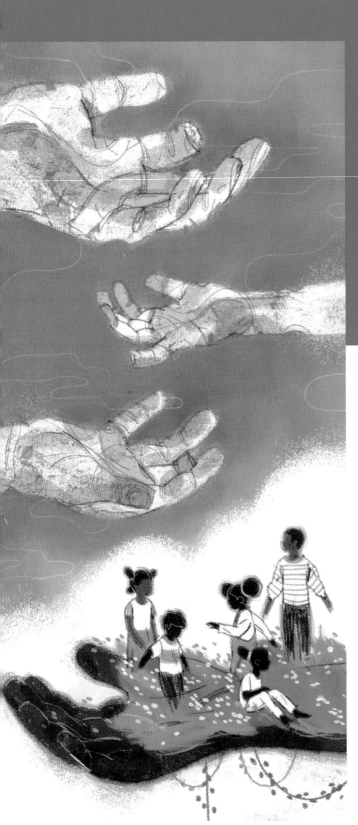

RICHIE POPE

Sending kids of color to the classrooms of teachers of color for time-outs on a continual basis is hurting everyone, including the teachers who send them away.

As a Black, female, no-nonsense middle school teacher, dating back to the days of my student teaching, white teachers in the building have asked if I wanted to be in on a "difficult" phone call, if I would "talk" to a Black boy who was "acting out" or a Black girl who "needed a mentor." I've gotten used to responding with professional, helpful words, though at times I'd like to choose otherwise: "Baby Boy spends more time in your class than anywhere else. He is looking for praise and mentorship from you. It's phony coming from me. You can call home. His mother doesn't want him acting up, but she wants you to do *your* job too. So, sorry — no, he cannot come to me for time-out."

Don't get me wrong, I appreciate when teachers come to me for advice and understanding regarding students and families of color, but using me solely for repeat time-outs and phone calls does not help anyone involved.

A couple of Januaries ago, I was called into my building administrator's office. I had assumed that I would be asked to do something, write something, or lead something. Instead, I was informed that my child's teacher had written her a referral.

I spent six years teaching at the same school that my children attended, which also happened to be statistically the Blackest school in the city. The school was full of amazing, unique educators who had a good grasp on cultural competence. My child's teacher was a white man who taught on the same floor as I did. I sat with this man through many good and not-so-good staff meetings and trainings. He asked me for writing lessons, which I shared. So how is it that I could share my expertise with him and simultaneously have no idea that my child was having trouble behaving herself in class — until it was crammed into one discipline referral at the end of the fifth month of school? The discipline referral went nowhere, but the confusion remained. I confronted her teacher to clear it up. "Why did you not tell me anything if she'd been doing this since September?"

I was met with a wheelbarrow full of excuses. "I don't want to interrupt your teaching or use you as a crutch," he said.

"Interrupt my *life*? That's my child."

It was my suspicion that his fear of the situation crippled his feet and his dialing fingers, just as fear has defeated many well-meaning white teachers of Black and Brown students. I tell my students, "Don't go running your mouth unless you have multiple reliable sources on which to draw your conclusion." So one day I sent out a special focus group invitation to the students who frequented my classroom time-out leather couch. I grabbed the envelope where I had collected the students' time-out slips (I claimed to have lost them, but was secretly stockpiling them) and began writing invitations.

While most of the class was snuggled into silent reading and Josh had finally succumbed to the quiet, warm, dark room and put his head down, I scribbled out 13 invitations. One was for Josh, but I'd wake him later. They read:

You're invited

A big bucket of Red Vines in exchange for your honest opinions today at lunch
Use this invitation
as a hall pass
Don't tell other students — they'll eat up our candy

Some of these kids were sent by other teachers for a time-out, and some decided to come for their own time-outs; nevertheless, my room was a revolving door with these same students of color, constantly in and out. Some were in my class at least one period a day; others weren't on my class rosters at all. Some were girls, most were boys. All of them were Black or Brown except Josh, a white boy who had attended this school since kindergarten and was now in 8th grade.

What I wanted to know from these kids was: What makes my class so different from their other classes? Why do they behave while they're here but misbehave elsewhere, always get busted, and always get sent to me? I knew that the entire middle school team wanted students to be successful. Some can be sarcastic, but I am the queen of sarcasm. Some yell at times, but so do I . . . a little . . . OK, maybe a lot. So what makes Mrs. Lathan's class different? Why were they always circling back to me?

The lunch bell rang and I quickly pushed my class along to get out of the room and get their coats for lunch and recess. I discreetly handed out the invitations to some students. Kids who didn't get one begged to see what they said while I marched the line down to the cafeteria, and drank my soup before I got back upstairs. I set the bucket of licorice in the middle of the hexagonal table, grabbed my flower journal to take notes, and sat. Five minutes later, three kids were escorted in by another teacher, followed by 10 other kids filtering in with their lunches.

I started with my reasoning for asking them to this forum. "Y'all," I said, "I've been teaching for a while, but not long enough. I come to school to learn too. What I learn from you helps me to be a better teacher, for you and for the next year's class. Most of you are in my class at some point in the day, and a few of you aren't. But you guys always come to me for time-out. Look, I counted your time-out slips —"

> **"Mrs. Lathan, you know they're scared of us and our parents, too. That's why they don't be calling home. They just send us to you."**

"Who has the most?" Shawn butted in. He had a quick wit, but mine traveled faster than light.

"You," I said, looking over the top of my glasses at him.

The table laughed and grabbed another Red Vine.

"Anyway, I counted your time-out slips. That's why you were invited. And I really need you guys."

"You need us?" Josh asked.

"Yes, Joshie. I need all of you to answer this perplexing question. Right now I'm like the Godzilla meme, with his finger to his brain, thinking, because I can't answer this question: Why y'all always comin' to me for time-out?"

The room fell silent, except for a few munches of licorice.

So far, Mai had sat with her head down, picking at an overcooked grilled cheese sandwich, silent. This was common for Mai; she rarely spoke to teachers. She came to me for time-out once and I asked her if she was ready to return — and she growled. Today would be different.

"You really want to know the truth, Mrs. Lathan?" she asked, never looking up. "You're not scared."

"Scared of what? Who? Tell me more, Mai."

"Mrs. Lathan, you know they're scared of us and our parents, too. That's why they don't be calling home. They just send us to you."

Mai's words prompted a firestorm of responses, some funny, some serious, coming so fast and hard that finally I had to conduct this small lunch group as a class. "One at a time — raise your hand — I can't write that fast."

"It's because he ain't got no control of the classroom, Mrs. Lathan!"

"Because we can still do our work in here and go back knowing how to avoid getting picked on by the teacher."

"My mom don't like her because she gave me an F without once calling my mom and telling her I wasn't doing my work."

"Because everybody in here knows Mrs. Lathan does not play."

"You talk to us like our moms and aunts; you expect us to do right, and if we don't, you make us tell our parents what we're not doing."

"They send us here when they get tired of us."

"Only certain kids get sent out for doing the same things white kids do, maybe just a little louder or bolder, so we get caught."

"I think they be watching us as soon as we come in the building."

"You know why, Mrs. Lathan, we ain't gotta tell you why we always get sent to you for time-out. It's because you're Black."

"They don't just send us to you. They send us to the other Black teachers and aides too, Mr. Jones, Ms. Johnson . . ."

"You're not scared of us. We're scared of you, though. Just kidding. I mean, scared in a good way. We're scared to disappoint you. We're scared to go into other classes because we know they're gonna start out talking crazy before we even sit down."

Students spoke of my familiar demeanor and tone, my classroom routines, my allowance of personal space when needed, my low tolerance for work avoidance or refusal, my refusal to kick students out but instead expecting them to work hard, my classroom environment of respect for one another, and so on. All of this sounded like what any good teacher would do.

The "it" factor that lingered was fear. There were two types of fear that the students spoke of: the teachers' fear of them and their fear of the teacher.

As an adult and a professional, there were clearly some issues that I dared not discuss with the group of kids. One is the fact that I'm basically doing another adult's job by doing out-of-class disciplinary work. I work hard, but I have a small lazy bone. I don't want to do portions of other people's jobs, as I'm sure no one else wants to do part of mine.

Another issue is that I am teaching students of color how to navigate a classroom with routines and rules centered in ideals of whiteness, where there is only one "right" way to be a successful student: show in ways recognized by white culture that you respect authority, work to a standard, don't challenge, don't make waves, apologize when you do. I question my own ethics every time I tell a student: "I understand you, your teacher may not. That is a reason to follow their rules." And then I push them right back into that room.

The main issue, though, is the time I spend putting out the fires burning in kids, cooling the burns of the previous classroom mishaps, bandaging them up, and telling them not to play with fire, when I know full well that they aren't playing with fire at all. They are walking into a furnace every time they step into the classroom. That furnace is failure, and it is fueled by fear.

"I Don't Want to Be Called Racist"

Based on conversations with colleagues and my observations, I think that many whites live in fear of their good faith actions being labeled as racist. Rather than facing that fear and seeing what they can learn about themselves from the process, many white teachers seem to believe that a better alternative would be to pair students with teachers who look and sound like them, or like people in their families, in the name of having a positive role model or mentor. There's no doubt that we need more teachers of color in our schools, but we also have to deal with the situation that exists today. Many white teachers are discouraged, believing that they are ill-equipped to meet the needs of students of color simply because they don't have the same experiences as them. In response, they freeze.

They freeze when students like Mai are disengaged and not doing work. She may have issues going on that they can't identify with, and she's probably not going to open up to them anyway because she knows that, too. Does that make it OK to ignore what is clearly work avoidance and instead go to help students who have eager hands in the air? They freeze when students like Isaac storm out and say that they hate the school and every brick in it. Does that justify punting Isaac to Mr. Jones because Mr. Jones goes to church with his family? They freeze when Shauna is watching twerk videos on her phone during science class. Sure, there are rules about phones in school, but do we tell her to put away her personal property and risk a class-melting blowout? They freeze when it's time to call Julius' father because Julius needs a tutor. Julius' father just got out of jail. Does that justify letting Julius fall by the wayside? Or deflecting Julius directly to the principal because his father has a record?

> **I think many whites live in fear of their good faith actions being labeled as racist. Rather than facing that fear and seeing what they can learn about themselves from the process, many white teachers seem to believe that a better alternative would be to pair students with teachers who look and sound like them, or like people in their families, in the name of having a positive role model or mentor.**

"Phone Conversations with Parents Don't Go Well"

I've had my share of literal and metaphorical hang-ups when it comes to calling parents, but most conversations have been helpful. When I call parents or guardians, I follow these guidelines:

1. Address them as Mr., Ms. or Mrs., followed by their name on record. No assumptions. If needed, I ask how to say their name properly — and remember it.
2. Refer to their child by their given name.
3. Talk to the parents. Highlight the positive, academically and socially.
4. When explaining the issue to parents, have concrete evidence without interpretation, and give the parent a chance to respond. For example, "Today when James was with another student, he pulled her chair out, and the student fell," instead of "James hurt another student at his table and caused disruption to my lesson."
5. Ask for the parent's help. The student is their child forever, I am their teacher for one year. Look to the parent as an expert.
6. Make a deal among parent, student, and yourself as to how all three will help the child be successful in the area of concern.
7. Call back in two weeks to update and thank the parent.

"I'm Giving Them Someone Positive to Identify With. What's Wrong with That?"

Although white teachers may feel that they are doing a service to children by sending them to someone identifiable, it's actually a backfire. Each time a child is sent to another adult in the building to manage behavior, the teacher loses a little power, no matter what race the child or teacher is. However, there's a subliminal message that many white teachers are blind to, yet it's a bold, glaring truth to parents and students of color: This teacher does not care. Today, I implore you to care. Care enough about this student to build and fortify your own special relationship with them. Care enough about this student to work at figuring out where communication breaks down between you. Care enough about this student to make them pull their weight and work when it's time to work. Care enough about this student to see if there are academic, health, social, or emotional reasons for their work avoidance. Care enough about this student to call on their parents for help, knowing that a parent is more of an influential teacher than you are. And care enough about your colleagues of color to stop using them to clean up your mess.

> Sending kids of color to the classrooms of teachers of color for time-outs on a continual basis is hurting everyone, including the teachers who send them away.

Clearly, being uncaring is not the message that any teacher is trying to send. It is inherent that teachers care about the people in their schools. Otherwise, they'd look for jobs that pay more and do less. And just like I don't know of parents who condone misbehavior, I don't know of teachers of any race who intentionally seek to send a message that they don't care.

"I Can't Control that I Am White. How Can I Show My Students of Color that I Care?"

Allowing fear to cripple your ability to develop relationships in your personal life would have devastating emotional effects, so why allow fear to shroud your intelligence as a compassionate educator? The fear of a race of people fuels the furnace of failure for students of color. Just because you are a white teacher and do not experience life through the same lens as your students of color doesn't mean you can't build an environment where realness, rigor, and relationships abound in your classroom.

If you are a teacher of a student of color, and you have ever asked a co-worker of color to "help," "guide," "mentor," or "just talk to" a student of color that you've had difficulty working with, it's time for you to wake up. Trust me, there's a time in every classroom where a kid needs to go so that either she — or you — can cool off. The revolving door of kids of color, however, needs to stop.

When you send your students to teachers like me, you are inadvertently forcing me to contribute to a racist system, asking me to tell kids how to behave within your four walls and sending them back. That is not fair to them, and it's not fair to me. You need to find that bone in your body that tends to recoil when it comes time to deal with people of color and purposely straighten it back out. You must confront your own discomfort at all costs. Find out why you really don't want to call home, hold the child after school, tell him to sit down, or tell her to finish that essay.

> **If you are a teacher of a student of color, and you have ever asked a co-worker of color to "help," "guide," "mentor," or "just talk to" a student of color that you've had difficulty working with, it's time for you to wake up.**

To effectively teach children of color, you need to understand this: I know that you don't look or sound like me, but that doesn't mean that you have no power. My strength in the classroom does not come from my racial identity, and neither does yours. It comes from the way we treat — and what we expect from — kids and families. It is time for you to take back the power in your classroom. By all means, seek out the advice of colleagues of color, but don't send your students to us without first examining the patchwork needing to be done in your teacher practice. ■

Chrysanthius Lathan (clathan@pps.net) is a public school 8th-grade teacher and writing coach in Portland, Oregon.

Black Boys in White Spaces

One mom's reflection

By Dyan Watson

Right away I recognized her. Ruby Bridges. The courageous girl who defied white racists and became the first to integrate an all-white elementary school. My 7-year-old son pulled a handout out of his backpack with her face on it. He is in a bilingual, two-way immersion program at our local elementary school. As is our custom on Friday, we emptied his backpack and sorted the contents. We determined what needed to be recycled, what would be hung on our whiteboard, and what needed to be stored in my Things-to-take-care-of box by the fridge. I smiled, because as a former history teacher and lover of Black history, I was happy to see my son learning about this important historical moment. And then, I took a closer look and saw that it was in Spanish. I was elated as it dawned on me that my son truly is emergent bilingual. "Caleb, what's this about? Did you read this in school?"

"Oh, yes. Her name was Ruby Bridges and they wouldn't allow her to go to school with the white people."

"That's so cool that you learned about her. I learned about her too."

"Yes, but Mama, I shouldn't have been there that day."

I frowned and looked him in his eyes, "Why not? What do you mean?"

"Everyone stared at me when we read it because I'm the only Black kid in my class."

"Oh sweetie. I'm so sorry. What did the teacher do? What did she say?"

"Nothing."

"Did anybody say anything to you?"

"No, they just stared at me. I didn't like it."

I didn't know what to say. My eyes welled up with tears. I put my arm around him as I tried to figure out what reaction would best serve him. Should I show him my anger? Do I simply weep and say nothing? Should I offer him a snack and ignore it altogether?

I was so disappointed in my lack of words and that I didn't know what to do in that moment. It wasn't a secret to Caleb that we're Black and that on some level that makes us different from most of the people around us. We attend a white church. We live in a white neighborhood. We shop in white stores. And even though his bilingual class is 40 to 50 percent Latino, most of their faces are white or light-skinned. So far, I haven't had any planned conversations about race with my boys. Not sure what I'm waiting for or even that I am waiting. Race is funny that way. As a reality, it's ever present; as a topic it slips in and out of our lives, attaching to everyday things like hair and clothes, to speaking, to how my boys comport themselves in a grocery store. And like many difficult topics about life, the explicit conversations and lessons often come in reactionary waves.

ERIN ROBINSON

Once I was really angry with both of my sons. Can't remember what it was exactly but I remember having this colossal adult tantrum yelling at them about not listening to me. Through tears I shouted, "Don't you get it? Do you think these white people are going to care that you're good kids or that I love you? They will shoot you without even thinking!"

Then there was the time that Caleb came home and reported that two kids were making fun of his skin color in the lunchroom. Teasing him that he must eat a lot of chocolate and that's why his skin is black. As soon as my son told me, I ran upstairs and emailed his teacher:

> Caleb came home today and told me that Santiago and Matt were teasing him about being Black. Santiago and he seem to have had trouble all year long. I haven't said anything to you because I was encouraging Caleb to learn to problem-solve and to speak up for himself but clearly it hasn't worked and this time

it's gone too far. It happened in the lunchroom and Caleb said he raised his hand to tell the teacher but she never called on him. I asked Caleb to talk to you about it tomorrow. It has been tough being the only Black kid in his class. I am trying to prepare him for this life since he lives in Oregon and this will be a regular occurrence. But I also want others to be accountable for their actions. If you could please check in with the boys about this and let me know what you find out and decide to do, I would really appreciate it.

Turns out the kid who "said it first" was from a different class. Caleb's teacher followed up with the boys to find this out and spoke to the other teacher, who subsequently had a class meeting. I don't know the details of this meeting but am glad she acted. She also spoke with Santiago and two other kids who were there when it happened. I applaud her for not letting this go and dismissing it as "boys will be boys," or "good-natured teasing," or "I'm sure they were just joking around." All of which are responses I have heard over the years.

So yes, race is not a stranger to us and we talk about it. But in this moment, with my little boy expressing his sadness and feeling invisible yet overly seen, I was speechless. And then I was sad. And then I was angry.

Here's what I wished would have happened instead.

I wish Caleb's response to my enthusiasm about him learning a moment in Black history would have been him saying, in his own excited voice, "And you know what else we learned? We learned that even though there were white people who didn't want Ruby Bridges in that school, there were some who did." I wish his teacher told him about allies, about the various people of all races committing to stand up against injustice. I wish the teacher noticed everyone staring at my son. I wish that she would have explicitly prepared the class for an age-appropriate conversation about difference.

I wish I felt comfortable asking him my customary "And how did that make you feel?" But I was afraid of his response. And my reaction.

If the teacher had been more thoughtful about the implementation of the lesson, maybe his answer would have been that he felt good. Maybe he would have felt validated if she had talked with him prior to the lesson and explained that sometimes when we're the only one, it can feel lonely and embarrassing, but she was there. That she cared about him. That she would protect him.

Don't misunderstand me. This teacher is thoughtful and definitely cares about my son. But she was not skillful in this circumstance. Part of me wants to be quick to forgive. Here I was also not knowing what to do. Is it OK for me to criticize the actions of a teacher who has too many students and has perhaps been undertrained in how race mediates teaching and learning?

I choose to forgive her.

But I will also hold her accountable for the learning that took place that day. And the learning that should have taken place.

I wish that later that evening, when he was in bed closing his eyes to sleep, he was fantasizing about wildly unrealistic adventures he and his brother would have with the Six Million Dollar Man, how maybe they'd be social justice superheroes righting the wrongs of racism. He could have imagined what he'd do the next day, what he'd get to eat for snack, or if he'd be able to go over Uncle Kevin's house and play on his old Wii. But instead, I have a feeling that he thought about how he didn't want to go to school the next day. How he "shouldn't have been there."

I want Nehemiah and Caleb, my Black sons, to be free to dream, to go to bed with nothing on their minds but how much they are loved and cared for. Black boys deserve to be boys — to be young, carefree, and nurtured. To be seen as human — capable of being hurt, bullied, and afraid. They deserve a school system that will educate them with intentional love. They deserve teachers who will hold the learning space as sacred in all aspects and think through who their students are as they plan lessons and activities. We all deserve schools that will think about how race plays with learning — everyone's learning. White students, especially, deserve to have teachers who will empower them as white allies.

Every neighbor, every teacher, all of the church members and friends of our family have a role in my boys' development. As I think about the conversations I am having with my sons, I wonder what conversations white mothers are having with their sons and daughters. What are they saying — or not saying — that results in their children staring at someone who looks different from them, or teasing a Brown boy's chocolate skin, or accent, or hair texture.

When I asked Caleb how his day went, at some point he answered, "I shouldn't have been there that day." The truth is, son, no one should have been there. No student — Latinx, white, or Black — was served well that day. At the same time, he should have been there; I just wish he was better served and felt like he belonged. ■

> As I think about the conversations I am having with my sons, I wonder what conversations white mothers are having with their sons and daughters. What are they saying — or not saying — that results in their children staring at someone who looks different from them, or teasing a Brown boy's chocolate skin, or accent, or hair texture.

Dyan Watson, an editor for Rethinking Schools, *is an associate professor in teacher education at the Lewis & Clark Graduate School of Education and Counseling. She is also one of the co-editors of the popular book for teachers,* Rhythm and Resistance: Teaching Poetry for Social Justice.

MAYA FREELON, *NURTURE*, 2014, 21.5" x 11.5", TISSUE INK MONO PHOTO PRINT, COURTESY OF THE ARTIST AND MORTON FINE ART

"Raised by Women"
Celebrating our homes

By Linda Christensen

When I first read "Raised by Women" by Kelly Norman Ellis, I knew the poem would be a hit with my students. I love Ellis' celebration of the women in her life, her use of home language, and the wit and wisdom of her rhythmic lines. And from reading student tributes to their mothers over the years, I knew most of my students would relate to the topic. "Raised by Women" also had qualities I look for in poems I use to build community and teach poetic traits: a repeating line that lays down a heartbeat for the students to follow, delicious details from the writer's life that could evoke delicious details from my students' lives, and a rhythm so alive I want to dance when I read it.

Part of my job as a teacher is to awaken students to the joy and love that they may take for granted, so I use poetry and narrative prompts that help them "see" daily gifts, to celebrate their homes and heritages. Ellis' poetry provides a perfect example. As she wrote, "I was just lucky enough to have been born into a loving Southern, Black family. I want these poems to stand as witness to the beauty and abundance of that life: a Black Southern woman's life, a good life, a proud life, a life as rich and sweet as the pies I bake with Mississippi pecans. There are others like me, folks raised in the Brown loving arms of family."

I also use poetry to build relationships with students and between students. Ellis' smart and sassy poem helped launch our yearlong journey to establish relationships as the students and I learned about each other, but also their journey in developing their writing.

In each stanza of the poem, Ellis lists the kinds of women who raised her — from "chitterling eating" to "some PhD toten" kind of women. Ellis' poem follows a repeating but changing pattern. She writes that she was raised by women, sisters, and queens. She includes both description and dialogue in most stanzas:

> I was raised by
> Chitterling eating,
> Vegetarian cooking,
> Cornbread so good you want to lay
> down and die baking
> "Go on baby, get yo'self a plate"
> Kind of Women.

The full poem, as well as a video clip of Ellis reading the poem, can be found at the Coal Black Voices website (coalblackvoices.com), which was developed by Media Working Group to "honor contemporary African American culture and celebrate regional expressions of the African Diaspora through the works of the Affrilachian Poets."

Filling the Bucket with Delicious Details and Style

After reading "Raised by Women" twice, I asked students, "Who were you raised by?" Although Ellis discusses only women, I wanted to open other possibilities. I salted the pot by generating a few: mother, father, coaches, church. I also wanted them to reach out beyond the traditional, so I encouraged them to think about neighbors, neighborhoods, musicians, novelists, civil rights activists, the halls at Grant or Jefferson High School.

After students wrote their lists, we shared them out loud so they could "steal" more ideas from each other. I pushed students to get more specific as they shared. For example, when Melvin said, "Coaches," I asked which coaches raised him — all of them? What did his football coach say or do that helped raise him? When Alex said the men at the barbershop, I asked which men and what did they contribute. Because the best poetry — and writing in general — resides in specific details, I pushed students to move beyond their first response and get deeper.

> "The verb is the workhorse of the sentence. Look at how it harnesses the rest of the stanza and moves it forward. Think about your verbs. What other verbs could you use besides raised?" We played around with alternatives: brought up, taught, educated, nurtured. This is the weightlifting function of teaching poetry.

I wanted them to see that they weren't limited by the original verb, raised, so I asked, "The verb is the workhorse of the sentence. Look at how it harnesses the rest of the stanza and moves it forward. Think about your verbs. What other verbs could you use besides raised?" We played around with alternatives: brought up, taught, educated, nurtured. This is the weightlifting function of teaching poetry. Instead of grammar worksheets, I teach students about the functions of language as we discuss how verbs work in the poem.

When we completed our initial brainstorming about the repeating line, we went back to the poem. I asked, "What kinds of specific details does Ellis include?" The first stanza was about food, the second stanza focused on hair, the third was about physical appearance — skin color and clothes — the fourth about choices, the fifth about music, the sixth about attitude, and the seventh about professions. Because I didn't want each poem to turn out the same, I said, "When you write your poem, you can use these as potential categories, but you can use other categories as well. What else could you list in your poem?" Students shouted out: cars, songs, languages. I encouraged them to create a list of categories like Ellis' — food, clothes, music — and to fill in each category with specific details.

After they brainstormed, we returned to the poem's form. "What do you notice about how Ellis developed the poem? Look at the lines. Where does it repeat? Does it repeat in the same way?" Kamaria noticed the repeating, but changing line. Damon talked about how Ellis' dialogue gives her poem flavor. Tanisha noted that she named specific people — Angela Davis and James Brown. Destiny pointed out that Ellis used home language rather than Standard English. As students noticed these details, I listed them on the board. "Take a look at this list — a repeating but changing line, dialogue, naming people, home language. When you write your poems, I want you to try to include some of these techniques. I know some of you speak another language at home. Experiment with using pieces of that language in your poems. Also, notice how Ellis catches a rhythm in her poem. See if you can create a heartbeat when you write."

The Read-Around and Collective Text: Structuring Response

Before students read their poems, we arranged the desks in a circle so they could see and hear the reader. I asked students to pull out a piece of paper to take notes on what they learned about each classmate through their poem: "Who raised them? What's important to them? Who's important to them?" I discovered that students pay more attention during the read-around if I give them a specific task. For the most part, student poems were stellar, and even those that lacked the style and sassiness of their classmates' gave us a glimpse into their lives.

Students found their own ways into the poems by celebrating more than one person. Anaiah Rhodes, for example, wrote a stanza each for her mother and father, grandmother and grandfather, church folk, music, cousins, and track. Her classmates loved how she used language and details to capture each one in turn, but they especially loved how Anaiah wrote about her church:

> I was taught by a tongue talkin'
> Sanctified, holy ghost filled, fire baptized,
>   shoutin'
> "'Member to keep God first, Baby!"
> Kinda church folk
>
> Some aisle runnin', teary-eyed, joy jumpin',
> Devil rebukin', seed sowin'
> "How you doin', Baby?"
> Type of church folk

Ellis' poem provided an opportunity for us to celebrate the brilliance and linguistic richness of my students' cultures. Destinee Sanders, who also chose to write about a variety of people in her family — mother, aunts, sisters, and *abuelita* — switched languages throughout her poem:

I was raised by *Mi Abuelita*,
Es mi abuela favorita,
Ella es mi corazón, mi amor, mi amiga
Mi noche, mi todos los días, mi siempre.
Yo amo a mi abuelita

[I was raised by My Grandma,
My favorite grandmother,
She is my heart, my love, my friend
My night, my every day, my always.
I love my grandma]

Like Destinee, students shared information in the poem that helped us know their family and backgrounds. Jessica Chavez wrote about her "tortilla making/Grease usin'/ cumbia dancin'" family. Adiana Wilmot wrote, "I was raised by that/curry goat and chicken cookin'/'Eat your vegetables, pickney,'/type of Jamaican woman." Kirk Allen wrote about his family — the Allens — rather than selecting out individuals:

I was raised by the gas, brake dipp'n,
Cadillac whip'n, Wood grain grip'n,
Old school, big body, pimp'n,
Ain't you bullshit'n Allens

I was raised by the show stopp'n,
Hater droppin',
Hat tilted to the side,
Look like a bad mutha,
Shut yo mouth Allens

In this and all class writing, I encouraged students to abandon the prompt and my suggestions and find their own passion and their own way into the assignment. Shona Curtis did that and forged her way to a poem about music instead of people:

I was raised by smooth jazz
Make you want to sit down and
Cry kind of music

Some move your feet and shake
Those hips feel like you dancin'
Down the streets of Argentina
Kind of music

When students wrote at the end of the assignment, many pointed to Shona's straying from the prompt as a strength in her poem. Details from poems brought shouts of laughter or nods as students recognized their own family in Destiny Spruill's description of her family's "Found Jesus/Church goin'/Your mouth can get you in trouble" and "Gumbo makin'/Hat wearin'/Mother of the church/Kinda grandmothers." They understood Ebony Ross' "I was raised to get the belt/If I was talking that lip." But it was Jessica's repeating line — "I wasn't raised by my daddy" — that brought the most affirmations from other students.

Framing Reflection: Milking the Learning

After students shared, I handed out note cards and asked them to look back over their notes and write about what they learned about each other and poetry through our lesson. Kayla Anderson wrote that she learned "that you can completely change a poem but still keep the meaning. Shona made her poem fun by using words like 'hip-hoppin', pop lockin', shake your dreads.'" She noted that many students used strong verbs and imagery. Shona pointed out that "when you say your poem with attitude it sounds better."

But it was students' revelations about each other that made me realize this poetry assignment is a keeper. Students wrote about how much they learned about each other in a short amount of time. "I learned that Adiana is from Jamaica, that Bree was raised by foster parents, and that a lot of us have been let down by our fathers." Destinee wrote:

> I learned that I have something in common with every single person in this room. I realize that we have all been through a lot of the same things. I learned that most of us weren't raised by our dads. I learned that Shaquala loves soul food. I learned that although Bree is Latino like me, she was raised by different types of Latinos, and I can relate to that. . . . I learned that we're different . . . yet we're the same.

Out of the 30 students in the class, the majority were raised without fathers. This became a repeating "aha" for most of the class. Virginia Hankins, for example, wrote that she "learned a lot about my classmates that I would have never known. I was surprised that so many of us were raised without our fathers."

Knitting together poetry that teaches about our lives as well as the craft of writing builds the kind of caring, risk-taking community I hope to create. ∎

Linda Christensen (lmc@lclark.edu) is director of the Oregon Writing Project at Lewis & Clark College in Portland, Oregon, and a Rethinking Schools *editor. She is author, most recently, of* Reading, Writing, and Rising Up: Teaching About Social Justice and the Power of the Written Word (*2nd edition*).

RESOURCE

For additional resources related to this article, go to teachingforblacklives.org

Ellis, Kelly Norman. 2003. "Raised by Women." *Tougaloo Blues*. Third World Press.

RAISED BY WOMEN
By Kelly Norman Ellis

I was raised by
Chitterling eating
Vegetarian cooking
Cornbread so good you want to lay
down and die baking
"Go on baby, get yo'self a plate"
Kind of Women.

Some thick haired
Angela Davis afro styling
"Girl, lay back
and let me scratch yo head"
Sorta Women.

Some big legged
High yellow, mocha brown
Hip shaking
Miniskirt wearing
Hip huggers hugging
Daring debutantes
Groovin
"I know I look good"
Type of Women.

Some tea sipping
White glove wearing
Got married too soon
Divorced
in just the nick of time
"Better say yes ma'am to me"
Type of Sisters.

Some fingerpopping
Boogaloo dancing
Say it loud
I'm Black and I'm proud
James Brown listening
"Go on girl shake that thing"
Kind of Sisters.

Some face slapping
Hands on hips
"Don't mess with me,
Pack your bags and
get the hell out of my house"
Sort of Women.

Some PhD toten
Poetry writing
Portrait painting
"I'll see you in court"
World traveling
Stand back, I'm creating
Type of Queens.

I was raised by
Women.

RAISED

By Anaiah Rhodes

I was raised by a lovin'
Church goin', home cookin', belt whoppin',
Non-stop children bearin'
Money arguin',
"You're going to be something great one day"
Mom and Dad

I was raised by a Jesus lovin', behind tearin'
Bomb cookin', hair pressin', garage sale givin'
Grandma

A politic lovin', money givin', pipe puffin',
Fish fryin', Cadillac whippin', wine sippin',
"Study hard now!"
Grandpa

I was taught by a tongue talkin'
Sanctified, holy ghost filled, fire baptized,
    shoutin'
"'Member to keep God first, Baby!"
Kinda church folk

Some aisle runnin', teary-eyed, joy jumpin',
Devil rebukin', seed sowin'
"How you doin', Baby?"
Type of church folk

I was brought up with that hold on,
Wait on God, don't give up,
Weepin' may endure for the night,
But joy comes in the mornin'
What a friend we have in Jesus, music

By some double darin', house playin',
Fightin', scratchin', teasin', tauntin',
Crumb snatchin'
To football playin' and track runnin'
"I got cha back!"
Cousins

I was brought up by that race
Everybody on the block, barefoot,
    wind in my face,
win or lose, spirit of runnin'
To that sweatin', trainin', muscle tearin',
Shin splintin', intense burnin',
Heavy workout, deep breathin' crazy
Type of runnin'.

Raised.

RAISED
By Elizabeth

I was raised by
swift hands, sturdy words, and strong minds.
"Do what I say,
not what I do.
Think for yourself,"
Kind of women.

I was raised by,
"He ain't no good.
We don't need him,
better off without him.
Never lower your standards.
You better demand respect."
Kind of women.

I was raised by
tears, doors slapping,
trying not to cry,
get outta my face.
"You don't need to see this, baby,"
Kind of women.

I was raised by
head bowing, god fearing,
holy ghost worshipping,
"Never forget your morals.
Praise the lord,"
Kind of faith.

I was raised with pride.
I was raised with pain.
I was raised with faith
I was raised with swift hands,
sturdy words, and a strong mind.

Ode to the Only Black Kid in the Class

By Clint Smith

You, it seems,
are the manifestation
of several lifetimes
of toil. *Brown v. Board*
in flesh. Most days
the classroom feels
like an antechamber.
You are deemed expert
on all things Morrison,
King, Malcolm, Rosa.
Hell, weren't you sitting
on that bus, too?
You are every-
body's best friend
until you are not.
Hip-hop lyricologist.
Presumed athlete.
Free & Reduced sideshow.
Exception and caricature.
Too black and too white
all at once. If you are
successful it is because
of affirmative action.
If you fail it is because
you were destined to.
You are invisible until
they turn on the Friday
night lights. Here you are
star before they render
you asteroid. Before they
watch you turn to dust.

Clint Smith is a doctoral candidate at Harvard University and the author of Counting
Descent *(Write Bloody Publishing, 2016), which has won numerous awards. This poem
was originally published in the fall 2015 issue of* Watershed Review.

#MeToo and *The Color Purple*

By Linda Christensen

uring a recent conversation, a former high school classmate said, "I always wondered why you left Eureka. I heard that something shameful happened, but I never knew what it was."

Yes, something shameful happened. My former husband beat me in front of the Catholic Church in downtown Eureka. He tore hunks of hair from my scalp, broke my nose, and battered my body. It wasn't the first time during the nine months of our marriage. When he fell into a drunken sleep, I found the keys he used to keep me locked inside and I fled, wearing a bikini and a bloodied white fisherman's sweater. For those nine months I had lived in fear of his hands, of drives into the country where he might kill me and bury my body. I lived in fear that if I fled, he might harm my mother or my sister.

I carried that fear and shame around for years. Because even though I left the marriage and the abuse, people said things like, "I'd never let some man beat me." There was no way to tell them the whole story: How growing up and "getting a man" was the goal, how making a marriage work was my responsibility, how failure was a stigma I couldn't bear.

The #MeToo movement has highlighted the breadth of sexual assault and violence against women in this country, and how we might challenge it in every aspect of our lives, including in our schools and our curriculum.

One powerful antidote is literature. Celie, Shug, Sofia, Nettie, and Mary Agnes from *The Color Purple* taught me that the shame I carried wasn't mine, that the fear was real and necessary for survival, but they also taught me to question the roles and rules about womanhood that I learned at my mother's knee. And they taught me about solidarity with other women, about finding my voice and using it.

As I write this article four decades after that foggy night, 120 students sit in a restorative justice circle in the hallways at Madison High School in Portland, Oregon, talking about the sexual harassment they've experienced at school and demanding that the school create and enforce sexual harassment policies. Hallelujah! What I experienced wasn't unique — from catcalls to unwanted attention to my body to forced sex to physical and emotional abuse — but because schools refuse to acknowledge these issues, too many of us who experienced it covered our bruises and believed it was our fault.

At this #MeToo moment of history, this wake-up call for the women — and children and LGBTQ people — who have been physically, emotionally, and sexually abused and

HANNA BARCZYK

harassed, language arts teachers must be courageous enough to teach novels like *The Color Purple.*

I say courageous because *The Color Purple* has been banned across the country. The reasons vary: explicit sex, rape, "vulgar" language, and homosexuality. Novels with sexual abuse, violence, and gay characters are often deemed "inappropriate" for classroom use. What the #MeToo moment demonstrates is that the attempt to protect high school students from literature that exposes them to sexual abuse and sexual harassment has not protected them from experiencing it. Many students in our classrooms have already been abused, already watched their fathers berate or beat their mothers, already been ogled or touched without their consent, already learned that girls need a boy to be OK, that boys can have sex and enjoy it, but girls who enjoy sex are sluts.

In order to teach students how to act differently, we must use our educational space to work for change. The issues most critical in our students' lives are not taught in our curriculum: How to love yourself, how to select a partner who respects you, how to reject social boxes that perpetuate fixed gender roles, how to reject social and familial words and actions that promote harm, how to report sexual abuse.

The #MeToo movement has highlighted the breadth of sexual assault and violence against women in this country, and how we might challenge it in every aspect of our lives, including in our schools and our curriculum.

One powerful antidote is literature.

As teachers we need to ask which systems in our schools and classrooms create conditions for these actions and perspectives to flourish and how can we fashion a different kind of classroom. When we look at our syllabus we need to ask, "Whose voices are heard and what stories are told? How are students nurtured to be their better selves?" If we want schools to prefigure the kind of society we want to live in, we need to change the syllabus.

In my work with a number of school districts in our area, I have asked members of high school language arts communities to make a list of each book they teach by grade level and then to note the gender and race of the main characters and authors. Every single district discovered that during their four years of high school language arts, students rarely encountered main characters or novels by women, writers of color, or LGBTQ authors. The novels most frequently taught: *The Great Gatsby, Catcher in the Rye, To Kill a Mockingbird, The Odyssey, The Scarlet Letter,* and *Lord of the Flies* — all books with mostly male protagonists, written by men, deal with male issues, where women are objects of desire, absent, befuddled, or stoic.

To their credit, these school districts have spent the last five years updating their bookrooms with novels by authors of color and women. But as language arts teachers, we have to do more than weave women, queer folks, and authors of color into our classes. We have to consciously construct a curriculum that talks back to a society that allows sexual harassment to flourish like a virus in a hothouse. We need to fill the curriculum with issues most critical in our students' lives. We need books that teach students about healthy relationships, finding their voices, and understanding their sexuality, and we need to teach them in a way that allows for students to wrestle with these issues in the literature and in their lives instead of building quizzes and tests about quotes and literary motifs. How else will young men learn to be empathetic partners in relationships? Where else will they learn that kindness and masculinity are not opposites? Where else will they understand how much harm their hands, bodies, and words can inflict?

We need to construct writing assignments that promote passageways into our students' lives, and we need to provide safe spaces for students to share their stories — including ones like mine, filled with fear and shame — because those stories teach that we all are vulnerable and need caring communities to support us.

Our curricular choices demonstrate who we believe counts and what beliefs about society we promote. I want us to create curriculum that would have educated me enough to trust my first inklings of fear that said, "This isn't right" instead of a curriculum that taught me that my job was to find, save, serve, or satisfy a man.

The Color Purple is the perfect vehicle for this re-education because the women in the novel suffer abuse and rejection, rise together in strength, and the men learn that instead of using their power to beat women, they can find courage to discover their humanity. Every character in the book teaches students how to overcome their past in order to become stronger human beings.

From Celie's first letters to God, students learn that sexual abuse is about brutality, force, oppression; it is not about pleasure. Celie also teaches that women have the right to love and passion. When Celie and Shug find sexual pleasure with each other, they teach queer kids coming into their own sexuality that queer love is just as natural and beautiful as heterosexual love. And they teach straight kids that lesson too.

When Celie stands up to Mr._____, fueled by anger and her growing sense of her right to be in the world as a woman, Mr._____ is taken aback, as if a rug found a backbone and waved goodbye. Celie says, "I'm poor, I'm Black, I may even be ugly, but, dear God, I'm here, I'm here! . . . Time for me to get away from you, and enter into Creation." Celie's transformation telegraphs that when we assert our right to be in the world, to be seen and heard for who we are, we find our strength — strength enough to walk away from the fear and abuse and lies told about us.

Recently, one of my former students reached out, telling me that she has been in a relationship with a partner who physically and emotionally abused her. I helped her locate a program that finds housing and support for women and children experiencing abuse. If I hadn't taught this book and told my story, would she have stayed?

When Sofia fights back against Harpo's repeated attempts to rule over her, students learn how to refuse to bow to anyone's fists:

> All my life I had to fight. I had to fight my daddy. I had to fight my brothers. I had to fight my cousins and my uncles. A girl child ain't safe in a family of men. But I never thought I'd have to fight in my own house. She let out her breath. I loves Harpo, she say. God knows I do. But I'll kill him dead before I let him beat me.

In this scene, Sofia also teaches Celie — and us — about solidarity by confronting Celie for telling Harpo to beat Sofia into submission. When the two women finish their conversation, they take the pieces of Celie's curtain that Sofia has cut up in her anger at Celie's betrayal and they make a quilt. This is how we learn to confront injustice and use it as a tool to move forward.

The Color Purple also shows that people aren't beyond redemption. Mr.____ learned abuse from his father and he handed it to his son Harpo. At one point in the novel he tells Harpo, "Well how you spect to make her mind? Wives is like children. You have to let 'em know who got the upper hand. Nothing can do that better than a good sound beating." But Mr. _____, like Celie, is transformed. He comes to learn the error of his ways, to find pleasure in the conversation of women, and joy in sewing and cooking, traditionally women's work.

> *The Color Purple* is the perfect vehicle for this re-education because the women in the novel suffer abuse and rejection, rise together in strength, and the men learn that instead of using their power to beat women, they can find courage to discover their humanity. Every character in the book teaches students . . . to become stronger human beings.

By teaching *The Color Purple*, and other content that helps our students critique oppressive patterns of gender and sex, by opening our classrooms to discuss all of the topics that book-banners want us to lock away and look away from, we teach students to name harassment and rape, we teach them to call out actions that belittle, shame, or hurt others. And we teach them to start a movement toward healing, through stories, through action, like the 120 students at Madison High School who sat in a hallway and called out for a different future. ∎

Linda Christensen (lmc@lclark.edu) is director of the Oregon Writing Project at Lewis & Clark College in Portland, Oregon, and a Rethinking Schools *editor. She is author, most recently, of* Reading, Writing, and Rising Up: Teaching About Social Justice and the Power of the Written Word (*2nd edition*).

Queering Black History and Getting Free

By Dominique Hazzard

I am a queer Black woman. By this I mean that my sexuality exists outside the margins, between the approved boundaries, beyond the limits of most imaginations. A queer thing is a thing that existing words cannot yet adequately describe, a thing that our language and our boxes have not yet evolved to capture. So, what does queering something mean? To me it means turning the thing on its head: questioning its assumed narratives, reworking its categories, and upending its status quo.

Let's queer Black history.

Lifting Up the Stories of Black LGBTQ People

Queering Black history means lifting up the stories of Black LGBTQ people. It means resolving that not one more student learns about the "I Have a Dream" speech without learning about Bayard Rustin, the man who led the planning of the March on Washington — at least not on our watch. It means really learning about him: knowing his contributions to the Civil Rights Movement, reading *Time on Two Crosses* right next to *The Autobiography of Martin Luther King Jr.*, having discussions in our classrooms and on our social media about "Letter from a Birmingham Jail" while also discussing why Bayard Rustin too was arrested, how he was relegated to the background by his peers, and what we must do to prevent that from ever again happening in the Black freedom movement.

> **Queering Black history means canonizing Marsha P. Johnson as a matriarch of Black America. Putting her face on those calendars and poster collages right next to Harriet Tubman, Sojourner Truth, Coretta Scott King, and Michelle Obama.**

Queering Black history means canonizing Marsha P. Johnson as a matriarch of Black America. Putting her face on those calendars and poster collages right next to Harriet Tubman, Sojourner Truth, Coretta Scott King, and Michelle Obama. It means studying her ACT UP campaigns in high school classrooms. It means mourning her too-early death just as we mourn the deaths of cisgender men like Malcom and Medgar. It means examining why it took 20 years for the NYPD to investigate that death as a murder, and having conversations about the role of the Black freedom movement in bringing about trans liberation today.

Complicating the Stories of the Historical Figures We Know

Queering Black history goes wider and deeper than the inclusion and re-centering of queer folks. Remember that "queering" also means reworking. We must rework and complicate the stories we tell about the Black figures we are familiar with.

Rosa Parks, for example, was not only told to get to the back of the bus. She was also told by Montgomery NAACP president E. D. Nixon, with whom she served as chapter secretary, that women should stay in the kitchen. As we study her resistance against both attacks on her Black womanhood (and her organizing against sexual violence), a queering of Black history requires us to ask why we leave out that piece of the story, and how we can ensure that our contemporary movements are safe spaces for people living at the intersections.

> Remember that "queering" also means reworking. We must rework and complicate the stories we tell about the Black figures we are familiar with.

Billie Holiday was a prolific jazz singer. She was also addicted to heroin, and the first major target of the federal government's war on drugs. Harry Anslinger, virulent racist and first head of the Federal Bureau of Narcotics, intentionally turned a blind eye to the addictions of prominent white entertainers while obsessing over Holiday and his dream of bringing the full force of the federal government down upon her head. She died shackled to a hospital bed, denied appropriate treatment by the federal government, with police officers at her door. Billie Holiday has an important place not only in the history of Black music, but in the history of Black people, the police state, and resistance.

Seeking Out New Stories

But if we are to queer Black history then we must dig deeper, do more than adding nuance to the narratives of those we already know and love. We also have to study and celebrate the Black people who have been erased, hidden from our collective memories. We have to move beyond the shiny Negroes — the astronauts, entrepreneurs, athletes, entertainers, and organizers who have been deemed respectable enough to be worthy of our memory. We have to look between the cracks and find our incarcerated heroes, our undocumented leaders, our luminary sex workers, the people who systems of oppression most desperately want us to forget. And we have to teach those stories to each other.

We have to do the work of intentionally remembering people like Carol Crooks. I learned her name while doing research for this essay. She doesn't have a Wikipedia page. But she is worth remembering. Crooks was a woman who became an organizer while incarcerated at Bedford Hills, a maximum security prison in New York.

In February of 1974, Crooks had a severe migraine and asked to be taken to see the prison nurse. When her guard denied her request, she tried to push past her and get to the nurse anyway. In response to this incident, Crooks was beaten, stripped naked, and placed into a solitary confinement cell for three days. Crooks later filed a lawsuit

NO PRIDE for SOME of US without LIBERATION for All of US

MARShA "Pay It No Mind" JohNSon was a mother of the trans+ QueeR LibeRation movement. She dedicated her life to helping tRaNs youth, sex workers and pooR and incaRceRated queers.

We HONOR her LeGACy by Supporting TRaNS WomeN of COLOR to LIVE+LEAD.

MICAH BAZANT

challenging the practice of sentencing inmates to solitary confinement with no trial or formal charges. She won her case, and the warden was found guilty of unconstitutional treatment of a prisoner.

That August, Crooks was returned to solitary with no formal charges. The next morning, a group of women went to the warden and demanded Crooks' release, alleging that the solitary confinement of Crooks was retaliatory. The women were ignored and told to go to bed three hours earlier than usual. They refused to comply. The guards began to assault the women in response to the insubordination. The women seized the guards' weapons and fought back. They took over the prison in what is now known as the August Rebellion, until state troopers subdued them about four hours later.

Carol Crooks is part of a queered Black history.

Disrupting the Centralized, Charismatic Leader Narrative

Next we must question the very ideal of Black history through the lens of the individual. We must ask ourselves: Why does the history we choose to remember so often come in the form of charismatic and solitary pioneers, centralized leadership, and the folks out front?

Queering Black history means remembering everyday people, the struggles they faced, and the work they did. It means recognizing ordinary Black people who were told their lives didn't matter, but who still contained a fierce will to live, and love, and fight for freedom. It means valuing all different types of Black leadership — the folks who were behind the scenes, who were quiet, who were less than charming, who didn't win but set the stage for those who later would, who rose to the occasion because they had to and then went back to their regularly scheduled lives. It means celebrating collectives, and group efforts, and conglomerations of movers, shakers, and neighbors whose names we won't ever know.

> Queering Black history means remembering everyday people, the struggles they faced, and the work they did. It means recognizing ordinary Black people who were told their lives didn't matter, but who still contained a fierce will to live, and love, and fight for freedom.

I want us to upend the status quo by including the Contract Buyers League in our Civil Rights Movement narrative. The Contract Buyers League was a group of more than 500 people living on the South Side of Chicago in the 1960s who had bought their homes through predatory loans after being shut out of the mainstream home loan market by racist laws. They banded together, filed suit against the speculators who were cheating them, and demanded their money back. They lost. But the Contract Buyers League is part of a queered Black history.

I want us to queer Black history by teaching about the residents of the Arthur Capper public housing community in Washington, D.C. These residents saw businesses, and particularly grocery stores, disinvest from their Southeast community in the 1970s. They decided to take matters into their own hands. As the mythology of entitled Black welfare queens and lazy project thugs was gaining steam across the country, the residents worked together to start a community-owned small business. They built the Martin Luther King Jr. Co-Op Food Store and harnessed the power of cooperative economics to nourish a Black community trying to survive in a hostile white world. We don't know the names of everyone who accomplished this feat, but the residents of the now-demolished Arthur Capper public housing project are part of a queered Black history.

Acknowledging Our Dirt, Holding Our Pain

A queered Black history cannot be sanitized. Filing down Black history's sharp edges would make sense if the only point of studying it was to make ourselves feel good. Sweeping the flaws of our Black icons under the rug would be reasonable if the goal of Black history was to convince a white society that Black people are good and smart, that we can be honorable too, that our lives matter. But I don't believe that either of these goals are what Black history is about.

I believe that we learn Black history because doing so will help us to get free. And in order to accomplish this goal, to be able to learn from the fullness of our past, we have to approach it with a queer lens. We have to bring to Black history a quality that the Black queer community embodies at its best — the unconditional acceptance of people's full and real selves.

> I believe that we learn Black history because doing so will help us to get free.

Our history is what it is. Sometimes we didn't overcome. Sometimes our faves were misogynists. Sometimes our idols were reckless and led movements into the ground. Sometimes effective and powerful Black leaders were on crack. Sometimes our stories are not glistening tales of hope and triumph and movin' on up, but stories of mistakes made. Sometimes they are stories of pain and loss, death, and things being taken from us. But they are stories that have something to teach us nonetheless.

Let's queer Black history. Let's reimagine it as an opportunity to celebrate Black heroes, leaders, and everyday people. Let's use it to remember and mourn the Black lives that white supremacy has ripped from our arms. Let's use it as a chance to learn from the lives of Black people at all different intersections, Black people whose sweat and tears, laughter and joy, victories and mistakes have brought us to where we are today. Let's make learning Black history about getting free. ∎

Dominique Hazzard is a food justice advocate, a Black freedom organizer, and a doctoral student at Johns Hopkins University studying the history of racial capitalism, land use, and the environment. This article originally appeared on Black Youth Project.

Rethinking Islamophobia

Combating bigotry by raising the voices of Black Muslims

By Alison Kysia

The increasing violence against Muslims, Sikhs, South Asians, and others targeted as Muslim, suggests we, as Americans, are becoming less tolerant and need educational interventions that move beyond post-9/11 teaching strategies that emphasize our peacefulness or oversimplify our histories, beliefs, and rituals in ways that often lead to further stereotyping. Although I support religious literacy — increasing our knowledge of religious texts, beliefs, and rituals — as a common good and believe increasing religious literacy in schools challenges stereotypes, my experience teaching Islam makes me question whether it is an effective antidote to Islamophobia.

Hate crimes against Muslims increased 67 percent from 2014 to 2015 and were also up a frightening 91 percent in the first half of 2017 compared to the first half of 2016, according to the FBI and the Council on American-Islamic Relations. And in a recent survey conducted by the Institute for Social Policy and Understanding (ISPU), 42 percent of Muslims reported bullying of their school-aged children, and even more disturbingly, 25 percent of those cases involved a teacher.

In reviewing current pedagogies around Islam, I haven't seen many lessons that address the historical connections between Islamophobia and anti-Black and anti-immigrant racism, yet through my own study of U.S. history those connections are clear and relevant. Instead, the teaching strategies and content I see reproduced most often in textbooks, teacher workshops, online teaching lessons, and even in graduate lectures is what I call the "Five Pillars of Islam" teaching approach, which represents Islam as a religion that can be summed up in a memorizable list of beliefs and rituals. This approach reduces Muslims to a set of stereotypes that reinforce media caricatures of Islam as foreign and unidimensional and Muslims as automatons who blindly follow an inflexible faith. It also does not allow students to make critical connections between Islamophobia and racism.

There is a set script with certain narrative threads that the Five Pillars of Islam teaching approach follows and it comes with a number of profound weaknesses. The story often contains references to violence without providing examples or any real context, making it easy for readers to assume Islam is a foreign religion from a foreign land that is inherently violent. For example, under the heading "The Homeland of Islam," *Ways of the World*, a popular high school and college world history textbook published by Bedford/

St. Martin's, explains that "The central region of the Arabian Peninsula had long been inhabited by nomadic Arabs. . . . These peoples lived in fiercely independent clans and tribes, which often engaged in bitter blood feuds with one another." After describing Muhammad's 22-year prophecy from 610–632 CE, which is collected in the Quran, the textbook says, "The message of the Quran challenged not only the ancient polytheism of the Arab religion and the social injustices of Mecca but also the entire tribal and clan structure of Arab society, which was so prone to war, feuding, and violence."

@KHALIDALBAIH

How are students supposed to make sense out of these statements? Free from examples and context, readers can assume that there is something fundamentally violent about the place and people, reinforcing the terrorist stereotype. Nor are these descriptions ever followed by an explanation of the differences between Muslims and Arabs, mimicking the way they are often confused as identical (the majority of Arabs are Muslim; the majority of Muslims are not Arabs).

The *Ways of the World* textbook then launches into a description of this new religion: The Five Pillars of Islam. A quick Google search for "teaching lessons on Islam" or "teaching lessons on Muslims" illustrates the dominance of the Five Pillars teaching approach. For example, a PBS lesson states that "students explore and understand the basic beliefs of Islam as well as the Five Pillars that guide Muslims in their daily life: belief, worship, fasting, almsgiving, and pilgrimage. They will view segments from *Religion & Ethics NewsWeekly* and information from internet sources to look closely at each pillar. Then, as a culminating activity in groups, students will create posters about the Five Pillars for classroom display."

> I haven't seen many lessons that address the historical connections between Islamophobia and anti-Black and anti-immigrant racism, yet through my own study of U.S. history those connections are clear and relevant.

In this lesson, "Muslims" are represented as all one people and Islam is a fixed set of beliefs dating to 7th-century Arabia. It is instructive to think about what the lesson does not teach. It doesn't teach us the names of diverse identities that fall under the category of Muslim (Ithna'ashari, Ahmadiyya, Ismaili, or Druze, to name a few). It doesn't talk about the Muslims who don't follow all Five Pillars or add a few more to the list. It doesn't talk about the mind-boggling diversity of rituals and beliefs and texts that have been in continuous flux for 1,500 years across the entire world. Suspiciously, the Five Pillars script sounds a lot like the sanitized Saudi-sponsored version of Islam that is as popular in academic institutions as it is in the halls of government and missionary venues.

These simplistic descriptions have consequences. While describing the legal system that formed in the "Islamic empire" after the death of Muhammad in 632 CE, *Ways of the World* claims that "no distinction between religious law and civil law, so important in the Christian world, existed within the realm of Islam. One law, known as the sharia, regulated every aspect of life." This is incorrect. There was never a singular Islamic empire but rather multiple centers of power ruled by different leaders. Rulers used a variety of legal codes other than the sharia, like in the Ottoman Empire for example, where they included a secular code known as Kanun. There were no polities that exclusively used sharia in their legal systems. This kind of misinformation reinforces popular beliefs that sharia is an all-or-nothing totalitarian ideology that is intent on overthrowing the U.S. government — and it can lead to absurd, and racist, public policy. According to the Southern Poverty Law Center, 120 anti-Sharia law bills have been introduced in 42 states since 2010 and 15 of those bills have been enacted. One of the chief architects of such legislation, David Yerushalmi, noted the functional purpose of the laws "was heuristic — to get people asking this question: 'What is Sharia?'"

Even when I search for lessons on Islamophobia, I either get Five Pillars results or the lessons take the conversation out of the United States. For example, in a *Teaching Tolerance* article called "In a Time of Islamophobia, Teach with Complexity," the introductory paragraph says, "When teaching about the Middle East and North Africa (MENA), U.S. teachers are often confronted with a dearth of accurate and nuanced material about the history, politics, and people of the region." The authors suggest lessons about the MENA, which is great if you are teaching about the region. If the goal is to challenge Islamophobia, these lessons won't be as effective because they communicate that Islam, Muslims, and Islamophobia are from somewhere else rather than from here and that Islamophobia is not also rooted in U.S. history. Rather, I am looking for teaching resources that make Islamophobia personal by connecting it to shared American histories before taking the story global.

Disappointingly, some curricula on Islamophobia includes discussion of violent extremism, a choice that keeps terrorism central to any discussion of Muslims. In an article from *Teaching Tolerance* called "Expelling Islamophobia," the authors suggest "integrating Islam" more fully into the curriculum. One teacher explains that "We look at Islam from three different perspectives: history, violent extremism, and Islamophobia. . . . The history of Islam acts as the introduction . . . helping students get a handle on vocabulary and context. The course then pivots to violent extremism — who and where such groups are, their motivations, and how they compare to extremists in other major religions, including Christianity." The coupling of Muslims and extremism is troubling because it is a consequence of Islamophobia and fuels further pairing. We must talk about terrorism more, not less, but we need to do it in a way that acknowledges multiple relationships between Islamophobia and terrorism, like U.S. military interventions (it has been 27 years since the first Gulf War), drone warfare, and financial imperialism. And we also need to contextualize any terrorism committed by Muslims with the fact that among the more than 1,600 extremist groups being tracked by the SPLC, the majority are white supremacists and anti-government militias. Regardless, these lessons still don't give students the opportunity to make connections between Islamophobia and racism nor do they reinforce the fact that Muslims have been part of U.S. history since colonization.

I have seen how common it is to walk away from these Five Pillars recitations thinking that Islam can be summed up in a set of bullet points easily regurgitated on a test.

> The lesson empowers participants to fight Islamophobia by raising up voices we rarely hear in the media when we talk about Islam and Muslims — Black Muslims.

Yet Muslims are complicated people who have rich and varied relationships with their religious identity. The caricatures we see in the media become all that more believable when we are taught that 1,500-year-old traditions can be summed up in neat, formulaic ways. I'm not suggesting these caricatures are used intentionally on the part of educators; quite the opposite, I sympathize with these educators. I taught this way myself in my early years in a community college because the Five Pillars teaching strategy is how I was taught about Islam academically.

Through my teaching experience, I began to ask myself: Will learning about rituals I practice (or don't) with different levels of dedication over my life span effectively help students make connections between dehumanization and violence? Maybe we should begin our inquiry into Muslims and Islam and Islamophobia in the place where we live rather than in some other place. How does that choice shift our perception about what Islamophobia is and where it comes from? If Islamophobia is a process of dehumanization, who else has been demonized this way in U.S. history? Is there something we could learn from connecting those experiences that will aid our fight against Islamophobia?

After coming to the conclusion that religious literacy does not produce the outcomes I want to achieve in fighting Islamophobia, I decided to write a lesson I could share with other educators who want to teach about Muslims and Islam but don't want to teach from a religious studies perspective. I work in a variety of educational settings so I wanted the lesson to be effective in middle and high school classrooms and in activist or nonprofit professional development workshops. I wanted to share some of the stories I read in academic texts like *Black Crescent: The Experience and Legacy of African Muslims in the Americas* by Michael Gomez, *African Muslims in Antebellum America* by Allan Austin, *Servants of Allah: African Muslims Enslaved in the Americas* by Sylviane Diouf, *Islam in Black America* by Edward Curtis IV, *A History of Islam in America* by Kambiz GhaneaBassiri, *Inside the Gender Jihad* by Amina Wadud, and others that have enriched my thinking about the stories we use to teach about Muslims, Islam, and Islamophobia. In addition to narrative-changing content, I wanted to use a teaching strategy that reflects an active inclusivity rather than a passive authoritarianism between teacher and students. I wanted everyone to be part of the conversation. I wanted a lesson that would give all of us, Muslims and non-Muslims alike, the opportunity to think differently about our shared history as Americans. I wanted the lesson to blur the lines between who "us" and "them" are, since this is one of the steps of dehumanization we want to interrupt.

Taking all these goals into consideration, I developed a Black Muslim meet-and-greet teaching activity. The lesson empowers participants to fight Islamophobia by raising up voices we rarely hear in the media when we talk about Islam and Muslims — Black Muslims. The personalities included in the lesson are all Black, which not only teaches us about Islam in America but also advances themes in Black history.

Why Black Muslims and not all Muslims? I envisioned this lesson as the first in a series that help students see Islamophobia as a consequence of racism. American racism is an ideology borne out of white supremacy and of the need to steal land, resources, and labor. Islamophobia, like racism, is used to justify American imperialism or the stealing of land, resources, and labor in Muslim-majority countries. I want students to make con-

@KHALIDALBAIH

nections between the abuse of power at home and abroad. There are a lot of heavy topics to cover if we want to empower students to make these connections that must include lessons in both U.S. and global history. I wanted this first lesson to introduce students to a new way of learning about Islam and Muslims that raises awareness of stories most Americans have not heard, setting the stage for deeper inquiry.

I wrote half-page biographies of 25 Black Muslims who lived in the United States from colonization to the present. When identifying the characters who would populate my lesson, I soon discovered that there were too many examples to choose from.

In order to remedy this, I defined three time periods — colonization to the Civil War, Reconstruction to 1970s, and 1970s to the present — and then tried to balance out the names according to each time period. The earliest time period contained, predictably, almost exclusively male biographies. For this reason, I overrepresented women in the 1970s–present period, allowing me to also highlight the accomplishments of contemporary women. I chose to tell the story of Betty Shabazz rather than her husband, Malcolm X/Malik el-Shabazz, as I did for Clara and Elijah Muhammad. (Elijah led the Nation of Islam from 1934 to 1975.) These women were fierce activists and educators in their own right but their stories are almost always told in relation to their husbands. I mined a variety of sources — academic texts, documentaries, interviews — for the major events in their lives and then wrote about those experiences in a conversational first-person voice.

I reached out to a friend, Neha Singhal, who teaches social studies at John F. Kennedy High School in Silver Spring, Maryland, which serves the suburban communities within short commuting distance to Washington, D.C. The school is racially, ethnically, and financially diverse, and provided a welcome setting for piloting the lesson among 25 juniors and seniors.

I introduced myself to the class and asked, "Do you know any Black Muslims?" One of the students, Fatima, said, "I am a Black Muslim. I was born here but my parents emigrated from Senegal." Nino said there was a Muslim woman in the 2016 Summer Olympics, but no one could give me her name. Derrick offered Elijah Muhammad and told me he started the Nation of Islam. I corrected him that technically, Fard Muhammad started the Nation, but Elijah was the leader for many years. They couldn't list any other names. I explained to them, "I want to remedy this problem. Black Muslims have been in the United States for 400 years. Why can't we name more of them?"

I gave each student a half-sheet biography of one Black Muslim and asked them to take two minutes to read the descriptions quietly. I also told them that the names can be difficult for some students to pronounce and they should ask me if they needed help. While they read, I circulated around the room and said the name of the character for each student. I asked them to think quietly about which pieces of information were most important to share with someone who has never heard of their character. This was more challenging than I thought it would be for them. Later, I changed the instructions for the lesson, asking students to flip over their half-sheet biography and create this list in five bullet points. The content in this activity is unfamiliar to most students, so they need an extra minute to absorb the story, summarize the main ideas, and ask for clarification.

I then explained to the class, "In a minute, you will all get out of your chairs and meet and greet one another. How do you do that? You introduce yourself just like you would at a party, but instead of introducing the real you, you will introduce yourself as your Black Muslim character." Neha and I stood in the front of the room and briefly role-played for them. "Hello, who are you?" Neha answered, "I am Aisha al-Adawiya. I was born in 1944 and grew up in the Black church but I converted to Islam after reading the Quran in the early 1960s. I am the founder and president of Women in Islam Inc., an organization of Muslim women that focuses on human rights and social justice. I represent Muslim women at the United Nations. I make sure the stories of Muslims are included in Black history through my work at the Schomburg Center for Research in Black Culture at the New York Public Library." I explained that I would then introduce myself to Neha, and we could follow up with additional questions, particularly those listed on the worksheet.

I gave students the worksheet and explained, "These are questions to help guide your conversations and collect information we can use later in our discussion." I asked individual students to read them out loud: Find one person who was enslaved. Where were they from? Where did they end up? How did they resist? Find one person who experienced discrimination based on their race or religion. Describe their experience. Find two women. Describe some of their achievements. Find two people who worked for justice. Explain how they do/did that.

Some of the students got up and immediately launched into introductions. "Hi, I am Carolyn Walker-Diallo . . ." "I am Mahommah Gardo Baquaqua . . ." "Were you discriminated against because of your race or religion?" Others needed to be coaxed to get up. Sure, it was one of the last days of school before summer break. But as Neha noted in our post-activity feedback session, some students find it intimidating and uncomfortable when asked to take more responsibility for teaching one another, making it hard to get some of them to take their attention off the teacher. As the lesson progressed, we could see the students becoming more comfortable with the format and it made clear to Neha and me the way that inclusive pedagogies can help students more actively engage in their learning.

> Lessons like the Black Muslim meet-and-greet help students build vocabularies that increase their ability to talk about racism in ways that capture these intersections of oppression. We have to give them new ways of understanding racism if we want them to create solutions in the present and future that humanize all of us.

The students continued to meet one another for about 25 minutes. After we finished, I asked them to take a seat. I gave them each a handout and said, "At the top of the paper, please list three things you learned about Muslims from this activity."

After giving them one minute, I asked them to share their answers with the group. Melanie said, "I was shocked to find out that Muslims were enslaved in the United States. I never heard that before." Joon quickly added, "I like learning about the successes of Muslim women, so many of them are scholars." I asked her, "What do you hear about Muslim women in the media?" She looked up in the air inquisitively and said, "I don't really hear about them." I said, "OK, what comes to your mind when you think of a Muslim woman?" Another student, Carrie, yelled out, "They are oppressed." Joon added, "Yeah, I see that, but the women I learned about today, they are a strong group of people." Other students found it surprising that so many Black Muslims were from West Africa. When I asked why that is important, Nicole said, "We never hear anything about Black people before slavery. They were kidnapped and then end up picking cotton in the

South." Mika said, "I didn't know Mos Def was Muslim, he changed his name to Yasiin Bey and his music uses Islamic principles." I asked, "What kind of Islamic principles are reflected in hip-hop?" She had to look at her biography again but then answered, "like being worried about poor people and people who have to deal with discrimination."

On the same handout, there is a list of questions for students to discuss in small groups. Because we got started a little late, we decided to keep the group whole for the entire discussion, but given the full class period, I would have let the students discuss the questions in small groups before we debriefed together since this will maximize student participation.

I asked the class to give me a few examples of the first Muslims to come to the United States. Fatima offered, "Ayuba Suleiman Diallo was born in West Africa, he was enslaved and ended up in Maryland, on an island off the Chesapeake Bay. He eventually made it back to Africa." I quickly followed, "Where in Africa? It is a continent, not a country." She scanned her paper and replied, "Gambia."

Lydia relayed the story of Margaret Bilali, who we know about because her grand-daughter, Katie Brown, was interviewed by the Works Progress Administration (WPA). The WPA, the largest New Deal agency during the Great Depression, employed millions of Americans for public works projects, including the construction of buildings and roads, but they also supported art, music, and theater projects. Fortunately, they chose to collect oral histories of enslaved people and their descendants. It is from these interviews that we get Margaret's story. "Margaret's dad was enslaved on Sapelo Island off the coast of Georgia. She remembers seeing her dad and his wife praying on the bead and kneeling on a mat to pray," Lydia explained. "What does that mean — praying on the bead and kneeling on mat? Why would they do that?" I asked. One of the Muslim students explained that some Muslims use a string of beads to pray, called a tasbih or misbaha, that is similar to a rosary, japa mala, or other prayer beads. Muslims often use a small carpet or mat when praying because they fully prostrate by putting their forehead, knees, and hands on the floor. The prayer mat ensures you are praying on something clean. What's nice about this lesson is that it makes the connection between Muslims and Black history, and within those biographies, the stories can include religious literacy lessons without religion being the central focus.

We also talked about the ways Muslims fight injustice. Neha offered, "Kenneth Gamble fought injustice. He is the guy in Philadelphia who was a musician and then started a nonprofit to help fix houses in the South Philly community and then sell them to people who are from those neighborhoods. With gentrification taking over entire neighborhoods right now, this is important work." Sandra offered the story of Clara Muhammad, who started her own schools so they could teach their kids about their religion. "Her husband, Elijah, was put in jail because he wouldn't fight in WWII," she added. Marcus said, "Keith Ellison is a Muslim in the U.S. House of Representatives." I asked, "How does he fight injustice?" Marcus replied, "Being there is important so that when people have questions about Muslims, he can answer them." Lydia, who played Keith in the activity, added, "He also worked on police brutality issues before he came to Washington." As we were waiting for the bell to ring, a couple students pulled out their cell phones and started looking up photos of the Muslim characters they learned about. Once they saw Ibtihaj Muhammad's picture, for example, they made the connection between the face and the story about her shared in the meet-and-greet. After seeing how effective it was at grabbing their attention and making them continue talking about the lesson, I decided to add a PowerPoint presentation with as many open-source pictures of the characters as possible that teachers can use after the discussion.

After working with Neha and her students, I decided to add some questions to emphasize the fact that many of the characters in the activity are still alive. It is important that students be asked to connect the past to the present. In the worksheet, I included the prompt "Find at least one person who has been active during your lifetime. Describe some of their experiences." In the discussion, I added, "Who would you want to meet or research more? Why?" This last question gives the student a chance to make the story more personal and the character more relatable by thinking about who they admire and why.

In June 2017, a Somali American Muslim woman living outside of Columbus, Ohio, Rahma Warsame, was beaten unconscious and sustained facial fractures and the loss of teeth by a white man who screamed, "You will be shipped back to Africa" before he attacked her. As educators committed to pedagogies of equity and inclusion, we have to help students make connections between race, religion, and the racialization of Muslims. Our students are bombarded with violent images of Black men and women being killed by the police, immigrants being forcibly removed from their communities, and increasing hate crimes against Muslims. We cannot allow our students to think these are discrete events. The Movement for Black Lives platform reads, "We believe in elevating the experiences and leadership of the most marginalized Black people, including but not limited to those who are women, queer, trans, femmes, gender nonconforming, Muslim, formerly and currently incarcerated, cash poor and working class, disabled, undocumented, and immigrant." Lessons like the Black Muslim meet-and-greet help students build vocabularies that increase their ability to talk about racism in ways that capture these intersections of oppression. We have to give them new ways of understanding racism if we want them to create solutions in the present and future that humanize all of us. ■

Alison Kysia is the project director of "Islamophobia: a people's history teaching guide" at Teaching for Change. Previously, she designed Islamic studies and anti-Islamophobia teaching modules for adult education audiences, including religious leaders, social justice activists, and teachers. She taught U.S., world, and Islamic history in an urban community college and English language to adult immigrants. Alison holds a BA in race, class, and gender studies and a MA in history.

RESOURCES

For Alison Kysia's Black Muslim meet-and-greet, go to teachingforblacklives.org

Rethinking Identity
Afro-Mexican history

By Michelle Nicola

"**T**his is the country of my ancestors. It includes the fandango — music that takes Spanish instruments and plays them with African style, songs like 'La Bamba' that trace their way back to slavery and still influence music today, and a Mexican president with both Spanish and African ancestry. This is my history, but no one is talking to us about it," wrote Daniel as he reflected on the Afro-Mexican unit our class had just completed.

Several months earlier, I was searching for a way that my Spanish speakers class could support African American Heritage Month activities at our school. At De La Salle North in Portland, Oregon, students organize month-long activities to celebrate and critically consider the histories of the many heritages represented in the student body. I wanted to support these student-led projects with lessons in my classroom, but how? Driving home one night, the solution hit me: Nicholas Marshall.

Nicholas was a memorable student from my first year of teaching. One day he looked at me, eyes wide, and said: "Wait, Señorita! There are Black people who speak Spanish?"

"Yes," I said. "There most definitely are." I developed a whole unit for my Spanish World Language class based on Nicholas' question. I decided to adapt that unit to meet the needs of my current students. I hoped that, by the end of the unit, they would be able to identify ways that enslaved Africans and their descendants shaped Mexican culture, and describe the historical and political forces that led to Afro-Mexican invisibility. I wanted students to complicate their narratives about Mexican identity and realize that Afro-Mexican resistance weaves through the fabric of that heritage.

My students at De La Salle were heritage language speakers. Heritage students have both a cultural and a linguistic connection to a language other than English. Our class of 23 juniors and two seniors each shaped the definition of heritage Spanish speaker in their own way. For example, Marta didn't consider Spanish her native language — she favored English, although she spoke Spanish with her parents. Ana Maria emigrated from Mexico at the age of 10. She learned to read and write in Spanish, and then learned to do the same in English. Daniel grew up in the United States but spoke Spanish at home and often with his friends. Itzel was from Guatemala and English was her third language, after Mayan and Spanish. Alex's father was from Ecuador and his mother from Chile, so his Spanish was peppered with words that differed from those of his peers.

They all spoke, read, and wrote with high levels of fluency in Spanish, yet they weren't "native" Spanish speakers because most of their formal schooling had been in English.

RAFAEL LÓPEZ

They switched between cultures and languages and, in Daniel's words, sometimes felt "stuck between two countries I'm not wanted in." In that sense, the definition of a heritage speaker is not just about language; it also includes socio-emotional factors.

Where Did the Africans Go?

On our first day, I announced that we would be uncovering the history of Black Mexicans. "Does anyone already know anything about this topic?"

My students' faces were blank.

"When I was preparing this unit for you, I found out that many people believe the first Africans arrived with the first conquistadores. By the 16th and 17th centuries, one out of every two Africans who were enslaved and taken to the so-called "New World" was sold in Mexico. In fact, until 1650, the number of African-heritage Mexicans equaled the number of Spanish-heritage Mexicans. Yet today, no one seems to know much about the story of Afro-Mexicans and their descendants. So where did they all go? How did they become invisible?"

"Maybe they left the country," Josué called out.

"It's possible," I replied. "Any other ideas?"

"Maybe they got kind of mixed," Lalo ventured.

I pulled out my trusty teacher phrase: "Tell me more."

"You know, Ms. Nicola, the birds and the bees, and then the kids got lighter skin or something." The class laughed.

"You may be on to something, Lalo. I want you to keep these ideas in the back of your minds throughout the unit. Keep asking the question: How does a history, a culture, and a people become invisible? I want you to collect stories of things you didn't realize had a connection to Africa, but that are deeply rooted in African cultures and that have shaped what we think of as 'Mexican.'"

In fact, until 1650, the number of African-heritage Mexicans equaled the number of Spanish-heritage Mexicans. Yet today, no one seems to know much about the story of Afro-Mexicans and their descendants. So where did they all go? How did they become invisible?

"Now grab your bags," I said. "We're going to the computer lab."

Once in the computer lab, I gave my students a piece of paper with the URL for the Afropop Worldwide website "La Bamba: The Afro-Mexican Story." "*Chicos*," I called out, moving to the center of the lab. "Remember that even though the website is in *inglés*, your notes need to be *en español*." Although I wanted our class to read, write, think, and speak in Spanish 100 percent of the time, the reality was that my students don't live in a 24/7 Spanish-speaking world. Too often, I ended up resorting to English-language resources.

The website contained a wealth of information, and I wanted to give students the autonomy to explore what they found interesting. So the only instruction I gave them was to spend time reading and writing down what they found interesting. At the end of the unit, students would need their notes for their essays, but I didn't bother them with that detail for the moment. Instead, I gave them time to let their curiosity lead the exploration. As they clicked from page to page, I wandered around the room, checking on their notes and gathering snippets of their conversations.

"What? The fandango is African?!" I heard Eduardo exclaim.

"Eduardo, don't forget to write down what you are learning," I reminded him.

"*Estamos hablando de cómo el son jarocho tiene raíces Africanas* (We're talking about how *son jarocho* music has African roots)," Evelyn commented to me as I walked by.

"*Maestra*, what is this about the 'third root'?"

"*Bueno*, Alex, read it and you will see. That part is important, so write it down."

Alex jotted notes on *la tercera raíz* (the third root). In 1992, as part of the 500th anniversary of the arrival of the Spanish in the Americas, the Mexican government officially acknowledged that African culture in the country represented *la tercera raíz* of Mexican culture, along with Spanish and Indigenous peoples. Since then, many Mexicans (especially those living on the west coast) have reconnected with their African heritage through dance, theater, radio, and political mobilizations.

Daniel called out to me. "I'm interested in this guy Vicente Guerrero. He was a hero in the war for independence, and it says here that he was Mexico's first Afro-Mexican president — the Barack Obama of 1829!"

I smiled. My students were already rethinking some of their ideas about Mexico. They were collecting stories of things that they had taken for granted as "just Mexican" and uncovering a more complex version of those stories.

By the time we had finished our first lesson exploring the Afropop site, students were hooked and energy was high. It was a good launching pad for our next question: If Afro-Mexicans have been living in Mexico since the days of the slave trade, why wasn't anyone talking about it?

The Black Grandma in the Closet

If the goal for the first part of the unit was to challenge students to rethink Mexican identity, and specifically Black Mexican identity, parts two and three were about discovering the historical and political forces that led to the invisibility of Afro-Mexican roots, and the activism and resistance that occurred throughout history and into the present.

I decided to show an episode from the Henry Louis Gates series *Black in Latin America* titled "Mexico & Peru: The Black Grandma in the Closet." Gates documents the ways that Black Mexicans were oppressed and made invisible, and how they have fought against Spanish oppressors and modern-day discrimination. I gave students lots of freedom to explore the Afropop Worldwide website however they wished, but I took a different tack for this next activity.

"Mexico & Peru: The Black Grandma in the Closet" is full of information about why we don't often hear about Black Mexicans. Before students viewed the documentary, I created a note-taking template so they could work together to capture the relevant facts. I listed important names, dates, and ideas in the order they were mentioned in the documentary. Then I chose four items for each 15-minute segment of the documentary. I made a copy of the note-taking template for each student, and had students get into groups of four.

> **If Afro-Mexicans have been living in Mexico since the days of the slave trade, why wasn't anyone talking about it?**

"*OK, clase, vamos a ver el documental,*" I said, moving about the room. "We've already discussed some ideas about why no one knew the African roots of the fandango, or that Mexico had important military and political leaders who were Black." Josué suggested maybe all the Afro-Mexicans left the country, and Lalo talked about interracial relationships. Now we're going to dig a little deeper and see what Mexican anthropologists and historians have to say. You can see on your papers that important terms from the documentary are divided into sets of four. Each person in your group will be responsible for taking notes on just one term. When we've heard all four terms,

I'll stop the documentary and as a group you will write one summary that includes all of those terms. OK?"

Students decided how they wanted to divide the terms and ideas among themselves, and I hit "play." By the time we finished, I was happy with my decision to have students share the work of understanding and synthesizing the reasons behind Mexico's hidden Black culture. They collectively gathered and analyzed more information than students working on their own. And, because each person was responsible for one term per video segment, everyone had a responsibility to listen and share.

In one of their summaries, Lalo, Ana Maria, Itzel, and Evelyn wrote: "Tlacotepec is the city where the documentary opens. They say that if the 'one-drop' rule were applied to this city, everyone would be Black! The fandango uses Spanish instruments but played in an African way. The documentary says that slaves were singing 'La Bamba' in 1683!!! (So, does that mean that Ritchie Valens broke copyright? LOL)"

Marta, Alex, Daniel, and Miguel wrote: "Vicente Guerrero, Mexico's first Black president (1830), said, 'The country comes first,' a common saying in Mexico. After that, they abolished racial categories on birth certificates and other official documents."

This act, though progressive in purpose, contributed to the systematic erasure of Afro-Mexican history. The simple act of eliminating racial categories did not eliminate racism, and some present-day activists are seeking to reinstate racial categories into the Mexican census so that Afro-Mexicans can benefit from public policy. Miguel in particular was uncomfortable with the idea that a reintroduction of racial categories would fix the problem: "Father Hidalgo started our nation's independence with *El Grito de Dolores*, and he believed that we should not have racial categories. Activists like Israel Reyes, a teacher in Mexico, are trying to boost Afro-Mexican pride with their radio shows and activism to reintroduce racial categories. I think the radio show is a good idea, but new census categories will divide the people."

Eduardo's group focused on the story of Sagrario Cruz-Carretero, professor of anthropology at the University of Veracruz. Cruz-Carretero did not discover that she was Black until she was 19, when she traveled to Cuba and started recognizing herself and her family in the faces of the Cubans she met. The foods they made were the same foods — like fufú — that Cruz-Carretero's grandma made, foods that can be traced back to Africa. When she returned to Mexico, she asked her grandfather why he had not told the family that they were Black. Her grandfather responded that they were not Black, they were *moreno*. According to Cruz-Carretero, "This happens in most families — you hide the Black grandma in the closet."

Camila, Sofia, and Adán wrote: "Yanga is a town and a man. The town of Yanga is named after a slave who freed himself and lived for 30 years in the mountains fighting off the Spanish and defending his community. If the TV show *Survivor* had existed in the 16th century, he definitely would have won. And he did win against the Spanish — in 1609 they finally grew tired of fighting him and gave him the land. Yanga became one of the first towns in Mexico where Blacks could live free!"

Lalo snapped to attention when the film started talking about interracial relationships. The Catholic Church allowed marriage between races and so, from early on, Africans, Europeans, and Indigenous Mexicans mixed bloodlines. The Spanish already had a heritage that was more open to interracial relationships than other European countries, thanks to the centuries-long dominance of the Moors in Spain, so those relationships weren't as taboo as they were in the United States. Interracial marriages continued over time, to the point that one's African roots could only be heard in the dropped *d* from the word *helado*, a certain hue in skin tone, or the taste of an old family recipe. "See?" Lalo said with a smug smile. "I told you they were making babies."

Pros and Cons of Racial Statistics

By now, I had a degree of guilt about the resources I was providing them with — our two main sources had been in English. I needed to get my students back to reading in Spanish. So next we looked at *Afrodescendientes en México* by the Consejo Nacional para Prevenir la Discriminación (National Council for Preventing Discrimination).

This document describes the problems, including the difficulties connected with the lack of racial statistics in Mexico, and offers concrete actions that both the Mexican government and its citizens should take to counteract this history of invisibility and oppression. Specifically, it calls for more research and a way to document the numbers and experiences of Afro-Mexicans.

Once again, I had a resource full of important information that I wanted my students to capture. Therefore, I annotated the text before making copies for my students. I starred main ideas, wrote definitions and synonyms for high-level vocabulary in the margins, added footnotes with questions for students to consider. I noted a few questions that I had while reading. Some students did not need this extra support, and for easier texts students would do this annotation work themselves. However, because this was a complicated government document, I wanted to make sure all my students had access to the information presented.

> Questions such as *"Maestra, ¿qué es el racismo interiorizado?* (Teacher, what's internalized racism?)" were an indication that students were being exposed to a broader understanding of systems of oppression.

Then I divided the class into heterogeneous groups so that students could help each other as needed. I told them that each group would decide who would be the reader, summarizer, director, and question-asker.

"One person is going to read aloud," I explained. "Another is going to write a summary of the main ideas from the text. The director is in charge of watching the clock, and also making sure that everyone speaks and no one dominates the conversation. The question-asker will jot down questions that the group has while reading."

Students got busy reading and writing, and I walked around the classroom, listening in and answering questions.

Questions such as "*Maestra, ¿qué es el racismo interiorizado?* (Teacher, what's internalized racism?)" were an indication that students were being exposed to a broader understanding of systems of oppression.

The text did not have hard data in the form of statistics on achievement gaps, poverty, or access to services — how could they provide this when the Mexican census had no system for identifying those of African heritage? But the authors described the myriad ways that the ideology of racial superiority has spread into the language, education policy, and throughout Mexican society.

Mateo focused in on *Memín Pinguín*, a popular cartoon from the 1940s based on racist caricatures that could be compared to Sambo in the United States. The text reinforced information we had learned in the documentary. Mateo took notes on how the government had issued a commemorative stamp featuring *Memín Pinguín* in 2005 that had caused such an international stir that Jesse Jackson flew to Mexico City to speak with then-President Vicente Fox. Mateo told me that he wanted to write his final essay on this character.

Sofia and Camila were curious about the experience of Afro-Mexican women. They began to write down questions about how basing beauty standards on *lo blanco* (whiteness) affected women. They were also struck by the information that Afro-Mexican women are the most vulnerable targets of racism in Mexico, to the point that many of them leave the country, primarily heading to the United States.

> **Sofia and Camila were curious about the experience of Afro-Mexican women. They began to write down questions about how basing beauty standards on *lo blanco* (whiteness) affected women.**

Miguel called me over. "They're saying that they want to reintroduce racial categories in Mexico. I think that will divide the people more." He shook his head. Miguel, a senior, had often encouraged the juniors to step out of their comfort zone and hang out with students of other races at our school. I admired his willingness to challenge his peers and the text. I also wanted him to consider multiple perspectives before solidifying his view.

"Miguel, I hear your concern about dividing people, but can you think of any ways that Black Mexicans would benefit from reintroducing racial categories? What does the article say?" Miguel returned to the text, searching the document for answers.

My students were asking important questions, and it was time for them to give voice to what they were learning. For their end-of-unit project, I asked them to write an explanatory essay, either highlighting an unsung Afro-Mexican historical figure or explaining how African ancestry has shaped the Mexico of today.

Eyes Wide Open

Before this unit, my students had little to no knowledge of the African presence in Mexico. By the end of the unit, students were asking important questions about race, defining racial categories, and what it really means to be Mexican. Many walked away with a different view of their family's country of origin, one whose history and cultural identity was infinitely more complex than they had previously imagined. Their final essays demonstrated that we had met our goals of rethinking identity, identifying ways that Afro-Mexicans helped shape the nation, and reflecting on the present-day implications of Afro-Mexican invisibility.

"Many people do not know the history of Afro-Mexicans," wrote Ana Maria, "but it's thanks to them that we have various walls, cities, food, and dance. It may be that you have to look with eyes wide open to see it, but their presence is there for those who wish to see it."

Miguel's paper was a response to the position of *Afrodescendientes en México*. He decided to stay true to his original stance: "I fear that reintroducing racial categories in Mexico will have the opposite effect of what they want. I don't think that they should divide people in this way because they may start to divide the country."

> By the end of the unit, students were asking important questions about race, defining racial categories, and what it really means to be Mexican.

As sometimes happens, this six-week unit evolved into about 10 weeks of learning. There were a few things that I ended up cutting, and others that I will do differently next time. For example, I'll build in more time for small-group discussion, and plan for students to struggle with the questions present-day activists are facing: how to undo the legacy of invisibility and oppression. In addition, I would provide some more journaling time for students to self-reflect. For high school students deep in the throes of identity development, extra time for journaling may have allowed them to question assumptions they had about themselves, and the groups they identify with.

There is more work to do — more counter-stories to offer, more questions to ask, Afro-Latina/o history from countries other than Mexico to explore. Yet, my students began to understand that national identity is something we construct together and that, just like in our classroom, everyone has something to contribute. ■

Michelle Nicola currently teaches middle school language arts and Spanish at Bridger School in Portland, Oregon. Nicola was a recipient of the 2014 Teaching Tolerance Award for Excellence in Teaching, and she is a frequent contributor to Rethinking Schools.

RESOURCES

Afropop Worldwide. 2013. "La Bamba: The Afro-Mexican Story." Public Radio International. afropop.org

PBS four-part series. 2011. "Mexico & Peru: The Black Grandma in the Closet"; "Brazil: A Racial Paradise?"; "Cuba: The Next Revolution"; and "Haiti & the Dominican Republic: An Island Divided." *Black in Latin America.* PBS

Velázquez, María Elisa, and Gabriela Iturralde Nieto. 2012. *Afrodescendientes en México: Una historia de silencio y discriminación.* Consejo Nacional para Prevenir la Discriminación.

Brown Kids Can't Be in Our Club

Teaching 6-year-olds about skin color, race, culture, and respect

By Rita Tenorio

I sat down one day with seven of the children in my 1st-grade class. It was early in the year and we were getting to know each other. We talked about how we were alike, how we were different. "Our skin is different," one of the children said. I asked everyone to put their hands together on the table, so we could see all the different colors.

One African American student, Dana, simply would not. Scowling, she slid her hands beneath the tabletop, unwilling to have her color compared to the others.

It was a reaction I had seen before. I was teaching at La Escuela Fratney, an ethnically diverse dual-language school in a racially mixed working-class Milwaukee neighborhood. My students typically included Black kids, white kids, and Latinos; Spanish speakers and English speakers. They had many things in common. Recess was their favorite time of day. Friendships were a priority. They wanted to "belong" to a group and they were very conscious of where they fit in a social sense.

And they all "knew" that it was better to be light-skinned than dark-skinned, and that English was better than Spanish.

Even though my students had only six years of life experience by the time they reached my classroom, the centuries-old legacies of bias and racism in our country had already made an impact on their lives. I would see fair-skinned children deliberately change places in a circle if darker-skinned children sat down next to them. An English speaker wouldn't play with a Latino child because, he said, "He talks funny." On the playground, a group of white girls wouldn't let their darker-skinned peers join in their games, explaining matter-of-factly: "Brown kids can't be in our club."

Dealing with issues of bias against language or race is perhaps the most complicated problem I encountered as a teacher. For many years, the problem didn't seem to "exist," and was glossed over by teachers as part of the view that "all children are the same — Black, white, or Brown." Yet I've learned that it is not the awareness of racial and cultural differences that leads to prejudice and racism, but how people respond to those differences.

I realized I needed to do two things. First, I had to immediately respond to unacceptable behavior by children, such as racist put-downs or slurs. Second, I had to develop a curriculum that included anti-bias lessons that help students recognize and respond to stereotypes and prejudice.

An Anti-Racist, Multicultural Focus

When I began my career, I worked in a specialty school where the students were learning Spanish as a second language. Moving from holiday to holiday, we learned about cultures

KEITH HENRY BROWN

all over the world. I changed bulletin boards and literacy activities to correspond to the holidays, and proudly integrated the activities into our daily lessons. We learned about our "differences" and celebrated our "similarities." I insisted that "we can all live together" and forbade words or actions that would "hurt" anyone.

It worked. At least I thought it worked.

But as I learned more about multicultural, anti-racist teaching, I began to recognize that just because the atmosphere was calm and children were not overt about their biases did not mean that bias and prejudice were not present. I began to observe and listen more closely to my students, especially in situations where they interacted independently with their peers both in and out of the classroom.

Later, I was part of the founding staff of La Escuela Fratney, a two-way, Spanish/English bilingual elementary school. Our vision was to explicitly explore issues of race and language. The language component was part of a broader framework that had a multicultural, anti-racist curriculum at its core. We wanted our multicultural, multilingual students to not only learn about the history and culture of major ethnic groups, but also to understand racism's influence on all of us. We developed a series of activities and projects that helped us discuss issues of language, race, and social justice in meaningful, age-appropriate ways.

> **Even though my students had only six years of life experience by the time they reached my classroom, the centuries-old legacies of bias and racism in our country had already made an impact on their lives.**

We built classroom community by learning about each other's lives and families; students collected and shared information about their families and ancestry. We talked about how they got their names, how their families came to live in Milwaukee, which holidays they celebrated and how.

Together we defined our classroom rules and discussed what "fairness" meant to each of us. Playground problems became the topics for class discussions or role plays during which students heard from each other how they might more peacefully resolve their disputes. We learned about people who have worked for fairness and equality. At every step we helped the children explore the nature of racial and cultural differences and to overcome simplistic notions of who is "better" or who is "like us" and who isn't, whether it related to language, color, or culture.

Responding to Students' Comments

Even in a school with a social justice focus, I sometimes observed frustrating conflicts. Sometimes these centered on a verbal put-down or involved body language. Even the children's "make-believe" stories were at times defined by race or language. Comments like "You can't be the queen; there are no Black queens" or "If you want to play with us you have to speak English" caught me off guard. Equally disturbing, the children often accepted these statements without complaint. Interactions where children put each other down or where children reflect the discrimination that is so prevalent in our world provide opportunities for strong lessons in counteracting stereotypes and racism. They are as much a part of the curriculum as teaching a science lesson or reading a story.

When these incidents arose, I first put a stop to the behavior and made clear that it was inappropriate. Then I tried to explain why it was inappropriate and acknowledge the feelings of the targeted child.

Often the remark was unrelated to the conflict at hand, and I tried to help the parties focus on the real problem. The child who told her classmate that "there are no Black queens," for instance, needed to understand not only that her remark was incorrect, but also that she has insulted her friend. Next, she had to see that her real motivation was that she wanted to wear the rhinestone crown and sequined dress that were part of the play-house scenario. Beyond that moment, it would also be good to have discussions of the queens throughout African history, perhaps using a piece of literature like John Steptoe's *Mufaro's Beautiful Daughters* or *Ashanti to Zulu* by Margaret Musgrove.

Some of the stereotypes at Fratney were related to our two-way bilingual program and the fact that some students were hearing Spanish for the first time. For example, I remember when an English-speaking student, Sean, referring to Miguel, a Spanish-speaking student, said, "I don't want to sit next to him. He talks funny."

One response might have been "Miguel is very nice, Sean. In our room we take turns sitting next to all the kids." But such a response would not have addressed Sean's bias or curiosity about a different language. It may have merely caused Sean to be less verbal about his feelings while still avoiding Latino classmates. In my view, Sean's remark was really a question to the adults as he tried to understand and get used to an unfamiliar situation. Most Spanish-speaking students come to school having experienced being in situations where everyone around them is speaking English. In our society, most English-speaking students have little or no experience being in a situation where they don't understand the language being spoken.

A more appropriate response might be "Miguel is speaking Spanish like the other people in his family. You and I are speaking English. In our classroom, we'll be speaking in both Spanish and English. It's fine for you to ask questions about what Miguel is saying, or say that you don't understand. But it's not OK to say that he talks funny. That's a put-down to all of us who speak Spanish. You'll be learning to speak in Spanish, too, so you can learn a lot from Miguel."

Another constant source of comments is skin color. A child may say, for instance, "Jonathan is too brown. I'm glad I'm lighter than him." One response from the teacher might be "We're all the same. It doesn't matter what color you are." Although meant to promote equality, it doesn't address the child's view that "being lighter is better." In addition, it might send Jonathan a very negative message. Such a comment from a child indicates that child is quite aware that we are not all the same.

At first I found it difficult to respond to these types of insults, particularly because an explanation of why society views lighter skin as superior to darker skin, or one language more positively than another, is rooted in our history and may be developmentally difficult for young children to conceptualize. Yet it's important to intervene immediately to contradict the notion of "brown is bad" or "English is better." In this case, I would ask Jonathan how that comment made him feel. I would remind the other child that what was said sounds like a put-down to me and is not OK. Then, I would address the issue of skin color through specific curriculum activities — stories, interviews, and projects offer opportunities for children to learn and respond to these issues.

Activities

Over the years, I've gathered a variety of teacher-developed activities that can be used to address some of these issues with students. Although it's vital to respond to student comments in the moment, developing curriculum activities to address racial and linguistic prejudice is also essential. With young children, this can begin with activities to get to know each other and learn about similarities and differences. It can then progress to a more explicit exploration of skin color and privilege.

Me Pockets. This is always a class favorite. Each child takes home a letter-sized clear plastic sleeve, the kind used to display baseball cards. I ask students to fill the pockets with photos, pictures, drawings, or anything else that will help us know more about them and the things that are important in their lives. They return the pockets within a week and each child presents their work to the class. I put them into a three-ring binder that becomes the favorite classroom book to read and re-read. Students learn about the home language and culture of their peers.

The individual pockets reflect the cultural and socioeconomic diversity of the families. Some students put lots of photos in their pockets. Others cut pictures out of magazines or make drawings. My experience is that every family is eager to share in some way, and family members take time to help their children develop the project.

If someone doesn't bring their Me Pocket sheet back, the teachers step in to help him or her find pictures or make the drawings they need to add their page to the binder.

I'm always amazed at how quickly children learn the details about each other's lives from this project: who has a pet, who takes dance classes, who has family in Puerto Rico, who likes to eat macaroni and cheese. The children know there are differences among them, but they also love to share the things that are alike: "Look, Rachel has two brothers, just like me." "I didn't know that Jamal's family likes to camp. We do, too!"

Each of the teachers also completes a Me Pocket sheet. The students loved looking at the picture of me as a 1st grader, seeing my husband and children, and learning that chocolate cake is my favorite food.

Partner Questions. Each day I take time to teach the social skills of communicating ideas with others and listening to another person's perspective. I practice those skills with role-playing activities and problem-solving situations students or teachers bring to the group. This activity is done in both English and Spanish, with those learning the target language of the day getting support and scaffolding from the teachers and their peers. For example, I might ask such simple questions as "Do you like to speak Spanish? Why or why not." Or other more difficult questions: What is the meanest thing anyone has ever said to you? Why do you think some people like to use put-downs? The children take a few minutes to talk with a partner. Afterward some are willing to share with the whole group. We might then role-play the situation as a group and look for ways to respond, such as speaking back to insults.

Someone Special. By the end of October, during the time of Halloween, Día de los Muertos, and All Souls' Day, we learn about how people remember their ancestors and others who have died or who are far away. I set up a table and students are encouraged to bring in pictures or artifacts to display. They bring a remarkable variety of things: photos, jewelry, a trophy won by a departed relative, a postcard that person sent them, or perhaps the program from a funeral. And they bring many, many stories. Again, the teachers also participate and share stories of those who have gone before us.

Let's Talk About Skin Color. Another important conversation I have with my students focuses on the varieties of skin color we have in our group. Usually when we begin this discussion, some children are uncomfortable about saying "what they are" or describing the color of their skin. In particular, children with very dark skin — like Dana, who would not even put her hands on the table — are often reluctant to join in. Meanwhile, the white kids often boast about being "pink." Though we've never talked about this in class before, there is definitely a strong implication that it is better to be lighter. Many children are amazed that this topic is put out on the table for discussion. The looks in their eyes, their frequent reluctance to begin the discussion, tell me that this is a very personal topic.

As part of the lesson, I ask the students if they have ever heard anyone say something bad or mean about another person's skin color. The hands shoot up.

"Grandma says that everyone should speak only English."

"My mom says that you can't trust Black people."

"My sister won't talk to the Puerto Rican kids on the bus."

"Mara said that I couldn't play, that I was too black to be her friend."

They continue to raise their hands and this conversation goes on for a while. We talk about ways we've heard others use people's language or skin color to make fun of them or put them down. We talk about what to do in those situations.

As we continue to discuss issues of race, I often introduce my personal experiences. I tell them about the first time I realized that Black and white people were treated differently. I share my experience being one of the few Latinas in my school. And we try to ask questions that really intrigue the students, that invite them to try to look at things with a different perspective, to learn something new about the human experience and be open-minded to that idea: Do people choose their first language? Where do you get your skin color? Is it better to be one color than another? Lots of our conversations revolve around a story or a piece of literature.

> **It is not the awareness of racial and cultural differences that leads to prejudice and racism, but how people respond to those differences.**

With a little work, this discussion can expand in ways that incorporate math lessons, map lessons, and other curricular areas. I ask children to interview their relatives to find out where the family came from. We create a bulletin board display that we use to compare and learn about the huge variety of places our students' relatives are from. We graph the data of where families come from and the languages that are spoken there.

Skin Color and Science. Our class discussions of skin color set the stage for lots of "scientific" observations. For example, I bring in a large variety of paint chips from a local hardware store. The students love examining and sorting the many shades of beige and brown. It takes a while for them to find the one that is most like their own skin color. *All the Colors We Are/Todos los colores de nuestra piel* by Katie Kissinger is an excellent resource.

In *The Colors of Us*, by Karen Katz, Lena learns from her mother that "brown" is a whole range of colors. Like the characters in the story, we take red, yellow, black, and white paint and mix them in various combinations until we've each found the color of our own skin. Then we display our "research" as part of our science fair project.

In another exercise, inspired by Sheila Hamanaka's *All the Colors of the Earth*, students are asked to find words to describe the color of their skin, and to find something at home that matches their skin color. Then we display the pieces of wood and fabric, the little bags of cinnamon and coffee, the dolls and ceramic pieces that "match" us.

> **Although it's vital to respond to student comments in the moment, developing curriculum activities to address racial and linguistic prejudice is also essential. With young children, this can begin with activities to get to know each other and learn about similarities and differences. It can then progress to a more explicit exploration of skin color and privilege.**

As we continue these explorations, dealing concretely with a topic that so many have never heard discussed in such a manner, students begin to see past society's labels. It is always amazing to children that friends who identify as Black, for example, can actually have very light skin. Or that children who identify as Puerto Rican can be darker than some of the African American children.

Writing About Our Colors. As children begin to understand the idea of internalizing another's point of view, they can apply that understanding by examining different ideas and alternatives to their own experiences. As they learn to express themselves through reading and writing in two languages, they can learn to challenge stereotypes and speak back to unfair behavior and comments.

Once students have had a chance to reflect on skin color, they write about it. Annie wrote: "I like my skin color. It is like peachy cream." James wrote: "My color is the same as my dad's. I think the new baby will have this color, too." And Keila wrote: "When I was born, my color was brown skin and white skin mixed together."

When Dana wrote about mixing the colors to match her skin, she said: "We put black, white, red, and yellow together. I like the color of my skin." How far she had come since the day she would not show us her hands.

These activities have an impact. Many children have taken steps toward awareness of race. They are not afraid to discuss it. They now have more ways in which to think about and describe themselves. The activities challenge my consciousness, too.

These activities are powerful, but it is also important to remember that there are no guarantees that children have internalized anti-racist ideas. So much still depends on the other forces in their lives and on the other ways that we deal with race in our classrooms.

Are They Too Young for This?

We rely on our schools to be the place for a multicultural, multiracial experience for our children. We want to believe that learning together will help our students to become more understanding and respectful of differences. Yet so often we do not address these issues head-on. Without specific instruction it is unlikely that sensitivity and tolerance will develop, that children will bridge the gaps they bring to school from their earliest days.

Many people would say that 6-year-olds are too young to deal with these serious issues. I, too, had real questions at first about what was actually possible with young children. Can you have "real" conversations with 6-year-olds about power, privilege, and racism in our society? Can you make them aware of the effects that racism and injustice have in our lives? Can they really understand their role in the classroom community?

The answer to all of these questions is "yes." Even very young children can explore and understand the attitudes they and their classmates bring to school each day. They have real issues and opinions to share, and many, many questions of their own to ask. In this way, they can begin to challenge some of the assumptions that influence their behavior toward classmates who don't look or talk the same way they do.

In more than 30 years of teaching I have learned that, contrary to what adults often believe, young children are not "blank slates." Instead, they have an unstated but nonetheless sophisticated understanding of issues of race and power. One of our most important roles as teachers, I believe, is to recognize society's effect on children, address the issue directly, and give students the beginning skills and strategies they will need to combat racism and bias in their lives.

Early childhood educators hold an incredible amount of influence over the minds of the children they teach. As the cliché goes, "All I really need to know I learned in kindergarten." For today's students, "all they need to know" goes beyond the traditional formula of playing fair and putting things back in their place. It includes developing the skills and strategies to counteract the racism in their lives. ∎

Rita Tenorio is a retired bilingual early childhood teacher. She is one of the founding editors of Rethinking Schools *and taught at La Escuela Fratney for 24 years. This article was adapted from two previously published pieces by Tenorio: "Race and Respect Among Young Children" (Rethinking Our Classrooms, Volume 1, 2007) and "Brown Kids Can't Be in Our Club" (Rethinking Schools, Spring 2004). A version of this article has previously been published under the headline "Not Too Young."*

RESOURCES

Hamanaka, Sheila. 1999. *All the Colors of the Earth.* HarperCollins.

Katz, Karen. 2002. *The Colors of Us.* Square Fish.

Kissinger, Katie. 2002. *All the Colors We Are/Todos los colores de nuestra piel.* Redleaf Press.

Musgrove, Margaret. 1992. *Ashanti to Zulu: African Traditions.* Puffin Books.

Steptoe, John. 2008. *Mufaro's Beautiful Daughters: An African Tale.* Puffin Books.

A Message from a Black Mom to Her Son

By Dyan Watson

DEAR CALEB,

When you were almost 2, we would drop off your cousin, Sydney, at her K–8 elementary school. The ritual went something like this:

"OK, Syd, have a good day."

"OK," she'd groan as she grabbed her backpack. "Bye, Caleb."

"Bye," you'd wave and grin with your entire body.

"Bye," Sydney would say one last time as she shut the door. I'd roll down the car window.

"Byeeeee," you'd sing.

"Bye," Sydney would laugh as she caught up with friends.

I'd roll up the window as you said "bye" a few more times, then start to whimper. "It's OK, sweetie, she'll be back before you know it. And you'll be off joining her before I know it."

And it's true. Before I know it, Caleb, you will be throwing your backpack on and waving goodbye as you run off across the playground. I think about that moment often and wonder about the condition of schools you'll enter. I worry about sending you, my Black son, to schools that over-enroll Black boys into special education, criminalize them at younger and younger ages, and view them as negative statistics on the dark side of the achievement gap.

> **I worry about sending you, my Black son, to schools that over-enroll Black boys into special education, criminalize them at younger and younger ages, and view them as negative statistics on the dark side of the achievement gap.**

Son, my hope for you is that your schooling experiences will be better than this, that they'll be better than most of mine.

For three years of my K–8 schooling, from 7:40 a.m. until 3:05 p.m., I was Black and invisible. I was bused across town to integrate a white school in southeast Portland, Oregon. We arrived at school promptly at 7:30 a.m. and had

HANNA NEUSCHWANDER

10 full minutes before the white children arrived. We spent that time roaming the halls — happy, free, normal. Once the white children arrived, we became Black and invisible. We were separated, so that no more than two of us were in a class at a time. I never saw Black people in our textbooks unless they were in shackles or standing with Martin Luther King Jr. Most of us rarely interacted with a Black adult outside of the aide who rode the bus with us. I liked school and I loved learning. But I never quite felt right or good. I felt very Black and obvious because I knew that my experience was different from that of my peers. But I also felt invisible because this was never acknowledged in any meaningful way. I became visible again at 3:05 p.m. when I got back on the bus with the other brown faces to make our journey home.

Caleb, I want your teachers to help you love being in your skin. I want them to make space for you in their curricula, so that you see yourself as integral to this country's history, to your classroom's community, to your peers' learning. I want your teachers to select materials where Blacks are portrayed in ordinary and extraordinary ways that actively challenge stereotypes and biases. Most of all, Caleb, I want your teachers to know you so they can help you grow.

One day a teacher was trying to figure out why I was so angry since I was generally a calm, fun-loving kid. She said to me: "I know you, Dyan. You come from a good family." But did she know me? She knew that I lived on the other side of town and was bused in as part of the distorted way that Portland school authorities decided to "integrate" the schools. But did she know what that meant? My mom — your grandma — got us up at 6 a.m. in order for me to wash up, boil an egg just right, fix my toast the way I liked it, and watch the pan of milk so that it didn't boil over, so I could have something hot in my stomach before going to school. You know Grandma, she doesn't play. We had to eat a healthy breakfast before going to school, and we had to fix it ourselves. Maybe that's what that teacher meant by "good family." My teacher didn't know that we had to walk, by ourselves, four blocks to the bus stop and wait for the yellow bus to come pick us up and take us to school. It took us a half hour to get to school. Once there, I had to constantly code-switch, learn how not to be overly Black, and be better than my white counterparts.

Caleb, I want your teachers to know your journey to school — metaphorically and physically. I want them to see you and all of your peers as children from good families. I don't want you to have to earn credit because of whom you're related to or what your parents do for a living. And I don't want your teachers to think that you're special because you're Black and have a family that cares about you and is involved in your life. I want them to know that all children are part of families — traditional or not — that help shape and form who they are.

The summer before beginning 4th grade, I started teaching myself how to play the clarinet. It was the family instrument in that both of my older sisters played it when they were younger. For years I wanted to be a musician. It was in my blood. My grandfather was a musician, all of my uncles can sing very well, and my dad — your grandfather — was a DJ in Jamaica once upon a time. At the end of 5th grade, my band director took each member aside to provide feedback on whether or not she or he should continue music in middle school. My teacher told me that I just didn't have it and should quit. I was devastated. I had dreams of becoming a conductor and I loved playing music. I learned to read music and text at the same time before entering kindergarten, so I couldn't understand what my teacher saw or heard that made him think that I, at the tender age of 11, didn't have what it took to pursue playing in a middle school band. He knew nothing about me and had never asked any questions about me, our family, my aspirations. He didn't seek to make me a better musician.

Caleb, I hope that you will have teachers who realize they are gatekeepers. I hope they understand the power they hold and work to discover your talents, seek out your dreams and fan them, rather than smother them. I hope they will see you as part of a family, with gifts and rich histories that have been passed down to you. I hope they will strive to know you even when they think they already know you. I hope your teachers will approach you with humility and stay curious about who you are.

When I was in 4th grade, my elementary school held a back-to-school night that featured student work and allowed families to walk the halls and speak with teachers. In each classroom was a student leader, chosen by teachers. I was not sure what my role was supposed to be. But at one point, a couple came in, desiring to speak with Mrs. S. She was busy, so I thought I'd chat with them while they waited. As I approached them, they recoiled in fear and, with panicked looks, turned away from me and said, "Mrs. S.?" My teacher looked away from the folks she was working with and said, "It's OK, she's not like the rest." I don't remember what happened next. All I remember is that this seemed to be one of the first in a long line of reassurances that I was special and not like other Black boys and girls. For many years afterward, I was told on more than one occasion, "You're not like other Blacks." This was supposed to be a compliment.

Caleb, I pray that your teachers will not look at you through hurtful racial preconceptions. I pray that they will do the work necessary to eliminate racist practices in themselves and in those around them. I pray that they stand up for you in ways that leave you feeling strong and capable. I pray that they will nurture your spirit, and that you, in turn, will desire to be a better you.

> **Caleb, I want your teachers to help you love being in your skin. I want them to make space for you in their curricula, so that you see yourself as integral to this country's history, to your classroom's community, to your peers' learning.**

Son, I end this letter by sharing a story that Grandma has told me many times, that I hope will one day resonate with you. On the first day of kindergarten, many of the kids were crying and clinging to their parents. But not me. I was ready! I wanted to be like my three older siblings and go to school. So I gave my mom a hug, let go of her hand, waved goodbye, and found my teacher. And remember how I told you that my oldest sister taught me how to read before I went to school? The teacher found this out and used this skill, along with my desire to be at school, to teach the other kids the alphabet and help them learn how to read. I believe, in part, that is why I became a teacher. She saw something in me and encouraged me to develop my passion — even at this young, sweet age.

That, my son, is my hope for you. I hope your teachers will love you for who you are and the promise of what you'll be.

Love,
Mama

Dyan Watson, an editor for Rethinking Schools*, is an associate professor in teacher education at the Lewis & Clark Graduate School of Education and Counseling. She is also one of the co-editors of the popular book for teachers,* Rhythm and Resistance: Teaching Poetry for Social Justice.

Black Is Beautiful

By Kara Hinderlie

For years, I have struggled to find authentic ways of helping young children — kindergarteners and 1st graders — learn, remember, and appreciate Black history. Come January, the halls of my school are plastered with a variety of Martin Luther King Jr. tributes and artwork that conveniently find their way to being relabeled for February's Black History Month displays — and disappear in time for March's green living tips to save the planet.

But here is what my students need to know: Black is beautiful.

And here is why they need to know it . . .

Currently, in my predominantly white kindergarten class of 27, I see the few Black boys in my class targeted as the ones who did something wrong, as the kids who are called mean, as the kids who are not named as a friend. I see my one Black girl sad on the playground, or looking for a spot at the table with her white peers, unsure how to make space for herself. They are on the periphery of play, usually the "it" in tag, and it reminds me of my own story: In high school a teacher told us that, in our society, the color black symbolizes bad and evil, and white symbolizes good and pure.

I also remember when I was in a human development college class watching a video clip of children choosing a white baby doll instead of a brown one. I remember a little Black girl in the study saying the brown dolls were not as pretty, and the little white girls saying the brown dolls looked dirty. The video and the study itself made me sad for the little Brown girl I once was, trying to fit in and make friends in school.

One day I came across a stack of books the former librarian volunteer at my elementary school was going to throw out marked "Free books." In it were two copies of *Black Is Beautiful*. It was published in the '70s by Ann McGovern and made up of black-and-white photos of simple black subjects: a black bird, black jelly beans, black puppies, a black butterfly, a young Black girl in dress-up. The words in the book were written like a free verse poem. I loved the simplicity and took both copies to use in my classroom.

The students listened to me read aloud using a voice of wonderment and adoration — some pages I whispered in reverence. I stopped at the page of the Black girl playing dress-up in her mom's clothes, the only page mentioning black skin being beautiful:

> Black lace, black face.
> Black is beautiful.

"Do you see her wearing her mama's fancy clothes? So beautiful and fun," I said. When I finished, I asked what they noticed in the book.

KESHA BRUCE, *WE HAVE BUT FAITH*, 2008, 12" x 9", ARCHIVAL PIGMENT PRINT, EDITION OF 15, COURTESY OF THE ARTIST AND MORTON FINE ART

"I notice the pictures only had black."

"I notice a black bird."

"I noticed beautiful."

"The horse was black!"

"I noticed the candy!"

"Yeah!" the class responds in a chorus of agreement.

I wrote down what they noticed on chart paper. Then I asked, "What can we add to this *Black Is Beautiful* book that the author didn't mention?"

"The tire swing!" Chris said.

"Some people may not see a tire swing as beautiful. How can we convince them it is? I think about how some of you love to push it, and some of you love to ride on the tire swing. Hmm . . . what would some beautiful movement words be that you could say with tire swing?"

"It twirls!"

"It spins around and around!" said Chris, who was now on his knees, having popped up during his share out.

"Oooh! I can't wait to see how you write that!" I popped up too, and smiled.

I moved on, asking for more ideas. I framed their answers in the style and context of the book we read, modeling how to expand their list to sound like a poem. I wrote down their new ideas, and pointed to the ones already mentioned or from the original text: a kitten, a dog, sneakers, a witch.

"I notice the author wrote this like poetry to help us remember how beautiful the things in the book were. What words and descriptions can we add to our ideas to make people see the beauty and goodness of the color black?"

"My dress is soft and cozy," Lori gently patted her black fuzzy skirt, smiling into her own shoulder.

Nadira, who had been gazing away, raised her hand. "Black bird floating in the night sky."

I wrote what they said on the board and asked them to tell a friend three black things they are going to write about in a beautiful way. I know some will only get a picture or a word down while some will fill the page, but I want them all to start by telling someone three things. It gives them a goal and sets the expectation with a starting point.

I sent them off to write their ideas and have "Black is beautiful" written on sentence strips at each writing table for reference. I collected their work, went home, and typed them up.

The next day we reviewed: "Who remembers something that is black and beautiful?"

"Horses!"

"Birds!"

"Sneakers!"

"Rain clouds!"

"Yes!" I said. "Today we are going to look at a different kind of black is beautiful. We know that there are things that are black and beautiful, and people who are Black and beautiful. But it can be a little confusing because is people's skin the color of black paper

or a black shirt? No! Black people are all different shades of brown. We just call it black sometimes. Today we are going to write about beautiful Black people and I have a few books to share with you to help give you ideas."

I started off by reading *My People* by Langston Hughes.

"Sunshines, I love this book," I told my students. "The words in this book are so simple and so powerful. This book is actually a short poem that was stretched across the pages so the photographs could illustrate each line of the poem. When I read this poem to you, I want you to study the pictures as you hear the words I say. Look at the faces and features of these Black people and notice their beauty. Notice what Langston compares the beauty to. In one place he compares me to the sun! I always feel so great when I read this poem."

> The night is beautiful,
> So the faces of my people.
>
> The stars are beautiful,
> So the eyes of my people.
>
> Beautiful, also, is the sun.
> Beautiful, also, are the souls
>   of my people.

I tell them to listen to ways Langston knows Black- and Brown-skinned people are beautiful. It's a slow book, with only a few words per page, which allows my students to study the sepia-toned photos. Using the same format from the last lesson, we try to translate the idea of black is beautiful to features of Black and Brown people. After I finish the book, I ask the students to tell me about beautiful Black people. "What did Langston say?"

"Beautiful like the sun."

"The stars are beautiful!"

I am explicit when I talk to the students about the metaphor in this poem. It is hard to understand when you are 5 years old and the world is a literal, concrete place. Some do not make the connections I want them to make, they are not thinking about the Black people of the poem but of their metaphors as the thing of beauty. So I make the connection for them and carry them with me through an example.

"Now you understand why I love this poem. Langston compares beautiful people with the sun and stars. Look at this page." I show them the page of an elderly man, face raised and smiling at something unseen to the reader. "When I look at this page, I see joy and happiness. I see lines around his mouth that say he smiles a lot. His skin looks soft to touch. That is why he looks beautiful to me, and I think that's why they chose this picture to go with the word 'also' in the poem. Sometimes we think of beauty one way and then discover, like in this book, there are other ways that we can see beauty!"

I re-read the poem and asked for "Black is beautiful" examples again. This time there are more accurate answers:

"Eyes are beautiful!"

"Brown skin is beautiful."

"Hands are beautiful."

Brandon, a Black boy who often sits quietly as if in meditation, raised his hand. "Souls are beautiful." He looks at me and we smile.

We also read *Hair Dance!* by Dinah Johnson, another book with photos of Black and Brown kids playing outside. There is so much visual movement in this book; kids are jumping and hair is swinging. This book is special because the children in the book are from our neighborhood: The author is a parent and the kids were previous students in our school. This interests the children and they study the pictures and recognize some of their playground in the artwork. This time around when kids answer what is beautiful, they move their heads as if flipping their own imaginary beaded braids. They are holding their own hair in the air to mimic the pictures they saw while I read the rhythmic words in the book. The resounding agreement is that Black hair is beautiful — and so is jumping! We spend two minutes trying to jump high and fast to get our own hair to dance.

But here is what my students need to know: Black is beautiful.

But this time when I sent them to write, they were less confident. Maybe I moved too quickly, or maybe the metaphor was too big of a jump. They stuck pretty close to the examples given in the books: hands, hair, skin. They focused on the metaphor and less on the physical attributes of people as beautiful.

And this was what my students deserve to know: Black is beautiful.

I tell the kids why I think it's important to celebrate Black history. I tell them my story, of learning about history where no one looked like me or my family. "We have Black History Month as a reminder to teachers that there is not much written about all of the things that Black and Brown people have contributed to our lives. When I was a kid, I only learned about the ways white people changed our lives. There were no books or activities in our school that let us know who those Black people were, or how they affected the way we live. I will share inventors and leaders who paved the way, or made an important discovery through diligence and hard work." They seemed intrigued. Some looked surprised, some totally bored. Buy-in to the unknown is hard, so I gave them an example.

Fresh off the heels of a presidential election with an unexpected outcome in 2016, where girls were coming in wearing pussycat hats and pant suits, I told the class about Shirley Chisholm.

I then told them mostly about inventors or "real firsts," as opposed to firsts for Black people, because they are the most tangible for young learners to understand. It is a clear, concrete contribution to bettering our daily lives: refrigeration, open-heart surgery, stoplights, peanut butter. I want my students to have a basis for appreciating Black people. Later, when they learn about the more complex concepts of slavery, Jim Crow, and civil rights, somewhere in the back of their mind I hope they will remember the beauty of Black and the ways Black people made life better for them. And then maybe, in the front of their eyes, they will see the injustice for what it was and what it still is.

For the next writing exercise, to retain the feeling of reverence, we stayed with the free verse poetry writing style of the first book I introduced by Ann McGovern. The tone of that piece set the mood for the beauty on the page, and allowed them to transition into that poetic mode of writing, thinking, and seeing their ideas in a different light. I had them talk in pairs and instructed them to tell each other who they remember learning about and liked. When I asked them to write, they quickly jotted down their choices: *Stoplights speak to cars in colors, tasty peanut butter on sandwiches for lunch every day, open-heart surgery saving lives.*

When writing with young children, I have to make publishing decisions. In this unit, I wanted the kids to see their ideas from these lessons typed up and put together as a collective piece. If I made them do the extra combining work it could make the unit drag on too long, its message losing potency. So, in this instance, I did it for them.

Once all the parts were typed into one poem, I brought in craft and scrapbook supplies all in black: pipe cleaners, pom-poms, feathers, beads, stickers, textured felt, and dozens of patterned papers; all glittery, soft, and shiny — the jewels of the crafting world. I cropped their poems and let them collage them into beautiful black works of art. I read the poems aloud as I handed them out one at a time, so they could hear each other's work as inspiration.

Resistance

Some years when I do this lesson, I get backlash in the form of parent emails to the principal, disengagement from students, or the fairness argument from both students and parents: "Why just black, why not all colors?" This year it was Andrew, a tall blue-eyed white boy, and a proficient reader and writer.

When he learned about Black inventor Lyda Newman's improved hairbrush, Andrew whispered to a friend, "That's not special."

When he saw the sentence strips with "Black is beautiful" written on them for a second day, he turned them face down on the tables and exclaimed, "We already did these!"

When Jasmin told her friends something Black was beautiful, he responded, "Black is not beautiful."

Andrew, whose humor sometimes runs in the center of insulting, who often finds delight in others' misfortune, exclusion, or embarrassment, was creating another opportunity for me to change his mind.

When he turned the sentence strips face down exclaiming their completion, I explained this project was going to last the entire month. "Sometimes we remember things better and learn more when we stick with it. It feels like we finished because we did finish one part, but there's more I want to show you and more I want you to try." Andrew said, "OK."

When he said Ms. Newman's invention wasn't special, I noted there is a difference between flashy and noteworthy. "Raise your hand if you have a brush like this one in your house. Raise your hand if you've seen one before. Isn't that cool you're learning about the person who made something we've all seen or used every day? That's why I wanted you to learn about Ms. Newman. She gave us things we use so much they seem boring, but every time someone uses or buys it, she is getting affirmation that what she created was needed, even still today!" I make eye contact with Andrew when I say this, and he nods in agreement.

When Jasmin came to me upset that Andrew told her Black wasn't beautiful, I took him aside and told him about the power of an ally.

"Why did you say Black isn't beautiful to Jasmin?"

"I was kidding. It is." He tries to get the early exit card by placating me.

"I'm spending a lot of time on black is beautiful because I want you on my team, Andrew. I want you to be the person who stands up and defends black when someone else tries to do what you just did, tries to make a joke about it, and tries to hurt someone's feelings about black. Black isn't just a color of clothes, right?"

"No, it's people and brown skin."

"So when someone jokes about black, it makes us, people with that skin, feel less important. But you have a chance to be a leader. Friends look to you to include them and they follow your lead. If you decide not to treat black as a joke, if you tell a friend why it's not funny to joke like that, you'll be helping the unfairness that is all around us. You will be making this place a better place for more of us. Can you try to do that? Help us feel welcomed and proud of black?"

Andrew nods, "OK, yeah! I'm sorry I hurt Jasmin's feelings, Ms. Kara."

"I know, Andrew. Thank you for apologizing. I'm glad you're on my team." Andrew smiles shyly and takes a big breath.

Then I take a big breath as he goes back to his seat.

Yeah, the work is weighty, little one. Deep breaths help. ∎

> **"I'm spending a lot of time on black is beautiful because I want you on my team, Andrew. I want you to be the person who stands up and defends black when someone else tries to do what you just did, tries to make a joke about it, and tries to hurt someone's feelings about black. Black isn't just a color of clothes, right?"**

Kara Hinderlie teaches at Irvington School in Portland, Oregon. She works with the Oregon Writing Project.

Index

Note: Page numbers in italics indicate illustrations.

Rethinking Ethnic Studies

Edited by R. Tolteka Cuauhtin, Miguel Zavala, Christine Sleeter, and Wayne Au

Built around core themes of indigeneity, colonization, anti-racism, and activism, *Rethinking Ethnic Studies* offers vital resources for educators committed to the ongoing struggle for racial justice in our schools.

Paperback • 368 pages • ISBN: 978-0-942961-02-7
$24.95*

Rhythm and Resistance
Teaching Poetry for Social Justice

Edited by Linda Christensen and Dyan Watson

Rhythm and Resistance offers practical lessons about how to teach poetry to build community, understand literature and history, talk back to injustice, and construct stronger literacy skills across content areas — from elementary school to graduate school. *Rhythm and Resistance* reclaims poetry as a necessary part of a larger vision of what it means to teach for justice.

Paperback • 262 pages • ISBN: 978-0-942961-61-4
$24.95*

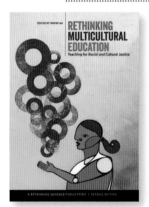

Rethinking Multicultural Education SECOND EDITION
Teaching for Racial and Cultural Justice

Edited by Wayne Au

This new and expanded second edition demonstrates a powerful vision of anti-racist social justice education. Practical, rich in story, and analytically sharp, *Rethinking Multicultural Education* reclaims multicultural education as part of a larger struggle for justice and against racism, colonization, and cultural oppression — in both schools and society.

Paperback • 418 pages • ISBN: 978-0-942961-53-9
$24.95*

Teaching a People's History of Abolition and the Civil War
Edited by Adam Sanchez

Teaching a People's History of Abolition and the Civil War is a collection of 10 classroom-tested lessons on one of the most transformative periods in U.S. history. These lessons encourage students to take a critical look at the popular narrative that centers Abraham Lincoln as the Great Emancipator and ignores the resistance of abolitionists and enslaved people. The collection aims to help students understand how ordinary citizens — with ideas that seem radical and idealistic — can challenge unjust laws, take action together, pressure politicians to act, and fundamentally change society.

2019 • Paperback • 181 pages • ISBN: 978-0-942961-05-8
$19.95*

TO ORDER ONLINE AND FOR A COMPLETE LIST OF OUR BOOKS, GO TO: **rethinkingschools.org**
CALL TOLL-FREE: **800-669-4192**

> *"Whenever teachers ask me for resources, I refer them to the work of Rethinking Schools."*

HOWARD ZINN
(1922–2010)
Author of *A People's History of the United States*

Subscribe to the leading social justice education magazine.

Every issue of *Rethinking Schools* overflows with creative teaching ideas, compelling narratives, and hands-on examples of how you can promote values of community, racial justice, and equality in your classroom — while building academic skills. Plus: news and analysis by and for education activists.

> *"As a teacher and researcher, I rely on Rethinking Schools for information, insight, and inspiration. It has become an indispensable part of my reading regimen."*

SONIA NIETO
Professor Emerita, University of Massachusetts Amherst

rethinkingschools.org/subscribe
CALL TOLL-FREE: **800-669-4192**

Use discount code **RSBK19** for a
10% discount on your next order.